NEOCLASSICAL THEATRE

Ronald W. Vince

NEOCLASSICAL THEATRE

A Historiographical Handbook

GREENWOOD PRESS
New York
Westport, Connecticut
London

Library of Congress Cataloging-in-Publication Data

Vince, Ronald W.
  Neoclassical theatre.

  Includes bibliographies and index.
    1. European drama—18th century—History and
criticism—Sources—Handbooks, manuals, etc.
2. Neoclassicism (Literature)—Sources—Handbooks,
manuals, etc.   3. European drama—18th century—
Bibliography.   4. Neoclassicism (Literature)—
Bibliography.   I. Title.
PN1841.V56   1988   792'.094   87–17803
ISBN 0–313–24445–6 (lib. bdg. : alk. paper)

British Library Cataloguing in Publication Data is available.

Library of Congress Catalog Card Number: 87–17803
ISBN: 0–313–24445–6

First published in 1988

Greenwood Press, Inc.
88 Post Road West, Westport, Connecticut 06881

Printed in the United States of America

The paper used in this book complies with the
Permanent Paper Standard issued by the National
Information Standards Organization (Z39.48–1984).

10 9 8 7 6 5 4 3 2 1

Copyright Acknowledgment

Grateful acknowledgment is hereby given for permission to quote from the following
source: John A. Cook, *Neo-Classic Drama in Spain: Theory and Practice* (Dallas,
Texas: Southern Methodist University Press, 1959) and is reprinted by permission.

For
my mother
and in memory of
my father

CONTENTS

PREFACE

Neoclassical Theatre, is, as its subtitle indicates, a *handbook*, intended to serve as an introductory guide to the source materials and interpretations of a major but circumscribed aspect of eighteenth-century European theatre. The principles on which the neoclassical theatre was based were initially enunciated in Italy in the sixteenth century, but they reached fruition in a wedding of precept and practice in France in the seventeenth century. While the national theatres of England and Spain developed and flourished during the early years of the seventeenth century with little regard to neoclassical rules, the French theatre reached maturity in mid-century in a context of theoretical debate and well-articulated neoclassicism. By the end of the seventeenth century, French theory and practice had established themselves as the standards by which cultivated Europeans judged all theatre. The history of the neoclassical theatre in Europe is largely the history of the interaction of French neoclassicism with other theatrical traditions. The only theatre strong enough to resist French domination and develop a parallel but independent neoclassicism was the theatre of England, where the process of adapting the rules to a native tradition and the exigencies of production had begun with the restoration of the monarchy in 1660, and where by the turn of the century a theatrical tradition peculiarly English had been established. When we speak of the neoclassical theatre of Europe, then, we are in fact referring mainly to the French and English theatres. Elsewhere, neoclassical principles encountered an entrenched resistance, or were introduced late in the eighteenth century at a time when even in France they were being challenged by new ideas.

Neoclassicism was a highly artificial, supranational system that—except in France and England—was imposed upon, rather than developed from, national cultures. And the theatre based on its principles was a deliberately cultivated institution whose rules had to be learned, not only by playwrights and actors, but also by audiences as well. The built-in tendency for neoclassicism to foster the creation of an elite theatre for an elite audience, however, was balanced in practice by the increasing integration of the theatrical enterprise into a larger political and cultural context, into the world of an expanding middle class, whose politics were democratic, whose interests were commercial, and whose tastes were sentimental. Although it seems clear that neoclassical theatre was not the only kind of theatrical activity to be found in eighteenth-century Europe, as an organizing and informing historical phenomenon it remains the single most important force in eighteenth-century European theatre.

The theatre historian's task is to reconstruct and describe the theatrical forms and conventions, the audiences, and the playing spaces that determined the dynamic and the style of past performances, and to attempt to account for particular conditions and styles as they change through time. The theatre historiographer's task is in part to describe and explain the processes by which history is made out of data and interpretation. The present volume follows the pattern established in the two previous volumes in this series of historiographical handbooks, *Ancient and Medieval Theatre* (1984) and *Renaissance Theatre* (1984). *Neoclassical Theatre* provides an introduction to the sources of information available to the theatre historian, and to some of the methods that have been used in the interpretation of those sources. It offers an analytical survey of the principal written and artifactual evidence for the history of the neoclassical theatre of eighteenth-century Europe. It thus includes a discussion of dramatic texts and prompt books, public and legal records, playbills and account books, stage plans and scene designs, contemporary history and dramatic theory, biography and memoirs, stage iconography and theatrical portraiture. Particular attention is paid to those specific sources that have proved to be of central importance in the writing of theatre history, and where possible the reader is directed to a source where the original evidence is reproduced. Each chapter opens with an evaluative sketch of relevant modern scholarship and concludes with a full bibliography of the sources consulted. Except where indicated otherwise, translations of passages quoted from non-English sources are my own.

My debts to the hundreds of scholars whose labors furnished much of the material for this book are documented in the bibliographical references. I also wish to thank the staff of the Department of Interlibrary Loans at Mills Memorial Library, McMaster University, for their unfailingly courteous diligence in locating books widely scattered and printed in sundry languages. Others assisted as well. Dr. R. H. Johnston of the Department of History at McMaster came to my aid in the transliteration of Russian titles, and Maria DiCenzo of the Department of English graciously translated some difficult Italian passages. I am grateful too to my McMaster colleagues Antony Hammond and Richard Morton, and to members of the American Society for Theatre Research, particularly Rosemarie Bank, Cary Mazer, Bruce McConachie, and Robert Sarlós, for their support and encouragement in the enterprise.

1

THE ENGLISH THEATRE, 1642–1800

INTRODUCTION

Theatre historians have traditionally treated the years 1642–1800 in England as a unit distinguishable from the periods that preceded and succeeded it. The generalized impression of homogeneity sometimes produced as a consequence is in fact undermined by more specialized efforts to understand the period by isolating less extensive periods of time for analysis. Not that such efforts always result in clarification. On the contrary, the varying notions of when a subperiod begins and ends, the various bases on which historical divisions are based, and the overlapping and seldom agreed upon nomenclature used to designate periods and subperiods often combine to produce what appears, to the uninitiated, to be chaos.

Political events that had an obvious effect on the theatre do determine certain key dates in English theatrical history: the closing of the London theatres by Act of Parliament in 1642; the Restoration of the Monarchy and the reopening of the playhouses in 1660; the Licensing Act of 1737. But other dates, like that of the fall of the Bastille in France (1789), are at worst arbitrary and at best simply symbolic. Similarly arbitrary and, because they hint at a definition of style as well as a delineation of time, clearly misleading are designations derived from the names of monarchs (e.g., ''Carolean'' or ''Georgian'' periods). The term *Augustan*, derived from literary history, is also occasionally used, to add to the confusion. Somewhat more appropriate to the study of the theatre is the use of clearly theatrical criteria to describe a period (e.g., the Age of Betterton or the Age of Garrick) or to indicate the end of one period and the beginning of another (e.g., the great increase in the size and number of English theatres in the 1790s and the early years of the nineteenth century). The difficulty of assigning specific dates—and specific meanings—to even widely used and accepted terms can be illustrated by the differing interpretations given to the word *Restoration*. It is possible to find in scholarly literature at least half a dozen periods so designated, the differences depending upon the criteria used to define the period. All designations agree that the Restoration began with the restoration to the throne of Charles II in 1660, but the period can end at 1685 with the death of Charles, at 1688 with the deposition of James II, at 1700 with the death of John Dryden, at 1707 with the death of George Farquhar, at 1714 with the death of Queen Anne, or even at 1737, the year of Walpole's Licensing Act. (For convenience, *Restoration* in this book refers to the years 1660–1700.)

Most of these distinctions, nevertheless, are made on the basis of perceived changes in dramaturgy and dramatic literature. A more or less historically contiguous, homogeneous group of plays and the period in which the plays were produced are given what we must admit is an arbitrary designation. In fact, what at first glance appears to be a confusion born of scholarly pedantry is a revealing reflection of the number and variety of dramatic types and theatrical forms that characterize this long period. Tragedy (heroic, domestic, "high"), comedy (of wit, of manners, laughing and sentimental), farce, afterpiece, burlesque, opera (English, Italian, ballad), pantomime, ballet—Polonius' list pales in comparison.

Equally complex is the history of the playhouses between 1660 and 1800. Most attention has been paid to a handful of major theatres within the confines of the City of Westminster: Drury Lane (1674; rebuilt 1791), Lincoln's Inn Fields I (1661–1714), Dorset Garden (1671–1709), Lincoln's Inn Fields II (1714–1732), King's Theatre (1705–1789; called the Haymarket or Queen's Theatre until 1714), the Haymarket (1720), Covent Garden (1732–1808). The history of these houses is, nevertheless, only part of the story. From 1642, dozens of different structures and locations were utilized for the performance of plays, including tennis courts, the old Red Bull and the Cockpit, court theatres, the fairs of Saint Bartholomew and Southwark, the Inns of Court, and the so-called nurseries (schools for young actors) of the Restoration, as well as unlicensed theatres and places of specialized and spectacular entertainments such as pleasure gardens and amphitheatres, which appeared as the eighteenth century wore on. Moreover, theatrical activity was not confined to London. Indeed there may have been as many productions in the provinces as in the capital. In Dublin, Smock Alley opened in 1662 and the Crow Street Theatre in 1758; by the 1760s Parliament had begun to authorize theatres in other cities, until by the end of the century almost every major town had its "Theatre Royal." By 1805 there were over 280 places of regular entertainment throughout Great Britain. Information concerning these theatres is plentiful but tangled, and the reconstruction and explanation of their form and development continue to occupy the attention of theatre historians. (Private theatricals also flourished. See Sybil Rosenfeld, *Temples of Thespis* [1978].)

Scholars are, nevertheless, used to dealing with complex questions and incomplete or confusing data. A far greater impediment to a clear conception of

English theatre in the Restoration and eighteenth century has been the tendency to separate dramatic criticism and theatrical history. The result among students of dramatic literature has been an attitude of condescension often reflected in neglect or even disapproval of the drama, and among theatre historians an emphasis on sterile factual studies of the purely "theatrical" aspect of dramatic performance, each side sometimes spicing its comments with barbs aimed at the other. A leading scholar of the period has recently drawn attention to this "awkward distinction" between theatre history and criticism and has called upon scholars in both camps to bridge the gap between text and the circumstances of production:

We now have rather considerable resources available in theatre history. Most scholars would agree in principle that study of actors and physical theatre is ultimately arid without attention to the plays, and conversely that critical study of plays is at best limited and at worst unsound without an understanding of production circumstances and a sense of the meanings arguably communicable in performance. [Robert D. Hume, "English Drama and Theatre 1660–1800: New Directions in Research" in *Theatre Survey* XXIII, 74]

Although Hume blames the dominance of New Criticism in English departments for much of the problem, the dichotomy did not originate with critics who preferred the textual complexities of metaphysical poetry over dramatic texts that even Hume admits present few problems of interpretation. The problem has its roots in the nineteenth-century conviction that Restoration comedy in particular was immoral. "Its indecency," wrote Thomas Macauley, "though perpetually such as is condemned, not less by the rules of good taste than by those of morality, is not, in our opinion, so disgraceful a fault as its singularly inhuman spirit" (quoted by John Loftis in his introduction to *Restoration Drama*). Macauley at least conceded entertainment value to the plays. Later critics have seen them as, in the words of L. C. Knight, "trivial, gross and dull" (quoted in Loftis, pp. 18–19). And in spite of the vigorous efforts by scholars such as Robert Hume to defend the value of the plays as entertainment, the charge has stuck. In fact, a more common response to the charge of literary inferiority has been to concentrate on the theatre rather than on the plays, on the "whole show" of eighteenth-century entertainment, and to find in it the value that the drama lacks. The history of drama thus becomes the history of the stage, with dramatic action yielding to spectacle as the object of analysis, and literary value giving way to popular success as the appropriate criterion for judgment. Literary critics may deplore the substitution of "the average London theatregoer" as the arbiter of eighteenth-century taste and may lament what seems to be a confusion between commercial success and artistic worth, but from a historian's point of view, the thrust of much current scholarship is in the right direction. The only value judgments that a historian ought to be concerned with are those of the past, for those judgments are part of the stuff of history, and the recording and explaining of changing values are part of the historian's job of work. Eighteenth-century theatre is not twentieth-century theatre, and leaving aside a handful of classic plays, understanding must be derived from the history of that theatre rather than from an immediate literary or theatrical experience. Such understanding is not easily come by. A distinguished historian of the stage, Charles Shattuck, has drawn attention to a truth too seldom acknowledged:

The eighteenth century was a long time ago. We can perceive it only through many layers of darkened glass—the limited keeping of records at that time, the loss of records since that time, the inability of all of us but the most deeply committed students of eighteenth-century life to see with eighteenth-century eyes, to bypass two centuries of human experience and reconstitute ourselves citizens of that remote time. [In G. Winchester Stone, Jr., ed., *The Stage and the Page*, p. 164]

The best criticism that has emerged in recent years has largely abandoned efforts, rightly decried, to elevate George Lillo or Samuel Foote to major literary status, and has instead sought to understand the plays in the light of their theatrical and generic contexts, to see them as the products of a deliberate ideology and craft, performed under specific theatrical conditions before specific and diverse audiences, and reflecting the assumptions and concerns of a specific social, political, and intellectual milieu. (See Robert Hume's review essay, "English Drama and Theatre 1660–1800," in *Theatre Survey* XXIII [1982].) The approach treats plays primarily as historical documents rather than as literary texts: they become an "abstract and chronicle of the times," and the criticism of them a form of history. "To the extent that it was represented by contemporary audiences," writes James Lynch, "society itself . . . may be a principal object of study even in a book on theatrical history" (*Box, Pit and Gallery*, p. vii). Yet another scholar comments:

We have long discussed the connection between politics and the theatre and the social implications of theatrical trends, and we have at least hinted at the relationship between the theatre and the novel; we have recognized dramatic poets as the darlings of the Restoration court and the scapegoats of Augustan poets; we have known that plays were important to the reading public as well as to theatregoers. We have considered pit, box, and gallery as the site of social interaction and intrigue, as the essayists, novelists, and poets reiterated throughout the period. [Shirley Strum Kenny in *British Theatre and the Other Arts, 1660–1800*, p. 9]

Dramatic criticism has met cultural history.

Criticism thus oriented is impossible without sufficient data, but fortunately, in spite of the lost or incomplete records that prompted Shattuck's regret, the eighteenth century at least has provided a plethora of information, far more than for any earlier period in English theatrical history. This is due in part to the rise of popular journalism during the early years of the century and its expression in biography, autobiography, memoirs, and theoretical books as well as in pamphlets and periodicals. Moreover, the century saw the beginnings of theatre history itself, attempts to chronicle the stage from the reopening of the theatres in 1660. More than a dozen titles of books published between 1699 and 1832 promise a history of the stage. This commentary on matters theatrical, together with various kinds of iconography, playbills, theatrical accounts, and public and legal records, provide the substance of the standard histories of the Restoration and eighteenth-century theatre written over the past century. The presentation rather than the interpretation of evidence has been their forte as well as the source of their lasting value.

The Reverend John Genest's *Some Account of the English Stage from the Restoration in 1660 to 1830*, published at Bath in 1832 and usually taken as the first history of the theatre of the period, is in fact a remarkable work. Genest was not perfect and he did not, of course, have access to every pertinent document, but he was familiar with the plays and the London theatrical world, and for the earlier part of the period he could rely on John Downes' *Roscius Anglicanus* (1708), Samuel Pepys' *Diary* (written 1660–1669), Colley Cibber's *An Apology for the Life of Mr. Colley Cibber* (1740), W. R. Chetwood's *A General History of the Stage* (1749), and the latter author's *The British Theatre* (1750). Downes and Chetwood had been prompters in the theatre; Cibber had been an actor, playwright, and manager; and Pepys had been an inveterate playgoer during the reign of Charles II. Later scholars have been able to refer to other material, but no one has been able to impugn Genest's authorities. *Some Account of the English Stage* remains an important work of reference.

Toward the end of the nineteenth century, more of the gaps in documentary evidence were filled in with the publication of Percy Fitzgerald's *A New History of the English Stage From the Restoration to the Liberty of the Theatres* (1882). Fitzgerald was also indebted to Downes, Pepys, Cibber, and Chetwood; in addition, he included among his authorities the histories of Benjamin Victor, published in 1761 and 1771, and Charles Dibdin, published 1797–1800. More important, he was the first to undertake a methodical examination of papers in the Lord Chamberlain's office and the State Paper Office. He argued in his preface that

to understand the stage and its growth, as a social element, it becomes necessary to consider its titles, pedigrees, parents, licences, and other official documents, which . . . will best show its rise and the various changes it has undergone. Only in this way can we follow its many relations to the Court and magistrates, as well as to the society of the day, which supported or opposed it.

Almost entirely abandoned in the process is any serious consideration of playwrights, plays, and players—the staple of earlier histories, including Genest's. Fitzgerald is uninterested in criticizing the drama in terms of its theatrical dimension or in using plays as documents of theatre history, both twentieth-century concerns. Rather he concerns himself with the theatre as an institution reacting to political pressures, commercial necessities, and personal rivalries and prejudices publicly expressed. His main theme is made clear in his title, which refers to the breakdown in the nineteenth century of the monopoly enjoyed within the City of Westminster by the patent theatres of Covent Garden and Drury Lane. Clearly he saw government regulation of the theatre as a form of servitude. Fitzgerald claims to set out "almost every document of importance relating to the stage," and he considered his use of public and legal documents and his plan for his history "most scientific and certain, besides having analogy with the schemes of histories of other subjects" (preface). Fitzgerald's determinism and positivism place him directly in the main tradition of late nineteenth-century historiography.

In spite of Genest's and Fitzgerald's pioneering work, interest in the theatre of the Restoration and eighteenth century was not high in either scholarly or theatrical circles during the early years of the twentieth century. During the second decade of this century, however, two small sparks were kindled. George C. D. Odell began his work on the production of Shakespeare, which resulted in 1920 in the two volumes of *Shakespeare from Betterton to Irving*, and groups of amateur theatre enthusiasts set about reviving interest in the plays of the older English dramatists. By 1925 the Stage Society, founded in 1899, and its offspring the Phoenix Society, founded in 1919, had produced almost a dozen plays by Congreve, Dryden, Buckingham, Otway, Vanbrugh, and Wycherley.

Odell includes among his sources those used by Genest and Fitzgerald and a good many more of a similar nature, but he also makes extensive use of playtexts, iconographical evidence, and periodical literature. Unlike Fitzgerald, Odell is interested in the texts of the plays performed and in the details of their production, with the methods of staging: "stage presentation—scenery, machinery, costumes, pageantry, spectacle, music, song, dancing" (I, xviii). Odell's conclusions concerning the staging practices—especially during the years before 1775 where he himself acknowledges we "grope for definite details of staging" (I, 391) "in half-lights and visible gloom" (II, 81)—have of course been refined, corrected, and added to, but Odell's work remains in many ways remarkably reliable and informative.

Odell's interest in the staging practices of the Restoration and eighteenth century was prompted by an even stronger interest in Shakespeare and the stage history of his plays. Shortly after the publication of his work, however, in 1923, the first volume appeared of Allardyce Nicoll's *History of English Drama, 1660–1900*, devoted to the period 1660–1700. A second volume, treating the period 1700–1750, was published two years later, and a third on the years 1750–1800, in 1927. All three volumes have gone through several editions and have remained standard reference books. The format for each volume is the same: a discussion of the theatrical conditions (audience, scenery, actors); discussion of the forms of dramatic literature (tragedy, comedy, miscellaneous forms); and appendices providing a history of the playhouses, a selection of original documents, and a handlist of plays. Thus for the first time we find a reference work that attempts to integrate the kind of information provided by Fitzgerald with a complete listing and discussion of the dramatic texts which formed the period's theatrical repertory. It is true, as Hume points out, that Nicoll makes almost no attempt to determine the effect of theatrical circumstances upon dramaturgy, but criticism, of course, was not Nicoll's intention. He had no illusion about the quality of most of the drama he was chronicling. Beyond what he refers to as "the few gems," he acknowledges the general inferiority. His information serves as an initial charting of terrain previously known almost exclusively in terms of its promontories or "gems." And the plays are at least treated as part of theatrical history. Leslie Hotson's *Commonwealth and Restoration Stage* (1928), described by Hume as "a magnificent compilation of information, largely from lawsuit sources" ("English Drama and Theatre 1660–1800," *Theatre Survey* XXIII, 72), is in a sense a throwback to Fitzgerald in its emphasis on the commercial and legal aspects of theatrical history, without the earlier writer's organizing theme.

The first writer to insist on the necessary connection between theatrical conditions and dramatic texts—and the author of the last major works on the Restoration theatre to appear before World War II—was another clergyman, the Reverend Montague Summers. *The Restoration Theatre* was published in 1934; *The Playhouse of Pepys* in 1935. In the prefaces to both books Summers drives home his thesis:

Without some knowledge, some visualization of Restoration stage conditions the reader of a play by Dryden, Congreve, or any contemporary, must often find himself hopelessly puzzled and at sea. . . . [*The Restoration Theatre*, p. xv]

Before the student . . . can at all adequately appreciate the merits and genius of the dramatists of the latter half of the seventeenth century, he must have some knowledge of the conditions under which the authors of the days of Charles II wrote their plays, and if he is to form any estimate of their craft and skill, he must be able to visualize . . . the stage for which they fitted their work, since the technique of an acting play is inevitably to a large extent determined by the contemporary theatre. [*The Playhouse of Pepys*, p. xi]

Summers goes on in *The Restoration Theatre* to discuss in detail the systems of advertisement and admission; the audiences; and the use of the curtain, scenery, and changes of scene, costume, and lighting. Continuing in *The Playhouse of Pepys*, Summers deals mainly with plays and playwrights, the latter "considered more or less biographically" (p. xii). Summers was cranky, opinionated, and overbearing. For instance, he took Harley Granville-Barker to task for his discussion of Restoration dramaturgy in *On Dramatic Method*, which Summers describes as "undiluted nonsense," "neither very intelligent nor very discerning," the product of a man "lamentably ignorant of the technique of the Restoration theatre" (*Restoration Theatre*, pp. xviii, 149–50 n.3). Nevertheless, like the equally quirky Hotson, he provides a great deal of information about the theatre, and few scholars or critics would now disagree with his insistence on the relationship between theatrical conditions and dramaturgy or critical analysis.

The dramatic criticism that evolved over the next four decades, however, ignored both Summers' injunctions and his information on Restoration staging conventions. This is not the place to undertake a full review of dramatic criticism, but in the words of one commentator, "the bibliography in this field is mountainous, but the mountain has brought forth a mouse." The same writer goes on to point out that, "with few exceptions, the critics have made what should be conclusions reached after examining the plays into preconceptions to limit examination of the plays. The comedies are said to be 'immoral,' or 'purely social,' or 'artificial,' or 'brilliant,' and then dismissed" (Norman H. Holland, *The First Modern Comedies*, p. 209). Holland's own work, together with that of Thomas H. Fujimuro (*The Restoration Comedy of Wit*) and Dale Underwood (*Etherege and the Seventeenth-Century Comedy of Manners*), provided a triad of brilliant and influential studies during the 1950s, but even in these instances the writers remain oblivious to the theatrical aspect of their subject. They did, however, spark a renewed interest in the plays and, more important, in the theatre that originally gave them life. Since 1960 two major reference works devoted to the study of the theatre have appeared.

Arguably the more significant of the two is *The London Stage, 1660–1800*, prepared by a team of scholars including William Van Lennep, Emmett L. Avery, Arthur H. Scouten, George Winchester Stone, Jr., and Charles Beecher Hogan, and published in eleven volumes by Southern Illinois University Press between 1960 and 1968. The work's subtitle indicates its scope: "A Calendar of Plays, Entertainments and Afterpieces Together with Casts, Box-Receipts and Contemporary Comment Compiled from the Playbills, Newspapers and Theatrical Diaries of the Period." The authors discern five practices that strongly influenced English drama and stagecraft during the period: (1) the creation in the patent theatres of a monopoly; (2) the introduction of actresses; (3) the alteration of playhouse design to accommodate three distinct areas for the audience (pit, boxes, galleries); (4) the increasing emphasis on scenes and machines and spectacle; and (5) the increasing enlargement of the program by means of entr'acte and music. It is these practices that are documented in *The London Stage*. (A computerized index to *The London Stage* is housed at Lawrence University in Wisconsin. The entire work is currently being revised and corrected.)

The second of these monumental reference works is *A Biographical Dictionary of Actors, Actresses, Musicians, Dancers, Managers, and Other Stage Personnel in London, 1660–1800*, by Philip H. Highfill, Jr., Edward A. Langhans, and Kalman A. Burnim, also published by Southern Illinois University Press. The projected sixteen volumes are still in progress; the first appeared in 1973. These imposing volumes are providing theatre historians with fundamental data for the pursuit of their craft. What will be provided are biographical notices "of all persons who were members of theatrical companies or occasional performers or were patentees or servants of the patent theatres, opera houses, amphitheatres, pleasure gardens, theatrical taverns, music rooms, fair booths, and other places of public entertainment in London and its immediate environs from the Restoration of Charles II in 1660 until the end of the season 1799–1800'' (I, preface). The magnitude and the thoroughness of the project are evident in the number of persons to be covered (8,500) and in the variety of sources of information to be examined—diaries, letters, and memoirs published and unpublished; legal, theatrical, and parish records; playbills and newspapers; paintings, engravings, and illustrated books; local histories, maps, poetry, catalogues, genealogies, and shop lists—every source, in the authors' words, ''that ingenuity could suggest.''

As evidence that even historians can have a foreshortened temporal perspective, we might note that *The London Stage* and *A Biographical Dictionary* are now referred to as ''pioneering'' works, and a younger generation of scholars and critics is busily exploiting this newly available information. There is in fact no doubt that the *amount* of data now readily available places Genest, Fitzgerald, Summers, and even Allardyce Nicoll in the shade, but historiography is not a purely ''progressive'' activity, nor does more information necessarily make for better or more satisfactory history. The constant interaction of data and model only very occasionally results in a revolutionary interpretation. Moreover, modern historical scholarship is the inheritor of a nineteenth-century positivism that places almost all theatrical historiography in the same tradition, that is, the belief that the collection of data and its interpretation are invariably sequential steps in the writing of history. We nevertheless ignore earlier historians at our peril, for in them we find the seeds of our own assumptions and concerns.

The most prevalent current explanatory model for the changing theatrical circumstances and dramatic styles that characterize the period 1660–1800, for example the commercial model, differs little in its essence from the ideas expressed by Fitzgerald in 1882. The editors of *The London Stage* themselves thought of this theatre in terms of ''show business,'' a notion that both explains and justifies the attention they devote to ''the management, finances, operations, and practices of the houses devoted to drama and opera'' (Emmett L. Avery, *The London Stage*, Part Two, Vol. I, p. xviii). And, of course, as Hume notes in ''English Drama and Theatre 1660–1800'' in *Theatre Survey* (1982), ''*The London Stage* is set up to help us study repertory theatres in competition'' (p. 76). According to this commercial model, theatrical competition underlies the changing dramaturgy and the increasingly spectacular performances of the Restoration and eighteenth century. (Judith Milhous' *Thomas Betterton and the Management of Lincoln's Inn Fields, 1695–1708* [1979] is a chronological, detailed analysis of one phase of such theatrical competition.) The commercial theatre, it is assumed, is invariably a popular theatre, with theatre managers constantly compelled to tailor their offerings to the tastes of a growing and diversified theatrical public.

The commercial model, linked to its modern equivalents in London's West End or New York's Broadway, has an undeniable appeal, but it is occasionally presented as though it is somehow the ''natural'' state of the theatre. ''Drury

Lane and Covent Garden,'' writes Ralph G. Allen, "were not subsidized theatres.
There was no National Endowment for the Arts to rescue the managers from
faulty assessments of the public taste. . . . And what man of the theatre would
have it otherwise? If drama as performed were responsive only to the enthusiasms
of high-minded critics, it would smother in its own delicacy'' ("Irrational Entertainment in the Age of Reason" in G. Winchester Stone, Jr., *The Stage and
the Page*, p. 90). As a reaction to earlier characterizations of the period as one
of "decay and disintegration" (the phrase is Allardyce Nicoll's), Allen's comment is perhaps understandable but surely overstated. A moment's reflection on
the possible results of catering exclusively to popular taste might in fact give us
some pause. The fact that a theatre is popular might very well justify it as an
object of historical study, but it does not necessarily endow it with intrinsic
merit. In *The Development of English Drama* (1976) Robert Hume traces the
vagaries of theatrical fashion, season by season from 1660 to 1710. It is difficult
to avoid the impression of a seventeenth-century equivalent of modern television
programming, with successful shows breeding imitations, spinoffs, and down-
right schlock in the manner of *Dallas* or *Dynasty*. It is now recognized too that
the theatre was part of a wider commercial enterprise: the marketing of leisure
and the creation of a consumer society. (See J. H. Plumb, *The Commercialisation
of Leisure in Eighteenth-Century England* [1973].) Historians of the theatre are
correct to document the phenomenon, but there is no reason either for assuming
the workings of natural law or for substituting commercial success for artistic
worth as a basis for value judgment.

The confusion of commercial and artistic success is in fact a charge often laid
against theatre historians, but the confusion, if it exists, is not inherent in the
discipline, and it is certainly possible to distinguish between the theatre as a
commercial institution and the theatre as an artistic medium. We might, for
example, distinguish between *ulterior* and *immediate* intention, between the
intention on the part of managers, actors, and playwrights to attract an audience
or to make a profit, and the artistic intention involved in writing a play or staging
a performance. The former is part of the context for a consideration of the latter,
but it is not to be identified with it. Theatre historians are concerned with the
theatre as an institution dependent upon resources which, in some societies and
in some ages, must be gotten by persuading patron or public to provide them.
The nature and extent of this support may affect the artistic enterprise, even
determine the artist's ulterior intention. But it does not determine the art. The
tracing and evaluating of artistic choices is the aesthetic branch of theatre history,
but it is a task relatively few historians have attempted. We are as yet in the
process of determining which choices artists have thrust upon them, and which
they choose for the sake of their art.

DRAMATIC LITERATURE AND DRAMATIC TEXTS

Whatever their value as dramatic literature—and few critics would grant the
vast majority of them more than entertainment status—dramatic texts provide

the first level of entry into the world of the English theatre in the Restoration and eighteenth century. Such is not the case on the Continent, where scene designs, drawings and plans of theatres and stage machinery, and many theoretical and practical treatises on the theatre might claim first attention instead. Whether the English predilection for preserving playtexts rather than scene designs or theatre plans is, as Edward Langhans suggests, a reflection of a traditional English interest in the written word rather than in the pictorial image, or is simply the result of accident, the end for the historian is the same. The historian has, as prime material evidence, several thousand playtexts—in print, in manuscript, and most important, in the form of prompt books. Most of these were of course written between 1660 and 1800, but a large number of older plays, particularly Shakespeare's, continued to be performed throughout the period, often in versions quite different from what the playwright originally wrote or what we have grown accustomed to reading in modern editions. The systematic analysis of the performance texts that made up a constantly changing repertory is essential if we are to understand the theatre and theatrical tastes, as opposed to the literature of the period. And as the eighteenth century wore on, and plays from the Restoration and the early part of the century joined pre-Restoration and new plays in the repertory, it becomes increasingly prudent to determine, where possible, the specific text performed on any single occasion. In most instances, unfortunately, such detailed information is inaccessible, and scholars must content themselves with cautious generalization based on an examination of the texts we have, together with information gleaned from other sources concerning staging practices and habits. The complexity of the task—and the value of *The London Stage* and computers—are reflected in the figures offered by George Winchester Stone, Jr., in "The Making of the Repertory" in *The London Theatre World, 1660–1800* (edited by Robert Hume). Comparing the periods 1700–1728 and 1747–1776, Stone notes 11,837 performances of 876 plays for the first period, and 24,870 performances of 929 plays for the second.

Our primary source of dramatic texts consists of printed editions. In order to make the best use of these as evidence, the historian needs full bibliographic information, including a knowledge of publication practice, editing procedures, if any, and the dates of both publication and performance. There have been several attempts to provide the beginnings of a bibliographical guide, especially for the Restoration period, but there is as yet no full descriptive bibliography for the entire period 1660–1800. (The best overall guide to the printed drama is provided by Nicoll in the "Handlist of Plays" appended to each of the first three volumes of *A History of English Drama*.) The potential difficulty of distinguishing between performance text and published text is reflected in the various dates associated with eighteenth-century plays: the date of application for a performance license (after 1737), the date(s) of performance(s), the date of the publication license (recorded in *The Stationers' Register*) or copyright (after 1710), and the date of publication. (Much of the information concerning performance is available in *The London Stage*.)

The serious collecting of eighteenth-century plays actually began with David Garrick, whose collection of over 1,300 plays was willed to the British Museum in 1779 and forms the basis for that library's current collection. (George M. Kahrl provides a catalogue of the Garrick Collection.) Other libraries also have large collections of plays, but the most convenient source for most scholars is *Three Centuries of English and American Plays*, a microcard edition published by the Readex Corporation. Here we have reproduced early editions of nearly every English play printed before 1800. A less eye-taxing facsimile collection is provided in the Garland eighteenth-century drama series, *Eighteenth-Century English Drama*, edited by Paula R. Backscheider.

The limitations and possibilities of published texts as evidence for theatre history are clear when we consider not only publishing practices but also the repertory tradition that developed after 1660, and the censorship and licensing procedures that prevailed after passage of the Licensing Act in 1737.

Plays were published, not for the benefit of actors or managers or even primarily of playwrights, and certainly not for the benefit of theatre researchers, but in order to provide literary entertainment for the reading public, and profit for the publisher. The habit of reading playtexts as literature intensified during the Interregnum, and dramatic publication of older dramatists such as Beaumont and Fletcher increased. With the reopening of the theatres, the plays of new dramatists were added to the stock. By the last half of the eighteenth century, the published play had, to a large extent, become a form of fiction, sharing with the novel both a reading public and various literary devices. After 1710, the Copyright Act gave the author rights in the published play for fourteen years, once renewable, but there is little evidence that playwrights, who derived much more income from the performance than from the publication of their plays, were much concerned with the printed texts. It appears, in fact, that no one saw any reason for printed and performance texts to agree. They were prepared to meet quite different requirements.

The main reason for the discrepancy between the printed and the acted versions of a play was that any additions, deletions, or revisions made in a text prior to its performance were only rarely incorporated into the printer's copy. The nature of the copy sent to the printer is difficult to determine. In a recent survey, "The Publication of Plays" in *The London Theatre World, 1660–1800*, Shirley Strum Kenny notes that about thirty printed Restoration plays show traces of the playhouse, but that in some instances it is impossible to separate a prompter's notes from those of the playwright. More commonly, it appears that a separate copy was sent to the printer, who published it without reference to cuts and revisions made during rehearsals, and without reference to any deletions required by the censor. "The history of play publication in this period," writes Kenny, "is one of expanding runs of plays, accelerating republication of successful plays, increasing interest on the part of booksellers, and ever-growing numbers of partners in the publication of old plays as booksellers divided, sold, or willed their copyrights" (p. 323). Without other evidence to guide us, we cannot be sure of the relationship between the resulting texts and playhouse copies. Under these circumstances the best we can hope for from stage directions is that they provide evidence of what could be done, but not necessarily of what was done.

Prologues and Epilogues

The texts of prologues and epilogues, which accompanied 90 percent of Restoration plays, present their own textual difficulties. The majority of the twelve hundred or so that have been located are to be found in early quarto editions of the plays, but a number were printed as broadsides or leaflets and evidently sold in the streets or at the theatres. Others were published in poetical miscellanies, and still others exist only in manuscript. In those instances where a piece is found in more than one edition or in more than one form, it often appears in different versions. A number are preserved in the Bindley Collection in the Bodleian Library. And at least two incomplete collections, consisting only of previously published pieces, were published in the eighteenth century. A complete edition of the prologues and epilogues of the Restoration is being prepared by Pierre Danchin of the Université de Nancy. Danchin argues their use as stage documents, noting that they not only give an indication of the general atmosphere of the period, but also enable us to learn something of stage conditions (the physical features of playhouses, the nature of the spectators, the fortunes of the rival companies). This "direct communication" between actor and audience resulted in a new type of stage oratory. Nevertheless, as Judith Milhous points out in a review in *Theatre Notebook* (1983), these documents must be used with caution: "They often incorporated several messages—topical, political, theatrical, personal—aimed at different parts of the audience, and the printed page rarely gives any hint of the tone and attitude with which a given piece was to be delivered" (XXXVII, 90). At any rate, prologues and epilogues are now available for an appropriate analysis.

Collections of Plays

While publishers generally ignored the theatrical aspect of the playtexts they published, during the last third of the eighteenth century several collections of plays appeared that made some claim to playhouse or promptbook provenance. Collections of plays, generally of the most popular plays, had been published early in the century by Thomas Johnson, William Feales, and others, but it was not until *The New English Theatre*, published in twelve volumes (1776–1777) that any attempt was made to indicate the acting text by indicating stage cuts, printing songs, and providing cast-lists. Possibly the best known of such collections is *Bell's British Theatre*, published by Francis Gentleman, which appeared in 21 volumes between 1776 and 1781, and in a new edition of 36 volumes between 1791 and 1802. All the plays included in the several series published by Elizabeth Inchbald between 1808 and 1815 were asserted to have been printed "from the prompt books under the authority of the managers." "If we recognize such attention to the theatre as purely commercial enterprise," observes Kenny, "one feels nevertheless some satisfaction in knowing that these plays . . . occasionally touched, however lightly, the stage that had launched them as literary properties" ("The Publication of Plays" in *The London Theatre World, 1660–1800*, p. 336). Small praise, but for theatre historians these texts represent evidence of a different order from that of other printed editions.

Similarly, *Bell's Shakespeare* (1773–1776), also edited by Francis Gentleman, was "regulated from the prompt-books, by permission of the managers." Of the twenty-four acting versions printed, eighteen are from Drury Lane and six from Covent Garden. Gentleman included the remainder of Shakespeare's plays (save *Pericles*) with indications of lines he thought might be cut in production, but he does not pretend that these are acting versions. From Genest to the present there has been almost universal agreement that this is the most execrable edition of Shakespeare ever published. From the point of view of the stage historian, it is a treasure in that it gives us not what Shakespeare wrote—or what a modern textual editor believes he wrote—but rather what was actually performed in the theatre.

Between 1789 and 1812 the scholarly John Philip Kemble systematically published his own acting versions of Shakespeare as pamphlets to be sold at the box-office. While lacking some of the technical data of true promptbooks, these editions do describe scenes, indicate some stage business, and provide cues for music and sound effects. In 1814–1815, twenty-six of Kemble's Shakespeares were reissued in uniform editions. His non-Shakespearean adaptations, performed 1800–1815, were published as *A Select British Theatre* (1816). The Kemble editions not only reflect playhouse practice but also were in turn used by other managers in the playhouse, and thus influenced play production for a generation. Given the common identity of stage producer and editor, they have an even greater claim to playhouse authenticity than does *Bell's Shakespeare*.

The Larpent Collection

In 1737 the British Parliament passed the Licensing Act, which required that plays offered for performance in the public theatres be licensed by the Lord Chamberlain. In practice, the task of censor was performed by a subofficial of the Lord Chamberlain's Office, the Examiner of Plays. From 20 November 1778 until 18 January 1824 this office was held by John Larpent who, with no authority to do so, assumed ownership of all the plays that had been submitted for licensing since 1737. At his death in 1824 the collection, numbering over 2,500 items, passed to his widow, who sold it to John Payne Collier and Thomas Amyot for the equivalent of about $350. Collier's offer in 1853 to sell the collection to the British Museum for the same amount was refused. The collection was subsequently owned by the Earl of Ellesmere until purchased in 1917 by Henry E. Huntington and housed in the Huntington Library in San Marino, California.

Allardyce Nicoll brought it to the attention of students of the theatre in 1927 in the third volume of his *History of English Drama*. In 1939 Dougald MacMillan published his *Catalogue of the Larpent Plays in the Huntington Library*.

The significance of the Larpent Collection is obvious. These copies, most of them in manuscript but those dating before 1737 in printed form, are far more likely to approximate performance texts than do published versions of the plays. The precise relationship among the text sent to the playhouse, the text sent to the printer, the text sent to the Examiner, and the text actually performed is, however, a complex one to determine, and each case ought to be, as MacMillan suggests, solved individually. What we can say with surety is that the Examiner's copy rarely conforms to the published edition.

The collection does present some difficulties. It includes manuscript plays, printed copies, and three scrapbook volumes containing prologues, epilogues, occasional addresses, and some undated and unidentified short pieces. Most of the manuscript copies were evidently prepared by professional copyists, although some appear to be in their authors' handwriting. Most plays too are accompanied by a formal application for license, signed by the theatre manager. But a number of plays have been removed from the collection; the Examiner's marks are not always easy to distinguish from those that may have been made by the author or manager or prompter; and Collier added his own notes in the nineteenth century, "often mistaken and sometimes unintelligible" (MacMillan, *Catalogue*, p. viii). The difficulty of sorting through this evidence and arriving at some notion of the text actually performed is emphasized in a rueful comment by Leonard Conolly, whose *Censorship of English Drama, 1737–1824* (1976) depends very heavily on the Larpent Collection. "Even when a text had survived the scrutiny of managers, actors, and the Examiner," he observes, "it could still be ruthlessly altered by the audience. Common . . . are accounts of audiences demanding the omission or revision of speeches deemed objectionable on moral, political, religious, or personal grounds" (p. 3).

Two other documents at the Huntington provide additional information concerning the activities of the Examiner during Larpent's tenure. One is Larpent's account books (ms. 19926). The other is a collection of diaries and a journal by his wife, Anna Margaretta Larpent (ms. 31201), "easily the most informative source that has yet been found about the man who for nearly fifty years had a very important say in what appeared on the British stage" (Conolly, p. 9).

Promptbooks

Promptbooks, copies of plays in print or manuscript marked for playhouse use, are of considerable interest to theatre historians. The term is used in a general way to refer to playtexts in a variety of states: stage-managers' or prompters' workbooks, from which the performance was directed; study books or part books belonging to specific individuals associated with the production; "master-copies" revised and cleaned up, kept as permanent records of performances and occasionally published. Promptbooks normally indicate the cuts, alterations, restorations, or additions to a text; provide information concerning scenic devices, stage properties, sound effects, and stage business; and give cues for entrances and exits. For the Restoration and eighteenth century, they could also include call lists (for actors), property lists, groove numbers (for flats), and bell-and-whistle cues.

In spite of their obvious usefulness to theatre historians, it has been only in the fairly recent past that promptbooks have drawn intense scholarly attention. As recently as 1956, for example, there were only half-a-dozen known promptbooks for the period 1660–1700. We now know of at least twenty, and thirty other printed texts show traces of prompt copy. Nor do promptbooks give up their secrets easily. Notations are often cryptic and idiosyncratic, rough and ready. (See Charles H. Shattuck's discussion of "Symbols and Abbreviations in the Older Promptbooks" in *The Shakespeare Promptbooks*, pp. 14–23.) Toward the end of the eighteenth century, promptbooks began to be prepared with some eye to order and intelligibility, but we are still in the process of finding, describing, and analyzing them.

Charles Shattuck's *The Shakespeare Promptbooks* (1965) locates and describes 106 Shakespeare promptbooks dating between 1660 and 1800. Edward Langhans, in *Restoration Promptbooks* (1981), reproduces eleven in facsimile and transcribes and prints the prompt markings from nine others. He also provides descriptions of seven "very full" promptbooks from the eighteenth century. Langhans', *Eighteenth-Century British and Irish Promptbooks* (1987) is a descriptive bibliography of eighteenth-century promptbooks and related documents such as part books and call books. We also have a good number of Shakespeare promptbooks from Smock Alley Theatre in Dublin dating from the 1670s and 1680s. (Several have been printed by G. Blakemore Evans in *Shakespearean Prompt-Books of the Seventeenth Century*.) A manuscript promptbook from the same theatre, John Wilson's *Belphegar* (Folger Library ms. V.b.109), contains more information concerning notes and properties than is usual for the period. Thomas Killigrew's copy of the 1664 folio of his own plays, now in the Worcester College Library, Oxford, contains annotations in the playwright-manager's own hand. All eight plays in the collection were originally written for performance in private playhouses before the closing of the theatres in 1642, and the interest of the alterations lies in the fact that apparently no radical changes were necessary to perform the plays on the Restoration stage. (See "The Killigrew Folio: Private Playhouses and the Restoration Stage" by Colin Visser in *Theatre Survey* XIX [1978].) Harry William Pedicord is preparing an edition of David Garrick's promptbooks, eighteen of which have thus far been discovered. But finding them has proved to be more a matter of luck and serendipity than the product of systematic search.

The best-known and most carefully prepared promptbooks of the late eighteenth century are those of John Philip Kemble (1757–1823), actor and successively manager of Drury Lane and Covent Garden theatres. We have already seen that Kemble habitually published his acting texts, and his methodical and

careful practices carried through in his original promptbooks. Nevertheless, although many of the promptbooks have come down to us, they were all prepared
or reconstructed after 1808. In 1802 Kemble had left Drury Lane for Covent
Garden, leaving behind the promptbooks of productions he had mounted since
1783. He seems to have prepared new versions for Drury Lane. Unfortunately,
both theatres and both sets of promptbooks were destroyed by fire, Covent Garden
in September 1808 and Drury Lane in February 1809. Kemble now had to prepare
promptbooks for yet a third time, and seems to have gone about it with his
customary thoroughness. Using his own published acting versions where possible, he made four copies of each new promptbook, two for the theatre, and
two for personal use. Those labelled "PB" (Prompt Book) on the spine, originally
numbering about sixty-five, show signs of heavy playhouse use and were obviously used for production. (Seven are at the Shakespeare Centre at Stratford;
four at the Folger; two at Indiana University—all plays by Shakespeare.) The
second theatrical set, each volume labelled "MB" (Master Book?) consisted of
"control copies" for use should the "PB" copy be lost. (The only three known—
Julius Caesar, *Othello*, and *Twelfth Night*—are in the Folger; two others, at
Harvard and Smallbythe, may also belong to his set.) A third set, belonging to
Kemble's brother Charles, is now in the possession of the Garrick Club in
London. The last set, presumably brought to Philadelphia by Fanny Kemble in
1834, was presented to the Folger Shakespeare Library by Mrs. Charles K. B.
Wister in 1969. It is this set that Charles Shattuck used for his facsimile edition
of 1974. He reproduces the twenty-five Shakespeare plays from this set, *The
Tempest* from the Indiana collection, and six of the non-Shakespeare plays in
the set. (In addition to the promptbooks, the Folger also has thirty-three quartos
of Kemble's most important parts, written out in the actor's own hand.)

    While promptbooks continue to be discovered, and continue to inform us
concerning matters of special effects, properties, scene changes, and so on, in
at least one crucial respect they are disconcertingly silent. They are, in the words
of Charles Shattuck, "tricky, stubborn informants" that rarely "give us a hint
of voice, or temper or histrionic manner" (*Shakespeare Promptbooks*, p. 3).

    Two brief publications related to texts by a writer who was himself a prompter
might well be noted here. John Brownsmith's *The Dramatic Timepiece* (1767)
provides the acting time, by act, of plays performed at Drury Lane, Covent
Garden, and the Haymarket (where Brownsmith was the prompter). The same
author's *The Theatrical Alphabet* (1767) is a catalogue of actor's parts, noting
in each case the number of "lengths" (units of forty-two lines of dialogue).

                              *   *   *

Dramatic texts are central to the study of the theatre. From them we learn
what was performed and something of the method of performance. Discussions
of staging procedures on the London stage have traditionally relied very heavily
on printed texts. George C. D. Odell's *Shakespeare from Betterton to Irving*,

for example, relies almost exclusively on such evidence. Odell was a sophisticated scholar who distinguished in general between reading texts and editions prepared from acting versions, but he had few promptbooks to work with, and the Larpent Collection was unknown to him. The printed stage directions, from which Odell derived many of his ideas about the physical structure of the theatres, remain still the first line of evidence on this subject. Some sceptics doubt their value, and others counsel caution in their interpretation. But taken in conjunction with the evidence from promptbooks and other sources, printed stage directions can help us arrive at a generalized conception of theatrical performance. Finally, some texts are valuable because they take as their subject matter the theatre itself, its playwrights, its actors, and its audiences. (See Dane F. Smith, *Plays about the Theatre in England from the Rehearsal in 1671 to the Licensing Act in 1737*, and Smith and M. L. Lawhon, *Plays about the Theatre in England, 1737–1800*.)

THEATRICALIA

Dramatic texts may be the most obvious evidence for theatrical history, but as we have seen, there are sometimes difficulties in determining the precise relationship between published and acted versions of a play, and there are limits to what can be inferred about theatrical conditions. Other evidence directly associated with the theatre can also be brought into play: theatrical account books, inventories, playbills and programs, newspaper advertisements and press cuttings, notebooks and scrapbooks. And fortunately, much of this material has been gathered into major theatrical collections at various libraries: the British Library (especially the Charles Burney Collection of notebooks, press cuttings, playbills, and theatrical registers); the Folger Shakespeare Library in Washington, D.C.; the Huntington Library; the Harvard Theatre Collection; the New York Public Library; the Victoria and Albert Museum in London; the London Theatre Museum; the Library of the University of Texas. (See Rosamund Gildes and George Freedley, *Theatre Collections in Libraries and Museums: An International Handbook*, and Freedley's article on American collections in the *Bulletin of the New York Public Library* LXII [1958]. See also André Veinstein and Alfred S. Golding, eds., *Bibliothèques et musées des arts du spectacle dans le monde*.)

Advertising Materials

Playbills and newspaper notices, together with oral announcements made at the conclusion of dramatic performances, were the principal means of advertising plays. Few playbills are extant before the early years of the eighteenth century, although there are numerous references to them in prologues and epilogues. In fact, Ifan K. Fletcher notes only seventeen bills of performance at legitimate theatres before 1718 (*Theatre Notebook* XVII, 48–50). But the number increases dramatically as we move through the eighteenth century and as the provincial theatres are added to the patent playhouses of Westminster. There are significant collections of playbills in over thirty locations in England and the United States. The Burney Collection in the British Library alone includes 1,800 playbills for the period 1773–1800; and the York Public Library has no fewer than 6,000 for the provincial York circuit. Another important collection is held by the Victoria and Albert Museum. In the United States, the Harvard Theatre Collection and the Folger Shakespeare Library each own several hundred playbills, most of them dating from the last quarter of the century and associated with provincial theatres; and the Huntington Library has the Kemble-Devonshire Collection of 111 volumes acquired in 1914 by Henry Huntington. The total is well over 11,000. (A valuable list of collections is provided by Frederick T. Wood in *Notes and Queries*, CXC [1946].) Newspaper announcements carried essentially the same information as playbills, often in the same format. Many of these have been clipped and collected. The British Library and the Harvard Theatre Collection, for instance, each have substantial holdings of newspaper clippings. In general, this material provides information concerning forthcoming performances, special attractions, and so forth, and the material increases in volume as we move through the eighteenth century.

Account Books and Registers

Account books and registers provide an incomplete but important record of the commercial side of play production in the eighteenth century and provide data useful in the preparation of calendars of performances. Although no proper account books survive from the Restoration, two documents in the Chancery Masters Exhibits at the Public Records Office (C105/34/16) list payments to the managers of Dorset Garden and Drury Lane between 1682 and 1692. From them we learn something of the United Company's calendar of activities as well as details of the managers' salaries. (Edward A. Langhans prints and discusses the documents in "New Restoration Theatre Accounts, 1682–1692," in *Theatre Notebook* XVII, 118–34.)

The most extensive collection of account books for Covent Garden is held by the British Library (Add. Mss. Egerton 2268–2298). The earliest is for the 1735–1736 season; others cover the years 1746–1747, 1749–1750, 1757–1758, 1760–1761, 1766–1770, 1771–1774, 1776–1778, 1779–1784, 1785–1792, and 1794–1800. In addition to these the Folger has accounts for 1740–1741, 1793–1794, and a manuscript cash book for 1759–1760. Harvard University has a list of performances and receipts at Covent Garden for the years 1767–1770. The Folger also has an important collection of account books for Drury Lane theatre: the Treasurer's Book for 1749–1750 prepared by George Garrick; similar books for 1766–1767 and 1771–1776 prepared by Benjamin Victor; and a Memorandum Book of nightly accounts for 1776–1779, which sets out in detail the attendance and receipts for boxes, pit, and gallery. To these we might add J. P. Kemble's Memoranda Books for the years 1788–1815, now in the British Library (Add.

Mss. 31,972–5), and receipts in manuscript for 1747 and 1748 held in the Harvard Theatre Collection. (Harvard also has an account book from Lincoln's Inn Fields for the years 1726–1728.)

The earliest extant account books, however, are the four manuscript registers of John Rich (ca. 1682–1761), failed tragic actor, sometime Harlequin, and manager of Lincoln's Inn Fields (1714–1732) and later Covent Garden (1732–1761). The first of Rich's four volumes, now at the Folger, consists of records kept between 1714 and 1723. It is of particular interest because Rich entered both the plays performed at Lincoln's Inn Fields, where he was manager, and the plays offered at the rival Drury Lane theatre. Other volumes of Rich's registers are housed in the Garrick Club in London (for the period 1723–1740), the Harvard Theatre Collection (1740–1750), and Chatsworth House, Bakewell (1750–1773).

Finally, in the Bristol Public Library is an account book of Jacob's Wells theatre for the years 1741–1748. Here we have an invaluable record of the financial affairs of a strolling company from London operating in a provincial city. Expenses are listed, with occasional comments appended, for personnel, advertising, printing, properties, wardrobe, lighting, and rent. The account book is discussed by Sybil Rosenfeld in *Strolling Players and Drama in the Provinces, 1660–1765* (pp. 205–15). "Our bookkeeper," she writes, "has raised the curtain a little on the conditions under which an actor laboured and performed his task in the provinces" (p. 215).

Prompters' Diaries

Manuscript diaries by two successive prompters at Drury Lane theatre covering four decades between 1740 and 1780 provide valuable firsthand information concerning the day-to-day activities at a major London theatre. Richard Cross evidently began keeping his diary during the 1740–1741 season when he served as prompter at Covent Garden theatre, but the following season saw him take up a similar position at Drury Lane, where he continued his entries until a month before his death in February 1760. Cross' diary, part of which is in the Folger Shakespeare Library and part in the John Rylands Library, besides noting some of his own activities and offering estimates of box-office receipts, provides very interesting insights into audience reactions to specific performances. Cross' replacement as prompter at Drury Lane, William Hopkins, continued his predecessor's practice of keeping a diary during the twenty years preceeding his death in 1780. The thirteen manuscript volumes are housed in the Folger. In addition a manuscript memorandum book by Hopkins is now in the British Library, and some notes transcribed by J. P. Kemble on playbills are in the Kemble-Devonshire Collection at the Huntington Library. It is worth noting as well that it was Hopkins, as keeper of the promptbook library of the company's repertory, who furnished the prompt copies to Gentleman for *Bell's Shakespeare* and *Bell's British Theatre*.

Inventories

Between 1660 and 1800 it was the normal practice for English theatres to use stock scenery, to refurbish and reuse standard painted wings, borders, and shutters according to generalized notions of type and place. An anonymous pamphlet of 1757(?), *The Case of the Stage in Ireland*, lists the necessary stock scenes as temples, tombs, city walls and gates, exteriors and interiors of palaces, streets, chambers, prisons, gardens, and rural prospects of groves, forests, and deserts. These might occasionally be supplemented by castles, camps, seashores, and caves. This report by an anonymous author is supported by three documents that provide lists of just such scenes used in specific theatres. Two of these inventories are relatively late and reflect theatrical activities outside London. The first is an inventory of scenes and machines prepared in 1776 when Spranger Barry sold the Crow Street theatre in Dublin to Thomas Ryder. (See James Boaden, *Memoirs of the Life of John Philip Kemble*, I, 469.) The second is a list prepared by Tate Wilkinson (1739–1803), a provincial theatre manager who administered the so-called York circuit (which also included Hull and Leeds) for thirty years. Tate's inventory, which dates from 1784 and is currently housed in the York Public Library, indicates the repairs and alterations made to fit old scenes to new plays and to make specific scenes into generalized scenes; it also records the movement of the scenes among the three points of the circuit.

By far the most important inventory of scenes, however, is that listing the scenes and properties at Covent Garden theatre in 1744. In 1743 the manager, John Rich, assigned the original lease as security for a loan, and among the papers (B.L. Add. Ms. 12201) is an inventory of the scenic materials in the theatre at the time. An incomplete transcript was published by Henry Saxe Wyndham in *The Annals of Covent Garden from 1732 to 1897* (1906); but a full transcript, including references to costumes as well as scenery, is provided by Philip H. Highfill, Jr., in *Restoration and 18th Century Theatre Research* (1966–1967). Richard Southern, who analyzes the document in *Changeable Scenery: Its Origin and Development in the British Theatre* (1952), notes that the various kinds of scenes are listed in six separate groups—flats, back flats, wings, pieces, properties, and ''stuff''—but that of the forty-three flats and back flats (backing flats?) only seven can be associated with particular plays. It is in fact difficult to distinguish between scenes deliberately designed for general use and those intended for specific plays but later put to general use. Nevertheless, the scenes are generally in line with the list from the 1757 pamphlet. Also included in the inventory are numerous references to stage machinery and mechanical devices, and historians have found it useful in their analysis of the document to refer to articles in contemporary encyclopedias such as those of A. Rees (1819) or Denis Diderot (Vol. X, 1772).

A list of properties at Covent Garden in 1767–1768 is also to be found in a volume of press cuttings dating from 1760 to 1789 in the British Library. Included is a valuation of the women's wardrobe at Covent Garden in 1769, and an *après-*

mort inventory of Christopher Rich's wardrobe. (The wardrobe lists are printed by Sybil Rosenfeld in "The Wardrobes of Lincoln's Inn Fields and Covent Garden" in *Theatre Notebook* V 15–19.)

PUBLIC AND LEGAL DOCUMENTS

The tracing of at least the outer dimensions of theatrical activity between 1660 and 1800 is dependent upon the patient, systematic, and diligent examination of an intimidating mass of official documentation: records of patents, charters, contracts, agreements, leases, deeds, warrants, and lawsuits; birth and death records, wills; acts of Parliament and Royal decrees. Theatre historians have recourse to several general collections and guides—*The Statutes of the Realm*, *Calendars of State Papers*, *Historical Manuscripts Commission Reports*—and scholars since Fitzgerald have quoted and summarized pertinent materials found in the Public Records Office. But until now there has not been a convenient guide to those records relating specifically to the theatre. A project announced by two American scholars promises to provide just such a guide, at least for the first half of the period. Judith Milhous and Robert Hume plan *A Register of English Theatrical Documents, 1660–1737*, which will consist of "a chronological register of documents . . . bearing on the operation and regulation of the professional theatre in England" ("Notes and Queries," *Theatre Notebook* XXXVIII [1984], 41). We can only hope that this example will spur a similar enterprise devoted to the rest of the eighteenth century.

Lord Chamberlain's Records

The great repository of much of this material is the Public Records Office in London, which holds the Accounts of His Majesty's Office of Works and the Chancery Proceedings of Bills and Answers. The former were used extensively by Eleanore Boswell in *The Restoration Court Stage* (1932), while the Chancery records were used by Leslie Hotson in *The Commonwealth and Restoration Stage* (1928). (Hotson lists 119 documents "of greatest importance for stage history" and prints several of them in his appendix, pp. 315–97.)

But the single most cited collection of public documents in the Public Records Office is *The Records of the Lord Chamberlain's Department*, in 87 volumes, described by Fitzgerald in 1882 as "admirably kept and carefully indexed" (*A New History of the English Stage*, App. A). Fitzgerald was in fact one of the first investigators to make use of these documents. It was Allardyce Nicoll, however, who summarized and partially quoted them in a more or less systematic way in the appendices to Volumes I and II of *A History of English Drama*, first published 1923–1925, and it is to Nicoll that several generations of theatre students have gone to consult the documents. Several factors combine to make this procedure less than satisfactory. In the first place, Nicoll confines his references to documents from 1660 to 1720, and even within this limited period he is incomplete. Second, summaries and edited and/or abbreviated excerpts can be misleading. And finally, some of his conjectural dates are questionable. All in all, in recent years theatre historians have found it advisable to consult the original documents.

To consult these records can be a formidable task. Since the Lord Chamberlain had a good many responsibilities besides supervising dramatic activities, references to theatrical affairs are scattered throughout the collection, and we have no systematic account of them. Fortunately, however, two circumstances make the task easier. First, for reasons that are not altogether clear, effort was made on a couple of occasions to gather theatrical materials together, and these collections constitute the series with the shelf mark LC7. In total, there are 242 documents, most of them from the period 1660–1720, but some concerning the opera from the 1780s. Second, those two indefatigable researchers, Judith Milhous and Robert Hume, have provided an annotated guide to these documents in "An Annotated Guide to the Theatrical Documents in PRO LC 7/1, 7/2 and 7/3" in *Theatre Notebook* (1981). The LC7 series consists of three collections:

a. LC7/1: A collection of thirty-six orders relating to the theatre, issued by the Lord Chamberlain between 1663 and 1700. Milhous and Hume suggest that about the year 1700, someone collected these orders, perhaps to provide a kind of source of case law. The handwriting is uniform, and some of the documents are duplicated in other volumes. There are two indexes, undoubtedly the same that stirred Fitzgerald's admiration.

b. LC7/2: A collection of eleven actors' contracts, eight dated 1706, three from 1714.

c. LC7/3: Two large scrapbooks consisting mainly of loose papers sent to the Lord Chamberlain's Office. As Milhous and Hume note, these "routine nuisances"—requests for action, petitions for redress, drafts of orders theatre managers would like to have had issued—were sometimes dealt with by the Lord Chamberlain and sometimes by a deputy. These papers total 195.

Other series have also yielded their treasures: LC3, devoted to registers; LC9, Great Wardrobe accounts and bills; and especially LC5, a miscellaneous collection of warrant books and original warrants. It is in this latter series that we find documents allotting plays to Davenant and Killigrew in 1660 and 1668, the Articles of Union of the two companies in 1682, various company leases issued between 1704 and 1720, and the order closing Drury Lane theatre on 6 June 1709. This closing is also the subject of a compilation of copies of documents—the originals mainly housed in the Public Records Office—preserved in the British Library (Add. Ms. 20726). Milhous and Hume, to whom we are again indebted for providing a summary of the contents of the collection ("The Silencing of Drury Lane in 1709," *Theatre Journal* XXXII, 427–47), point out that these documents were assembled about 1711 for Charles Killigrew and offer a corrective to Colley Cibber's "rather biased account" of the silencing in his autobiography.

Theatrical Papers of Vice Chamberlain Coke

As we have already noted, the supervision of theatrical activity in London was one of the Lord Chamberlain's responsibilities, but it was a minor one. We have also seen that after 1737 a subofficial was designated the Examiner of Plays, a circumstance that has provided us indirectly with the Larpent Collection (see above). A similar circumstance has provided us with another collection of theatrical material. In 1706, Thomas Coke was appointed "Vice Chamberlain to the Queen," an office he held until his death in 1727. Coke appears to have had a particular interest in the theatre, and it was he who was largely responsible for theatrical matters between 1706 and 1715. The existence of documents relating to the theatre among Coke's papers has long been known, but little use has been made of them. (Percy Fitzgerald was one of the few early historians to refer to them.) The story of the papers from the early eighteenth to the early twentieth century is a complicated one. (See the edition of the papers by Judith Milhous and Robert Hume, eds., pp. xxix–xxxiv.) For our purposes, it is enough to know what the documents are, where they are currently held, and what transcriptions are available. Eighty-two of a total of 153 known documents were acquired by Harvard University in 1928; the remaining items are scattered throughout various libraries and private collections: the Folger, the Pforzheimer Library, the Huntington, Texas, Yale, and Westminster Public Library. Eight are known only from the descriptions in sale catalogues (and one of these may be a ghost). There are in addition two partial transcriptions of the documents. One was made by James Winston, manager of Drury Lane in the 1820s and a close friend of Coke's great-grandson George Lamb, who owned the collection of theatrical papers from 1834 to 1843. This transcription is in the British Library (Add. ms. 38607). The second transcription, which bears no relationship to Winston's, was once in the possession of the music historian E. F. Rimbault (1816–1876), was privately acquired in 1888, and is now part of the collection of the New York Public Library (Drexel ms. 1986). The contents of the papers are succinctly summarized by their editors:

The documents include rough drafts of orders by the Lord Chamberlain regulating the theatre; complaints against managers by actors, singers, and dancers; costume and sundries bills; performers' contracts; orchestra rosters; salary lists; tradesmen's bills; financial estimates for the opera; lists of daily receipts; complaints in fractured French by angry Italian castrati about breach of contract; and the only daily box-office reports for opera that we possess for any time in London before the 1730s. Two major clusters of documents are of special interest. They concern, respectively, Vanbrugh's disastrous plunge into the Italian opera at the Haymarket in the spring of 1708, and the ferocious row during 1713–15 which saw Booth replace Doggett in the Triumvirate. [Milhous and Hume, *Vice Chamberlain Coke's Theatrical Papers 1706–1715*, p. x]

This material represents indeed the nitty-gritty of theatrical scholarship. From the point of view of theatre administration and theatrical rivalries, the Restoration and early eighteenth-century periods were particularly complex. Together with the earlier records of Sir Henry Herbert (Master of the Revels 1623–1673) and the Lord Chamberlain's documents discussed above, Coke's theatrical papers provide the underpinning for the legal and commercial history of the theatre. (*The Dramatic Records of Sir Henry Herbert* were edited by Joseph Quincy Adams in 1917.)

The Licensing Act of 1737

The Licensing Act of 1737, to which we have several times referred, was the most significant piece of government legislation concerning the theatres that was passed in the eighteenth century. Indeed, according to the author of a recent study, "Next to the laws protecting copyright, the 1737 act has probably had the most profound influence on English literature of any official measure in the last three centuries. . . . " (Vincent J. Liesenfeld, *The Licensing Act of 1737*, p. 3). Nevertheless, the genesis of the act lay in a combination of social, religious, economic, and political conditions, the complexity of which is evident both in Liesenfeld's discussion and in the documents he lists and prints in his appendices. Two bound volumes of printed sheets and pamphlets are the sources of many of the documents: "*Dramatic Tracts and Papers* collected by Mr. Haslewood" (B.L. 11795.K.31) and "Sir John Barnard's Bill and Related Papers—1735" (Harvard Theatre Collection TS 297.25.35F). The manuscript of the act itself is in the House of Lords Record Office (10 George II, Chap. XXVIII) and is printed by Liesenfeld (pp. 191–93). The act reestablished and codified earlier methods of controlling the theatre: a provision for outlawing vagrancy was joined to the establishment of the Lord Chamberlain as the official responsible for censorship and the enforcement of the act. (The Master of the Revels was ignored.) As is usual when considering such legislation, we must try to distinguish between the intentions of the government—to increase its own security by censoring an institution that was increasingly holding both government and crown up to public ridicule—and the effects, intended or not, on the history of the theatre. In order to achieve its own aims, Walpole's government needed a mechanism whereby it could impose prior censorship on all theatrical performances. To make the mechanism effective it was expedient to limit the number of performances; thus the number of theatres licensed to offer dramatic performances was limited to two. This measure had the effect of strengthening the commercial positions of the two patent theatres in Drury Lane and Covent Garden, by restricting the opening of rival theatres.

The act also abolished the right of provincial companies to perform. Nevertheless, strolling companies continued to act outside London, and in the last third of the eighteenth century Royal patents were granted for the building of new theatres in Bath (1768), Norwich (1768), York (1769), Hull (1769), Liverpool (1771), and Chester (1777). In 1788, another act (28 George III, Chap. XXX) gave justices the power to license theatrical representations—in the provinces—of plays that had been presented at the patent theatres. In spite of some arbitrary restrictions on place (outside London, Edinburgh, the King's residence, and the universities), the provinces were now officially a part of Britain's theatrical enterprise. (See Sybil Rosenfeld, *Strolling Players and Drama in the Provinces, 1660–1765.*)

WRITTEN EVIDENCE

Within the boundaries of the large and unwieldy category of written evidence, we find formal treatises and histories; diaries, letters, and memoirs; pamphlets and periodical literature; and theatrical biography and autobiography. And as we move through the eighteenth century, we discover that the volume of published material swelled in response to the growing demands of an increasingly literate public and the understandable desires on the part of the writers to profit by meeting that demand. That the product is sometimes drivel, or puffery, or self-serving, or designed more to titilate than to inform (the historian of course) is a fact that the historian must deal with. All products of human activity are evidence of something. Only through analysis and interpretation can the historian select that which is relevant to his concerns—in this instance the organization, presentation, and reception of theatrical events and their place in the sociocultural context of their time.

Dramatic Theory

Theatre history includes what was thought about the principles of dramatic art and the relationship between these principles and dramaturgical and theatrical practice. Dramatic theory in the Restoration and eighteenth century is scattered among dozens of prefaces, dedications, and prologues to printed plays, in pamphlets and periodical articles, and in a few formal treatises. (For a partial listing of dramatic and theatrical criticism see James Fullerton Arnott and John William Robinson, *English Theatrical Literature 1559–1900*, pp. 355–91. Marvin Carlson provides a succinct analysis in *Theories of the Theatre*, pp. 112–40. The most important documents are printed by Bernard F. Dukore in *Dramatic Theory and Criticism.*) The fact that playwrights—including Dryden, Congreve, Farquhar, Steele, and Goldsmith—were themselves major contributors makes the various statements of principle of particular interest.

By 1660 the principles of French classicism dominated European critical thought, and these were the principles that provided the foundations of English neoclassicism in the Restoration and early eighteenth century in England. Thomas Rymer's translation of René Rapin's *Réflexions sur la poétique* (*Reflections on Aristotle's Treatise of Poesie*) appeared in 1674; Nicholas Boileau's *Art poétique* was translated in 1680; the Abbé d'Aubignac's *The Whole Art of the Stage* in 1684. Even earlier, in *An Essay of Dramatic Poesy* (1668), John Dryden had set out the parameters of the critical debate: ancients versus moderns, French versus English practice. Although Dryden intellectually approved neoclassical principles, he was never able to resolve the tension between, in Carlson's words, "classic principles and traditional English practice" (*Theories of the Theatre*, p. 120). Indeed, the same might be said of Dryden's contemporaries and successors, for after his death in 1700, the authority of neoclassicism, at least as narrowly defined in terms of rules, began to weaken. Both common sense reason and a new sense of psychological verisimilitude underlay the pronouncements of Samuel Johnson (1709–1784), who distinguished between rules of custom and rules of nature, approved the mixing of comic and serious elements in Shakespeare, expressed doubts about the concept of poetic justice, and supported domestic tragedy.

The increasing emancipation of English criticism from French theory is reflected too in the new translations of Aristotle's *Poetics*. Until 1775, the standard version of the *Poetics* in English was actually a translation of André Dacier's French translation of 1692. In 1775 an anonymous English translation based on the Greek text was published, to be followed by the important translations of Henry James Pye (1788) and Thomas Twining (1789). (See Marvin T. Herrick, *The Poetics of Aristotle in England*.

The modified and moderate neoclassicism of late eighteenth-century England is illustrated in William Cooke's *The Elements of Dramatic Criticism* (1775). Cooke's primer is of course based on Aristotle's *Poetics*, but contemporary dramatic practice is reflected in his discussions of manners, sentiments and sentimental comedy, pantomimes, and farce. Perhaps the key indicator of how emancipated popular neoclassical theory had become is Cooke's treatment of the unities. Provided the underplot is connected to the main plot, he will allow that the unity of action is not breached, and he suggests that although the unities of time and place were necessities in the Greek theatre, their observance by modern playwrights must be a matter of choice.

The standard anthology pieces, however, present only the tip of the iceberg. Throughout the century, occasional writings and periodical essays reflected contemporary taste and thought in ways that may not always have been original, but that can help us to determine the relationship between the classic documents and the general cultural context for both theory and practice. In *Theatrical Criticism in London to 1795*, Charles Harold Gray surveys over two hundred periodicals and traces "the growth of criticism of theatrical entertainments in London" (p. 27). Gray draws few conclusions, but the criticism he traces is an important part of the body of commentary that, taken together, provides a picture of the tastes and concerns of playwrights, critics, and theatregoers from various segments of society. A knowledge of this material is useful for an understanding of the general milieu of the theatre. That the opinions expressed seem often to be at variance with the facts of repertory and box-office does not lessen their value as social documents.

Much of the periodical and pamphlet literature concerning the theatre was controversial, but one episode in particular needs to be singled out. In 1698

Jeremy Collier, a dissenting clergyman, published *A Short View of the Immorality and Profaneness of the English Stage*, prompting a pamphlet war that featured more than eighty documents over the following twenty-five years. (See Sister Rose Anthony's *The Jeremy Collier Stage Controversy 1698–1726* for a complete list of documents, and *The English Stage: Attack and Defense 1577–1730*, which reprints the most important contributions.) *A Short View* is in one respect another contribution to the series of anti-theatre documents that had begun in the sixteenth century and had reached a zenith (or nadir) in William Prynne's *Histriomastix* (1633). But Collier proved much more difficult to refute. He was familiar with neoclassical doctrine and vocabulary and was able to cite critical authority in support of his argument that, contrary to Horace's dictum that poetry was intended to delight and instruct, the contemporary English stage offered neither proper pleasure nor proper (i.e., moral) instruction. It is generally agreed that the most effective response to Collier was made by the critic John Dennis (1657–1734), especially in his *Usefulness of the Stage to the Happiness of Mankind* (1698). Collier nevertheless remains a force for the theatre historian to reckon with. A century ago a stage historian wrote that "Collier was completely victorious, and the best proof of his success, and of the necessity for his attack, was the marked improvement in decency which it produced" (Robert W. Lowe, quoted in Arnott and Robinson, *English Theatrical Literature 1559–1900*, p. 283). Modern historians are less inclined to such value judgments, but few have seriously questioned the general validity of Lowe's assertion.

Restoration Material

The main written evidence of the Restoration theatre consists of diaries, occasional comments, a couple of short treatises, a major work of dramatic bibliography, the reminiscences of a theatrical prompter, and an anonymous gossipy work evidently intended to stimulate controversy but ignored until resurrected by modern scholarship. To this we may add the comments and accounts of various foreign visitors.

It can be something of a shock to discover that our knowledge of the theatrical world of the Restoration period depends so heavily upon references in the diaries and letters of spectators who were for the most part writing for themselves and whose observations have only accidentally remained available to us, often still in manuscript. The twenty almanacs of Sir John Nicolas of Surrey, for example, dating from 1667 to 1703 and now in the British Library, contain diary entries and household accounts that suggest the possibility of the Restoration theatre as family entertainment. But of course other references convey a great variety of impressions. On the one hand, we have the sparse notations of James Brydges, who records his attendance at the theatre but usually neglects to tell us what play he saw. On the other hand, we have the occasionally alarming comments of Godwin Wharton, whose close associations with fairies and the deity lend a bizarre coloring to the most mundane report. (For a review of these and other occasional observers of the theatrical scene, see R. Jordan "Some Restoration Playgoers" in *Theatre Notebook* XXXV [1981].) A better-known and more sober example is the memorandum book, in the British Library, of Edward Browne, a Cambridge medical student and son of Sir Thomas Browne. Browne notes the plays he saw, the playhouses he attended, and the cost. The only date mentioned is 1662. (Selections are printed in Arthur C. Sprague, *Beaumont and Fletcher on the Restoration Stage*, pp. 21–24.)

The diaries of John Evelyn (1620–1706) and Samuel Pepys (1633–1703) are undoubtedly the masterpieces of the genre in the Restoration. But however valuable as evidence of English life, Evelyn's work pales in comparison with that of Pepys so far as the theatre is concerned. The publication in 1818 of Evelyn's *Diary*, however, stimulated interest in Evelyn's friend, and by 1825 Pepys' shorthand had been deciphered and a two-volume selection from the diary published. It was immediately clear that here was important new evidence concerning the theatre during the first decade following the return of Charles II. Genest paid tribute to Pepys in *Some Account of the English Stage* (1832): "The theatrical intelligence contained in two large 4to. Vols. is not very great in quantity, but it is highly valuable, on account of dates—and because Pepys mentions the revival of several old plays not noticed by Downes or Langbaine as having been revived" (I, 39). Pepys was a close observer of and had an abiding interest in the social world in which he lived, and when that world coincided with the theatrical world, his descriptions are detailed and comprehensive. He tells us about actors, actresses, scenes, costumes, and music, and about the action in the auditorium as well as on the stage. He inspected the tiring rooms and the stage machinery, and he reports an interview with Thomas Killigrew in 1667, in which the theatre manager contrasts his theatre with the stage of the previous age. Since Pepys is our only source of information on some points, his general accuracy has been difficult to assess. In those instances where it has been possible to compare his information with that provided by Evelyn or Herbert, he has often been corroborated, and in no instance has he actually been contradicted. Pepys' firsthand evidence remains of prime importance for the theatre historian. (Pepys' *Diary* was edited by Henry B. Wheatley, 1893–1899. A collection of passages relating to the theatre, *Pepys on the Restoration Stage*, was published by Helen McAfee in 1916.)

Pepys' general picture of the Restoration stage is supplemented by several peripheral works of literature. Sam Vincent's *The Young Gallant's Academy* (1674) is an adaptation of Thomas Dekker's *The Gull's Hornbook* (1609) and consequently may owe as much to its literary progenitor as to the author's observations of the contemporary playhouse. The anonymous *Country Gentleman's Vade Mecum* (1699) provides a description of an audience on a "third day," the day on which the profits went to the playwright. The satirist Tom Brown, in his *Amusements Serious and Comical* (1700), includes a description of a playhouse at the turn of the century. (Selections from all three writers are printed in A. M. Nagler, *A Source Book in Theatrical History*.)

And finally, we should perhaps compare Pepys' descriptions with the later observations of John Macky, who in the first volume of *A Journey Through England*, published in 1714, contrasts English and Continental theatres. He comments

that between the Acts you are as much diverted by viewing the Beauties of the Audience, as while they act with the Subject of the Play; and the whole is illuminated to the greatest advantage: Whereas abroad, the Stage being only illuminated, and the Lodge or Boxes close, you lose the Pleasure of seeing the Company; and indeed the *English* have reason in this, for no Nation in the World can shew such an Assembly of shining Beauties as here. [pp. 170–71]

Pepys would undoubtedly have agreed.

Restoration writers were often self-consciously insistent on the differences between contemporary drama and theatre and that of the "previous age." Both Richard Flecknoe's *A Short Treatise of the English Stage* (1664) and James Wright's *Historia Histrionica* (1699) profess admiration for Elizabethan dramatists and actors, but find the circumstances of theatrical production wanting in comparison with that of their own time. Flecknoe refers to the "cost and ornament" of the contemporary stage, making for plays more suited to sight than hearing. Wright too laments the deterioration of dramatic literature that accompanied the introduction of "scenes," music, and actresses, although he approved the new delights.

A far more scholarly and substantial work is Gerard Langbaine's *An Account of the English Dramatick Poets* (1691), a revised edition of which was prepared in 1699 by Charles Gildon and published as *The Lives and Characters of the English Dramatick Poets*. Langbaine was a literary scholar rather than a man of the theatre; his knowledge of plays and playwrights was bibliographical rather than theatrical. In fact, English dramatic bibliography really began with Langbaine who, although more interested in plagiarism than in stageworthiness or commercial success, provided remarkably complete biographies and accurate lists of plays. He has been called brash, tactless, and pedantic, but he did his work well. "Perhaps alone among seventeenth-century students of the English drama," writes John Loftis, "he continues to be cited not merely as a contemporary or near-contemporary witness but as an authority whose opinion is valued by reason of his comprehensive research" (*The Revels History of Drama in English*, V, i).

In some respects John Downes' *Roscius Anglicanus* (1708) is a book at opposite poles from Langbaine's *Account*. It is uncertain when Downes was born, but it is clear that he was an elderly man in 1708 and was looking back over a long career as prompter for the Duke's Company. Thus his anecdotal, matter-of-fact survey of the theatrical nitty-gritty is based on his own experience, on theatrical records to which he undoubtedly had access, and on a view of plays as commercial commodities rather than as literary works. While Downes attempted to write a coherent history, the real value of his work lies in its unimaginative listings of

roles and actors, dates and finances. Scholars have detected errors in his anecdotes, for which he had to rely on his memory, but they have found fewer
mistakes in his theatrical data, for which he probably had notes and records.
The view of the Restoration stage as essentially a commercial enterprise has its
roots in Downes' account.

The anonymous *A Comparison Between the Two Stages* (1702), at one time
mistakenly attributed to Charles Gildon, appeared at a time of intense interest
to the theatre historian. In 1695, the actor Thomas Betterton broke with the
management at Drury Lane, and with a group of other actors he opened at
Lincoln's Inn Fields. The "two stages" are the two playhouses. In 1698 Jeremy
Collier's *A Short View* appeared. The anonymous *A Comparison* then was written—in a week, according to its author—in the seventh year of the separation
of the united company and during the height of the Collier controversy. *A
Comparison* provides a brief survey of the two theatres and their fortunes together
with a more detailed look at some particular productions. (Sixty pages are devoted
to an analysis of Bevill Higgons' otherwise forgotten *The Generous Conqueror*.)
The author reveals himself as a moderate neoclassicist who cites the obvious
"rules" and concedes Collier his basic point. The modern editor of *A Comparison*
summarizes the work neatly:

Replete with contemporary allusions and gossip, it is a storehouse of fact and opinion.
The varying fortunes of Drury Lane and Lincoln's Inn Fields are traced in detail. The
older dramatists, Shakespeare, Jonson, and Beaumont and Fletcher, are discussed and
their contemporary appeal and popularity indicated. Current productions of plays by such
writers as Congreve, Vanbrugh, Farquhar, Steele, and Rowe are surveyed as well as
those of their less capable competitors. Actual stage conditions are reflected in an amusingly cynical manner, and the tendency of the theatre toward the vaudeville type of
entertainment is clearly indicated. [*A Comparison*, p. xviii]

Wells notes that he found no contemporary allusions or references to the book.
If it was intended to stir controversy it failed. But in the twentieth century it
has become an irreplaceable document concerning the English stage at the turn
of the eighteenth century.

Visitors from abroad offer their own views of the English stage, although few
early visitors add substantially to our knowledge of the Restoration theatre.
Samuel de Sorbière and Balthasar de Monconys, both of whom visited London
in 1663, refer in their published accounts to the stage being covered with a green
cloth. Henri Misson a few years later observed that it was the benches in the
auditorium that were so covered. While Misson may have sowed some confusion
here, his general description of the second Theatre Royal in Drury Lane, which
he attended in 1698, can be compared with an earlier description of Dorset
Garden by François Brunet in his *Voyage d'Angleterre* (1676). Another detailed
description of a theatre, by Conte Lorenzo Magalotti, who accompanied the
Duke of Tuscany on a tour of England in 1669, has usually been assumed to

refer to the first Theatre Royal in Bridges Street. According to Magalotti, the Duke visited the Theatre Royal twice and the Duke's Theatre, Lincoln's Inn Fields twice. In 1980, however, John Orrell pointed out that a supplementary account of the same visits by Filippo Corsini, housed in the state archives in Florence (Archivo Mediceo 3987), indicates that Magalotti's description is actually of the Duke's Theatre. Since Corsini himself offers a description of the Theatre Royal, we now have full descriptions of each theatre. (See "Filippo Corsini and the Restoration Stage" in *Theatre Notebook* XXXIV, 4–9.)

Finally, we should note *Lettres sur les Anglois et les François* (1725) and *Lettres sur les voyages* (1725) by the Swiss moralist Beat Ludwig Muralt (1665–1749), who visited England in 1694–1695. Both volumes were translated into German and English and served to introduce the London stage to continental Europe. In fact, most early accounts of the English theatre by foreign visitors are of more significance as contributions to the intellectual climate of the countries the visitors came from than as documents of English theatrical history. And even so, we ought to heed the words of John Alexander Kelly, who in his survey of the accounts of German visitors, noted that "these works [of the late seventeenth and early eighteenth centuries] . . . are for the most part models of superficiality and shallowness" (*German Visitors to English Theatres in the Eighteenth Century*, p. 5). Fuller and more important descriptions of the Restoration court theatre, written over a period of twenty years, are provided in the diplomatic correspondence of Giovanni Salvetti, who with his father Amerigo functioned as a Florentine agent in London. Giovanni reported on the London scene for twenty-three years and made regular notes on the court theatre from 1660 to 1680. This important material has been translated and published by John Orrell in *Theatre Research International*, n.s. II (1976–1977).

Pamphlets and Periodicals

Pamphlets, occasional in nature, appeared in intermittent flurries throughout the eighteenth century, usually in response to controversial performances or plays, sometimes in response to yet other pamphlets. We find pamphlets that comment on specific plays or groups of plays; pamphlets that discuss specific performances or performers; pamphlets devoted to the theory of drama or acting; and pamphlets that simply form part of the theatrical quarrels of the period between and among actors, managers, playwrights, and the public. We have already had occasion to note the numerous pamphlets associated with the Collier controversy. Similar spates of pamphlets were prompted by the performances of Addison's *Cato* (1713) and Home's *Douglas* (1756, 1757), by the riots of 1763 and 1773 at Covent Garden; by actor-manager disputes of 1733 and 1743, and by a multitude of other events important and trivial. (The bulk of the pamphlets are listed in Arnott and Robinson.) Such material helps to fill in our picture of the sociopolitical dimension of the theatre.

This dimension, together with the beginnings of popular criticism and with data concerning places and dates of performances, can also be traced in the increasing periodical literature devoted to the theatre. The journals themselves varied in quality, nature, and purpose—from daily newsletters carrying political, financial, and commercial news and advertisements, to periodicals such as *The Tatler* and *The Spectator* containing serious essays, to monthly periodicals on the model of the *Gentleman's Magazine* (founded 1731), which tried to present a thoughtful retrospective on the events of the month. Later in the century, weekly and daily newspapers increased in prominence. More than two hundred periodicals appeared at various times during the eighteenth century, but only a handful of those from the late seventeenth and the first seven decades of the eighteenth century dealt in any regular or informative way with theatrical affairs. (Useful guides include Arnott and Robinson, *English Theatrical Literature*, pp. 392–434, and Carl J. Stratman's *Britain's Theatrical Periodicals, 1720–1967: A Bibliography*, both of which indicate library locations. John Loftis prints a selection in *Essays on the Theatre from 18th-Century Periodicals*.)

Among the important early periodicals is *The Gentleman's Journal* (January 1691/92–July 1694), edited by Peter Anthony Motteux, a Frenchman who had arrived in England in 1685. Motteux printed theatrical announcements but tended to go beyond mere advertisement. He commented on plays and discussed their reception by London audiences. His note on Dryden's *Cleomenes* (February 1691/92) has been called "the first effort in English journalism at criticism of the contemporary drama" (Charles Harold Gray, *Theatrical Criticism in London to 1795*, p. 33). A later journal, *The Muses' Mercury: or the Monthly Miscellany* (January 1707/8–January 1708/9), edited by the Whig pamphleteer John Old-mixon, promised a similar treatment of theatrical performances, but in practice provided far less. The first successful daily paper, the *Daily Courant* (founded 1702), either ignored the theatre or attacked it with a moralist's bludgeon.

Historians of the stage and the drama have found the publications of Addison and Steele of more interest. Many of the thirty-five papers in *The Spectator* (1711–1712) that are concerned either directly or indirectly with the theatre were written by Steele, who also contributed six articles on theatrical matters to *The Guardian* (March–October 1713) and in 1720 produced *The Theatre*, which in spite of its title was not exclusively or even primarily concerned with the theatre. Several issues, however, were devoted to affairs at Drury Lane theatre and formed part of a pamphlet debate on the strained relationship between the theatre's management and the Lord Chamberlain. Addison contributed a famous mock inventory of the sale of the properties at Drury Lane in 1709, by Christopher Rich in *The Tatler* (no. 42), and his series of four essays on tragedy in *The Spectator* (nos. 39, 40, 42, 44) is significant in the history of criticism. Addison's description of contemporary tragic costume (no. 42), which featured a headdress "so very high, that there is often a greater Length from his Chin to the Top of his Head, than to the Sole of his Foot," is amusingly informative, as are his comments on stage thunder and lightning in no. 592. The importance of these essays by Steele and Addison is attested by Odell: "Blessed be the Tatler and the Spectator. . . . One will look in vain for it [theatrical information] in other papers of the time, or of the years preceding or following. . . . Without them, my account of the staging of plays in Queen Anne's day would be meagre indeed'' (*Shakespeare from Betterton to Irving*, I, 296).

Steele's *The Theatre* notwithstanding, the first true theatrical journal to appear in London was *The Prompter*, produced by Aaron Hill and William Popple between November 1734 and July 1736. Hill was an experienced man of the theatre, and his discussions of practical theatre matters reflect this experience. He probably helped to pave the way for a revolution in acting. (Hill's ideas on acting were developed through several essays and poems and reached a final form in the posthumous *Essay on the Art of Acting*, published in his *Works* [1753].) Popple devoted most of his efforts to decrying the absurdities of Italian opera. Both men were intensely moral and viewed the stage as a moral institution. Their hope was to reform the theatre, and they therefore promoted and approved the legislation that became the Licensing Act of 1737. William Appleton and Kalman Burnim, who have edited a selection from *The Prompter*, note that the papers "provide for us the fullest and liveliest account of the London stage at a critical time in its history. They represent the earliest attempt to effect a journalistic discussion of theatrical events in the eighteenth century" (p. vii). (The only known complete run of *The Prompter*, possibly Popple's own copy, is in the Bodleian Library at Oxford.)

Between 1730 and 1770 periodicals increased in number, size, and scope. *The Grub Street Journal* (1730–1737) published a good deal of comment on theatrical affairs, mostly on the level of theatrical politics and personal quarrels. There were fresh imitations of *The Spectator* and the arrival on the scene of literary reviews such as *The Monthly Review* (1749) and *The Critical Review* (1756). Most newspapers continued to carry brief notices of plays, often "puffs" printed prior to performances, but the more important newspapers such as *The Gazetteer* or *The London Chronicle* joined the essay periodicals and magazines in a more regular coverage of theatrical affairs. *The London Chronicle* in particular is noteworthy for its column, "The Theatrical Register; or Weekly Rosciad" (1766–). In addition, newspapers often printed letters dealing with the theatre, along with plot summaries and advertisements.

After 1760, several important magazines undertook theatrical criticism. *The Gentleman's Magazine*, founded in 1731 by Edward Cave, which in its early years published plot summaries and occasional commentary, had by 1760 expanded its coverage to include theatrical as well as literary criticism. (The rival *London Magazine* on the other hand, which appeared between 1732 and 1785, confined its commentary to the printed text and usually provided little more than a plot summary.) Other magazines to take up theatrical criticism between 1760 and 1770 include *The Grand Magazine of Universal Intelligence*, *The Lady's Magazine*, *Court Magazine; or Royal Chronicle*, and *The Universal Museum*. In the meantime, several publications devoted exclusively to the theatre made brief appearances: *The Theatrical Review* (1763), *The Monitor* (later *The The-*

atrical Monitor (1767–1768), *Covent Garden Chronicle* (1768), and *The Macaroni and Theatrical Magazine* (1772–74). Many of these announced grandiose plans for treating all aspects of dramatic art, but few of them lasted more than a few issues.

The great newspapers founded during the last third of the century devoted considerable space to theatrical criticism. *The Morning Chronicle* (founded 1769) employed serious theatre critics, including, in the early years of the nineteenth century, William Hazlitt. *The General Evening Post* (founded 1771) printed theatrical news and criticism as well as memoirs of actors and actresses. *The Morning Post* (founded 1772) offered critiques of actors and actresses as well as theatrical reviews. Some articles, including the series, "The Prompter before the Curtain" (1776–1777), were evidently written by David Garrick.

Contemporary History and Commentary

The career of Colley Cibber (1671–1757) as actor, theatre manager, and playwright spanned more than forty years. Cibber's decision to record, explain, and justify that career has placed generations of theatre historians in his debt. *An Apology for the Life of Mr. Colley Cibber* was published in 1740, seven years after its author had "retired" from the stage. (Actually, Cibber's last recorded appearance on the stage was in 1745 at the age of seventy-four.) Cibber's themes are the struggle and ultimate triumph of the actor-manager over Christopher Rich, and the desirability of a unified theatrical enterprise. While we are given glowing portraits of older Restoration actors such as Betterton, Sandford, Mrs. Barry, and Mrs. Bracegirdle, many of whom are known to us only or principally through *An Apology*, we get far greater detail concerning the later period, especially 1704–1717, during which time Cibber was a main participant in the sometimes petty struggles and rivalries that marked the beginnings of the modern English theatre. We owe our knowledge of some crucial areas of theatrical history—the characters of actors, backstage machinations—almost entirely to Cibber. Cibber spanned the years between Betterton and Garrick, and his ongoing and intimate connection with the theatre makes his autobiographical history a central source of information for the period 1690–1733. Cibber was, of course, not a universally liked and admired man, and the appearance of *An Apology* sparked gossip, new quarrels, and a spate of pamphlets. But even Alexander Pope's devastating treatment of the old actor and poet laureate in the 1743 version of *The Dunciad* cannot detract from the importance of either Cibber's career or his autobiography. (In 1748 the actor Anthony Aston published *A Brief Supplement to Colley Cibber*.)

The year following the publication of Cibber's *Apology*, the publisher Edmund Curll issued *The History of the English Stage from the Restauration to the Present Time*, which he attributed to Thomas Betterton. Betterton had by this date, of course, been dead for over thirty years, and the volume seems to have been the work of Curll and William Oldys, based perhaps in part on notes by Betterton.

What is provided is a sketchy account of Davenant's company, the union of the companies in 1682, the opening in 1705 of the new theatre in the Haymarket, and the deaths in 1710 and 1713 of Betterton and Barry respectively. The remainder of the work is given over to notes on actors and actresses. The value of the discussion lies in the details provided on the duties of a player (chap. IV) and in the specific descriptions and instructions concerning the art of acting itself. There is an emphasis on gesture and motion, which are valued above "mere speaking" as "the support of Nature." We know little enough of the acting styles of the period, and if these descriptions are authentically Bettertonian, they are valuable indeed.

William Rufus Chetwood's *A General History of the Stage* (1749) delivers somewhat less than its title promises. Beginning with the Greek theatre, the "history" reaches *Gammer Gurton's Needle* (ca. 1552–1563) by page 12, and the Restoration by page 20. A paean to Betterton and a lengthy defense of acting and the stage follow. But the bulk of the book is devoted to memoirs of the principal performers on the English and Irish stages during the first half of the eighteenth century. Chetwood was prompter at the Smock Alley theatre in Dublin and Drury Lane in London, and therefore his incidental comments on the workings of the theatres, like the earlier observations of John Downes, are of immense value. It is Chetwood, for example, who provides the first positive reference to the use of machinery to move wings. He notes that a machinist "formed a Machine to move the Scenes regularly all together" but that this machine was later "laid aside" (p. 73). One of Chetwood's successors in Dublin, Robert Hitchcock, also refers to a barrel or drum "underneath," designed to shift scenery, in his *An Historical View of the Irish Stage* (1788, 1794). (For a discussion of the reference and its possible relation to both English and French methods of scene shifting, see Richard Southern, *Changeable Scenery*, pp. 213 ff.)

Another writer associated with the Smock Alley theatre and later Drury Lane, Benjamin Victor, in 1761 published *The History of the Theatres of London and Dublin* in two volumes; a third volume appeared in 1771. Victor thought of his work as a supplement to Cibber's *Apology*, and besides an annual register of performances at Drury Lane and Covent Garden from 1712, he also provides an insider's look at the workings of the theatrical enterprise—the personal relationships, the finances, the management. His work was continued by W. C. Oulton's *The History of the Theatres of London* (1796). A parallel work on the Edinburgh stage, John Jackson's *The History of the Scottish Stage* (1793), similarly reflects its author's career as manager at the Theatre Royal in Edinburgh and is most informative when dealing with his own time and responsibilities.

In many ways a much more interesting and informative work, this time on theatrical activity outside London, is provided in Tate Wilkinson's *The Wandering Patentee* (1795). Wilkinson (1739–1803) had previously published his memoirs in 1790. Taken together, these two works—totalling eight volumes—are a treasure-trove of information concerning theatrical activity on the so-called

York circuit. (Tate's dates and facts have been collated against other contemporary sources of information, such as playbills, by Charles Beecher Hogan in *An Index to the Wandering Patentee by Tate Wilkinson*.) Tate's intention and accomplishment are admirably expressed in his own words: "I will introduce a variety of sketches, incidents, anecdotes, and little dramatic adventures, that will, I hope, not only amuse, but in point of chronology, be often satisfactory and useful to some present and future theatrical virtuoso, and particularly so to a Yorkshire stage visitant" (I, 14).

Over a dozen accounts of the lives of strolling players were published between 1729 and 1830, from the obscure *Life of James Spiller* (1729), a pamphlet by George Akerby, to the *Life* of the eccentric and colorful Charlotte Charke (1755), daughter of Colley Cibber, to the possibly fictitious *Memoirs of Sylvester Daggerwood* (1806). (See Sybil Rosenfeld, *Strolling Players and Drama in the Provinces*.) But the only account in any way comparable to Tate's as an accurate source of information is *Memoirs of an Unfortunate Son of Thespis* (1818) by Edward Cape Everard, a protégé (illegitimate son?) of Garrick who, after the great actor's death in 1779, evidently lived out his life as an itinerant actor in the provinces. Everard's autobiography, described by the authors of *A Biographical Dictionary* (s. v. "Everard, Edward Cape") as "one of the best and most detailed of its kind," provides an accurate and reliable record of the life of a journeyman actor in a major London theatre and a strolling player during the last two decades of the eighteenth century.

Charles Dibdin, with *A Complete History of the English Stage*, published in five volumes between 1797 and 1800, continued the tradition of the man of the theatre turned historian. Dramatist, actor, and songwriter, Dibdin affirmed the primacy of firsthand experience as a historiographical principle, affirming its superiority to written documents as a basis for history. "I will venture to say," he wrote, "that any thing written upon the conviction of long experience will be more likely in its essence to be faithfully authentic, than a history composed, or rather vamped, from a whole library of printed and written documents. . . . " (I, iii). On the other hand, Dibdin is among the first historians of his kind to pay more than cursory attention to the history of the theatre in Europe as well as in England before his own time. The first three volumes of his work are devoted to the classical theatres, the European theatres (especially the French) to the death of Voltaire, and to the English theatre before 1625. Volume IV brings the account up to the time of Garrick, and the last volume ends with Garrick's death in 1779. The author clearly "vamped" much of his history. Dibdin nevertheless had the true historian's sense of purpose and point of view:

A mere history of theatrical events, I take to be a very insipid thing. I consider the Stage as a state branching from the empire of literature, and therefore an examination of its rulers, and the rise and operation of the various circumstances issuing from its general interest, cannot be related to effect without digesting different opinions and forming a rational judgment of them. [I, iii]

And at the centre of stage history is the actor: "That an actor is the main spring of the dramatic art it is impossible to deny. Vainly shall the poet paint a faithful portrait of men and manners; his labour shall remain a lifeless lump till it receive a promethean touch from the fire of the actor" (I, 5–6). In the eighteenth century only Luigi Riccoboni's *Reflexions historiques et critiques sur les différents théâtres de l'Europe* (1738) and Pietro Napoli Signorelli's *Storia critica dei teatri, antichi e moderni* (1787–1790) are comparable in their comparative treatment of the theatres of contemporary Europe. And only Napoli Signorelli can lay an equal claim to writing history in the sense that Dibdin's chronological survey is history.

Other discussions of the theatre were never intended as history. Thomas Wilkes' *A General View of the Stage* (1759) discusses dramatic genres, with examples from the contemporary and near-contemporary stage; provides the mandatory historical sketch of the ancient and modern stage to the Restoration; offers an extended commentary on acting; and devotes a third of its pages to remarks on the merits of the major performers that the author has seen. The value of Francis Gentleman's *The Dramatic Censor* (1770) and Thomas Davies' *Dramatic Miscellanies* (1784) lies mainly in their comparative descriptions of the various actors who performed in the plays they criticize. For both, Garrick represented the epitome of the actor's art, but Gentleman is capable of according earlier actors—such as James Quin (1693–1766)—their due as well. Gentleman also includes a brief, not wholly laudatory discussion of theatrical management (II, 451–56). Thomas Holcroft (1745–1809), whose novel *Alwyn, or the Gentleman Comedian* (1780) undoubtedly reflects its author's own experiences as a strolling player, was also the author of *The Theatrical Recorder*, a periodical that ran from December 1804 to November 1805. The collected numbers were published in 1805. "The plan of the Theatrical Recorder," he wrote, "is intended to be complete, with respect to every thing passing in the theatrical world, which is of a nature to be at all times interesting" (Preface). Holcroft was especially proud of the illustrations of costume that he included. Enterprises similar to Holcroft's had, as we have seen, been attempted at various times throughout the century, but like the earlier ones, this one too lasted but a brief time. Historians of the theatre must regret the circumstances that made these publications such short-lived affairs.

Biography and Autobiography

The preoccupation of much of the general theatrical history and commentary with acting and actors pales in comparison with the hundreds of publications, ranging from slight pamphlets to multivolume works, that were written by or about theatrical performers. These performers included—besides legitimate actors—singers, dancers, acrobats, equestrians, ventriloquists, magicians, and variety artists impossible to categorize. They performed in amphitheatres, pleasure gardens, fair booths, and taverns as well as in the patent theatres and opera houses. Moreover, the theatrical world included performers' private lives, real or imagined, and the traditional attacks on the immorality of the theatre were spiced by gossip and fueled by actors' own published confessions. Besides the pamphlet wars between the attackers and the defenders of the thespian art, the substantial volumes of biography, autobiography, and memoirs that proliferated, especially in the second half of the century, have contributed to a long-standing stereotypical impression of the profession as less than respectable.

It has fallen to theatre historians to examine this mass of material. (Most of it is listed in Arnott and Robinson, *English Theatrical Literature*, pp. 212–355.) From one point of view, this material is characterized by "diffuseness and anecdote" together with "inaccuracy, confused chronology and tedious irrelevancies" (Michael Booth, et al., *The Revels History of Drama in English*, VI, 273), and its usefulness is to be determined solely by its reliability in chronicling facts concerning audiences, playwrights and actors, copyright laws, the financial situation of theatres, and so on. These are, of course, central historical concerns. But another way to look at this material is to consider it as evidence of the mythology of the theatre, as "real" in its own way as the historian's documented "facts."

Some of the major actors of the eighteenth century were the subjects of serious biographies, several of which are still regarded as important historical sources and as significant works in their own right. The journeyman critic Charles Gildon's *The Life of Mr. Thomas Betterton* (1710) is, unfortunately, not among them; far more informed and informative comments are to be found in Cibber's *An Apology* and Aston's *Brief Supplement*. David Garrick was somewhat better served. While Arthur Murphy's biography of the actor, published in 1801, is ill-considered, petty, and self-serving, Thomas Davies' *Memoirs of the Life of David Garrick, Esq.* (1780), undertaken at the urging of the actor's friend Samuel Johnson (who provided information concerning Garrick's early years and in fact supplied the first sentence of the biography), not only brought fame and fortune to its author but also continues to be a highly regarded work. Charles Macklin was the subject of at least two early biographies, by James Thomas Kirkman (1799) and William Cooke (1804).

But possibly the best-known biographer of late eighteenth-century actors and actresses is James Boaden (1762–1839), who contributed lives of John Philip Kemble (1825), Sarah Siddons (1827), Dorothy Jordan (1831), and Elizabeth Inchbald (1833). Boaden was a critic and a journalist, with an intense, even scholarly, interest in the theatre. He wrote several plays and was among the first to expose the Ireland Shakespeare forgeries in his *Letter to Steevens* (1796). In addition, he was personally acquainted with his subjects. He was a close friend of Kemble and was thus able to present a fuller and more detailed and revealing portrait of the actor—especially in moments of crisis—than might otherwise have been possible. Boaden was present, for example, to witness and record Kemble's reaction to the destruction by fire of Covent Garden and Kemble's carefully kept library. Sympathetic and factually accurate, Boaden's biographies are among the best of their genre.

We have already had occasion to note the important autobiographies of Colley Cibber, Tate Wilkinson, and Cape Everard. We might well include in this honorable company the reminiscences and memoirs of George Anne Bellamy, the Dibdin family, and John Bernard. *An Apology for the Life of George Anne Bellamy* (1785), probably ghostwritten by Alexander Bicknell, was immensely popular in its own time and remains a useful source of information in ours. The actress's flamboyant reputation undoubtedly explains the work's initial success. Its usefulness to the theatre historian rests largely on the incidental information it provides, not only about Mrs. Bellamy, but especially concerning stage costume in the mid-eighteenth century. The portrait of George Anne is idealized, the tone overly moral, and both subject and author are vague on specific dates. But *An Apology* is undeniably entertaining and is perhaps best approached as a form of autobiographical fiction.

Charles Dibdin (the Younger) and his brother Thomas, like their father Charles, provided reminiscences of their theatrical careers. The Elder Charles' *The Professional Life of Mr. Dibdin* (1803) includes the words to over six hundred of the author's songs, and sixty prints taken from the subjects of the songs, but the work is most notable for its account of Dibdin's quarrels with managers and his relationship with Garrick. Charles Dibdin the Younger was for a time (1802–1819) proprietor and manager of Sadler's Wells Theatre, and his *Memoirs* (edited in 1956 by George Speaight) provide a lively account of a manager's life. His younger brother Thomas, who earned his living as an actor, scene painter, dramatist, and songwriter, also wrote *Reminiscences* (1827). As for John Bernard's *Retrospections of the Stage* (1830), we may allow the editors of *A Biographical Dictionary* to comment: "Though the style . . . is digressive, Bernard has a ready wit, an excellent eye for character, and an almost universal acquaintance among theatrical figures of the late eighteenth century; thus the volumes are valuable chronicles of theatrical life and repositories of amusing anecdote" (s.v. "Bernard John").

As the eighteenth century wore on, the initial interest of the age in the acting profession and the actors' lives degenerated into a taste for anecdote and gossip. In 1753 Theophilus Cibber published the first volume of *The Lives and Characters of the Most Eminent Actors and Actresses of Great Britain and Ireland*, an overly ambitious project that began and ended with the *Life* of Barton Booth included in this first volume. The anonymous *Theatrical Biography* (1772) provides sober commentary on the lives and merits of performers at Drury Lane, Covent Garden, and the Haymarket, "biased," according to the introduction, "by no stage connexions, prejudiced by no theatrical disappointments" (p. v). (A later and equally serious work is Thomas Gilliland's *The Dramatic Mirror* [1808], in which the author presents an alphabetically arranged discussion of major performers from the time of Shakespeare to 1807.)

By the end of the century, however, these reasonably serious endeavors gave way to collections of anecdotes, real or imagined. The anonymous compiler of *The Secret History of the Green Rooms* (1790) refers in his sub-title to "authentic memoirs of actors and actresses." However "authentic" they really were, the memoirs clearly found a ready public, and other publications followed the lead of *The Secret History*. The bookseller John Roach issued his totally unreliable *Roach's Authentic Memoirs of the Green Room* in 1796, and W. C. Oulton, author of *The History of the Theatres of London* (see above), was evidently responsible for six yearly volumes titled *Authentic Memoirs of the Green Room* (1799–1804). Little credence was placed in these "memoirs" even in their own day. Of Oulton's first volume, *The Monthly Mirror* (March 1799) snarled: "These *authentic* memoirs want but one thing to entitle them to that epithet, and that is . . . '*they are not true.*' They are manufactured by a needy and malignant scribbler, of the name of Oulton" (quoted by Arnott and Robinson, *English Theatrical Literature*, p. 213). *Green Room Gossip* (1809) by "Gridiron Gabble" (Joseph Haslewood) is a humorous addition to the genre. These publications may represent the nadir of their kind in eighteenth-century England, but they most certainly are the progenitors of the pseudobiography that continues to flourish on the periphery of the "entertainment industry." An honorable exception is *Crosby's Pocket Companion to the Playhouses*. *The Monthly Mirror* for January 1796 noted that the editor "has been particularly attentive to the accuracy of his materials" (quoted by Arnott and Robinson, *English Theatrical Literature*, p. 213).

Actors and actresses were also the objects of poetical appreciation, usually satirical, sometimes amusing, and occasionally informative. Among the best known is Charles Churchill's *The Rosciad* (1761), in which the actors discussed are, with the exception of Garrick, scathingly attacked. The poem went through eleven editions by 1772 and was almost immediately followed by *The Apology* (1761), in which Churchill pilloried those actors who had escaped his pen in the earlier poem. *The Apology* in turn went through six editions. (Both are reprinted in *The Poetical Works of Charles Churchill*, ed. Douglas Grant.) The two poems initiated a minor pamphlet war, as defenders of the maligned actors took up their cause against their oppressor. Several other "Rosciads" followed, and in 1766 another controversy evolved from the publication of Hugh Kelly's *Thespis*, a satire on the actors at Drury Lane. (A second part, on the performers at Covent Garden, appeared the following year.) Throughout the remainder of the century we find similar publications: *The New Rosciad*, *The Strolliard*, *The Children of Thespis*, *The Garriciad*, *The Druriad*, *The Histrionade*, *The Thespiad*. (See Arnott and Robinson, pp. 219–25.)

Actors' Handbooks

The art of acting received extensive treatment in some of the more general works that we have glanced at—in Cibber's *An Apology*, for instance, in the

History ascribed to Betterton, or in Wilkes' *A General View of the Stage*—and, of course, considerable commentary on acting is often included also in the various biographies and autobiographies. In addition, there were pamphlets that offered accounts of the acting styles of particular actors: Joseph Pittard's *Observations on Mr. Garrick's Acting* (1755), for example, or the anonymous *An Estimate of the Theatrical Merits of the Two Tragedians of Crow Street* (1760), a commentary on the acting of Spranger Barry and Henry Mossop.

A far more substantial work is Joshua Steele's *Prosodia Rationalis* (1779), in which the author attempts to provide a system of musical notation to record Garrick's delivery in the role of Hamlet. Alan S. Downer, whose 1943 essay on eighteenth-century acting in *PMLA* remains an important study, comments that unfortunately Steele's system is "intolerably complicated" and his "notation tells us little that we could not gather from . . . contemporary critics . . . " (John Loftis, ed., *Restoration Drama*, p. 367n.). The attempt is nonetheless noteworthy, as an indication of the serious attitude that characterized the writing about acting in the last half of the eighteenth century. A series of books attempted in various ways to establish and present the basic principles of elocutionary theory which, their authors maintained, underlay the actor's craft. The actor and theatre manager Thomas Sheridan (the father of the dramatist), in *A Course of Lectures on Elocution* (1762), argues that the revival of public speaking would improve religion, morality, and constitutional government and would pave the way for perfection in all the arts. Similar views were expressed by James Burgh (1761), John Walker (1781), and Gilbert Austin. The latter, writing in *Chironomia* (1806), elaborated a system of gesture and movement to accompany speech (illustrated in engravings) and expressed the wish that his work be of value to the clergy, parliamentarians, lawyers, and actors.

Pamphlets and handbooks equally seriously intended but devoted exclusively to acting also proliferated during the second half of the century. Downer points out that between 1741 and 1790, almost twenty such works were published. If a theme can be traced in these publications it is the desirability of grace in the realistic depiction of human passion. Two slight pamphlets by Samuel Foote— *A Treatise on the Passions* and *Roman and English Comedy Consider'd and Compar'd*, both printed in 1747—illustrate the actor's desire to understand and present his craft in scientific terms. In *A Treatise* Foote explains that his purpose is," . . . by tracing the Rise and Progress of the Passions, together with their Effects on the organs of our Bodies, [to] enable them [spectators] to judge how far the Imitation of those Passions on the Stage be natural, and give them not only an Opportunity of being rationally pleased, but of communicating to others, why they are so" (pp. 8–9). Roger Pickering's *Reflections Upon Theatrical Expressions in Tragedy* (1755) is similarly motivated.

We noted earlier that a primary concern of Hill and Popple's *The Prompter* was the art of acting. Most of the discussion was carried on by Hill, who approved of the "naturalistic" acting of Garrick and Macklin and prophesied the demise of the "fustian-and-feathers school" of Quin. About twenty of the numbers were devoted to actors and acting, and taken together they represent an important contribution to the eighteenth-century theory of acting. Hill also contributed a twenty-line poem, "The Actor's Epitome," to *The Prompter*, which later became an eighty-line poem and was finally published separately in 1746 as *The Act of Acting*. By this time its heroic couplets totalled 416 lines. Ultimately, a prose *Essay on the Art of Acting* was published as part of Hill's *Works* in 1753. (The relationship among *The Prompter* pieces, the poems, and the final essay is analyzed by Leo Hughes in "The Actor's Epitome" in *Review of English Studies* XX [1944].) Hill analyzed the passions into six "primary" passions (joy, sorrow, fear, scorn, anger, amazement) and four "secondaries" (jealousy, revenge, love, duty), although he later abandoned the distinction. His classification continues the scientific bias of the handbooks, but the author's experience in the theatre gives his theory a practical foundation.

A second Hill, John, described by A. M. Nagler as "quack doctor, actor, and pupil of Macklin" (*A Source Book in Theatrical History*, p. 394), was the author of two books titled *The Actor*, the first published in 1750, the second— a rewritten and shortened version of the first—in 1755. In the 1750 volume, Hill offers a highly categorized discussion of the desirable attributes of an actor, both those bestowed by nature (understanding, sensibility, gaiety of temper, and elevated soul; voice and figure) and those cultivated through art. The aim was truth in stage presentation. The 1755 version has a less complex organization and includes specific comments on various actors and actresses. Hill claims to have based his ideas on observation of working actors, and indeed he clearly knew and had spoken with several actors, including Cibber. He also suggests an erudite context for his attempt to "reduce to rules" the "science" of acting, citing Longinus, recommending the reading of *Paradise Lost* for the development of sensibility and sublimity, and referring to Aaron Hill's essay as a "classic." The theme of stage truth runs through both books, and Hill leaves little doubt as to what he means: "All representations on the stage please the more, the more they resemble real occurrences. . . . We express, by that term [truth], a concourse of all those appearances that may deceive the audience into an opinion, that they are attending to a real adventure" (1755, pp. 224–25).

The Actor was apparently in part a translation of Pierre Rémond de Sainte-Albine's *Le Comédien* (1749) and was in turn translated into French as *Garrick: ou les acteurs anglais* (1769). In this form the work prompted Denis Diderot's reply in his *Observations sur une brochure* and ultimately in his *Le Paradoxe sur le comédien* (written 1770–1778, published 1830). This was not, of course, the only instance of interaction on the subject with the Continent. J. J. Engel's *Ideenzu einer Mimik*, published in Berlin in 1785, was translated into English in 1807 by Henry Siddons as *Practical Illustrations of Rhetorical Gesture and Action*. Such instances should serve to remind us, however, that in the eighteenth century the world was shrinking and that a proper understanding of theatrical events and practices in a specific country depends in some instances on seeing issues from a pan-European perspective. (Such a perspective on acting is provided in an important five-part article by Dene Barnett in *Theatre Research International* [1977–1981], in which German, Dutch, French, and English sources are quoted and analyzed.)

Finally, we should note the comments on acting included in Paul Hiffernan's rather odd *Dramatic Genius* (1770, 1772). Of the five "books" which comprise the work, only one and a half are devoted to acting, but the remainder both provide a context for and are informed by Hiffernan's notions of acting. *Dramatic Genius* is dedicated to Garrick; the first book contains the plan of a Temple, to be erected in memory of Shakespeare; the second book discusses the human invention of drama and the neoclassical rules; the third book is concerned with acting, as is the second part of Book IV on "Dramatic Genius"; and finally, Hiffernan discusses the other arts—architecture, painting, sculpture, music—so far as they contribute to theatrical representation. "The end of dramatic writing, dramatic performing, and dramatic managing," he writes, "is to be honoured with crowded audiences . . . " (p. 218). The actor is of course subject to rules, just as the dramatist is, but he can also learn from music and sculpture the attributes of the beautiful and the sublime. Once more we find a version of the almost universal truth of representation: " . . . the general criteria of the truly beautiful of acting in comedy, as well as of the truly sublime of acting in tragedy, consists in the performers appearing to be the very characters they represent . . . " (p. 171).

Although many lesser publications are listed in Arnott and Robinson's *English Theatrical Literature* (pp. 74–78) and are cited in specialized studies, those discussed here are of particular importance and are the most likely to be referred to by theatre historians. As Downer points out, we must remain aware of prejudice or over-devotion to theory or authority (especially by those writers unconnected with the stage), but these limitations are no more endemic to actors' handbooks than to any other contemporary evidence. Of more significance is the necessity of recognizing that terms such as *natural, artificial, realistic*, and *truth of representation* had different meanings and connotations in the past than they do now and that they must be interpreted and understood in the context of eighteenth-century epistemology. (See Joseph R. Roach, *The Player's Passion: Studies in the Science of Acting*.)

Foreign Visitors

During the eighteenth century, Germans appear to have been the most likely visitors from the Continent to visit England. In *German Visitors to English Theatres* John Kelly discusses forty-seven travellers who made at least passing references to the theatre and notes twenty others. For the most part, however, he concludes that their comments "present not a great deal that is new and valuable as a contribution to the history of the English stage. . . . Most of what they say . . . may be found more fully and reliably recorded in some of the numerous English memoirs of the times, or in contemporary criticisms in newspapers and other periodicals'' (p. 2). The visits are nonetheless indicative of the cross-currents in cultural and intellectual affairs that came more and more to characterize eighteenth-century Europe, and visitors' observations, if not factually novel, offer a reciprocal if oblique light on affairs in both England and Germany.

The first German to give an account of actual performances was Zacharias Conrad von Uffenbach, who visited London in 1710. The first whose English was adequate for an accurate understanding of theatrical performances was the Protestant clergyman Georg Wilhelm Alberti, who was in England between 1745 and 1747 and who published a four-volume study of English culture. Alberti was properly shocked by what he encountered in the theatre and joined with ''wise Englishmen'' in condemning the stage on moral grounds. Johann Wilhelm von Archenholz, who travelled extensively in England between 1760 and 1775, returned to Germany to launch in 1781 a periodical, *Literatur and Volkerkunde*, for a quarter of a century the primary interpreter of English culture to Germans. Archenholz also published an account of English theatres in Volume III of *England und Italien* (1785). Another important visitor, Ernst Brandes, devoted an entire volume of his *Bemerkungen über das Londoner, Pariser und Wiener Theatre* (1786) to the English theatre. German visitors in the last third of the century tended to a theoretical preference for the English stage over that of the French, a possible reflection of Lessing's influence in Germany, but they were occasionally disappointed by the reality. This seems to have been the case with Justius Möser, who in 1763 found the English theatre an ''unmitigated disappointment'' (quoted by Kelly, p. 38). In general, however, later visitors were blinded by their adulation of Shakespeare and awed by the powerful acting of Garrick. Friedrich Grof von Kielmannsegge (1761–1762), Helferich Peter Sturz (1768), and Friedrich Justinian Freiherr von Günderode (called von Kellner) (1775?) all had high praise for England's greatest actor and offer good observations on his performances. Johann Christian Fabricius (1784) describes what he considered to be the deterioration of the stage after Garrick. (All of these travellers are discussed and in some instances quoted by Kelly.)

Undoubtedly the German visitor best known and most important to theatre historians is Georg Christoph Lichtenberg (1742–1799), physicist, sceptic, and wit, who visited England in 1770 and again in 1774. His *Briefe aus England* (1776–1778) was translated in 1938 as *Lichtenberg's Visits to England as Described in His Letters and Diaries*. Like other Germans, Lichtenberg was impressed by Shakespeare and Garrick, and he added a third Englishman worthy of admiration, the artist William Hogarth. (Lichtenberg published a commentary on Hogarth's engravings in 1794–1799.) He is an especially acute observer and reporter of Garrick, especially in his Shakespeare roles. Lichtenberg saw the actor eight times, twice as Hamlet, but also as Archer in *The Beaux' Strategem* and as Sir John Brute in *The Provok'd Wife*. Lichtenberg's descriptions of Garrick are wonderfully precise and detailed. But he has also left us a description of Macklin as Shylock, and he immortalized that actor's initial words in the role:

The first words he utters, when he comes on to the stage, are slowly and impressively spoken: 'Three thousand ducats.' The double 'th' and the two sibilants, especially the second after the 't', which Macklin lisps as lickerishly as if he were savouring the ducats and all that they would buy, make so deep an impression in the man's favour that nothing can destroy it. [Nagler, *A Source Book in Theatrical History*, p. 358]

The actor's ephemeral art has seldom been so successfully captured in a verbal description. Such precision is characteristic of Lichtenberg.

Shortly after Lichtenberg's last visit, the loyalist Samuel Curwen of Salem, Massachusetts, found it expedient to make London his home during the duration of the American War of Independence. He kept a diary for the years 1775–1783, and here we find recorded visits to the theatre on more than two dozen occasions. Curwen saw Garrick on at least three occasions, as well as Macklin as Shylock. Compared to those of Lichtenberg, however, his comments are of little interest. Garrick was "much more perfect to my eye and judgment . . . in the expression of his face than in the accent and pronounciation of his voice . . . " (*The Journal of Samuel Curwen*, I, 88–89). Macklin "manifests an exertion that would credit even youth" (II, 962). In two areas, however, Curwen provides significant description and comment. He occasionally visited lesser and peripheral houses of entertainment and witnessed acrobatic performances, puppet shows, and burlesque. At the Patagonian theatre, for example, he saw Henry Carey's *Chrononhotonthdogos*, "a burlesque farce but I know not of what; performance in puppetry, speakers below stage, invisible machinery, bungling, scenery pretty, audience here and there . . . " (II, 696–97). And he comments on the stage scene for a Harlequin performance at Covent Garden in December 1775:

there are views of a lumberyard, adjoining houses, apparently real smoke issuing out of the chimneys and a distant city prospect which by the artful disposition of the lights appear the most natural I have seen. The following I think . . . was in some degree a most agreeable *deceptrovisus*, the objects on the stage seeming to my eye not more natural than the Scenery. [I, 97–98]

In its own way, this is as informative on the scene as are Lichtenberg's comments on Garrick's acting. In both cases we get a clear notion of the effect produced.

The diary of one last visitor must be noted. Louis-Marie Fouquet, Comte de Gisors, visited England in 1754, and the diary he kept on that occasion is included in Volume I of *Mémoires et Documents* in the archives of the Ministry of Foreign Affairs in Paris. (Pertinent extracts are printed by Colin Visser in "The Comte de Gisors in London, 1754" in *Theatre Notebook* XXXVII, 51–54.) Fouquet, like Curwen, is most interesting when recording entertainments out of the main dramatic stream. He describes masquerades and balls and, perhaps of most importance, a performance of *Mrs. Midnight's Concert* at the Little Theatre in the Haymarket in April 1754. "Fouquet's description," notes Visser, "gives a vivid impression of a bizarre evening in the theatre that anticipates the music hall entertainments of a later age" (p. 53).

PLAYHOUSES

The physical theatre, the permanent arrangement of playing space and auditorium, is a central concern of theatre history, for evolving from these physical conditions of the playhouse are the theatrical forms and conventions that determine the dynamics and style of performance. The evidence for reconstructing playhouses improves in quantity and quality as we move from the Restoration period through the eighteenth century, but it remains incomplete at best, and the history of theatre architecture 1660–1800 depends upon a good bit of speculation and conjectural reconstruction. (The standard survey is Richard Leacroft's *The Development of the English Playhouse*.) We have the texts of plays, some promptbooks, and written descriptions of theatre interiors, usually of the auditoriums; we have the remains of several provincial playhouses built late in the century but evidentially in the manner of earlier London theatres; we have a variety of pictorial evidence, most of it in need of careful interpretation and evaluation; and we have a handful of architectural plans for theatres. The analysis of data derived from such a variety of sources is a time-consuming and specialist task, made ultimately frustrating by the fact that information is often too limited to allow for a reliable reconstruction of a playhouse. Edward A. Langhans' "A Conjectural Reconstruction of the Dorset Garden Theatre" in *Theatre Survey* (1972), for example, prompted a lively debate in *Theatre Notebook*, over ten years, between John R. Spring and Robert Hume, a debate that simply cannot be settled on the basis of the available data. Leacroft limits his scale reconstructions mainly to Drury Lane and Covent Garden, "theatres for which a reasonable amount of information was available" (*The Development of the English Playhouse*, p. xi), and it is these two Theatres Royal that are at the thematic centre of his book. The survey of evidence that follows focusses mainly on graphic and pictorial materials.

Extant Theatres

Six provincial theatres in varying states of repair and condition survive from the last half of the eighteenth century. Richard Southern, who surveyed the remains in *The Georgian Playhouse* (1948), notes that "the few [playhouses] that remain are generally in poor preservation or have been altered, or even cleared of all theatrical details, at a later date" (p. 28). A seventh theatre in Richmond, Surrey, built in 1765 and torn down in 1884, is known through drawings made at the time of demolition (Southern, figs. 10–13; Leacroft, fig. 80).

Bath is the location of two extant theatres, the Theatres Royal, Orchard Street (1750) and Beaufort Square (1805). The interiors of both houses have been completely altered, but the exterior shells remain fairly intact. Southern notes that a painting of the interior of the older theatre by a watercolorist named Nixon (pl. 15) is the earliest of several drawings of theatre interiors that help to reconstruct the changes in the playhouse through the years. The exterior of the Beaufort Square house can be compared with several sketches made by the architect George Dance (pl. 16–21). The theatre in Stamford, Lincolnshire, a town described by Southern as "one of the most perfect Georgian towns in England" (p. 43), offers less than its surroundings promise. The building dates from 1768, but everything from the interior was sold in 1871 and we do not even have the consolation of a sketch. We have the façade (Southern, pl. 32), and in the cellar a door that Southern believed might have been a proscenium door (pl. 33). Yet this is grandeur itself compared with the "forlorn four walls and a roof" that Southern found at Newbury in Berkshire. What had been built in 1802 as a playhouse, had later served as a cowshed and was serving after World War II as a furniture store (pl. 43). The shell can be compared with a print published in 1805 in James Winston's *The Theatric Tourist* (Southern, p. 44).

We are more fortunate with the Theatre Royal at Bristol, erected 1764–1766, and the theatre at Richmond, Yorkshire, built in 1788. The former is the earliest provincial theatre still standing, and although it underwent many alterations over the years, enough of the basic structure remained in 1948, and enough traces of its former form, to allow a reasonably reliable reconstruction of the original playhouse. In particular, four large pilasters that flanked the orchestra pit originally flanked the proscenium stage, which had been cut back by about two and one-half metres. There is evidence to indicate that the Bristol theatre was modelled closely on Garrick's Drury Lane Theatre. The architect, James Paty, evidently based his plan on a plan and section prepared by one "Mr. Saunders Carpenter of Drury Lane Play House," but it is not clear whether these plans were of Drury Lane or simply designs by Saunders. The drawings of the interior of the theatre at Richmond, Surrey (noted above), also designed by Saunders and quite distinct from Drury Lane, suggest the second alternative. So, at least, argues Richard Leacroft in *The Development of the English Playhouse* (pp. 112–16). The Theatre Royal, Bristol, was restored in 1948. (Southern provides illustrations of the unrestored theatre in *The Georgian Playhouse*, pls. 22, 23, 25–31; Leacroft offers a pre–1948 scale reconstruction, figs. 76, 79.) We have in addition a booking plan of the boxes at Bristol in 1773, preserved in the Avon County Reference Library. (See Allardyce Nicoll, *The Garrick Stage*, fig. 33.)

The playhouse at Richmond, Yorkshire (1788), was similarly restored to working order in 1949. It had long been abandoned as a theatre, and a wine cellar had been built beneath the auditorium and stage. Nevertheless, the remaining structure again allowed for a reliable reconstruction of the original. (The unrestored theatre is illustrated in Southern, pls. 34–39, 41, 42, and in Leacroft, fig. 104. Leacroft also provides a scale reconstruction, fig. 101.)

Architectural Plans

Architectural drawings of theatres, some in manuscript, some in printed form, are available from a very early date, although they increase markedly in number after 1770. Rarely do they tell us everything we wish to know about a particular playhouse or about the development of particular features over time, and they certainly need expert interpretation. But they do offer very important clues for reconstructing buildings and tracing historical change. The following are the most significant architectural drawings for the study of the English theatre of the period.

a. Among the papers of Sir Christopher Wren held at All Souls College, Oxford, are a plan and a sketch of the proscenium arch of an unnamed theatre labelled "Lecture Theatre Depository for the College of Physicians." Scholars have variously associated the drawings with Killigrew's Bridges Street Theatre of 1663, with the alterations made in the same theatre 1665–1666, with the Drury Lane of 1674, or with a court theatre. Edward Langhans notes that the semicircular seating arrangement anticipates Vanbrugh's Queen's Theatre, erected in 1705 ("The Theatres" *London Theatre World*, ed. Robert Hume, pp. 58–60). Richard Leacroft suggests the plan may represent an adaptation of the Tudor Hall (*The Development of the English Playhouse*, p. 84). And Donald C. Mullin thinks it likely that Wren's plan is a rough sketch of projected alterations made during the plague season of 1665–1666 (*The Development of the Playhouse*, p. 65). Although Leacroft thinks it "reasonable to assume a scale of 10 feet to 1 inch" (p. 84)—the same as that shown in Wren's section of a theatre (discussed below)—there is in fact no scale indicated, and estimates of the size of the structure range from Leacroft's 38'9" x 89'6" (11.8 m. x 27.3 m.)—coincidentally the measurements of the Tudor Hall—to Mullin's 58' x 135' (17.66 m. x 41 m.) ("The Theatre Royal, Bridges Street" in *Educational Theatre Journal* XIX, [1967]). Given the rudimentary nature of the drawings, the lack of detail sufficient to identify the structure, the obviously Serlian, even academic, design, it would seem best to consider them the result of preliminary thoughts on a projected theatre—possible at court— that was never built. (Leacroft reproduces the designs, fig. 57, and provides a reconstruction, fig. 58.)

b. Of far more significance is a sectional drawing by Wren, also in the All Souls collection, which, on the basis of the correspondence of its measurement with those recorded elsewhere, has been identified as the design for the Drury Lane Theatre built in 1674 to replace Killigrew's 1663 playhouse. This is the earliest known architectural drawing of the interior of an English playhouse. (The drawing is reproduced in Leacroft, fig. 60; a redrawn section based on the sketch is printed by George C. Izenour in *Theatre Design*, fig. 2.40.) While we cannot be sure of the exact relationship between the plan and the finished playhouse, Wren's sketch has served as the basis for detailed reconstructions of Drury Lane by Edward Langhans (Mullin, *The Development of the Playhouse*, fig. 101) and Richard Leacroft (fig. 63). The perceived compromise in the sketch, between the Italian scenic stage and the English thrust stage (or the masque stage and the older platform stage), has been taken as a nexus to describe and explain the subsequent development of the English playhouse. In Mullin's words: "The impact of the design of Drury Lane was great: Dorset Garden was abandoned and later theatres were based upon Wren's new plan. Covent Garden had an almost identical arrangement and design. . . . as long as Drury Lane stood, the iconographic stage was not entirely abandoned . . . " (*The Development of the Playhouse*, p. 69).

c. In the Property Services Agency Library, Whitgift Centre, Croydon, there is a book of drawings by Thomas Fort of various buildings about Hampton Court. Among them is a plan of the Great Hall with its theatre. Hampton Court Theatre, built in 1718, was only rarely used until 1721, and there is only one recorded later performance, in 1731. Graham Barlow, who discusses and reproduces the plan in *Theatre Notebook* XXXVII (1983), notes that its significance lies in the fact that it is a drawing of an actual theatre, presumably built to accommodate the requirements of the professional companies. It can serve, therefore, as evidence of minimal facilities available at Drury Lane and Lincoln's Inn Fields.

d. In the Harvard Theatre Collection there is a drawing by James Winston of a rough ground plan and one side of the stage of the Frankfort Gate Theatre at Plymouth (1758). Richard Southern first discussed the sketches in *Theatre Notebook*, I (1947), and Nicoll also reproduces them in *Garrick's Stage* (fig. 53).

e. Plans and sections for Queen's/King's Theatre, Haymarket (1764), and Covent Garden (1732) are to be found in G.P.M. Dumont's *Parallèle de plans des plus belles salles de spectacles* (1774), plates 20 and 21, although drawings for the first are reversed left to right and for the second top to bottom. Leacroft reproduces Dumont's drawings for both theatres (figs. 69, 72) and offers scale reconstructions (figs. 68, 73).

f. Robert and James Adam's remodelling of Drury Lane Theatre in 1775 is recorded in an engraving in Volume II of *The Works in Architecture of Robert and James Adam* (Set V, pl. VII) and in three scale drawings relating to the remodelling in the Sir John Soane Museum, where the bulk of the Adam architectural drawings are housed. Two of the drawings are designs for the ceiling; the third is a section through the side boxes showing the front of the stage. Leacroft adjusts the scale of the engraving in accordance with the Adams' section (figs. 81, 82) and attempts a reconstruction of the 1674 Drury Lane (fig. 63) by relating the ceiling plan (fig. 61) to Wren's section. (The Drury Lane of 1775 is reconstructed in fig. 83.) An earlier anonymous sketch, now in the Folger Shakespeare Library, shows a plan of the pit at Drury Lane. (See Nicoll, *Garrick's Stage*, fig. 29.)

g. The King's Theatre, Haymarket, was redesigned by the brothers Adam in 1778 and again by its resident designer, Michael Novosielski, in 1782. When the house burned down in 1789, it was rebuilt the following year, again by Novosielski. In the Soane Museum are superimposed plans of the 1782 and the 1790 playhouse (Leacroft, fig. 87). (The 1782 plan is redrawn and reproduced by Mullin, *The Development of the Playhouse*, fig. 122.)

h. The Enthoven Collection in the Victoria and Albert Museum contains a set of four architectural plans, ascribed to one Cornelius Dixon, and supposedly intended for the Royalty Theatre, which was built in 1787 by John Palmer but only sporadically used. The interpretation of the plans is rendered problematic by their lack of correspondence with known prints of the same theatre. (Richard Southern reproduces both the prints and the plans in *The Georgian Playhouse*, pls. 6–13.)

i. George Saunders' *A Treatise on Theatres* (1790) includes (i) a plan of the "Late Opera House in London" (Queen's Theatre, Haymarket) (pl. X, fig. 1); (ii) a plan of Edward Shepherd's 1732 Covent Garden (fig. 2, also reproduced in Mullin, *The Development of the Playhouse*, fig. 106; *cf* Dumont above); (iii) plans by William Capon of Covent Garden after the 1782 alterations (fig. 3); (iv) designs for an "ideal" theatre (pl. XI, XII; scale reconstruction in Leacroft, fig. 105) and an opera house (pl. XIII).

j. In 1792 Covent Garden Theatre was altered for the third time since 1784 by the architect Henry Holland. Holland's plans for the renovations, prepared in 1791, have been preserved and include a plan and section and a longitudinal section (Leacroft, figs. 88, 90). There may have been changes in the plans before the theatre was actually built, and changes continued to be made in the structure over the next several years, but Holland's proposal indicates the way in which the English theatre was being modified in the direction of Continental practice. Holland's designs for Drury Lane (1794), both preliminary and as executed, have also survived. (See *The Survey of London*, vol. XXXV, pls. 15, 16a–c; also Iain Mackintosh, *The Georgian Playhouse*, figs. 227e, 228a.) While the early designs include proscenium arch doors, the executed designs omit them. (The sleight of hand was completed in 1797 when the doors were restored.)

k. Edward Shepherd was also the architect of a theatre in Goodman's Fields, erected in 1732 for Henry Gifford. Gifford had an off-and-on-again career at Goodman's Fields and the theatre closed for good in 1742. It burned in 1802. The playhouse was visited in 1786 by the painter William Capon, who drew a plan of it, with notes (Leacroft, fig. 75). Capon's notes are a bit confusing concerning the dimensions of the structure: "88 feet exactly outside the walls/ 47 do width within do"; "The whole house from East to West in the clear is 90 feet width 52 feet." Edward Langhans, who quotes Capon's words in "The Theatres" in *London Theatre World* (pp. 35–65), draws attention to a ground plan preserved in the Folger Shakespeare Library, which shows the measurements 90'6'' outside depth by 49' inside width, and notes that Robert Wilkinson, in *Theatrum Illustratum* (1825), gives the dimensions as 88' by 48'6''. Whatever the precise dimensions, Goodman's Fields Theatre was smaller than either Covent Garden or Drury Lane.

l. Three late surveys of London theatres also provide illustrative material for earlier theatres, but are less likely to provide authentic information unavailable elsewhere. Wilkinson's *Theatrum Illustratum*, subtitled "Graphic and historic memorials of ancient playhouses, modern theatres, and places of public amusement, in London and Westminster," is a separate issue of part of the same publisher's *Londina Illustrata*, originally printed in thirty-six numbers between 1808 and 1826 and published in two volumes in 1819 and 1825. Most of the illustrations are pictorial renditions of theatre interiors, but a few architectural plans are printed, including one for Drury Lane in 1794. Edward Wedlake Brayley's *Historical and Descriptive Accounts of the Theatres of London* (1826) is similarly illustrated, although the author includes a few sections, ground plans, and views from Charles Dibdin's *History and Illustrations of the London Theatres* (1826). These surveys are naturally more concerned with theatre structures and alterations undertaken during the early years of the nineteenth century than with earlier forms, although the historical information they provide is useful as corroboration of other sources.

Theatre Exteriors

We are indebted principally to contemporary long views, maps, and surveys of London for exterior views of the Restoration and early eighteenth-century theatres. These show us the location and exteriors of the converted tennis courts normally used by Davenant and Killigrew, of Dorset Garden, Drury Lane, and Lincoln's Inn Fields. Edward Langhans, in a series of three articles published in *Theatre Survey* (1965, 1966) and *Educational Theatre Journal* (1968), reproduces a couple of dozen views from maps and surveys dating between 1660 and 1746. Other prints and engravings occasionally find their way into books on theatre history or theatre architecture, but it is sometimes difficult to determine their provenance or date. An engraving of the façade of the Queen's Theatre, Haymarket, reproduced in Mullin, *The Development of the Playhouse* (fig. 103), for example, was presumably done after the architect's elevation.

By contrast, exterior views from the last quarter of the eighteenth century are relatively numerous, and in the early years of the nineteenth century we find the beginnings of systematic surveys of the theatres with appropriate illustrations. We have already noted the attempts of Wilkinson, Brayley, and Dibdin to survey the theatres of London. A similar though far more ambitious project, for the provincial theatres, was undertaken by James Winston.

Winston (1779–1843), at various times a player, manager, and theatre owner, originally conceived of *The Theatric Tourist* as a work that would be published in thirty monthly parts (July, August, and September excluded), each featuring descriptions and exterior views of three provincial theatres. Only eight numbers were published, and in 1805 the twenty-four accounts and views were bound and published as a single volume. The twenty-four theatres were those at Bath, Andover, Margate, Turnbridge Wells, Reading, Brighton, Richmond (Surrey), Newbury, Portsmouth, Grantham, Lewes, Exeter, Newcastle, Edmonton, Maidstone, Liverpool, Windsor, Chichester, Birmingham, Manchester, Southampton, Plymouth, Winchester, and Norwich. (Arnott and Robinson, in *English Theatrical Literature* p. 151, note that a copy containing the original twenty-four drawings together with drawings for an additional sixty-six provincial theatres was sold at Sotheby's in June 1898.) In addition to this published work, a large amount of Winstonian material, including notes, sketches, scrapbooks, and correspondence, has survived in various collections in England (Garrick Club, British Library, Birmingham Reference Library), Australia (Mitchell Library in Sydney), and the United States (Folger, Harvard, Huntington). Of particular interest so far as playhouses are concerned are the sixteen volumes catalogued by the Folger as the "Dramatic Register." On the title-page of the second volume, Winston sets out his intention to present "a summary account of every public place of amusement where theatrical or vocal performances have been introduced: but more particularly an accurate account as far as it can be ascertained of every dramatic performance from the most remote period to the present time" (quoted by Alfred L. Nelson and Gilbert B. Cross in *Drury Lane Journal*, p. xiii). Winston mentions a total of 283 theatres, 253 of them on the mainland of England and Wales. The first volume covers the period 1300–1699 and contains few entries, but the detail increases as he approaches his own time, and the sixteenth volume (1789–1803) has much more extensive discussions. Scholars who have consulted this material have found errors, but it remains potentially an important contribution to our knowledge of theatrical building and activity at the end of the eighteenth century. (The "Dramatic Register" has not been published. The most useful guide to the Winston material is Alfred L. Nelson's doctoral dissertation, George Washington University, 1968.)

We also have a couple of pictorial surveys of theatres dating from the early nineteenth century. The theatrical plates to Rudolph Ackermann's *The Microcosm of London* (1808–1811), prepared by Augustus Charles Pugin and Thomas Rowlandson, depict seven theatres: Drury Lane (pre–1808), Covent Garden (pre–1809), Covent Garden (post–1809), King's Theatre Haymarket (after the renovations of 1796), Sadler's Wells (post–1804), Astley's Amphitheatre (1803), and the Royal Circus (pre- and post–1809). The original drawings for the plates are now part of the Charles Deering Collection at the Art Institute of Chicago. (See Iain Mackintosh, *The Georgian Playhouse*, nos. 328–34.) Robert B. Schnebbelie, who had provided many of the drawings from which the engravings in Robert Wilkinson's *Theatrum Illustratum* were produced, also painted a series of watercolors of minor London theatres of the early nineteenth century (*The Georgian Playhouse*, nos. 335–55).

Theatre Interiors

Interior views of Restoration playhouses are rare. We have a late print (1815) of the interior of Wren's Sheldonian Theatre, erected in 1663, a structure that was part academic assembly hall and part theatre (Mullin, *The Development of the Playhouse*, fig. 96). We have an engraved frontispiece to a collection of drolls by Francis Kirkman, titled *The Wits* (1672), which does not identify the stage it depicts (Mullin, fig. 95). We are shown a thrust stage, a rear curtain, members of the audience in a balcony above the rear stage, footlights, and candelabra. In spite of the obviously composite nature of the engraving, the stage at one time was held to be that of the old Red Bull, and the *Wits* picture has consequently played a larger role in discussions of the Elizabethan stage than it has in discussions of the Restoration stage. It is enough to remind us, nevertheless, that the traditions of Elizabethan staging did not die out with the closing of the theatres. We have as well two pictures of Joe Haines (or Haynes) mounted on a donkey on the forestage of Drury Lane, the first the frontispiece to Haines' *A Fatal Mistake* (1692), the second from Tom Brown's *Works* (1709). (Both are reproduced by Edward Langhans in "Pictorial Material on the Bridges Street and Drury Lane Theatres" in *Theatre Survey* VII, figs. 17, 18.)

Several scene designs and engravings also provide some information about the Restoration stage. The earliest are a set of six designs—for the proscenium and five scenes—by John Webb for a production of William Davenant's *The Siege of Rhodes* at Rutland House in 1656. As well, Webb provided a section and plan of the stage for the same production, showing the placement of wings and shutters. (The designs and plans are part of the Devonshire Collection at Chatsworth. Originally published by W. G. Keith in *The Burlington Magazine*

in 1914, they are often reproduced.) As Leacroft points out, the important thing
to note in the drawings is that the moveable perspective scenery formerly confined
to the court masque is here provided for a public performance. A set of five engravings in the printed text of Elkanah Settle's *Empress of Morocco*, performed
at Dorset Garden in 1673, presents an abbreviated view of the forestage, a decorated proscenium, and above the proscenium a music room. (Mullin reproduces
the designs in *The Development of the Playhouse*, fig. 97.) The frontispiece to
Pierre Perrin's opera *Ariane* (1674) gives the only contemporary view of the interior of Drury Lane Theatre. (See Mullin, fig. 99; Sybil Rosenfeld, *A Short History of Scene Design in Great Britain*, pl. 10.) Richard Southern in *Changeable
Scenery* draws attention to the frontispiece of John Eccles' *Theatre Musick* (1699–
1700), which presents a conventional scene labelled "The Theatre Royall" (fig.
5). While it is impossible to determine the specific theatre, if any, that the picture
is supposed to represent, Southern notes that it remains a rare example of a full
set on the English public stage before 1700. And finally, Odell cites and reproduces three frontispieces from the 1711 edition of the plays of Beaumont and Fletcher,
which he was convinced are accurate illustrations of the contemporary stage (*Shakespeare from Betterton to Irving*, I, 293). His confidence notwithstanding, the engravings shed little light on the architectural details of a theatre interior.

The interiors of the major playhouses of the eighteenth century, especially in
the later years, are documented pictorially much more frequently. (Mullin and
Leacroft reproduce many of the most significant illustrations, and the late Allardyce Nicoll's posthumous *The Garrick Stage*, published in 1980, contains a
number of little-known illustrations selected from over seven hundred that the
author possessed, selected by Sybil Rosenfeld. In addition, a catalogue devised
by Iain Mackintosh of an exhibition at the Hayward Gallery in London, *The
Georgian Playhouse*, should be consulted.) Late surveys such as those of Wilkinson or Brayley include a number of interior views of late eighteenth-century
and early nineteenth-century theatres. The views discussed here are a representative selection of those most often reproduced or cited, and represent in the
main Covent Garden and Drury Lane.

Two events in the long history of Drury Lane Theatre attracted illustrators.
Robert Adam's renovation of the interior in 1775 provoked mixed reactions in
the town, but the result seems to have pleased the architect. He included in his
Works in Architecture (II, pl. VII) the oft-reproduced engraving by B. Pastorini
showing the theatre as it appeared from the stage. (Colored copies of the engraving are held in the Harvard Theatre Collection, the Soane Museum, and the
Victoria and Albert Museum.) The figures depicted strolling across the stage,
however, are deliberately out of scale in order to emphasize the grandeur of the
architecture; a reproduction with the figures in corrected scale is provided by
Leacroft (figs. 81, 82). The equally famous engraving of the screen scene from
Richard Sheridan's *School for Scandal* (1777) more clearly shows the relatively
narrow width of the stage (about 9 metres or 30 feet) and also indicates the use
of flats as walls: the library and the window are painted on the back scene. "This

print," observes Odell, "with the stage-doors and stage-boxes, and with the actors far out of the scene on the 'apron,' is one of the most interesting and valuable in existence" (*Shakespeare from Betterton to Irving*, II, 83). Another engraving, titled "The Theatrical Oglers" (reproduced in Mackintosh, *The Georgian Playhouse*, no. 221) confirms the impression of the screen scene engraving. Yet a third engraving, depicting part of the riot of 3 February 1776, is a rare illustration of the green baize curtain lowered between the scene and the apron (Mackintosh, no. 222).

The second event occurred in 1791–1792, when Drury Lane was torn down and a new structure of the same name, designed by Henry Holland, was erected. Prior to the demolition, William Capon, who became the new playhouse's scenic director, sketched the interior of the old Drury Lane. (An engraving of the drawing was published in Robert Wilkinson's *Theatrum Illustratum*. See Mullin, *The Development of the Playhouse*, fig. 109; Leacroft, fig. 85.) A later drawing by Capon (Leacroft, fig. 94) is one of several illustrations of the interior of the new theatre before its destruction by fire in 1809. Others include an engraving by Isaac Taylor from the perspective of the stage (Mackintosh, no. 229); a watercolor by Schnebbelie, later engraved for inclusion in Wilkinson's *Theatrum Illustratum* (Leacroft, fig. 96); and a sketch and colored aquatint prepared for Ackermann's *The Microcosm of London* (Mackintosh, nos. 330a-b), featuring a scene from Shakespeare's *Coriolanus*. The difficulties inherent in interpreting such iconographic material as evidence for theatre history are apparent in the observation that the composition of the scene in the Ackermann engraving seems to be based on the frontispiece for Rowe's edition of Shakespeare published in 1709, a rendering that was in turn derived from a painting by Nicolas Poussin (1593–1665). And the situation is made more complex by the further conjecture that Pugin and Rowlandson (who prepared the engraving) were recalling Kemble's production of the play, which was itself patterned after earlier artistic renderings. (See Mackintosh, no. 330.) From the point of view of the theatre's architecture, fortunately, the picture is not so problematic.

The earliest known interior view of Covent Garden Theatre, opened in 1732, has as its subject the duel scene from Garrick's farce *A Miss in Her Teens*, acted by Garrick and Mrs. Pritchard early in 1747, during their only season at Covent Garden (Mackintosh, no. 245; Nicoll, *The Garrick Stage*, fig. 44). Two engravings of 1763, depicting the riots at the playhouse during a performance of T. A. Arne's opera *Artaxerxes* (Nicoll, fig. 18; Mullin, *The Development of the Playhouse*, fig. 108) show clearly the ringed chandeliers over the forestage, the stage-boxes and actors' entrance doors, the acting platform, and the scene behind. Nicoll notes that the artist neglected to indicate any distinction between what lies beyond the curtain line and what is in front, and he reproduces an anonymous oil painting (fig. 19) of a performance of *Macbeth* at the same theatre in 1765. Here the placement of the actors identifies the acting space as being well in front of the curtain line, and the platform and scene behind are clearly distinct areas (pp. 29–30). A colored engraving by Thomas Rowlandson, executed in 1786, complements the earlier pictures by showing us more of the audience and less of the stage (Mackintosh, no. 249). The figures are a delight; the architecture is confused.

Holland's 1792 alteration of Covent Garden is recorded in two basic configurations. A pencil sketch by William Capon, done about 1794 and now in a private collection, was the basis for Robert Schnebbelie's watercolor (Mackintosh, no. 252), which in turn was the basis for the engraving published in Wilkinson's *Theatrum Illustratum* (Leacroft, fig. 89; Mullin, *The Development of the Playhouse*, fig. 117). The second, depicting the playhouse after the alterations of 1803, consists of two drawings, in pen and pencil respectively, in the Charles Deering Collection, and a final execution as a colored aquatint for Ackermann's *The Microcosm of London* (pl. 27).

$$* \qquad * \qquad *$$

Even this incomplete sketch of the graphic and pictorial evidence for theatre architecture from the Restoration to the end of the eighteenth century is enough to demonstrate that, while details of specific playhouses at specific times may still be in doubt, the main outlines of the development of the playhouse seem reasonably clear. Leacroft's chapter titles for the period suggest the general process of change from the thrust stage to the picture-frame stage: "The fan-shaped auditorium"; "The retreat from the proscenium stage"; "The growth of spectacle"; "Picture-frames and proscenium walls." But while it is possible to describe the changes, it is harder to account for them. As Donald Mullin points out, "it is still not entirely clear why the seventeenth- and eighteenth-century English playhouse, in particular, assumed the form it did; why this form is associated almost exclusively with British theatres; and what effect, if any, this difference had upon production" ("Theatre Structure and Its Effect on Production" in *The Stage and the Page*, ed. G. Winchester Stone, p. 74). In his earlier *The Development of the Playhouse* (1970), Mullin attributed the radical change that had taken place over 150 years to the influence of Continental practice, "although the peculiarly English notion of the precedence of actor over scenery still managed to prevail" (p. 86). The perceived tension between the differing demands of scenery and actor informs most analyses of English theatrical architecture. Arthur H. Scouten in *British Theatre and the Other Arts, 1660–1800* (ed. Shirley Strum Kenny) attributes the shape of the Wren-designed Restoration playhouse to the Roman amphitheatre, and the alterations of the 1790s to Parisian and Italian models. His preference for the earlier form is posited on its ability to reconcile the tension:

With the Augustan theatre, with every aspect integrated in the fan-shaped auditorium, a deep stage showing perspective scenes, and an audience close enough and well-placed enough to see every facial movement and hear every word uttered as Betterton, Barry, and Bracegirdle appeared on that stage, we can now claim a Gestalt of our own. [p. 179]

This perhaps understandable preference is shared by Iain Mackintosh, who associates the English playhouse of the mid-eighteenth century with Shakespeare's Globe, an association surely calculated to seek approval. "Until it proved possible to increase the light on the scenic stage and dim the light in the auditorium," he writes,

the mid-Georgian playhouse with its audience and actor enclosed in a single space was closer in atmosphere to the Elizabethan Globe of a century and a half earlier than to the vast Regency theatres of Kean and his contemporaries. [*The Georgian Playhouse*, chap. X]

Richard Southern too sees the Georgian playhouse as a unique development of the Restoration playhouse, itself designed to serve and reconcile the two traditions—the scenic show and the Elizabethan dramatic form. The result was "a national creation of a decidedly individual pattern . . . differing markedly from anything to be seen on the Continent" (*The Georgian Playhouse*, p. 16).

Southern sees the design for the eighteenth-century English playhouse, then, as a reflection of its function, as a solution to a specific problem rather than in terms of foreign influence and native predilection. A similar tack is taken by Mullin in "Theatre Structure and Its Effect on Production" published in *The Stage and the Page* (1981). "Theatres," he notes, "like cathedrals and sometimes even palaces have always taken forms directly related to what takes place in them" (p. 74). He goes on to distinguish between what he calls the Continental "theatre of celebration" and the English "theatre of visitation," the first "intellectual and universal," and the second "personal, emotional, and domestic" (p. 78). The theatre of visitation persisted in England for one hundred years after it disappeared from the Continent until, in an ethos of "increasing illusion, realism, delusion, and finally disenchantment" (p. 88) it was replaced by the theatre of celebration. The attempts of Southern and Mullin to relate theatre architecture to theatrical content and the human instincts for involvement and detachment provide a rich context for a discussion sometimes weighted down with questions of date and dimension.

SCENE DESIGN AND SCENE DESIGNERS

> The Wise Italians first invented shows;
> Thence into France the Noble Pageant past;
> 'Tis England's Credit to be cozn'd last.
> > John Dryden, Prologue to *Albion and Albanius*

The reluctance of the English theatre to follow Continental fashion is reflected as well in the paucity of outstanding scene design. In *Stage Design: Four Centuries of Scenic Invention*, Donald Oenslager includes only one example from eighteenth-century England (fig. 128), an anonymous drawing of a palace chamber from about 1790, and he includes that only to illustrate "the old scenic doldrums of stock wings." The one designer of real significance, Philip de Loutherbourg, worked for Garrick at Drury Lane between 1771 and 1781, but then abandoned scene painting for easel painting. English drawings of scene designs of any quality are in fact very rare. Scenes were usually improvised from stock flats, few sketches were done, and those that were made were unlikely to survive. (The University of London library and the Victoria and Albert Museum house the most important collections.) Besides sketches, we have a few engravings, published on the title-pages particularly of operas and ballet scores. But, of course, these two kinds of evidence bear different relationships to the actual design that graced a given stage at a given time. The first, the drawing, precedes the painting of the flats and must be interpreted in terms of both artistic and theatrical conventions; the second, the published engraving, can be based on the drawing or on the actual scene design or both, and is executed according to the conventions of the engraver's art for inclusion in a non-theatrical medium— the book. And the fires that destroyed Drury Lane and Covent Garden helped to ensure that no actual scenery survived.

It is clear too that although scene painters were regularly employed throughout the late seventeenth and early eighteenth centuries, they were less highly regarded in England than were their counterparts on the Continent. Our knowledge of them is often derived from records of payments to them. Until the 1770s they were seldom named on playbills or in play advertisements. When the names of four scene painters were included on a playbill of 1727, the critic Lewis Theobald denounced the practice. (See Sybil Rosenfeld, *A Short History of Scene Design in Great Britain*, p. 60.)

Painters were engaged in several ways. Assistants or apprentices were paid by the day; regular "house" painters could be engaged for the season and paid a salary; or a scene painter might be brought in to do a particular job and paid by the piece. The last practice seems to have been the prevailing practice in the Restoration and through the first third of the eighteenth century. We know that John Webb (1611–1672) was employed by Davenant, and that Robert Streater (or Streeter), Samuel Towers, and Robert Robinson painted scenes for Thomas Killigrew. The first painters to be engaged by a theatre on an occasional basis were John Harvey and George Lambert at Lincoln's Inn Fields 1724–1727; in 1732 both men went to Covent Garden. John Oram worked at Drury Lane 1747– 1758, as did John French from 1763. Rosenfeld, who is the leading authority on the subject, notes that both Oram and French came from families of scene painters and that by mid-century, such work had become a profession in which father trained son to succeed him (*A Short History of Scene Design in Great Britain*, p. 61). Italian and other foreign scene painters were also engaged, especially for Italian opera, but while we know their names, none of their work is extant. De Loutherbourg brought new prominence to stage and scene design in the 1770s, but it was not until the nineteenth century that designs were preserved in any great number. So far as the eighteenth century is concerned, historians are more likely to lament the losses than to rejoice in the riches. The survey that follows draws attention to most of the designs that in one form or another have come down to us.

Restoration Scene Designs

The pictorial record for the Restoration stage is particularly poor and must be supplemented by stage directions, which may or may not have been carried out, and by the written evidence of diarists and visitors to the theatre. Most of the evidence we have encountered before. The earliest consists of the five scenes devised by John Webb for Davenant's *The Siege of Rhodes*, performed at Rutland House in 1656: a view of the city of Rhodes; a view of the besieged city, showing the Turks and their fleet; a scene of Solyman's throne; a picture of Mount Philermus with Solyman's army and a bastion on opposite sides; and a view of the final assault on the city, with the army painted on the canvas. (The originals are in the Devonshire Collection. See above.) A second series of four designs by Webb was prepared for Roger Boyle's *Mustapha*, acted at Whitehall in 1665. The scenes are very much like those for *The Siege of Rhodes*, and like the latter, they are also part of the Devonshire Collection. A set of five engravings in Settle's *The Empress of Morocco* is similarly familiar. Featured are a vaulted dungeon, a fleet of ships on a river, a hell scene, tortured bodies hanging from a rack, and a set of dancers before a palm tree. (See Mullin, *The Development of the Playhouse*, fig. 97.) We have as well the frontispiece to *Ariane* (1674), which is a model of classical restraint compared to some of the scenes for *The Empress of Morocco* (Mullin, fig. 99). We also have the frontispiece to John Eccles' *Theatre Musick* (Southern, *Changeable Scenery*, fig. 5). Finally, James Thornhill, later Sir James and the father-in-law of William Hogarth, has left us four drawings of scene designs for Thomas Clayton's *Arsinoe* (1705): two garden scenes, a room of state, and a great hall. The originals are in the Victoria and Albert Museum. Sybil Rosenfeld, who reproduces the drawings in *Georgian Scene Painters* (figs. 1–4), also reproduces another drawing by Thornhill of an arbor scene for an unidentified play (fig. 5). Another great baroque scene by Thornhill, again for an unknown play, is held by the Art Institute of Chicago (reproduced by Southern, *Changeable Scenery*, pl. 29).

Eighteenth-Century Scene Designs

The first half of the eighteenth century has yielded similarly few extant scene designs, either as drawings or as engravings. John Devoto (fl. 1708–1752), the scenographer associated with the staging of pantomimes at Drury Lane, Lincoln's Inn Fields, and Goodman's Fields, 1723–1733, is also significant as the designer of scenes of ancient Rome for a production of *Julius Caesar* at Drury Lane in 1723. Devoto's principal pictorial legacy is a book of sketches now housed in the British Library. The relationship between these drawings and Devoto's known work in the theatre is not clear. Thomas Lediard (1684–1743), who provides a lengthy account of the scenes he designed for the Hamburg Opera House between 1724 and 1730 in *The German Spy* (1738), also provided a scenic setting for his *Britannia* (1732), preserved as an engraving in the published text. Rosenfeld, who reproduces the design in *Georgian Scene Painters* (fig. 6), notes that it is the "only iconographical evidence we have of the full baroque treatment on the English stage" (p. 73). The most prominent European scene designer to work in England, however, Giovanni Niccolo Servandoni (1695–1766), has unhappily left no record of his work at Covent Garden in 1747. And even a long and stable career offers no guarantee that designs will survive. George Lambert (1699?–1765), for at least twenty-nine years (1732–1761) regularly employed as a scene painter at Covent Garden, has left a pitifully meager pictorial record. (His design for the farmhouse scene in *Harlequin Sorcerer*, 1752, is most frequently reproduced. See Odell, *Shakespeare from Betterton to Irving*, I, opp. p. 440. Rosenfeld prints a photograph of Odell's reproduction in *Georgian Scene Painters*, fig. 9 and in *A Short History of Scene Design in Great Britain*, pl. 14.)

Most of the scenes painters who worked in the latter half of the eighteenth century are represented by at most a handful of extant designs. (The most convenient selection is to be found in Rosenfeld, *Georgian Scene Painters*.) Lambert's pupil John Inigo Richards designed scenery at Covent Garden from 1759 to 1803. Rosenfeld reproduces three of his best-known designs, for *The Maid of the Mill* (fig. 22), *Harlequin Everywhere* (fig. 23), and *Raman Droog* (fig. 24). The work of the Italian Battista Cipriani (1727–1785) survives in a collection of prints published in 1789 and in a collection of several drawings and many prints in the British Library. He is nevertheless remembered mainly for his frontispiece design for the new proscenium frame for Covent Garden, painted in 1777 (Rosenfeld, fig. 12) and described by Rosenfeld as the "only pictorial evidence we have for the rococo on the stage in England" (p. 74). (The original is in a private collection.) Of the work of Michael Novosielski and Gaetano Marinari, scene painters at the Haymarket during the last two decades of the century, nothing remains. Similarly, the work of Thomas Malton (1748–1804), is known almost exclusively through account books and press reports. William Capon (1757–1827), as we have seen, left us plans for Goodman's Fields and Covent Garden, but his sketch book of theatrical drawings is also extant, and now in a private collection. (For illustrations see Rosenfeld, fig. 161, and Rosenfeld, "Scene Designs of William Capone" in *Theatre Notebook*, 1956.)

Michael Angelo Rooker (1743–1801) is represented in Rosenfeld by a couple of designs (figs. 13, 14), but his main claim to fame is a watercolor, now in the British Museum, depicting a painter (Rooker himself?) at work in the scene room of the Haymarket Theatre, where he worked between 1779 and 1797. This remarkably detailed picture is exceptionally valuable as evidence for the conditions under which scene painters labored. A painting roughly contemporary with Rooker's in the Tessin Collection in Paris by Nicolas Lafrensen (1737–

1807) also shows a scene painter at work. Sybil Rosenfeld, who reproduces the
Rooker painting in *Georgian Scene Painters* (frontispiece) and has examined the
Lafrensen painting, offers the following observations:

Rooker's [painting] shows a lofty, airy, well-lit room in which he is seen painting a
landscape in a scene frame. It was the British system to use these frames which could
be let down through a slot in the floor thereby rendering it much easier to paint the upper
portion of the backcloth. The Tessin water-colour shows a different system with the cloths
hung from above and rolled at the bottom. Presumably the cloth was lowered as the
bottom dried and was rolled up. On the left of Rooker's picture is a platform on which
stands a paint pot and brush by a ladder. A winch and pulley suggest that this may have
been used for suspending scenery and lowering it at the painter's convenience. Rooker
is working with a short brush and a mahlstick. There are several pots of paint and an
oven for warming the size. The same type of pots appear in the Tessin picture but the
brushes are much longer and no oven is visible. [pp. 10–11]

Thomas Greenwood the Elder (d. 1797), scene painter at Drury Lane from
1771 and at Sadler's Wells from 1778 until his death, was the busiest scene
painter in England during the last quarter of the eighteenth century. His legacy,
nevertheless, is small: (a) two watercolor sketches of Gothic exterior scenes for
an unidentified play, but indicated as acted at Covent Garden by Samuel Phelps,
who owned them in the nineteenth century; (b) two engravings, one for the
Prophecy of Queen Elizabeth at Tilbury, performed at Sadler's Wells in 1779,
and another for John Burgoyne's *Richard Coeur de Lion*, acted at Drury Lane
in 1786; (c) four engravings from the printed scores of *Lodoiska* (1794), *The
Pirates* (1792), *The Haunted Tower* (1789), and *The Siege of Belgrade* (1791).
(All of the designs, save those for *The Haunted Tower* and *The Siege of Belgrade*,
are reproduced by Rosenfeld, *Georgian Scene Painters*, figs. 25–29.)

De Loutherbourg

The one scene designer associated with the English theatre of the eighteenth
century who has at least a claim to whatever immortality theatre history can endow is the French-born Philippe Jacques de Loutherbourg (1740–1812), known
after his arrival in England in 1771 as Philip James. Shortly after his arrival he
outlined in a letter to David Garrick (now in the Harvard Theatre Collection, with
copies in the Victoria and Albert Museum) a proposal for the alteration and improvement of the entire lighting and scenic system at Drury Lane. He offered to
provide models and drawings, and to design the costumes for both actors and dancers. The upshot was a ten-year association with Garrick and Sheridan at Drury
Lane, during which time he designed scenery for sixteen new plays and afterpieces and for seven pantomimes, as well as for other productions to a total of
about fifty-five. De Loutherbourg's designs broke with the formal Italian architectural style and introduced an irregular, pictorially oriented style that not only
became the dominant scenic mode of the next century but also for a time made

England a leader in scene design, rather than merely a follower of Continental fashion.

De Loutherbourg's normal practice appears to have been to provide two-dimensional scene designs, as well as scene models or maquettes for productions. (The actual scene painting and construction was usually left to others.) When he died in 1812, the sale catalogue of his designs listed a total of 380 pieces covering a wide variety of scenes, and *The Times* of 19 June of that year referred to "a valuable collection of small painted models, for stage scenery" (see Rosenfeld, *Georgian Scene Painters*, p. 3 n.2, p. 22 n.54). Unfortunately, the following is all that remains. (The evidence is surveyed but not illustrated in an exhibition catalogue compiled by Rudiger Joppien.)

a. Two drawings of scenes for *A Christmas Tale* (1773), one in a private collection, the other at the Musée de Beaux Arts at Strasbourg. The settings for the production are also described in a manuscript in the Folger Shakespeare Library, quoted by Colin Visser in "Scenery and Technical Design" in *The London Theatre World* (ed. Robert Hume).

b. Drawings of five grotesque figures in the Ashmolean Museum, Oxford, the function or purpose of which is unknown.

c. Drawings that in 1874 came into the possession of Henry Irving, bearing in nineteenth-century handwriting the words, "the first practical bridge" and "sketch for the play 'Richard the 3rd.'—made for David Garrick by de Loutherbourg" (quoted in *A Bibliographical Dictionary*, s.v. "De Loutherbourg"). While the drawings seem undoubtedly to be by the designer, they do not appear to be for *Richard III*, and they certainly do not represent "the first practical bridge." (Photographs of the drawings were published by W. J. Lawrence in "The Pioneers of Modern English Stage Mounting: Philippe Jacques de Loutherbourg, R.A." in *Magazine of Art*, 1895.)

d. Several maquettes: one for *Robinson Crusoe* (1781); another for *The Wonders of Derbyshire* (1779); and two—Kensington Gardens and the interior of a dwelling—for *Omai* (1785), a pantomime commemorating the voyages of Captain Cook—based on drawings and prints by John Webber and William Hodges, artists who had accompanied Cook—and the only production designed by De Loutherbourg for Covent Garden. The maquettes are now in the Victoria and Albert Museum. (Allardyce Nicoll, who in *The Garrick Stage* reproduces the maquette for *Robinson Crusoe*, fig. 96, also includes watercolor designs for wings, pieces, and backdrop for the same production, fig. 97.) Another set of maquettes of ten scenes with variations, also purporting to represent the *Omai* production, were bequeathed in 1987 to the Claremont College library in California by Norman Philbrick. The maquettes, dated 1787, are signed in four places, "P. Munn." Munn, born in 1773, was only fourteen or fifteen years old in 1787, and it is therefore highly unlikely that the maquettes had any practical connection to either the original 1785 production of *Omai* or the 1787 revival.

e. Seventeen costume designs for *Omai*, in watercolor, now in the Commonwealth National Library, Canberra, Australia.

We have in addition a watercolor by Edward Francis Burney of De Loutherbourg's famous Eidophusikon, a "movable canvas" or miniature theatre that the designer exhibited in 1781–1782 and again in 1786–1787 and 1793. On a stage measuring less than 2 metres by 2.5 metres, constructed of wood, pasteboard, cork, and linen, De Loutherbourg contrived several scenes and "transparencies," which changed as light from lamps shining through stained glass played upon transparent and semitransparent surfaces. The discovery of Burney's watercolor in 1962 aided immeasurably in the visualization of the Eidophusikon, which hithertofore had been known through verbal description alone. (The painting is often reproduced; see Rosenfeld, *Georgian Scene Painters*, fig. 20.)

ART AND THEATRE

In the Introduction to the present chapter we saw that the theory of the commercialization of leisure in the eighteenth century espoused, among others, by J. H. Plumb provides a context for and supports the explanation of the theatre as a commercial enterprise responding to popular taste. The same theory helps to explain the proliferation through the century of a parasitic consumer art made profitable by the popularity of the theatre. Again, the commercial motive does not determine the quality of the art, and we have for examination a large collection of work of several kinds and certainly of varying quality, ranging from portraits by the leading artists of the time to workmanlike engravings and prints, to mass-produced porcelain figures of actors and actresses, and even playing cards featuring their faces. A related function was what can only be called publicity. Actors and actresses for example, particularly after mid-century, became theatrical "personalities" with an identity no longer confined to the stage. Consequently, they became popular subjects, willing and unwilling, for portraits, caricatures, and ceramics. (A useful discussion of this material is provided by Robert Halsband in *British Theatre and the Other Arts, 1660–1800*, ed. Shirley Strum Kenny.)

This close relationship between the fine and theatre arts may have enriched the lives of the public, and it seems also to appeal to the academic preference for integration and synthesis. But it is not always certain what such art can tell us specifically about stages and costumes. Most troublesome are those paintings and engravings that seem to represent actors in specific roles or scenes from specific performances. Caricature presents its own problems of interpretation, but at least the necessity of interpretation is manifest. Figurines, playing cards, and cane heads are less likely to lead the historian astray.

Theatrical Paintings

Eighteenth-century theatrical paintings and engravings, especially portraits of actors and actresses, number in the thousands and give us a sense of familiarity with the English stage and its artists unparalleled in earlier periods. It is altogether possible, of course, that so far as stages and stage productions are concerned, we are being misled by traditions and conventions related far more closely to iconography than to the theatre. Nevertheless, the pictorial record reflects the way the eighteenth-century public saw or wished to see its performers and theatres and therefore provides evidence of audience attitude and perception, even if it leaves some details of costuming and staging in doubt.

Portrait painting was the lifeblood of English artists during the eighteenth century, and theatrical portraiture was undertaken by outstanding painters, including William Hogarth (1697–1764), Francis Hayman (1708–1776), Joshua Reynolds (1723–1792), Johann Zoffany (1735–1810), Thomas Beach (1738–1806), and Thomas Lawrence (1769–1830). It is possible to trace in their work a development in style, from Zoffany's subdued but skillfully executed portraits of Garrick and his contemporaries, to Reynolds' neoclassical renderings, to what Iain Mackintosh refers to as Lawrence's "messianic portraits of Kemble" (*The Georgian Playhouse*, chap. V). Portraits of actors and actresses could be painted in private or in stage character, but while the latter are generally of more interest to the historian of the theatre, iconographic tradition and artistic considerations can make any painting misleading as theatrical evidence. Portraits of performers are in fact often indistinguishable from those of anyone else. And ironically the better the artist the greater the possibility of our being misled. Zoffany's paintings are considered to be of indifferent artistic merit by art historians but are valuable as accurate records of features and costumes. Sir Joshua Reynolds, on the other hand, the most successful portrait painter of the eighteenth century, frequently treats theatrical subjects non-theatrically, and non-theatrical subjects theatrically. He was also fond of portraying his subjects as allegorical or mythological figures. It has been noted, for example, that his portrait of Sarah Siddons as the Tragic Muse (*The Georgian Playhouse*, no. 98) takes its pose and gesture from Michelangelo's depiction of Isaiah in the Sistine Chapel and is emblematic of pity and terror. A theatre historian who ventures into such territory ignorant of the history and conventions of art will inevitably founder on such shoals.

A number of paintings of particular scenes have become famous through frequent reproduction: Hogarth's *Beggar's Opera*; the same painter's portrait of Garrick as Richard III; Zoffany's portrayal of Garrick and Mrs. Pritchard in the dagger scene from *Macbeth*; James Roberts' screen scene from *The School for Scandal*; Zoffany's portrait of Macklin as Shylock; Lawrence's portraits of Kemble as Coriolanus, as Rolla in Sheridan's *Pizarro*, as Hamlet, and as Cato in Addison's play of the same name. (Good selections of engravings and paintings are to be found in Odell's *Shakespeare from Betterton to Irving*, Nicoll's *The Garrick Stage*, and Mackintosh, *The Georgian Playhouse*.)

Although almost every performer who trod the boards in the eighteenth century was immortalized pictorially in some way, the most popular subjects were David Garrick, Sarah Siddons, and John Philip Kemble. Garrick was the subject of at least ninety portraits in twenty-nine stage characters; the total of original and engraved portraits exceeds 450 items. (See Kalman Burnim, "Looking upon His Like Again: Garrick and the Artist" in *British Theatre and the Other Arts*, ed. Shirley Strum Kenny.) Kemble was painted at least twenty-seven times in private character and another fifty-seven times in stage character; the total is 253 items. (See Burnim, ''John Philip Kemble and the Artists'' in *The Eighteenth Century Stage*, ed. John Browning.) The portraits of Mrs. Siddons approach in number those of her brother. (Convenient annotated lists of portraits of these and other performers are to be found at the end of each entry in *A Biographical Dictionary*.)

Not all theatrical paintings and drawings were flattering to their subjects. William Hogarth is the best-known English pictorial satirist of the eighteenth century (see below), but the full development of theatrical caricature and satire did not emerge until the last two decades of the century, twenty years after the death of Hogarth in 1764. James Gillray (1756–1815), Thomas Rowlandson (1756–1827), and the brothers Cruikshank, Isaac (1789–1856) and George (1792–1878), caricatured audiences as well as performers, and drew attention through exaggeration to details of costume and deportment that more polite artists might well have chosen to ignore or suppress. (See M. Dorothy George, *Hogarth to Cruikshank*, pp. 107–18, 203–5.) And to be honest, it is something of a relief after the near-idolatry of some serious portraiture to find satiric, even malicious, pictorial representations of the ''stars'' of the stage. James Gillray, for instance, like Reynolds, portrayed Sarah Siddons as the Tragic Muse, Melpomene (George, fig. 100), but made of her an emblem of shameless greed. Besides the leading players, theatrical rivalries and the addiction to spectacle were constant topics of caricature. But this represents only part of the story. Scenes from plays became a medium for contemporary political and social satire. As Shirley Strum Kenny notes:

The focus was changed. No longer was the stage scene and dramatic structure the key; instead the theatre as social and cultural phenomenon was central, with the audience becoming as important a subject as the actors and sets. The centrality of theatre in British cultural life and the market ability of prints based on theatrical scenes continued to encourage artists to produce prints based on the theatre, even if the prints had little to do with actual productions. [*British Theatre and the Other Arts, 1660–1800*, p. 22]

Again, a broadly based understanding of the cultural role of such art, as well as its social and political context, is necessary if we are to use it as evidence for theatre history.

William Hogarth

The artist best known to students of literature and the theatre is undoubtedly William Hogarth, whose work included theatrical subjects but was also influenced by dramatic conventions and conceptions. Hogarth engraved tickets for actors' benefits on occasion; provided frontispieces and illustrations for the editions of several plays, including Henry Fielding's *Tragedy of Tragedies* (1730) and Molière's *L'Avare* and *Sganarelle ou le cocu imaginaire* (1732); painted portraits of actors and actresses, including Quin and Garrick; painted scenes from plays, two from Shakespeare and one from *The Beggar's Opera*; and caricatured the theatrical world in several paintings and engravings. (The engravings are reproduced by Joseph Burke and Colin Caldwell in *Hogarth*, the paintings in R. B. Beckett's *Hogarth*. See also Ronald Paulson's *Hogarth's Graphic Works*.)

Of equal interest is the clear influence of the theatre on Hogarth's work in general. In his *Autobiographical Notes* the artist explained his method: "Subjects I consider'd as writers do, my Picture was my Stage and men and women my actors who were, by Means of certain Actions and expressions, to exhibit a dumb shew" (quoted by Sean Shesgreen, ed., *Engravings by Hogarth*, p. xxii). Hogarth is in fact credited with the popularizing if not the invention of the use of sequential, anecdotal pictures for moral and social satire. His most famous series—*The Rake's Progress, The Harlot's Progress, Marriage a la Mode*—are theatrical in conception, and they are readily analyzed in terms of plot, character, costume, set, and gesture. Other series, such as *Industry and Idleness*, seem to be deliberately designed to suggest the stage. We are presented with momentarily arrested dramatic moments whose implications take us both backward and forward from that moment. Just as the theatrical experience of Hogarth's audience enhanced their appreciation of his art, so a sympathetic and careful analysis of the prints can inform the theatre historian about the theatre that influenced the art.

Portraits of performers attributed to Hogarth include the following:

a. Lavinia Fenton, the original Polly Peachum in *The Beggar's Opera* (ca. 1740?). Beckett, who reproduces the painting in his *Hogarth* (pl. 115), notes that the identity of the lady was attested by Samuel Ireland but that there is no resemblance to other engraved portraits of the actress.

b. Peg Wolfington (Beckett, pl. 126). Beckett notes: "There is no particular reason to suppose that this portrait in fact represents the famous actress. . . . "

c. James Quin (Beckett, pl. 153).

d. David Garrick and his wife, Eva Maria Veigel (Beckett, pl. 187).

e. David Garrick as Richard III (Beckett, pl. 156; Burke and Caldwell reproduce the engraving, pl. 199). In spite of the subject, there is no hint in the painting of stage presentation. It is rather a historical painting, modelled on Charles Lebrun's *The Family of Darius before Alexander the Great*, and a study of fear. Garrick is presented not as an actor playing the part of Richard, but *as* Richard. Hogarth has rendered an artistic interpretation of the king's waking from his nightmare based on Shakespeare's text, probably Garrick's stage portrayal, and artistic tradition. What is significant for the theatre historian is not the detail, but the conception and the effect, which may well have approximated that of Garrick on the stage.

Other portraits of Fenton, Quin, and Garrick have been attributed to Hogarth, but those discussed above have been authenticated and are most likely to be reproduced as theatrical illustrations.

Early in his career Hogarth painted two other scenes from Shakespeare: *The Tempest* I.ii, before Prospero's cell (Beckett, pl. 3) and *Falstaff Examining his Recruits*, based on *2 Henry IV* III.ii (Beckett, pl. 4). The first appears to bear no resemblance to any stage performance, real or imagined; the second, according to Beckett, may have been based on an actual stage scene. The success of Colley Cibber's production of *Henry VIII* in 1727 is held to have inspired Hogarth's engraving of Henry and Anne Boleyn (Burke and Caldwell, pl. 120). The print may involve some contemporary political commentary, but there is little of the obviously theatrical about it.

Of more interest are the six versions of a scene from *The Beggar's Opera*. The earlier group (represented in Beckett by the third version, pl. 5) is usually taken as a matter-of-fact depiction of the modest stage at Rich's Lincoln's Inn Fields. Later versions (Beckett, pl. 17) show a much larger stage and have been taken in some quarters as representing the stage conceived by Rich for his new theatre at Covent Garden (1732). However, the presence in the sixth version of several extras, a Latin motto over the stage, and carved satyrs on each side of the stage has prompted the slightly different interpretation that Hogarth transformed his simple scene into self-conscious art. "Beginning with a simple stage scene," writes Robert Halsband, "Hogarth has created a theatrical conversation piece that comments on the stage and on the society that patronized it" (in *British Theatre and the Other Arts, 1660–1800*, p. 155).

Oddly, what may in the final analysis turn out to be the most important of Hogarth's scenes from plays is a large (130.8 cm. x 146.7 cm.) painting, done probably in 1731 or 1732, of a scene from John Dryden's *The Indian Emperor, or The Conquest of Mexico* as performed by children at the house of John Conduitt, Master of the Mint, before the younger members of the royal family (Beckett, pls. 52–54). Richard Southern, who discusses the painting at some length in *Changeable Scenery* (pp. 189–93), points out that there is no attempt, as there would have been on the professional stage, to hide the structural details of the scenery, and that consequently the picture is of particular value. The painting, he notes, "may turn out to be the earliest actual representation of grooves we possess after the Restoration." The practice in a private children's theatrical, of course, need not necessarily reflect professional practice.

Six of Hogarth's satirical engravings of the more general theatre world are also frequently cited and reproduced by theatre historians:

a. *Masquerades and Operas, or The Taste of the Town* (Burke and Caldwell, pl. 42). This early engraving (1723/4) depicts two crowds in front of Burlington Gate, one seeking admittance to a conjuring display and a masquerade, the other to a pantomime. In a wheelbarrow, the works of Shakespeare, Dryden, Otway, Congreve, and Jonson are labelled "Waste Paper for Shops." An Italian singer is featured on a signboard.

b. *A Just View of the British Stage* (Burke and Caldwell, pl. 53). The three managers of Drury Lane—Robert Wilks, Colley Cibber, Barton Booth—are planning pantomimes to outdo those of John Rich at Lincoln's Inn Fields. The banality and crudity of pantomime is emphasized by the trappings that clutter the room. The disregard of great drama is indicated by the toilet paper enscribed "Hamlet," "Macbeth," "Julius Caesar," and "The Way of the World." Odell, in *Shakespeare from Betterton to Irving* (I, 317), offers the suggestion that the drawing shows a stage set of a room with back flats and side wings, and he speculates that it might represent the stage at Drury Lane. He seems to have been alone in his belief.

c. *The Laughing Audience* (Burke and Caldwell, pl. 146). Here we are shown members of a theatre audience separated from the orchestra by a row of spikes, while in the boxes two gentlemen dally with the ladies. A fruit seller attempts to get their attention. One figure (a critic?) does not look pleased.

d. *Southwark Fair* (Burke and Caldwell, pl. 147; Beckett, pls. 61, 63). Executed 1733/ 4, the work depicts the efforts of a startling array of performers to attract an audience at Southwark Fair. Burke and Caldwell point out that nearly all the allusions are specific and topical.

e. *Strolling Actresses Dressing in a Barn* (Burke and Caldwell, pl. 181). The Licensing Act of 1737 made it illegal to perform plays outside London and Westminster. Hogarth produced this famous engraving the following year. The scene represents backstage preparations, rehearsal, and a generalized picture of the life of strolling players.

f. *The Charmers of the Age* (Burke and Caldwell, pl. 185). This etching, after Hogarth's 1741 drawing, caricatures the dancers Desnoyer and Barberini, as well as—in the figures of the enthusiastic spectators—the popular vogue for foreign dancers itself.

Book Illustrations

The practice of including frontispieces or illustrations in the printed editions of plays, particularly in collected editions, was not unknown even in the seventeenth century, but was becoming well established by the 1720s. The seventh edition of Addison's *Cato* featured an engraving by Louis Du Guernier as a frontispiece, and as we have seen, Fielding's *Tragedy of Tragedies, or Tom Thumb* has a frontispiece by Hogarth. The practice was normally confined to second and succeeding editions, and the plates were used, reused, pirated, and imitated in a myriad of ways for a variety of purposes. Under these circumstances, it is often difficult to determine the provenance of a given illustration or its precise relationship to the play or performance it purportedly represents. Such illustrations have nevertheless been scrutinized and analyzed by theatre historians and conclusions drawn with greater or less confidence concerning staging practices.

The most frequently reprinted and illustrated dramatist during the eighteenth century was Shakespeare. Nicholas Rowe's edition of the bard, published by Jacob Tonson in 1709, had each play illustrated with an engraving by Elisha Walker after a drawing by the French artist François Boitard. For the edition of 1714, Tonson had the original plates revised or replaced by Du Guernier. Theatre historians have in the past been convinced that the whole series of plates represents stage tradition and have examined the illustrations for evidence of costume, scenery, stage design, and acting. Certainly the engravings appear to have been based far more on contemporary staging practices than on the artist's interpretations of the plays. Nevertheless, we should temper our enthusiasm by recalling that the publisher, Tonson, was trying to emulate Continental practices and in fact, in the absence of qualified English artists, resorted to the use of a French one. The accuracy of the illustrations as reflections of English staging practice cannot be assumed, although they certainly remain weighty corroborative evidence, especially so far as costume is concerned. When a few years later Tonson printed the second edition of Alexander Pope's *Shakespeare* (1728), he reprinted the 1714 plates from Rowe's edition, again revised by a French artist. It seems unlikely that such revisions would be in the direction of an accurate portrayal of stage practice. In fact, the French artistic influence is clear in the rococo style of the illustrations, a style found as well in the plates included in the second edition of Lewis Theobald's Shakespeare (1740), prepared by Hubert-François Gravelot, who worked in England from 1732 to 1755.

The first prominent English artist to illustrate an edition of Shakespeare was Francis Hayman, who had begun his career as a scene painter at Drury Lane and Goodman's Fields theatres and who later designed scenery and painted theatrical conversation pieces. In 1744 he was engaged to draw the plates, engraved by Gravelot, for Thomas Hanmer's edition of Shakespeare. Robert Halsband, in an important piece on drama and art in *British Theatre and the Other Arts* (ed. Shirley Strum Kenny), observes that Hayman's work sometimes illustrates the printed text and sometimes the stage setting. For instance, Hayman's plate for *The Tempest* is based on the text, while that for *Macbeth* appears to illustrate the stage setting for Lady Macbeth's sleepwalking scene (p. 152). (Tonson also hired Hayman to design the plates for an edition of William Congreve, published in 1753. The plates were used again in another edition of 1761.)

Later in the century John Bell commissioned several lesser-known English painters—Edward Edwards, John Sherwin, James Roberts—to provide engravings for a twenty-volume edition of Shakespeare's plays, edited by Francis Gentleman and published in 1773–1775. *The New English Theatre* (1776–1777) and *Bell's British Theatre* (1776–1781) were similarly illustrated. In 1791 Samuel DeWilde (1748–1832) was engaged to provide portraits for a new edition of *Bell's British Theatre*. DeWilde produced more than ninety illustrations for the thirty-six volumes, sometimes scenes from plays but more often small, full-length portraits of actors and actresses in character.

One of the most ambitious projects devoted to Shakespearean illustration was undertaken late in the century by John Boydell (1719–1804), engraver and print publisher, who in 1790 became Lord Mayor of London. In 1786 Boydell commissioned several of the leading artists of the day to provide 162 large oil paintings illustrating Shakespeare's plays. These he exhibited in his Shakespeare Gallery in Pall Mall. Boydell evidently intended to bequeath the collection to the state, but in 1804 it was sold to pay debts and was thus broken up. Fortunately, *A Collection of Prints from Pictures Painted for the Purpose of Illustrating Shakespeare by the Artists of Great Britain* was published in 1803; and engravings in a smaller format were also used to illustrate an 1802 edition of Shakespeare. The artists were encouraged to paint after their own inclinations and interpretations of Shakespeare's text; consequently very few reflect stage practice. They are for the most part examples of history painting, the mode that Boydell hoped to encourage by his enterprise. From an artistic point of view, some of the paintings are of considerable interest—the illustrations for *Hamlet*, *Lear*, and *Macbeth* by Henry Fuseli for instance—but they can tell us little about the life of the plays on the eighteenth-century stage.

Finally, we must take note of two further series of theatrical illustrations. The first, *Dramatic Characters, or Different Portraits of the English Stage*, was published in 1770 and a second edition in 1773. The work consists of twenty-five plates of actors in character (thirty-eight in the 1773 edition), engraved after drawings by Jean Louis Faesch (who also produced a similar series of French actors in character). The second is a series of about one hundred watercolors of Shakespearean scenes, executed between 1769 and 1782 by Samuel Hieronymus Grimm (1733–1794). The paintings are manifestly dramatic, but it is impossible to pinpoint them on the line ranging from accurate representation of stage as reality, to an artistic impression of what was seen and heard, to totally imaginative rendering.

The interpretation of graphic and pictorial art as evidence for the study of theatre history involves determining as closely as possible the relationship between the work of art and an actual stage presentation. As we have just noted, this relationship depends upon the artist's attitude and purpose. If based upon what was witnessed on the stage, a picture may in fact show us exactly what the artist saw, or it may reflect the impression the scene made on the audience. Even if the picture is simply a work of the imagination, it may have theatrical significance in that it influenced the costuming and presentation of subsequent productions.

Yet these are not the only considerations. Allardyce Nicoll, whose discussion of iconographical evidence in *The Garrick Stage* (pp. 145–56) provides salutary reading for students of theatre history, draws attention to two further considerations: first, the problem of deliberate falsification or erroneous ascription; and second, the question of accuracy. He cites as an example of deliberate falsification the famous mezzotint of *Garrick in the Greenroom*, executed in 1829 by W. J. Ward and supposedly based on a work by Hogarth (Nicoll, fig. 100). The work is in fact based on a drawing by Alessandro Longhi, *A Poet Declaiming His Verses*, and therefore, as Nicoll notes, "must now be deemed to have nothing whatever to do either with Garrick or with the English stage" (p. 146). Less consciously dishonest but equally misleading examples can be found among the illustrations for *Bell's Shakespeare* and *Bell's British Theatre*. Some of the plates show performers in roles that they never performed during the period and must therefore be either imaginary or studio portraits. The portrait of Garrick as Demetrius in Edward Young's *The Brothers* (Nicoll, fig. 104) shows the great actor in a role he had last played a quarter of a century earlier and is thus almost surely the product of the artist's imagination. Such examples serve as reminders that each illustration has to be evaluated on its own terms in the light of all the available information. So far as accuracy is concerned, we have no way of knowing how closely a given portrait approximates the stage figure in costume and gesture. We know from comments recorded by Lichtenberg that we certainly cannot take accuracy for granted (*Lichtenberg's Visits to England*, pp. 26, 70–71), and so far as costume is concerned we are left with Nicoll's cautionary conclusion:

All that can be said with assurance is that the colourings serve to reflect in general the diverse and often startling hues displayed on the stage: the ordinary civil dress of the period was rich in tone, and the costumes worn by the actors are likely to have outdone the bright variety to be seen among the spectators in the house.

"Beyond that," he continues, "we cannot go" (pp. 154–55).

MUSIC IN THE THEATRE

Music has always had a place in the theatre, including the English theatre, but two factors have combined to make music of particular significance for the historian of the Restoration and eighteenth-century theatre. First, the period is the first for which a substantial amount of theatre music has survived; and second, the use of music in stage presentations expanded dramatically—pun intended. Music was used in the theatre in a variety of forms and for a variety of purposes. The forms included dramatic opera (English and Italian), ballad opera, comic opera, burletta, masque, as well as regular plays accompanied by music. There is, nevertheless, often no clear distinction to be made among these forms; a more useful categorization of theatre music has been devised by Curtis A. Price in *Music in the Restoration Theatre* (1979). Music, Price suggests (p. xvi), was either (a) *dramatic*, "integral to plot and meaning, growing directly from the dramatic situation"; (b) *para-dramatic*, "irrationally accommodated within the action, but not part of it"; or (c) *incidental*, played between the acts of the play. For the critic of the drama, the first is clearly the most important use, but for a full appreciation of the theatrical experience of any given performance, all music—whatever its relation to the drama—must be taken into account. Unfortunately, in the past it has too often been ignored. Editions of Restoration plays rarely indicate the use of music and even less frequently reproduce it. As a consequence, students of English literature almost invariably remain ignorant of the musical dimension of the plays they study. This neglect is especially detrimental to the understanding of drama and performance between 1660 and 1705, when the great majority of plays were accompanied by vocal or instrumental music, but music continued to be an important feature of the drama throughout the eighteenth century. We can no longer turn a blind eye and a deaf ear to its impact.

This state of affairs was not simply the result of the failure of theatre historians and musicologists to communicate, although such cross-disciplinary failure is common enough. It was also the consequence of the fact that English theatre music has been little valued or discussed even as music. The idea persists that the premature death of Henry Purcell in 1695 effectively ended any hope there had been for the development of a native English opera, and that the importation of Italian opera in 1705 dealt English music a final blow. In the light of the rise of ballad opera in the 1720s and the number of "dialogue" operas performed in London theatres during the last half of the eighteenth century, it seems patently clear that musical drama—whether or not classified as "opera" in the purist's sense—continued to be performed throughout the century.

Whatever else might be said of the musical drama that persisted on the English stage, for music historians in general, the term *opera* was reserved for the Italian variety. It was so used by Roger North (1653–1734) in his *Memoirs of Musick* (1728; see John Wilson, ed., *Roger North on Music*), and by the anonymous author of *A Critical Discourse on Operas and Musick in England* (1709). The great eighteenth-century musicologist Charles Burney confirmed the usage in *A General History of Music* (1776–1789). Like earlier critics of the opera such as John Dennis and Joseph Addison, Burney implies that English dramatic genius flourishes best in the absence of music, particularly English music. Music is used simply to support "weak plays and unattractive actors of our national theatres" (IV, 631):

It is only in times of distress that managers have recourse to Music and dancing: when the actors are good and in favour, they are sure of the national attention and patronage; but if, as is often the case, the attempts at opera on the English stage are awkward, and the agents possessed of but ordinary talents, this good effect is produced, that, after quickening appetite in the public by abstinence, they return with eagerness to their natural food. [IV, 193]

Music historians found English theatre music unworthy of their attention, and stage historians were assured that it was an element extraneous to true drama. Little wonder it could for so long have been ignored.

The first substantial study of seventeenth-century English music-drama was Edward J. Dent's *Foundations of English Opera* (1928). Dent traced the development of these dramatic productions from the masques of Ben Jonson to the "semi-operas" of Purcell. To his credit he took into account the contributions of librettist and composer, designer and producer, and consulted scores, librettos, designs, and contemporary critiques. And he tried to establish a more sophisticated "operatic principle" to replace the cruder definition of opera as a drama entirely sung. This operatic principle arises when musical and dramatic principles interact and modify one another. Ultimately, however, Dent finds himself unable to define what he calls "clarity of form." He writes: "The music is itself the drama; that is the fundamental principle of opera. A composer of opera must choose a dramatic idea which will lend itself to musical principles of development; the poet must cast his thoughts in forms which definitely require music for their complete expression" (p. 233).

Given Dent's conclusion concerning music, it is more than a little puzzling to find not only that he quotes little music in his book, but also that he believes it possible to discuss an opera for which the music may not be extant:

For it is of comparatively little importance to know what the music sounded like—we can make a sufficient guess at that by looking at other compositions of the men who contributed to it—whereas it is of the greatest interest to know what relation the music bore to the dramatic action and how far it intensified the emotional values of the play. This we can find out to some extent by a careful examination of the libretto. [p. ix]

Dent was certainly not alone in his cavalier attitude toward musical notation as part of a dramatic text, but if this was the attitude of a musical scholar, we could hardly expect more of literary scholars or theatre historians.

There was in fact little attention paid to the subject for several years. Robert G. Noyes published several articles between 1934 and 1938; Willard Thorpe published *Songs from the Restoration Theatre* in 1934; and Edmond McAdoo Gagey's *Ballad Opera* appeared in 1937. But Noyes and Thorpe restricted themselves to songs, and Gagey was little concerned with the music.

Eric Walter White's *The Rise of English Opera* (1951) offers only a brief sketch of developments prior to 1800, but like Dent, White attempts "to illustrate the workings of the operatic principle" (p. 8). Also, like Dent, he finds "opera" to be based on musical principles, and distinguishes it from "light opera" or dialogue opera (described by White as "poor relations"), which rely on dramatic principles (p. 65). Given that music and drama had been artificially joined to make opera, after a considerable period of independent development, we are prepared to recognize a tension and an aesthetic problem in the resulting form. The desirability of discovering or establishing a quintessential operatic principle, however, is for theatre historians not initially a central concern. White quite rightly defines opera in broad terms as "a stage action with vocal and instrumental music" (p. 7), and it is that music that must be reintegrated into the history of dramatic performance. Only then can we turn to questions of aesthetics and form with any hope of answering them. Indeed in his later and more comprehensive *A History of English Opera* (1983), White abandons both his insistence on an operatic principle and the condescension towards non-Italian style operatic forms inherent in his "poor relations." He offers instead a first-rate study of "the composers of English operas and their librettists, the conditions under which their operas have been produced on the stage, the public reaction thereto, and the finances and administration involved" (p. 18).

While White chose not "to summarize librettos or analyze musical scores" (*The Rise of English Opera*, p. 8) in his search for the operatic principle, Robert Etheridge Moore in *Henry Purcell and the Restoration Theatre* (1961) eschews theoretical questions and "attempts to analyze both libretto and music in the light of their theatrical intentions and effectiveness" (p. xiii). Curtis A. Price's *Henry Purcell and the London Stage* (1984) similarly "examine[s] the music strictly in terms of its attendant spoken drama" (p. xi), although Price is able to go beyond Moore's analysis by drawing on an increasingly detailed and sophisticated knowledge of Restoration theatre conditions. Such analyses depend, of course, on the availability of librettos and scores; therefore before they can be practiced on works less known and documented than Purcell's, considerable preliminary spadework must be done.

This preliminary work—and more—is happily being done. Roger Fiske's *English Theatre Music in the Eighteenth Century* appeared in 1973; Curtis A. Price's *Music in the Restoration Theatre* in 1979. Fiske sensibly breaks free of restrictive value judgments, pointing out that "bad music is as much a part of history as good" (p. 581) and methodically describing every dramatic work of the period for which music survives. For the locations of the music, Fiske depends heavily on the *British Union Catalogue of Early Music*. Price is similarly helpful in providing a catalogue of instrumental music in plays during 1665–1713 (pp. 135–236), which taken together with *English Song-Books 1651–1702*, published in 1940 by Cyrus L. Day and Eleanore Boswell Murrie, provides a guide to most of the English theatre music of the Restoration. But the greatest boon to theatre history is the planned publication in facsimile of a large selection of theatrical vocal and orchestral music being undertaken by the British publisher, Richard MacNutt, under the editorship of several distinguished musicologists and historians, including Roger Fiske and Curtis Price. *Music for London Entertainment 1660–1800* is to be published in six series: Music for Plays 1660–1714; Music for Plays 1714–1800; English Opera and Masque; Pantomime, Ballet and Dances; Italian Opera; Music of the Pleasure Gardens. The first two series are comprehensive, the last four selective. The total number of volumes is expected to exceed one hundred.

The publication of theatre music was an enterprise quite independent of its role in the playhouse, a situation with two important consequences. First, it means that the complete musical score for a play or an opera was rarely published; and second, we are largely dependent upon the written text and published stage directions for information concerning the use of music in performance.

Important collections of Restoration instrumental act music include John Walsh's *Harmonia Anglicana* (1701–1710; see Price, Appendix II, and William C. Smith's bibliography of Walsh's publications), and *A Collection of Ayres . . . by the late Mr. Henry Purcell* (1697)—a major source for Dr. Burney. After 1710, publication of overtures and act music declined, but collections of songs and arias for home consumption continued throughout the eighteenth century. An early collection, Thomas D'Urfey's *Wit and Mirth: Pills to Purge Melan-*

choly—a vast anthology that in its final six-volume edition of 1719–1720 contained over one thousand songs together with their melody lines—included not only songs from the stage but also folk ballads. The work was in turn mined by the composers of ballad operas, including John Gay for *The Beggar's Opera*. The limitations of such publications as evidence for theatre history is obvious: recitatives and choruses were normally omitted; orchestration and musical notation were cut to a minimum; songs and arias were curtailed or left out. Even Italian operas rarely had a full score published. Improvements in publishing procedures late in the century are rendered less useful to the historian by other failures:

In the 1790s publishers no longer bothered to name the composer of a borrowed item or the instrument that played a solo. The title-page may say that the music has been 'selected and composed', but there is no way of telling which are the selected items, let alone who wrote them. Almost all eighteenth-century scores, whether full or vocal, tell you who sang each song at the first performance; they are much less conscientious about telling you the name of the character being represented. [Fiske, *English Theatre Music*, p. 298]

The use of the dramatic text or libretto as evidence of how music was used on the stage must also be undertaken with some care. Playtexts may in fact provide the best evidence, but they are not without their limitations. As Price points out, publication and printing practices make it possible that the implied musical practices "are just as attributable to printers, publishers, producers, directors, actors, and musicians, as to any 'original intention' of the author" (*Music in the Restoration Theatre*, p. xviii). And, of course, texts do not necessarily reflect actual theatrical practice. From the standpoint of the theatre historian, the playwright's lack of responsibility for the composition and performance of the music is not so important as the possibility that the printed directions for music may have been the responsibility of non-theatrical people such as printers or publishers.

There is in addition to the published music a relatively large amount of music in manuscript. In some instances these manuscript scores are more complete than those that found their way into print. Manuscript scores from the Restoration and early eighteenth century have proved most useful. (The dearth of manuscript copies of full opera scores after 1763 has been partially explained by postulating their loss in the fire that destroyed the King's Theatre in 1789.) Of particular interest are the manuscript scores for several famous Restoration productions. Matthew Locke's music for Settle's *The Empress of Morocco* (1673) is in Christ Church Library, Oxford; the 1696 score by John Eccles and Godfrey Singer for Davenant's *Macbeth* (first performed in 1664) is in the British Library; Purcell's music for Settle's *The Fairy Queen* (1692), the most complete manuscript of any Purcell opera, is held by the Royal Academy of Music; and the same composer's score for Naham Tate's *Dido and Aeneas* (1689), once held in the library of St. Michael's College, Tenbury, is now in the Bodleian Library at

Oxford. (This last manuscript, once thought to date from the early years of the eighteenth century, is now believed to be no earlier than 1750.) Perhaps the most significant of the Purcell manuscripts from a theatrical point of view is that for the operatic adaptation of Howard and Dryden's *The Indian Queen*, performed in 1695. The manuscript, now in the British Library (Add. ms. 31449) provides both text and music. The cast list is partially filled in, and we therefore know that the performers were the young and relatively inexperienced actors who remained at Drury Lane after Betterton and the senior actors left to form a rival troupe at Lisle's Tennis Court in Lincoln's Inn Fields.

Whether published or in manuscript, theatrical music for the period is scattered and difficult of access. Manuscripts are by their nature unique, and even published music often survives in only one or two copies. *The British Catalogue of Early Music* identifies locations of music in British libraries, but there is no similar listing for the considerable holdings of major libraries in the United States. Price lists twelve libraries in Britain and another four in the United States holding manuscript scores of Restoration music and also indicates the location of rare publications (pp. 135–236). Roger Fiske similarly provides lists—together with library locations—of operas that survive orchestrally and of theatre overtures published between 1698 and 1708 and again between 1740 and 1800 (pp. 585–96). Future work nevertheless will undoubtedly be facilitated by the publication of *Music for London Entertainment*.

A fundamental issue to be determined, of course, is the relationship between the music and the dramatic texts that the music was intended to accompany, enhance, or inform. Accurate bibliographical and musicological information is crucial. Also useful are several treatises on the subject—most of them from mid-century—by James Harris (1744), Francesco Geminiani (1749), Charles Avison (1753), and John Brown (1789). But in the final analysis, historical scholarship must join with a dramatic criticism that recognizes musical sound as an intrinsic rather than as a peripheral part of theatrical performance. Only during the past few years have some of the possibilities of such a criticism begun to be realized.

REFERENCES

Ackerman, Rudolph (publisher). *The Microcosm of London*. Text W. H. Pyne and William Combe. Plates A. C. Pugin and T. Rowlandson. 3 Vols. London, 1808–1811. [Facsimile ed., London, 1904]

Adam, Robert and James Adam. *The Works in Architecture of Robert and James Adam*, Vol. II. London, 1779.

Adams, Joseph Quincey. *The Dramatic Records of Sir Henry Herbert*. New Haven, Conn., 1917.

Alberti, Georg Wilhelm. *Briefe betreffend den aller neuesten Zustand der Religion und der Wissenschaften in Gross-Britannien*. 4 Vols. Hanover, Germany, 1752–1754.

Algarotti, Count Francesco. *An Essay on the Opera Written in Italian*. London, 1767. [Italian ed. 1755, French ed. 1773]

Allen, Ralph G. "Irrational Entertainment in the Age of Reason." In *The Stage and the Page*. Ed. G. Winchester Stone, Jr. Berkeley, 1981.

―――. "The Stage Spectacles of Philip James de Loutherbourg." Yale University Dissertation, 1960.

Altick, Richard. *The Shows of London*. London, 1978.

Antal, Frederick. *Hogarth and His Place in European Art*. London, 1962.

Anthony, Sister Rose. *The Jeremy Collier Stage Controversy 1698–1726*. Milwaukee, Wis., 1937.

Archenholz, Johann Wilhelm von. *England und Italien*. 5 Vols. Karlsruhe, Germany, 1785; 2d ed. 1787.

Arnott, James Fullerton and John William Robinson. *English Theatrical Literature 1559–1900: A Bibliography*. London, 1970.

Aston, Anthony. *A Brief Supplement to Colley Cibber, Esq. His Lives of the Late Famous Actors and Actresses*. London, 1748.

Austin, Gilbert. *Chironomia; or, a Treatise on Rhetorical Delivery* (1806). Eds. Mary Margaret Robb and Lester Thonssen. Foreward David Potter. Carbondale and Edwardsville, Ill., 1966.

Avery, Emmett L. *The London Stage 1700–1729: A Critical Introduction*. Carbondale and Edwardsville, Ill., 1968.

Avery, Emmett L. and Arthur H. Scouten. *The London Stage 1660–1700: A Critical Introduction*. Carbondale and Edwardsville, Ill., 1968.

Avison, Charles. *An Essay on Musical Expression*. 2d ed. London, 1753.

Backscheider, Paula R., gen. ed. *Eighteenth-Century English Drama*. 69 Vols. New York, 1979–1984.

Baker, David Erskine. *Biographica Dramatica, or, A Companion to the Playhouse*. Continued to 1782 by Isaac Reed and to 1811 by Stephen Jones. 3 Vols. London, 1812.

The Ballad Opera: A Collection of 171 Original Texts of Musical Plays Printed in Photo-Facsimile. 28 Vols. New York, 1974.

Barlow, Graham. "Hampton Court Theatre, 1718." *Theatre Notebook* XXXVII (1983), 54–63.

Barnett, Dene. "The Performance Practice of Acting: The Eighteenth Century." *Theatre Research International* N.S. II, no. 3 (1977), 157–86; III, no. 1 (1977), 1–19; III, no. 2 (1978), 79–93; V, no. 1 (1980), 1–36; VI, no. 1 (1980–1981), 1–32.

Beckett, R. B. *Hogarth*. Boston, 1955.

Bellamy, George Anne. *An Apology for the Life of George Anne Bellamy*. 6 Vols. London, 1785.

Bell's British Theatre: Consisting of the Most Esteemed English Plays. 21 Vols. London, 1776–1781. (36 Vols. 1791–1802) *Supplement*. 4 Vols. 1784.

Bell's Edition of Shakespeare's Plays, As They are Now Performed at the Theatres Royal in London, regulated from the Prompt Books of Each House. [*Bell's Shakespeare*] 9 Vols. London, 1774. Vol. X: *Plates*. London, 1773–1776.

Bernard, John. *Retrospections of the Stage*. 2 Vols. London, 1830.

Betterton, Thomas [Edmund Curll]. *The History of the English Stage from the Restauration to the Present Time (Memoirs of Mrs. Anne Oldfield)*. London, 1741.

A Biographical Dictionary of Actors, Actresses, Musicians, Dancers, Managers, and Other Stage Personnel in London, 1660–1800. Eds. Philip H. Highfill, Jr., Edward

A. Langhans, and Kalman A. Burnim. 16 Vols. (in progress) Carbondale and Edwardsville, Ill., 1973- .

Boaden, James. *A Letter to George Steevens*. London, 1796.

———. *The Life of Mrs. Jordan*. 2 Vols. London, 1831.

———. *Memoirs of Mrs. Inchbald*. 2 Vols. London, 1833.

———. *Memoirs of Mrs. Siddons*. 2 Vols. London, 1827.

———. *Memoirs of the Life of John Philip Kemble*. 2 Vols. London, 1825.

Booth, Michael R., Richard Southern, Frederick and Lise-Lonemarker, and Robertson Davies. *The Revels History of Drama in English*, Vol. VI: *1750–1880*. London, 1975.

Boswell, Eleanore. *The Restoration Court Stage (1660–1702)*. New York and London, 1966. [1932]

Boydell, John. *The Boydell Shakespeare Prints*. Intr. A. E. Santaniello. New York and London, 1968.

Boydell, John. *A Collection of Prints from Pictures Painted for the Purpose of Illustrating Shakespeare by the Artists of Great Britain*. London, 1803.

Brandes, Ernst. *Bemerkungen über das Londoner, Pariser und Wiener Theatre*. Göttingen, Germany, 1786.

Brayley, Edward Wedlake. *Historical and Descriptive Accounts of the Theatres of London*. Ill. Daniel Havell. London, 1826.

The British Union Catalogue of Early Music Printed Before the Year 1801. Ed. Edith B. Schnapper. 2 Vols. London, 1957.

Brown, John. *Letters on the Poetry and Music of the Italian Opera*. London, 1789.

Brown, Tom. *Amusements Serious and Comical, Calculated for the Meridian of London*. [1700] In Tom Brown, *Works*, Vol. III. London, 1709.

Browning, John D., ed. *The Stage in the 18th Century*. New York and London, 1981.

Brownsmith, John. *The Dramatic Timepiece: or Perpetual Monitor*. London, 1767.

———. *The Theatrical Alphabet*. London, 1767.

Brunet, François. *Voyage d'Angleterre*. Paris, 1676.

Burgh, James. *The Art of Speaking*. London, 1761.

Burke, Joseph and Colin Caldwell. *Hogarth: The Complete Engravings*. London, 1968.

Burney, Charles. *A General History of Music*. 4 Vols. London, 1776–1789.

Burnim, Kalman. "John Philip Kemble and the Artists." In *The Stage in the 18th Century*. Ed. John Browning. New York and London, 1981.

———. "Looking upon His Like Again: Garrick and the Artist." In *British Theatre and the Other Arts, 1660–1800*. Ed. Shirley Strum Kenny. Washington, D.C., London, and Toronto, 1984.

Campbell, Lily B. "A History of Costuming on the English Stage between 1660 and 1823." *University of Wisconsin Studies in Language and Literature* II (1918), 187–223.

Carlson, Marvin. *Theories of the Theatre: A Historical and Critical Survey, from the Greeks to the Present*. Ithaca, N.Y., and London, 1984.

The Case of the Stage in Ireland. Dublin, 1757(?).

Censor Dramaticus [pseud.]. *A Complete History of the Drama*. London, 1793.

Charke, Charlotte. *A Narrative of the Life of Mrs. Charlotte Charke, Written by Herself*. Facsimile Reproduction of the Second Edition, 1755. Intr. Leonard R. N. Ashley. Gainesville, Florida, 1969.

Chetwood, W. R. *The British Theatre*. Dublin, 1750.

————. *A General History of the Stage*. Dublin, 1749.

Child, Harold. *The Shakespearean Productions of John Philip Kemble*. London, 1935.

Churchill, Charles. *The Poetical Works of Charles Churchill*. Ed. Douglas Grant. Oxford, 1956.

Cibber, Coley. *An Apology for the Life of Colley Cibber*. Ed. B.R.S. Fone. Ann Arbor, 1968.

————. *An Apology for the Life of Mr. Colley Cibber*. London, 1740.

————. *An Apology for the Life of Mr. Colley Cibber written by Himself*. Ed. Robert W. Lowe. London, 1888.

Cibber, Theophilus. *The Lives and Characters of the Most Eminent Actors and Actresses of Great Britain and Ireland*. London, 1753.

A Collection of Ayres . . . by the late Mr. Henry Purcell. London, 1697.

A Comparison Between the Two Stages. Ed. Stanley B. Wells. Princeton, 1942. [1702]

Conolly, Leonard. "Anna Margaretta Larpent, The Duchess of Queensberry and Gay's *Polly* in 1777." *Philological Quarterly* LI (1972), 955–57.

————. *The Censorship of English Drama, 1737–1824*. San Marino, 1976.

————. "The Censor's Wife at the Theatre: The Diary of Anna Margaretta Larpent, 1790–1800." *Huntington Library Quarterly* XXXV (1971), 49–64.

————. "Some New Larpent Titles." *Theatre Notebook* XXIII (1969), 150–57.

Cooke, William. *The Elements of Dramatic Criticism*. London, 1775.

————. *Memoirs of Charles Macklin*. London, 1804.

Country Gentleman's Vade Mecum. London, 1699.

A Critical Discourse on Operas and Musick in England. London, 1709.

Croft-Murray, Edward. *John Devoto, A Baroque Scene Painter*. London, 1953.

Crosby, B. (ed.?). *Crosby's Pocket Companion to the Playhouses*. London, 1796.

Curtis, Julia. "A Theatrical Contract of 1773–1774." *Theatre Notebook* XXX (1976), 18–20.

Curwen, Samuel. *The Journal of Samuel Curwen Loyalist*. Ed. Andrew Oliver. 2 Vols. Cambridge, Mass., 1972.

Danchin, Pierre. *The Prologues and Epilogues of the Restoration (1660–1700): A Complete Edition*. 4 Vols. (of a projected 6). Nancy, France, 1981, 1984.

————. *The Prologues and Epilogues of the Restoration (1660–1700). A Tentative Checklist*. Nancy, France, 1978.

Davies, Thomas. *Dramatic Miscellanies*. 3 Vols. Dublin, 1784. [Reprinted 1971]

————. *Memoirs of the Life of David Garrick, Esq.* 2 Vols. London, 1780. [Reprinted 1969]

Day, Cyrus L. and Eleanore Boswell Murrie. *English Song-Books 1651–1702: A Bibliography*. London, 1940.

Dent, Edward J. *Foundations of English Opera: A Study of Musical Drama in England During the Seventeenth Century*, Intr. Michael M. Winesanker. New York, 1965. [1928]

Dibdin, Charles [the Elder]. *A Complete History of the English Stage*. 5 Vols. New York, 1970. [1797–1800]

————. *The Musical Tour of Mr. Dibdin*. London, 1788.

————. *The Professional Life of Mr. Dibdin*. 4 Vols. London, 1803.

Dibdin, Charles [the Younger]. *History and Illustrations of the London Theatres*. London, 1826.

Dibdin, Charles. *The Memoirs of Charles Dibdin the Younger*. Ed. George Speaight. London, 1956.

Dibdin, Thomas J. *The Reminiscences of Thomas Dibdin*. 2 Vols. London, 1827.

Diderot, Denis. *Encyclopédie. Recueil de planches, sur les sciences, les arts liberaux, et les arts mechaniques, avec leur explication*. Vol. X. Paris, 1772. [Readex Compact Edition]

————. *Le Paradoxe sur le comédien*. Paris, 1830.

Diderot, Denis and Jean le Rond d'Alembert. *Theatre Architecture and Stage Machines: Engravings from the "Encyclopédie, ou Dictionnaire raisonne des sciences, des arts, t des metiers"*. New York and London, 1969.

Doran, Dr. [John]. *"Their Majesties' Servants." Annals of the English Stage from Thomas Betterton to Edmund Kean*. Ed. and rev. R. W. Lowe. 3 Vols. London, 1888.

Downer, Alan S. "Nature to Advantage Dressed: Eighteenth-Century Acting." *PMLA* LVIII (1943), 1002–37. Reprinted in *Restoration Drama: Modern Essays in Criticism*. Ed. John Loftis. New York, 1966.

Downes, John. *Roscius Anglicanus (1708)*. Intr. John Loftis. Augustan Reprint Society, no. 134. Los Angeles, 1969.

Dramatic Characters, or Different Portraits of the English Stage. London, 1770; 2d ed. 1773.

Dukore, Bernard F., ed. *Dramatic Theory and Criticism: Greeks to Grotowski*. New York, 1974.

Dumont, Gabriel Pierre Martin. *Parallèle de plans des plus belles salles de spectacles, d'Italie et de France avec details de machines théâtrales*. Composite Edition. New York, 1968. [ca. 1774}

D'Urfey, Thomas. *Wit and Mirth: or, Pills to Purge Melancholy*. 6 Vols. London, 1719–1720. [Reprinted 1959]

Engel, J. J. *Ideerzu einer Mimik*. 2 Vols. Berlin, 1785.

The English Stage: Attack and Defense 1577–1730. Prefaces by Arthur Freeman. 50 Vols. New York and London, 1973–74.

An Estimate of the Theatrical Merits of the Two Tragedians of Crow Street. Dublin, 1760.

Evans, G. Blakemore, ed. *Shakespearean Prompt-Books of the Seventeenth Century*. 6 Vols. Charlottesville, 1960–1980.

Evelyn, John. *Diary*. Ed. E. S. de Beer. 6 Vols. Oxford, 1955.

Everard, Edward Cape. *Memoirs of an Unfortunate Son of Thespis*. Edinburgh, 1818.

Fabricius, Johann Christian. *Briefe aus London Vermischten Inhalts*. Dessau and Leipzig, 1784.

Fiske, Roger. *English Theatre Music in the Eighteenth Century*. London, 1973.

Fitzgerald, Percy. *A New History of the English Stage From the Restoration to the Liberty of the Theatres, in Connection with the Patent Houses*. 2 Vols. London, 1882.

Flecknoe, Richard. *Love's Kingdom, A Pastoral Trage-Comedy with a Short Treatise of the English Stage*. Pref. Arthur Freeman. New York and London, 1973. [1664]

Fletcher, Ifan K. "British Playbills before 1718." *Theatre Notebook* XVII (1963), 48–50.

Foote, Samuel. *Roman and English Comedy Consider'd and Compar'd*. London, 1747.

————. *A Treatise on the Passions*. London, 1747.

Freedley, George. "The Twenty-Six Principal Theatre Collections in American Libraries and Museums." *Bulletin of the New York Public Library* LXII (1958), 319–29.

Fujimuro, Thomas H. *The Restoration Comedy of Wit*. Princeton, 1952.

Gagey, Edmond McAdoo. *Ballad Opera*. New York, 1937.

Geminiani, Francesco. *A Treatise of Good Taste in the Art of Musick*. London, 1749.

Genest, John. *Some Account of the English Stage from the Restoration in 1660 to 1830*. 10 Vols. Bath, 1832. [Reprinted New York, n.d.]

Gentleman, Francis. *The Dramatic Censor*. 2 Vols. London, 1770. [Reprinted 1972]

George, M. Dorothy. *Hogarth to Cruikshank: Social Change in Graphic Satire*. New York, 1967.

The Georgian Playhouse: Actors, Artists, Audiences and Architecture 1730–1830. Intr. Iain Mackintosh. London, 1975.

Gildes, Rosamund and George Freedley. *Theatre Collections in Libraries and Museums: An International Handbook*. New York, 1936.

Gildon, Charles. *The Life of Mr. Thomas Betterton*. London, 1710.

Gilliland, Thomas. *The Dramatic Mirror*. 2 Vols. London, 1808.

Graham, Walter. *The Beginnings of English Literary Periodicals*. New York, 1926.

Gray, Charles Harold. *Theatrical Criticism in London to 1795*. New York, 1931. [Reprinted 1964]

Grimm, Johan Friedrich Karl. *Bemerkungen eines Reisenden durch Deutschland, Frankreich, England und Holland*. 3 Vols. Altenburg, Germany, 1775.

Grout, Donald J. *A Short History of Opera*. 2d ed. New York, 1965.

Günderrode, Friedrich Justinian Freiherr von. *Beschreibung einer Reise aus Teutschland durch einem Theil von Frankreich, England und Holland*. 2 Vols. Breslau, Poland, 1783.

Hall, Lillian A. *Catalogue of Dramatic Portraits in the Theatre Collection of the Harvard College Library*. 4 Vols. Cambridge, Mass., 1930–1934.

Halsband, Robert. "Stage Drama as a Source for Pictorial and Plastic Arts." In *British Theatre and the Other Arts, 1660–1800*. Ed. Shirley Strum Kenny. Washington, D.C., London, and Toronto, 1984.

Hanmer, Thomas, ed. *The Works of Shakespear*. 6 Vols. Oxford, 1744.

Harris, James. *Three Treatises*. London, 1744.

Haslewood, Joseph. *Green Room Gossip*. London, 1809.

Herbert, Sir Henry. *The Dramatic Records of Sir Henry Herbert*. Ed. Joseph Quincey Adams. New Haven, 1917.

Herrick, Marvin Theodore. *The Poetics of Aristotle in England*. New Haven, 1930.

Hiffernan, Paul. *Dramatic Genius*. London, 1770; 2d ed. 1772.

Highfill, Philip H., Jr. "Performers and Performing." In *London Theatre World*. Ed. Robert D. Hume. Carbondale and Edwardsville, Ill., 1980.

————. "Rich's 1744 Inventory of Covent Garden Properties." *Restoration and 18th Century Theatre Research* V (1966), 7–26; VI (1967), 27–35.

Highfill, Philip H., Jr., Edward A. Langhans, and Kalman A. Burnim. *A Biographical Dictionary of Actors, Actresses, Musicians, Dancers, Managers, and Other Stage Personnel in London, 1660–1800*. 16 Vols. (in progress). Carbondale and Edwardsville, Ill., 1973– .

Hill, Aaron. *The Art of Acting*. London, 1746.

————. *The Works of the Late Aaron Hill, Esq*. 4 Vols. London, 1753.

Hill, Aaron and William Popple. *The Prompter. A Theatrical Paper (1734–1736)*. Ed. William W. Appleton and Kalman A. Burnim. New York, 1966.

Hill, John. *The Actor*. London, 1750; rev. ed. 1755.

Hitchcock, Robert. *An Historical View of the Irish Stage*. 2 Vols. Dublin, 1788, 1794.

Hogan, Charles Beecher. *An Index to the Wandering Patentee by Tate Wilkinson*. London, 1973.

―――. *The London Stage 1776–1800: A Critical Introduction*. Carbondale and Edwardsville, Ill., 1968.

―――. *Shakespeare in the Theatre, 1701–1800*. 2 Vols. Oxford, 1952.

Holcroft, Thomas. *Alwyn, or the Gentleman Comedian*. 2 Vols. London, 1780.

―――. *The Theatrical Recorder*. 2 Vols. London, 1805.

Holland, Norman H. *The First Modern Comedies*. Bloomington and London, 1959.

Holland, Peter. *The Ornament of Action: Text and Performance in Restoration Comedy*. Cambridge, England, 1979.

Hook, Lucyle. "James Brydges Drops in at the Theatre." *Huntington Library Quarterly* VIII (1945), 306–11.

Hotson, Leslie. *The Commonwealth and Restoration Stage*. Cambridge, Mass., 1928. [Reprinted 1962]

Hughes, Leo. "The Actor's Epitome." *Review of English Studies* XX (1944), 306–97.

―――. *The Drama's Patrons*. Austin, 1971.

―――. "The Evidence from Promptbooks." In *The London Theatre World, 1660–1800*. Ed. Robert D. Hume. Carbondale and Edwardsville, Ill., 1980.

Hughes, Leo and A. H. Scouten. "Dryden with Variations: Three Prompt Books." *Theatre Research International* XI (1986), 91–105.

―――. "The Troublesome Play: A Promptbook of Oroonoko." *Theatre Notebook* XXXVIII (1984), 16–27.

Hume, Robert D. *The Development of English Drama in the Late Seventeenth Century*, Oxford, 1976.

―――. "The Dorset Garden Theatre: A Review of Facts and Problems." *Theatre Notebook* XXXIII (1979), 4–17.

―――. "English Drama and Theatre 1660–1800: New Directions in Research." *Theatre Survey* XXIII (1982), 71–100.

―――. "The Nature of the Dorset Garden Theatre." *Theatre Notebook* XXXVI (1982), 99–109.

―――. "Opera in London, 1695–1706." In *British Theatre and the Other Arts, 1660–1800*. Ed. Shirley Strum Kenny. Washington, D.C., London, and Toronto, 1984.

―――. *The Rakish Stage: Studies in English Drama, 1660–1800*. Carbondale and Edwardsville, Ill., 1983.

Hume, Robert D., ed. *The London Theatre World, 1660–1800*. Carbondale and Edwardsville, Ill., 1980.

Humphries, Charles and William C. Smith. *Music Publishing in the British Isles from the Earliest Times to the Middle of the Nineteenth Century*. London, 1934.

Hunter, J. Paul. "The World as Stage and Closet." In *British Theatre and the Other Arts, 1660–1800*. Ed. Shirley Strum Kenny. Washington, D.C., London, and Toronto, 1984.

Inchbald, Elizabeth, ed. *The British Theatre*. 25 Vols. London, 1808. (20 Vols. 1820)

Izenour, George C. *Theatre Design*. New York, 1977.

Jackson, Allan S. "Little-Known Theatrical Prints of the Eighteenth Century." *Theatre Notebook* XXII (1968), 113–16.

―――. "Restoration Scenery, 1656–1680." *Restoration and 18th Century Theatre Research* III (1964), 25–35.

Jackson, John. *The History of the Scottish Stage*. Edinburgh, 1793.

Joppien, Rudiger, ed. *Philippe Jacques de Loutherbourg, RA 1740–1812*. London, 1973.

Jordan, R. "Observations on the Backstage Area in the Restoration Theatre." *Theatre Notebook* XXXVIII (1984), 66–68.

———. "Some Restoration Playgoers." *Theatre Notebook* XXXV (1981), 51–57.

Kahrl, George M. *The Garrick Collection of Old English Plays, A Catalogue with an Historical Introduction*. Coll. Dorothy Anderson. London, 1982.

Keith, W. G. "The Designs of the First Movable Scenery on the English Public Stage." *Burlington Magazine* XXV (1914), 29–33, 85–89.

Kelly, Hugh. *Thespis: A Critical Examination into the Merits of all the Principal Performers belonging to Covent-Garden Theatre. Book the Second*. London, 1767.

———. *Thespis: A Critical Examination into the Merits of all the Principal Performers belonging to Drury-Lane Theatre*. London, 1766.

Kelly, John Alexander. *German Visitors to English Theatres in the Eighteenth Century*. New York, 1978. [1936]

Kemble, John Philip, ed. *The Kemble Shakespeares*. London, 1814–1815.

———. *A Select British Theatre Being a Collection of the Most Popular Stock-pieces*. 8 Vols. London, 1816.

Kemp, John. "The Work of Art and the Artist's Intentions." *The British Journal of Aesthetics* IV (1964), 146–54.

Kenny, Shirley Strum. "The Publication of Plays." In *The London Theatre World, 1660–1800*. Ed. Robert D. Hume. Carbondale and Edwardsville, Ill., 1980.

———. "Theatre, Related Arts, and the Profit Motive: An Overview." In *British Theatre and the Other Arts, 1660–1800*. Ed. Shirley Strum Kenny. Washington, D.C., London, and Toronto, 1984.

Kenny, Shirley Strum, ed. *British Theatre and the Other Arts, 1660–1800*. Washington, D.C., London, and Toronto, 1984.

Kerslake, J. F. *Catalogue of Theatrical Portraits in London Public Collections*. London, 1961.

Kielmannsegge, Friedrich Grof von. *Diary of a Journey to England in the Years 1761–1762*. Tr. (from ms) Countess Kielmannsegge. London and New York, 1902.

Kirkman, James Thomas. *Memoirs of the Life of Charles Macklin, Esq.* 2 Vols. London, 1799.

Kropf, C. R. "William Popple: Dramatist, Critic, and Diplomat." *Restoration and 18th Century Theatre Research*, 2d series, I, no. 1 (1986), 1–17.

Langbaine, Gerard. *An Account of the English Dramatick Poets*. Pref. Arthur Freeman. New York, 1973 [1691]

———. *An Account of the English Dramatick Poets (1691)*. Intr. John Loftis. 2 Vols. Los Angeles, 1971.

Langbaine, Gerard and Charles Gildon. *The Lives and Characters of the English Dramatick Poets*. London, 1699.

Langhans, Edward A. "A Conjectural Reconstruction of the Dorset Garden Theatre." *Theatre Survey* XIII (1972), 74–93.

———. "The Dorset Garden Theatre in Pictures." *Theatre Survey* VI (1965), 134–46.

———. *Eighteenth-Century British and Irish Promptbooks: A Descriptive Bibliography*. Westport, Conn.: Greenwood Press, 1987.

———. "New Restoration Theatre Accounts, 1682–1692." *Theatre Notebook* XVII (1963), 118–34.

————. "Pictorial Material on the Bridges Street and Drury Lane Theatres." *Theatre Survey* VII (1966), 80–100.

————. "Research Opportunities in Early Promptbooks." *Educational Theatre Journal* XVIII (1966), 74–76.

————. *Restoration Promptbooks*. Carbondale and Edwardsville, Ill., 1981.

————. "The Theatres." In *The London Theatre World, 1660–1800*. Ed. Robert D. Hume. Carbondale and Edwardsville, Ill., 1980.

————. "Three Early Eighteenth-Century Manuscript Promptbooks." *Modern Philology* LXV (1967), 114–29.

————. "Three Early Eighteenth Century Promptbooks." *Theatre Notebook* XX (1966), 142–50.

————. "The Vere Street and Lincoln's Inn Fields Theatres in Pictures." *Educational Theatre Journal* XX (1968), 171–85.

Lawrence, W. J. "The Pioneers of Modern English Stage Mounting: Philippe Jacques de Loutherbourg, R.A." *Magazine of Art* (1895), 172–77.

————. "The Pioneers of Modern English Stage Mounting: William Capon." *Magazine of Art* (1895), 289–92.

————. "Stage Scenery in the Eighteenth Century." *Magazine of Art* (1895), 385–88.

Leacroft, Richard. *The Development of the English Playhouse*. London, 1973.

————. "The Introduction of Perspective Scenery and Its Effect on Theatrical Forms." *Theatre Notebook* XXXIV (1980), 21–24.

————. "The Introduction of Perspective Scenery and Its Effect on Theatrical Forms. Part Two." *Theatre Notebook* XXXIV (1980), 69–73.

Lichtenberg, Georg Christoph. *Lichtenberg's Visits to England as Described in His Letters and Diaries*. Tr. M. L. Mare and W. H. Quarrell. Oxford, 1938. [Reprinted 1969]

————. *The World of Hogarth: Lichtenberg's Commentaries on Hogarth's Engravings.* Tr. Innes and Gustav Herdan. Boston, 1966.

Liesenfeld, Vincent J. *The Licensing Act of 1737*. Madison, Wisc., 1984.

Link, Frederick M. *English Drama, 1660–1800. A Guide to Information Sources*. Detroit, 1976.

Loftis, John. *Essays on the Theatre from 18th-Century Periodicals*. Los Angeles, 1960.

————. *The Spanish Plays of Neoclassical England*. New Haven and London, 1973.

Loftis, John, ed. *Restoration Drama: Modern Essays in Criticism*. New York, 1966.

Loftis, John, Richard Southern, Marion Jones, A. H. Scouten. *The Revels History of Drama in English*, Vol. V: *1660–1750*. London, 1976.

The London Stage, 1660–1800. Ed. William Van Lennep, et al. 11 Vols. Carbondale and Edwardsville, Ill., 1960–1968.

Lynch, James J. *Box, Pit and Gallery: Stage and Society in Johnson's London*. Berkeley, 1953.

McAfee, Helen. *Pepys on the Restoration Stage*. New York, n.d. [1916]

Mackintosh, Iain. *The Georgian Playhouse: Actors, Audiences and Architecture 1730–1830*. London, 1975.

Macky, John. *A Journey Through England*. 2 Vols. London, 1714, 1722.

MacMillan, Dougald. *Catalogue of the Larpent Plays in the Huntington Library*. San Marino, 1939.

————. *Drury Lane Calendar, 1747–1776*. Oxford, 1938.

Magalotti, Conte Lorenzo. *Travels of Cosimo the Third, Grand Duke of Tuscany, Through*

England, During the Reign of King Charles the Second, 1669. Tr. from Italian manuscript. London, 1821.

Milhous, Judith. "Company Management." In The London Theatre World, 1660–1800. Ed. Robert D. Hume. Carbondale and Edwardsville, Ill., 1980.

―――. Review of Pierre Danchin, The Prologues and Epilogues of the Restoration (1660–1700), in Theatre Notebook XXXVII (1983), 89–90.

―――. Thomas Betterton and the Management of Lincoln's Inn Fields, 1695–1708. Carbondale and Edwardsville, Ill., 1979.

Milhous, Judith and Robert D. Hume. "An Annotated Guide to the Theatrical Documents in PRO LC 7/1, 7/2 and 7/3." Theatre Notebook XXXV (1981), 25–31, 77–87, 122–29.

―――. Producible Interpretation: Eight English Plays, 1675–1707. Carbondale and Edwardsville, Ill., 1985.

―――. "A Register of English Theatrical Documents, 1660–1737," in "Notes and Queries," Theatre Notebook XXXVIII (1984), 41.

―――. "The Silencing of Drury Lane in 1709." Theatre Journal XXXII (1980), 427–47.

Milhous, Judith and Robert D. Hume, eds. Vice Chamberlain Coke's Theatrical Papers 1706–1715. Carbondale and Edwardsville, Ill., 1982.

Misson, Henri. Misson's Memoirs and Observations on His Travels over England. London, 1719.

Monconys, Balthasar de. Journal des voyages de Monsieur de Monconys. Lyon, 1666.

Moore, Robert Etheridge. Henry Purcell and the Restoration Theatre. London, 1961.

Mullin, Donald C. The Development of the Playhouse: a Survey of Theatre Architecture from the Renaissance to the Present. Berkeley and Los Angeles, 1970.

―――. "The Theatre Royal, Bridges Street: A Conjectural Restoration." Educational Theatre Journal XIX (1967), 20–29.

―――. "Theatre Structure and Its Effect on Production." In The Stage and the Page. Ed. G. Winchester Stone, Jr. Berkeley, 1981.

Muralt, Beat Ludwig. Letters Describing the Character and Customs of the English and French Nations. London, 1726.

―――. Lettres sur les Anglois et les François. Paris(?), 1725.

―――. Lettres sur les voyages. Paris(?), 1725.

Murphy, Arthur. The Life of David Garrick, Esq. 2 Vols. London, 1801.

Nagler, A. M., ed. A Source Book in Theatrical History. New York, 1959.

Nalbach, D. The King's Theatre 1704–1867. London's First Italian Opera House. London, 1972.

Nelson, Alfred L. "James Winston's Theatric Tourist. A Critical Edition, with a Biography and a Census of Winston Material." George Washington University Dissertation, 1968.

Nelson, Alfred L. and Gilbert B. Cross, eds. Drury Lane Journal: Selections from James Winston's Diaries, 1819–1827. London, 1974.

The New English Theatre. 12 Vols. London, 1776–1777.

Nicoll, Allardyce. The Garrick Stage, Theatres and Audiences in the Eighteenth Century. Ed. Sybil Rosenfeld. Manchester, 1980.

―――. A History of English Drama, 1660–1900. 6 Vols. London, 1952–1959. [Vol. I, 4th ed., 1955. Vol. II, 3d ed., 1955. Vol. III, 1955]

Noyes, Robert G. "Contemporary Musical Settings for the Songs in Restoration Dramatic

Opera." *Harvard Studies and Notes in Philology and Literature* XX (1938), 99–121.

———. "Contemporary Musical Settings of the Songs in Restoration Drama." *English Literary History* I (1934), 325–44.

———. "Conventions of Song in Restoration Tragedy." *PMLA* LIII (1938), 162–88.

———. "Songs from Restoration Drama in Contemporary and Eighteenth-Century Poetical Miscellanies." *English Literary History* III (1936), 291–316.

Noyes, Robert G. and Roy Lamson, Jr. "Broadside-Ballad Versions of the Songs in Restoration Drama." *Harvard Studies and Notes in Philology and Literature* XIX (1937), 199–218.

Odell, George C. D. *Shakespeare from Betterton to Irving.* Intr. Robert Hamilton Ball. 2 Vols. New York, 1966. [1920]

Oenslager, Donald. *Stage Design: Four Centuries of Scenic Invention.* New York, 1975.

Orrell, John. "Filippo Corsini and the Restoration Stage." *Theatre Notebook* XXXIV (1980), 4–9.

———. "A New Witness of the Restoration Stage, 1660–1669." *Theatre Research International,* n.s. II (1976), 16–28.

———. "A New Witness of the Restoration Stage, 1670–1680." *Theatre Research International,* n.s. II (1977), 86–97.

Oulton, W. C. *Authentic Memoirs of the Green Room.* 6 Vols. London, 1799–1804.

———. *The History of the Theatres of London.* 2 Vols. London, 1796.

Paulson, Ronald. *Hogarth's Graphic Works: First Complete Edition.* 2 Vols. New Haven and London, 1965.

Pedicord, Harry William. "The Changing Audience." In *The London Theatre World, 1660–1800.* Ed. Robert D. Hume. Carbondale and Edwardsville, Ill., 1980.

———. "Shakespeare, Tate, and Garrick: New Light on Alterations of *King Lear.*" *Theatre Notebook* XXXVI (1982), 14–21.

———. *The Theatrical Public in the Time of Garrick.* Carbondale and Edwardsville, Ill., 1954.

Pedicord, Harry William and Frederick Louis Bergmann, eds. *The Plays of David Garrick.* 7 Vols. Carbondale and Edwardsville, Ill., 1980–1982.

Pepys, Samuel. *Diary.* Ed. Henry B. Wheatley. 10 Vols. London, 1893–1899.

Petty, Frederick. *Italian Opera in London 1760–1800.* Ann Arbor, Mich., 1972.

Pickering, Roger. *Reflections Upon Theatrical Expressions in Tragedy.* London, 1755.

Pittard, Joseph. *Observations on Mr. Garrick's Acting.* London, 1755.

Plumb, J. H. *The Commercialisation of Leisure in Eighteenth-Century England.* Reading, 1973.

Pope, Alexander, ed. *The Works of Shakespear.* 2d ed. 9 Vols. London, 1728.

Powell, Jocelyn. *Restoration Theatre Production.* London, 1984.

Price, Cecil. *Theatre in the Age of Garrick.* Oxford, 1973.

Price, Curtis A. *Henry Purcell and the London Stage.* London, 1984.

———. "Music as Drama." In *The London Theatre World, 1660–1800.* Ed. Robert D. Hume. Carbondale and Edwardsville, Ill., 1980.

———. *Music in the Restoration Theatre, With a Catalogue of Instrumental Music in the Plays 1665–1713.* Ann Arbor, 1979.

Pry, Kevin. "Theatrical Competition and the Rise of the Afterpiece Tradition." *Theatre Notebook* XXXVI (1982), 21–27.

Rees, Dr. A. *Cyclopaedia, or Universal Dictionary of Arts, Sciences and Literature*. London, 1803–1819. [1778; 1784; 1786–1789]

Riccoboni, Luigi (Lewis). *A General History of the Stage*. 2d ed. London, 1754. [Reprinted 1978]

———. *Réflexions historiques et critiques sur les différents théâtres de l'Europe*. Paris, 1738.

Roach, John. *Roach's Authentic Memoirs of the Green Room*. London, 1796.

Roach, Joseph R. *The Player's Passion: Studies in the Science of Acting*. Newark, Del., 1985.

Rosenfeld, Sybil. "Dramatic Advertisements in the Burney Newspapers, 1660–1700." *PMLA* LI (1936), 123–52.

———. *Foreign Theatrical Companies in Great Britain in the 17th and 18th Centuries*. London, 1955.

———. *Georgian Scene Painters and Scene Painting*. Cambridge, England, 1981.

———. "The Restoration Stage in Newspapers and Journals, 1660–1700." *Modern Language Review* XXX (1935), 445–59.

———. "Scene Designs of William Capon." *Theatre Notebook* X (1956), 118–22.

———. *A Short History of Scene Design in Great Britain*. Oxford, 1973.

———. *Strolling Players and Drama in the Provinces, 1660–1765*. Cambridge, England, 1939. [Reprinted 1970]

———. *Temples of Thespis: Some Private Theatres and Theatricals in England and Wales, 1700–1820*. London, 1978.

———. *The Theatre of the London Fairs in the 18th Century*. Cambridge, England, 1960.

———. "The Wardrobes of Lincoln's Inn Fields and Covent Garden." *Theatre Notebook* V (1950), 15–19.

Rosenfeld, Sybil and Edward Croft-Murray. "A Checklist of Scene Painters Working in Great Britain and Ireland in the 18th Century." *Theatre Notebook* XIX (1965), 6–20, 49–64, 102–13, 133–45; XX (1966), 36–44, 69–72, 113–18.

Rowe, Nicholas, ed. *The Works of Mr. William Shakespear*. 6 Vols. London, 1709, 1714.

Sainte-Albine, Pierre Rémond de. *Le Comédien*. Paris, 1749.

Saunders, George. *A Treatise on Theatres*. London, 1790. [Reprinted 1968]

Sawyer, Paul. *Christopher Rich of Drury Lane: The Biography of a Theatre Manager*. Lanham, N.Y., and London, 1986.

———. *The New Theatre in Lincoln's Inn Fields*. London, 1979.

Scouten, Arthur H. "The Anti-Evolutionary Development of the London Theatres." In *British Theatre and the Other Arts, 1660–1800*. Ed. Shirley Strum Kenny. Washington, D.C., London, and Toronto, 1984.

———. *The London Stage 1729–1747: A Critical Introduction*. Carbondale and Edwardsville, Ill., 1968.

The Secret History of the Green Rooms. 2 Vols. London, 1790; new ed. 1795.

Shattuck, Charles H. "Drama as Promptbook." In *The Stage and the Page*. Ed. G. Winchester Stone. Berkeley, 1981.

———. *John Philip Kemble Promptbooks*. 11 Vols. Charlottesville, 1974.

———. *The Shakespeare Promptbooks. A Descriptive Catalogue*. Urbana, Ill., 1965.

———. "The Shakespeare Promptbooks: First Supplement." *Theatre Notebook* XXIV (1969), 5–17.

————. "Shakespeare Promptbooks of the 17th and 18th Centuries." *Restoration and 18th Century Theatre Research* III (1964), 9–11.

Sheldon, Esther K. *Thomas Sheridan of Smock-Alley*. Princeton, 1967.

Sheppard, F.H.W. *The Theatre Royal, Drury Lane, and the Royal Opera House, Covent Garden*. Survey of London, Vol. XXXV. London, 1970.

Sheridan, Thomas. *A Course of Lectures on Elocution*. London, 1762. [Facsimile reprint 1968]

————. *A Discourse. Being Introductory to his Course of Lectures on Elocution and the English Language* (1759). Intr. G. P. Mohrmann. Augustan Reprint Society, no. 136. Los Angeles, 1969.

Shesgreen, Sean, ed. *Engravings by Hogarth*. New York, 1973.

Siddons, Henry. *Practical Illustrations of Rhetorical Gesture and Action; Adapted to the English Drama*. London, 1807; 2d ed. 1822.

Signorelli, Pietro Napoli. *Storia critica dei teatri, antichi e moderni*. 6 Vols. Naples, 1787–1790. 10 Vols. Naples, 1813.

Smith, Dane F. *Plays about the Theatre in England from the Rehearsal in 1671 to the Licensing Act in 1737*. New York, 1936.

Smith, Dane F. and M. L. Lawhon. *Plays about the Theatre in England, 1737–1800*. Lewisburg, Penn., 1979.

Smith, Helen R. *David Garrick 1717–1779. A Brief Account*. London, 1979.

Smith, William C. *A Bibliography of the Musical Works Published by John Walsh during the Years 1695–1720*. London, 1948.

Sorbière, Samuel de. *Relation d'un voyage en Engleterre*. Paris, 1664.

Southern, Richard. *Changeable Scenery: Its Origin and Development in the British Theatre*. London, 1952.

————. *The Georgian Playhouse*. London, 1948.

————. "The Winston MS. and Theatre Design." *Theatre Notebook* I (1947), 93–95.

Sprague, Arthur C. *Beaumont and Fletcher on the Restoration Stage*. Cambridge, Mass., 1926.

————. *Shakespeare and the Actors. The Stage Business in His Plays (1660–1905)*. Cambridge, Mass., 1948.

Spring, John R. "The Dorset Garden Theatre: Playhouse or Opera House?" *Theatre Notebook* XXXIV (1980), 60–69.

————. "Platform and Picture Frames: A Conjectural Reconstruction of the Duke of York's Theatre, Dorset Garden, 1669–1709." *Theatre Notebook* XXXI (1977), 6–19.

The Statutes of the Realm. Record Commission. 11 Vols. in 12. London, 1963. [1810–1828]

Steele, Joshua. *Prosodia Rationalis*. London, 1779.

Steele, Richard. *The Theatre 1720*. Ed. John Loftis. Oxford, 1962.

Stone, George Winchester, Jr. *The London Stage 1747–1776: A Critical Introduction*. Carbondale and Edwardsville, Ill., 1968.

————. "The Making of the Repertory." In *The London Theatre World 1660–1800*. Ed. Robert D. Hume. Carbondale and Edwardsville, Ill., 1980.

————. "The Prevalence of Theatrical Music in Garrick's Time." In *The Stage and the Page*. Ed. G. Winchester Stone, Jr. Berkeley, 1981.

————. *The Stage and the Page. London's "Whole Show" in the Eighteenth-Century Theatre*. Berkeley, 1981.

Stone, George Winchester, Jr., and George M. Kahrl. *David Garrick, A Critical Biography*. Cardondale and Edwardsville, Ill., 1979.

Stratman, Carl J. *Britain's Theatrical Periodicals, 1720–1967: A Bibliography*. New York, 1972.

———. *Restoration and Eighteenth Century Theatre Research: A Bibliographical Guide 1900–1968*. Carbondale and Edwardsville, Ill., 1971.

Sturz, Helferich Peter. "Briefe, im Jahre 1768." In *Schriften*. 2 Vols. Vienna, 1819.

Summers, Montague. *A Bibliography of the Restoration Drama*. London, 1934.

———. *The Playhouse of Pepys*. London, 1935.

———. *The Restoration Theatre*. London, 1934.

The Survey of London. Ed. C. R. Ashbee, Sir Laurence Gomme, Philip Norman, et al. 37 Vols. London, 1900–1973.

Thaler, Alwin. *Shakespeare to Sheridan*. Cambridge, Mass., 1922.

Theatrical Biography: or, Memoirs of the Principal Performers of the Three Theatres Royal. 2 Vols. London, 1772.

Theobald, Lewis, ed. *The Works of Shakespeare*. 12 Vols. London, 1740.

Thorpe, Willard. *Songs from the Restoration Theatre*. Princeton, 1934.

Three Centuries of English and American Plays. Ed. Henry W. Wells. Catalogued by G. W. Bergquist. 5545 Microfiche Cards. New York, 1960.

Uffenbach, Zacharias Conrad von. *Merkwürdige Reisen durch Niedersachsen, Holland und Engelland*. 3 Vols. Ulm and Memmingen, Germany, 1753–1754.

Underwood, Dale. *Etherege and the Seventeenth-Century Comedy of Manners*. New Haven, 1957.

Veinstein, André and Alfred S. Golding, eds. *Bibliothèques et musées des arts du spectacle dans le monde/Performing Arts Libraries and Museums of the World*. 3d ed. Paris, 1984.

Victor, Benjamin. *The History of the Theatres of London and Dublin, From the Year 1730 to the Present Time*. 2 Vols. London, 1761.

———. *The History of the Theatres of London, from the Year 1760 to the Present Time*. London, 1771.

Vincent, Sam. *The Young Gallant's Academy*. London, 1674.

Visser, Colin. "The Comte de Gisors in London, 1754." *Theatre Notebook* XXXVII (1983), 51–54.

———. "The Killigrew Folio: Private Playhouses and the Restoration Stage." *Theatre Survey* XIX (1978), 119–38.

———. "Scenery and Technical Design." In *The London Theatre World*. Ed. Robert D. Hume. Carbondale and Edwardsville, Ill., 1980.

Walker, John. *Elements of Elocution*. London, 1781.

Walsh, John (pub.). *Harmonia Anglicana*. London, 1701–10.

Whincop, Thomas. *A List of all the Dramatic Authors*. In *Scanderbeg: or, Love and Liberty. A Tragedy*. London, 1747.

White, Arthur F. "The Office of Revels and Dramatic Censorship During the Restoration Period." *Western Reserve University Bulletin*, n.s. XXXIV, no. 13 (1931), 5–45.

White, Eric Walter. *A History of English Opera*. London, 1983.

———. *A Register of First Performances of English Operas and Semi-Operas from the 16th Century to 1980*. London, 1983.

———. *The Rise of English Opera*. London, 1951.

Wilkes, Thomas. *A General View of the Stage*. London, 1759.

Wilkinson, Robert. *Londina Illustrata*. 2 Vols. London, 1819, 1825. [Originally issued in 36 numbers, 1808–1826.]

———. *Theatrum Illustratum*. London, 1825.

Wilkinson, Tate. *Memoirs of His Own Life*. 4 Vols. York, 1790.

———. *The Wandering Patentee; or, A History of the Yorkshire Theatres, from 1770 to the Present Time*. 4 Vols. York, 1795. [Reprinted 1973]

Willard, Helen D. "The Harvard Theatre Collection." *Restoration and 18th Century Theatre Research* III (1964), 14–22.

Willet, C. and Phillis Cunnington. *Handbook of English Costume in the Eighteenth Century*. Ill. Barbara Phillipson and Phyllis Cunnington. London, 1957.

Wilson, John, ed. *Roger North on Music*. London, 1959.

Winston, James. *Drury Lane Journal: Selections from James Winston's Diaries 1819–1827*. Ed. Alfred L. Nelson and Gilbert B. Cross. London, 1974.

———. *The Theatric Tourist*. London, 1805.

Winton, Calhoun. "Dramatic Censorship." In *The London Theatre World*. Ed. Robert D. Hume. Carbondale and Edwardsville, Ill., 1980.

Wood, Frederick T. "Collections of Eighteenth Century Playbills." *Notes and Queries* CXC (1946), 222–26.

Woodward, Gertrude L. and James G. McManaway. *A Checklist of English Plays 1641–1700*. Chicago, 1945. *Supplement* by Fredson T. Bowers. Charlottesville, 1949.

Wright, James. *Historia Histrionica*. Ed. Arthur Freeman. New York and London, 1974. [1699]

Wyndham, Henry Saxe. *The Annals of Covent Garden from 1732 to 1897*. 2 Vols. London, 1906.

2

THE THEATRE OF EIGHTEENTH-CENTURY FRANCE

INTRODUCTION

Classical French theatre is traditionally held to have died with Racine in 1699, although the convenience of century's end is sometimes sacrificed in favour of 1715, the date of the death of Louis XIV. The recall of the Italian players the following year is reason enough for theatre historians to find the later date attractive. At the other end of the century, the outbreak of the French Revolution in 1789 seems an obvious point of conclusion. It is not unusual, therefore, for scholars to include the first fifteen years of the eighteenth century in discussions of the seventeenth century, and to treat the theatre of the Revolution as a phenomenon distinct from that of the rest of the century. The way in which the theatre of the remaining seventy-four years is interpreted depends upon whether it is viewed as a continuation of seventeenth-century theatre, slowly evolving new dramatic forms and temporarily interrupted by the political events at the end of the century, or as an institution whose change and upheavals reflect social, intellectual, and political tensions that point directly forward to revolution. A compromise position has it that the first half of the century was continuous with the seventeenth, but that developments after 1750 prove true harbingers of the revolutionary spirit. Add to this an uncertain evaluation of the drama produced on either side of the mid-century divide, and we are left with a somewhat blurred picture of eighteenth-century French theatre.

Writing of the entire period between 1600 and 1789, John Lough notes that it seems a coherent whole:

Indeed, it is an age which it is extremely difficult to divide into two parts; in any but the strictly numerical sense it is almost impossible to determine where the seventeenth century leaves off and the eighteenth begins. Although the theatre, like the society around it, was in a constant state of evolution, these two centuries do present a certain organic unity which enables one to treat them as a whole. [*Paris Theatre Audiences*, p. 2]

To speak of evolution implies some notion of the goal toward which changes are leading. In France it seemed easy to identify that goal. Thus Eleanor Jourdain:

The drama of the eighteenth century in France, while keeping to a large extent a traditional form, is . . . useful as an illustration of contemporary social and political progress. Its criticism of society prepares our minds for the Revolution of 1789. Beaumarchais . . . expresses, as well as any historian could do, the condition of the public mind; and other writers, earlier in the century . . . foretold, before Beaumarchais, the coming social conflict and class hatred. [*Dramatic Theory and Practice in France, 1690–1808*, p. 2]

Similarly Frederick Hawkins: "The philosophy of the age found utterance in the drama, and for about thirty years before the Revolution . . . the approach of that convulsion was at once hastened by and vividly reflected at the theatre" (*The French Stage in the Eighteenth Century*, I, viii–ix). These sociopolitical changes are traced by theatre historians specifically in three areas: in the content and changing forms of dramatic literature; in the increasingly heterogeneous theatrical audiences; and in the struggle among the various established and fringe theatres to maintain or gain privilege and attract audiences.

The strict decorum of French classical drama did in fact not long outlast the seventeenth century. Tragedy certainly continued to be performed—almost two hundred tragedies were acted at the Comédie Française between 1715 and 1789— but there is almost universal agreement that it had declined markedly in quality from that of the previous century. Voltaire alone, it is argued, prevented its actual death, and of his tragedies only *Zaïre* (1732) is likely to be known today. Even if we avoid the word *decline*, with its pejorative associations, we must admit that tragedy was changing. The emphasis on event and coincidence, the replacement of heroic passion with pathos and sentimentality, the shrinking status of the tragic protagonist, and the introduction of intellectual debate and even social and political propaganda all point to the emergence of the *drame*, a new form of bourgeois drama that represented the seriousness of everyday life. Comedy too moved towards this intermediate form. It became infused with a new underlying seriousness that required audiences to sympathize with rather than laugh at its characters, and these characters, like those of the new tragedy or *drame*, were representative of middle- and lower-class life. *Comédie larmoyante*, or tearful comedy, then was also absorbed into the *drame*. Technically, the term *drame* is applied to plays written in the second half of the eighteenth century according to guidelines set down by Denis Diderot in his *Entretiens* (Conversations) accompanying his play *Le Fils natural* (1757). Diderot cited as models George Lillo's domestic tragedy *The London Merchant* (1731) and the plays of the Roman dramatist Terence in stressing moral instruction over pleasure and in arguing for a dramatic verisimilitude governed by the perceptions of everyday life.

Changes in the audiences for whom the drama was written have also been traced. The essentially aristocratic and wealthy audiences of the earlier part of the century gradually gave way as arbiters of taste and acceptance to the bourgeoisie, who began to fill the *parterre* if not the *loges* of the Comédie Française and the Hôtel de Bourgogne and who were certainly the main supporters of the theatres of the Fairs of St. Germain and St. Laurent. The struggle between the monopolistic theatres—the Comédie Française, the Comédie Italienne, the Opéra—and the Théâtre de la Foire is the stuff of a complex history, but the evolution of new theatrical forms, the increasing opportunities for dramatic writers, even democracy itself, have been attributed to this competition. The peripheral and popular Théâtre de la Foire especially has in recent years been singled out. "The bustling world of popular theatre," writes Michèle Root-Bernstein, "serves as a microcosm, not just of the stage, but of the political and cultural forces that gave direction to experimentation, reform, and eventual revolution in the last decades of the eighteenth century" (*Boulevard Theater and Revolution in Eighteenth-Century Paris*, p. 3). Earlier scholars were less likely to approve of either the theatrical warfare or the popular theatre, since they tended to view the French theatre from the perspective of the ongoing tradition represented by the Comédie Française. Too, scholars interested primarily in dramatic literature were perforce attracted to the Comédie Française, where the vast majority of new plays were performed; therefore, they saw little reason to heed the Théâtre de la Foire. "Despite their popularity," writes Lough, "it cannot be maintained that these little theatres contributed anything of importance to the drama of the century . . . " (*Paris Theatre Audiences*, p. 166).

Some recent studies of the theatre of the French Revolution, however, have stressed not only the popular theatre of the fairs and the propagandistic nature of much of the regular drama, but also the clear desirability of the Revolution itself as a liberating force in the theatrical-dramatic sphere as well as in the sociopolitical sphere. From this perspective, the theatre comes to embody and focus the forces of social change. The eighteenth century, observes Jacques Boncompain,

a time of effervescence, of inquiry, of renewal, of social turmoil, found in the theatre a place of tension, of passion and of intrigue. This is the crucible in which the modern theatre was formed, where the authors and the public, more independent of royal power, were able to work out little by little the understanding that has not ceased to be theirs through the nineteenth century and to our own time. [*Auteurs et comédiens au XVIIIe siècle*, p. 11]

And so far as the theatre itself is concerned, the replacement of aristocratic patronage with the financial rewards of the marketplace changed the relationship among playwright, actors, and public. In particular, it resulted in a new freedom for the dramatist: "Money, far from being the instrument of his downfall, became the condition for his liberty" (Boncompain, p. 14).

It is worth noting, however, that Beaumarchais' founding of the Bureau Dramatique in 1777 (later the Société d'Auteurs Dramatiques) and the abolition of theatrical monopolies in 1791, as "liberating" as these measures undoubtedly were, neither derived from a conception of nor led to the realization of a laissez-faire commercial theatre in the English or American manner. The Comédie Française and, after 1723, the Comédie Italienne, although organized as sharing companies, were in effect state theatres, supervised on behalf of the King by the Four Gentlemen of the Chamber. The Comédie Française received an annual subsidy of twelve thousand livres or francs. Similarly, the Opéra was provided with a subsidy, and although an independent entrepreneur managed the company, he did so according to guidelines laid down by the Crown. Between 1749 and 1780, the Opéra was the responsibility of the City of Paris, but in the latter year it passed again into Royal control, and a court official was placed in charge. Even the fair troupes, ostensibly private enterprises, were subjected to a series of official rulings designed to protect the monopoly theatres and were actually suppressed for a five-year period between 1718 and 1723. It was largely in response to official prohibitions that the fair theatres introduced the irregular dramatic forms of *opéra comique*, pantomime, and *comédies-en-vaudevilles*. The success of a variant form sometimes worked against the interests of the minor theatres, for it could be expropriated by an official theatre and the fair troupe forced once again to find or develop a substitute. (In 1762, for example, the Comédie Italienne was given a monopoly on *opéra comique*.)

The abolition of theatrical monopolies certainly created a fluid, indeed chaotic, theatrical world during the last decade of the century, but it certainly did not create a truly commercial theatre. By 1803 a re-formed Comédie Française was safely ensconced in a state-owned theatre, its pensions and subsidies restored; the Théâtre Favart (formerly the Comédie Italienne) had been united with its competitor, the Théâtre Feydeau, to form the Théâtre National de l'Opéra-Comique, also state-subsidized; and the Opéra had been reestablished as the third state theatre. From the point of view of administration and finances little had changed. In fact, the author of a standard history notes that "the present system of administration of the state-run Comédie Française evolved logically and in a straightforward manner from the situation it enjoyed under the *ancien régime*" (Robert Niklaus, *A Literary History of France: The Eighteenth Century 1715–1789*, p. 286).

It is perhaps because of the ongoing tradition in France of subsidized theatres that, with one exception (see below), there has been little attempt by theatre historians to describe and explain the theatre of eighteenth-century France in terms of "show business." The commercial model lacks the explanatory power it has in the interpretations of the contemporary English theatre. Instead, the activities of the theatres and the nature of the drama they presented are most often explained, as we have seen, in terms of sociopolitical and intellectual history. "It is certainly as a mirror of social change and current values," writes Niklaus, "that it [eighteenth-century French theatre] is intellectually most significant'' (p. 291). In fact, divested of its function as a mirror of current French concerns, and viewed in the larger context of European theatre both earlier and later, French drama of the eighteenth century probably justifies its common reputation as the product of a declining neoclassicism.

At the same time, the amount of information available concerning theatrical production is substantial. The texts of hundreds of plays were published; the legitimate theatrical companies kept more-or-less complete records of performances and receipts; the private and public lives of actors and actresses were the subjects of biographies, autobiographies, and memoirs; information ranging from backstage gossip to theatrical reviews was included in periodicals of various kinds; playwrights and critics theorized and propagandized in print; books on architecture discussed theatre design and printed plans for theatres. And during the eighteenth century, *littérateurs* and scholars were writing the history of the theatre of their own time. The data that was slowly assembled in libraries and archives—private and public—or published in these early studies provided the raw material for more systematic collections and publications of theatricalia in the nineteenth century.

In general, nineteenth-century scholarship was little interested in historical interpretation or explanation in the modern sense. Rather it provided descriptive chronicles, usually devoted to a specific theatre or company. Jules Bonnassies produced half a dozen volumes on the Comédie Française between 1868 and 1875, and A. Joannides' *La Comédie-Française de 1680 à 1920* (1921) remains a standard history of France's national theatrical institution. (The first edition of 1901 concludes the account at 1900.) In 1902 Napoléon Maurice Bernardin published a history of the Comédie Italienne from 1570 to 1791. Maurice Albert covered the irregular theatres of Paris in *Les Théâtres de la foire (1660–1789)* (1900) and *Les Théâtres des boulevards, 1789–1848* (1902). Arthur Pougin provided a history of the Opéra in *Un Directeur d'opéra au dix-huitième siècle* (1914), and in *L'Opéra-Comique pendant la Révolution* (1891) he carried the history of the Théâtre Italien through to 1801. Adolphe Jullien, in a series of books published between 1874 and 1885, examined the vogue for private theatricals during the second half of the eighteenth century, emphasizing the intrigues as well as the entertainments of the Duchess du Maine, Madame de Pompadour, and Marie-Antoinette. Finally, we have Henri Welschinger's *Théâtre de la Révolution* (1880). The fact that these writers had interests or purposes different from our own ought not, of course, to be held against them. They sorted through thousands of documents and provided the basic outlines of institutional histories. Many of their books, in the form of modern reprints, maintain a respected place in theatre collections and are as likely as their modern counterparts to be consulted by students of theatre history.

These histories are nevertheless almost one hundred years old, and besides occasional lapses in accuracy and sometimes insufficient scholarly documentation—by modern standards at least—they reflect attributes and assumptions at odds with the social, cultural, political, and intellectual forces that are seen by modern historians as having both created and been imaged in the theatre. Oddly, this modern attitude also has its roots in the nineteenth century, not—to be sure—among the professors and archivists, scholars and historians whose works we have just noted, but among the *littérateurs* of Paris, those prolific journalists, essayists, and novelists for whom the theatre was simply a source of raw material for the practice of their craft. This is not to say that they did not write seriously, but in place of scholarly precision and analytical depth they brought to their work a dilletantish breadth of interest that throws fresh light on the theatre.

A case in point is that of Gustave Desnoiresterres (1817–1892). As a young man, Desnoiresterres studied law, but attracted to the world of letters, he gravitated to the cultural centre of Paris and for almost twenty years wrote for journals and produced a series of novels. About 1860, he developed an interest in history and set about writing some eighteen volumes on the social and cultural life of eighteenth-century France. His most substantial work was *Voltaire et la société française au XVIIIe siècle*, published in eight volumes between 1867 and 1876, but he is best known to students of the theatre for *La Comédie satirique au XVIIIe siècle* (1885), in which he attempted to provide a picture of French society based on the satirical allusions of the comic theatre.

A more profound exploitation of the relationship between theatre and the larger cultural context depended upon two things: a more searching examination of dramatic theory and staging practices, and a scholarly synthesis of specialized studies in order to provide a total picture of eighteenth-century French theatre.

In *Dramatic Theory and Practice in France, 1690–1808* (1921), Eleanor Jourdain traced the close relationship between criticism and dramaturgy during the period, noting that most critics were also playwrights. The hundreds of theoretical pamphlets and critical prefaces to plays pointed to a struggle of ideas only partially resolved in the plays actually performed. One of the results of this struggle according to Jourdain was the replacement of "symbolism" with "realism." "Since the remoteness of the stage was being given up," she writes, "all symbolism of representation was bound to disappear. Dress and scenery became realistic and intonation natural" (pp. 182–83). The point was taken up by Edith Melcher in *Stage Realism in France Between Diderot and Antoine* (1928), in which the author argues that Antoine's naturalistic theatre at the end of the nineteenth century was the culmination of an evolutionary process that began with the decline of French classicism in the eighteenth century. Both Jourdain and Melcher point to the importance in this process of the theory of Denis Diderot and the practice of Louis Sébastien Mercier (1740–1814), and tend to see the first half of the century as a continuation of the literary and theatrical traditions of the seventeenth century.

This notion was challenged in 1936 by Elbert B. O. Borgerhoff in *The Evolution of Liberal Theory and Practice in the French Theatre 1680–1757*. Borgerhoff agrees that Diderot's writings, especially his *Entretiens sur le fils naturel* (1757), mark a turning point in dramatic theory, but Borgerhoff insists that "the first half of the century must be viewed as a period of advance in theory and

experiment in practice leading up to developments that took place after the middle
of the century'' (pp. 1–2). The process that Borgerhoff sees at work is the
replacement of a ''classic general reality'' with ''a more specific, material and
individual reality.'' He stresses this transformation in the tone of the drama, in
staging practices, in the attitude toward rules and conventions, and in the attitude
toward the purpose and morality of the theatre. In particular, the growing connection of the theatre with the social order is reflected in the substitution of the
idea of absolute morality with the notion of social utility. Borgerhoff suggests
that whether the transformation he analyzes is better described as decadence or
renaissance depends upon whether the observer is liberal or conservative, but
he leaves little doubt as to his own perspective. The movement, he says

was fundamentally a *rapprochement* between the theater and an audience for whom the
material, present and immediately recognisable reality was becoming more and more the
important reality and who therefore demanded from the drama a greater familiarity of
tone. . . . [Diderot's contribution] is but another step on the road to the final victory or at
least high point of individualism, which where the drama is concerned will be reached
only with nineteenth century Naturalism. [p. 113]

Historical change here seems to reflect a teleological necessity, with every period
an age of transition in the movement towards some ideal.

    In the meantime, serious attempts were being made to provide comprehensive
surveys of the theatre. In *Le Théâtre à Paris au XVIIIe siècle* (1926), Max
Aghion observed that what was needed was

a general work, which shows the development, the general perfecting of dramatic art and
its evolution under the irresistible pressure of ideas, a work, indicating not only literary
progress, but also the considerable material changes arising in an art where so many
complex factors contribute to a work and are necessary to realize the thought of the
author, where so much is important and contributes to success: the auditorium, the lighting,
costume, the mise en scène.

''This work,'' continued Aghion, ''remained to do and we have undertaken it''
(p. 7). In fact, Aghion does an admirable job, tracing the development of dramatic
genres, discussing the fortunes of the Comédie Française, the Comédie Italienne,
and the Opéra, and surveying the many peripheral theatres of Paris, private
theatricals, actors and actresses, costumes, and decor. But Aghion's overriding
concern is with the relationship between social customs, ideas, and sentiments
and their expression in the theatre, and like others before him he saw the sociopolitical tensions and their reflections in the drama intensify during the last
forty years of the century. During this period social forces acted upon the theatre,
but in its turn the theatre was used as an instrument of social change, becoming
in the hands of the *philosophes* ''a precious instrument of proselytization and
combat'' (p. 20).

    The theatre outside Paris is the subject of Max Fuchs' *La Vie théâtrale en*

province au XVIIIe siècle (1933). This is a still-valuable, well-documented study
of the French provincial theatre and includes consideration of theatre architecture,
stage construction, actors and actresses, staging practice, administration, and
audiences. Freed from the preconceptions attending the study of the Parisian
theatre and indeed dealing with quite different theatrical circumstances, Fuchs
argues for a fundamental commercialism as the governing motive of the provincial theatre during the years 1715–1790:

Little by little the troupes regularized themselves; the theatre, installed in a public building,
became a commercial affair, staged by shareholders, managed, more or less honestly,
by an *entrepreneur de spectacles*. [pp. 7–8]

The Revolution, rather than representing the inevitable culmination of tensions
reflected in the theatre, brought to an end this "capitalist transformation of the
acting profession" (p. 8).

Since World War II, several excellent specialized studies have explored particular aspects of eighteenth-century French theatre. In 1957 John Lough, drawing on a very wide variety of contemporary sources, sought in *Paris Theatre
Audiences* to define the changing French audiences of the seventeenth and eighteenth centuries and to determine their influence on the plays produced for them.
Since the best actors and the most important playwrights practiced their crafts
in the capital, Lough excludes the provincial theatre from his analysis and concentrates, even in Paris, almost exclusively on the Comédie Française. While
the procedure is undoubtedly useful so far as changing dramaturgy among established dramatists is concerned, it is also based on the assumption that there
was little or no overlap between the audiences at the Comédie Française and
those patronizing the Opéra or the Comédie Italienne or the Théâtres de la Foire.

The sophisticated economic analysis of Claude Alasseur's *La Comédie Française au 18e siècle* (1967), based as it is mainly on documents from the archives
of the Comédie Française—especially the *registres*—is similarly limited. Pierre
Peyronnet attempts in *La Mise en scène au XVIIIe siècle* (1974) to define the
basic ideas of a theatrical presentation in the eighteenth century, the ideas that
determined staging independent of a particular dramatic text. He concludes that
the modern "*metteur en scène*," although born in the nineteenth century, was
conceived in the eighteenth. Jacques Boncompain in *Auteurs et comédiens au
XVIIIe siècle* (1976) concentrates on the changing socioeconomic conditions of
actors and playwrights during the last quarter of the century and concludes that
the distinguishing characteristic of the century was the expansion of theatrical
activity beyond the stages of the monopoly theatres into society at large. The
acting of plays became, he argues, a social game, a universal pastime, a "*théâ-
tromanie.*" A panoramic view of all theatrical activity in the eighteenth century,
he suggests, would prompt interesting questions concerning the status of actors,
the attitude of the Church, dramatic criticism, and censorship. "It is an agitated
world, full of oddities, of passions, and of concerns" (p. 12).

The opening up of theatre history—apparent in Lough's relating of Paris theatre audiences to the changing state of the world outside the theatre, in Alasseur's relating of theatre economics to the general economy, and in Boncompain's placing of actors and playwrights in a wide social context—is reflected as well in recent books on the theatre of the French Revolution. Marvin Carlson in *The Theatre of the French Revolution* (1966) is less interested in the plays of the period than in "the stories behind the plays, how and why they were presented and how they were received" (p. vi). Fernando Mastropasqua, concentrating particularly on the Terror of 1793–1794 in his *Le feste della Rivoluzione Francese* (1976), translates a similar interest into a sophisticated analysis of the French national psyche. Examining the mass festivals sponsored by the leaders of the Revolution, he finds that these served as propaganda and as quasi-religious public rites designed to sublimate a collective sense of guilt and to celebrate a national moral regeneration.

What stands out in the historiography of eighteenth-century French theatre is the continuing emphasis on the theatre as a sociopolitical institution, the significance of which, even its meaning, is derived from its role in the evolution of French civilization. The theatre is seen as either reflecting or affecting the changes taking place in society at large. But if the job of theatre historians also includes the reconstruction and description of theatrical forms and conventions, the audiences, and the playing spaces that have determined the dynamics and the style of past performances, it is occasionally necessary to refocus attention on the internal writings of the theatre itself, even if at the same time its relationship to the greater society is acknowledged. This is the tack taken by Henri Lagrave, whose *Le Théâtre et le public à Paris de 1715 à 1750* (1972) is the best introduction to the period it represents. Lagrave's overall purpose is threefold: to describe administrative conditions, theatre architecture, and theatrical techniques; to describe the components of the theatrical public in its social context; and to show how the interaction between dramatic art and society gave rise to the collection of practices, conventions, and rules that defined the theatrical art of the period. Although two-fifths of the study is devoted to a social and psychological portrait of the theatre-going public of the time, Lagrave is careful to distinguish between this public and society in general. He pays considerable attention not only to the relationship between audiences and dramatic form and content, but also to the interaction of audiences and theatrical space: "The theatrical place reflects the social composition, the mentality and the habits of the public, at the same time as it shapes the dramatic creation" (p. 16). One of Lagrave's innovative strengths is his statistical method whereby the *registres* of the acting troupes are carefully analyzed to provide several time-confined pictures of theatrical activity—daily, weekly, monthly, seasonal, over the run of a given play, and so on. His generalizations about the period, therefore, are presented in terms of a final temporal perspective. His statistical analyses, he argues,

clarify the methods of programming of the actors, adapted to public exigencies, the effects of competition, the evolution of [dramatic] genres, and even certain tastes of spectators.

The figures allow us in particular to understand the reality of theatrical life at all levels, days, months, seasons, years, periods, to measure the variations in all domains and to give, finally, an accurate picture of the dramatic period that we are studying. . . . [p. 15]

Lagrave clearly saw his work as a continuation of Pierre Mélèse's excellent study *Le Théâtre et le public à Paris sous Louis XIV* (1934). We await a similar book on the period 1750–1789.

DRAMATIC TEXTS

Compared with the contributions of seventeenth-century France to the world's theatrical repertory, the plays of the eighteenth century seem poor indeed. Beyond an occasional comedy by Alain-René Lesage or a tragedy by Prosper Jolyot Crébillon, most students of the drama would recognize only Voltaire's *Zaïre*, Beaumarchais' *Barbier de Séville* and *Le Mariage de Figaro*, and a play or two by Pierre Marivaux. Yet French drama and dramatic theory, firmly based—or so it seemed—in a century-long tradition of neoclassical dramaturgy and staging practice, provided models and precepts for the rest of Europe. The history of the theatre in eighteenth-century Spain was in a large measure shaped by the struggle between those who advocated and imitated French dramatic practice and those who urged the revival of a native tradition exemplified in the earlier drama of the Golden Age. In Germany, Johann Gottsched and Carolina and Johann Neuber attempted during the 1730s to reform the theatre by establishing a repertory of plays that were either translations or imitations of French neoclassical plays. In the Scandinavian countries and in eastern Europe dramatic principles, repertory, and even acting troupes were French or French inspired. Moreover, a historian cannot afford the luxury of ignoring evidence that might lack aesthetic appeal. It is, of course, unlikely that anyone would be masochistic enough to devote a lifetime—or several lifetimes—to reading the thousands of plays that were first produced in France in the eighteenth century. But to proceed to use any part of the total number as the basis for generalizations concerning the drama or its staging, it is imperative to have some notion of the size and nature of the repertories and the provenance of the texts. (Still the standard surveys in English of the dramatic literature of the period are three volumes by Henry Carrington Lancaster: *Sunset: A History of Parisian Drama in the Last Years of Louis XV, 1701–1715*, *French Tragedy in the Time of Louis XV and Voltaire, 1715–1774*, and *French Tragedy in the Reign of Louis XVI and the Early Years of the French Revolution, 1774–1792*. See also Geoffrey Brereton, *French Comic Drama from the Sixteenth to the Eighteenth Century*.)

Clarence D. Brenner in *A Bibliographical List of Plays in the French Language, 1700–1789* (1947) lists 11,662 titles, but also notes that he makes no pretense that the list is complete and that even the accuracy of the bibliographical descriptions cannot be guaranteed. He tries to indicate the place and date of first performance and of first publication, but contemporary sources are sometimes contradictory, particularly with respect to the theatres of the fairs and the popular theatres that appeared and disappeared during the second half of the century. The establishing of repertories for these theatres is therefore a difficult if not an impossible task. Fortunately, we have more accurate information concerning the monopoly theatres. (See Henry Carrington Lancaster, *The Comédie Française 1701–1774* and Clarence D. Brenner, *The Théâtre Italien*. Spire Pitou provides a chronologically arranged repertory of the Opéra for the years 1671–1815 in the first two volumes of *The Paris Opera*.)

The difficulties of establishing accurate repertories and performance texts are compounded by performance and publishing practices. Plays were sometimes performed privately or in the provinces before they appeared on the public stage in Paris; they were sometimes performed and/or published in several different versions; these versions could be given different titles; some plays exist in both printed and manuscript forms. In the case of the *opéras comiques*, entertainments performed at the fair theatres and featuring a considerable use of music and spectacle, we know that the texts were printed and distributed at the performances as *livrets*. Most of these pamphlets have disappeared, but others are scattered throughout French libraries, and still others were collected and republished in *recueils factices* or nonce collections. This was the case, for instance, in the publication of the plays of Charles Simon Favart (1710–1792), the first writer to earn his reputation by writing librettos for the *opéra comique*. (Francis J. Carmody indicates the place of performance—fair theatre or Theatre Italien— in *Le Répertoire de l'opéra-comique en vaudedilles de 1708 à 1764*.) Finally, the ultimate effect of official censorship is not clear. Authors normally submitted their plays in manuscript to the secretariat of the Lieutenant of Police, where they were examined by the censor. The censor prepared a written report recommending that a play be prohibited, authorized for performance, or subjected to corrections. The final decision, however, belonged to the Lieutenant Générale of Police. An approved text usually remained with the police for the duration of the performance. The problem is this: Since the approved, and presumably the performed, manuscript version has rarely survived, we have no way of knowing how closely the printed version corresponds to what was actually played. We are left in general with plays in printed editions designed, perhaps revised, to sell as literature, but always with the potential of being used in a revival.

Scholars who wish to examine eighteenth-century dramatic texts can, of course, avail themselves of the large collections in the Bibliothèque Nationale, but several early published collections are more widely available and have the added advantage of reflecting contemporary taste and notions of worth and popularity. *Nouveau recueil choisi et mêlé des meilleures pièces du théâtre françois et italien* was published in eight volumes between 1733 and 1743. *Le Nouveau Théâtre Italien*, edited by Luigi Riccoboni, went through several editions after 1716, culminating in the ten volumes of 1751. Included are plays in both French and Italian. The playwright Alain René Le Sage included eighty-eight of his plays in his *Le Théâtre de la Foire*, published in ten volumes between

1721 and 1737. In the latter year there also appeared another collection, *françois, ou Recueil des meilleures pièces de théâtre* in twelve volumes. In 1756 Thomas Simon Gueullette published his *Théâtre des boulevards ou Recueil des parades*. By the turn of the century, large collections had canonized what were evidently the most popular and significant dramas of the eighteenth-century repertory. Between 1803 and 1825, C. B. Petitot published over two hundred volumes of plays in several collections. The best known is the *Répertoire du Théâtre Français* (1817) and its supplement of 1819–1820, a total of thirty-three volumes. Unlike their English counterparts, the French texts that were printed leave no evidence to suggest that they were playhouse texts or were based on promptbooks. (Indeed, during the eighteenth century promptbooks outside England are very rare.) Stage directions are generally spare, although they did increase in number during the 1730s, indicating perhaps an increased interest on the part of dramatists with the staging of their plays.

One early nineteenth-century *répertoire*, however, which lists plays performed at the Théâtre Français to 1818, provides important supplementary information concerning staging. The *Répertoire du Théâtre-Français, ou details essentials sur 360 tragédies et comédies*—prepared by Jean-Baptiste Colson, *regisseur* of the Grand Théâtre de Bordeaux, and published in 1818—includes the following data: the date of first performance; the names of the actors; the playing time; the length of each role; a description of the decor; and a list of properties. These notes, writes Edith Melcher, constitute "more accurate information as to the way in which the play was staged than can be gathered from the author's directions in the printed play" (*Stage Realism in France*, p. 3n.). And Colson's *Répertoire* may even be in fact what Peyronnet suggests it is: a collection of the first printed examples of specific *mises en scène*. Colson, the son of a "*chef des figurants*," possibly with the Comédie Française, made his own debut with the company as an actor in 1809, but in 1816 left for Bordeaux where as *regisseur* he published a *Manuel dramatique* (1817) as well as the *Répertoire*. Both works were intended as guides for provincial theatres, and the *Répertoire* therefore lists those plays that could be conveniently staged by a provincial company. While his parentage and early career would indicate that his ideas of *mise en scène* were probably based on the practices of the Comédie Française in the late eighteenth century, the descriptions themselves are undoubtedly of at least equal value as evidence for provincial practices in the early nineteenth century.

Historians sensitive to the possibilities can learn a great deal from printed dramatic texts. They are central, for instance, to the study of the playwright/actor-audience relationship. "The dialogue is constant between the stage and the auditorium," writes Lagrave:

it is easily established, not only owing to the rapport between actors and spectators, but through the speeches and the compliments that the players address to the *parterre*, and through the prologues in which the authors place themselves on stage, pleading their causes before their judges. Prologues, compliments, satirical ballads, playlets on current affairs, parodies, various *impromptus* build up the "representations" of the actor, of the author, of the very theatre and the public, comprising a mass of documentation of prime interest. [*Le Théâtre et le public*, p. 15]

Reading texts in this way takes us far from simple questions of staging and into the sociocultural milieu that provides the context for so much interpretation of the eighteenth-century French theatre.

Early Dramatic Libraries and Catalogues

Several eighteenth-century personalities acquired substantial collections of French playtexts, including the Comtesse de Verrue, "La Dame de Volupté," whose library was sold in 1736, and the Marquise de Pompadour, whose collection included that of the scholarly Pierre François Godard de Beauchamps, author of *Recherches sur les théâtres de France* (1735). Mme de Pompadour's library was sold after her death in 1764 to Antoine de Ferriol, Comte de Pont-de-Vesle (1697–1744). Pont-de-Vesle's collection of French plays was one of the largest in France and was used in the preparation of several works on the theatre: Mouhy's *Tablettes dramatiques* (1752), Léris' *Dictionnaire portatif* (1754), La Porte's *Dictionnaire dramatique* (1776), and various volumes by the frères Parfaict (see discussion below). There was a concerted effort, after his death, to sell Pont-de-Vesle's theatre books as a single collection. "It is a precious thing in France," states the sale catalogue, "and even more so in foreign countries where our theatre has come to be admired and where it would not be possible, for the sake of detail, to assemble a collection so large" (quoted by Paul Lacroix, *Bibliothèque dramatique de M. de Soleinne*, p. x). Fortunately the Comtesse de Montesson expressed a desire to have the collection, and the Duc d'Orléans, who wished to marry the lady, bought it for her. At her death, the collection passed to one General Valence and thence in 1823 to M. de Soleinne.

De Soleinne's library, the product of a forty-year preoccupation and passion, included a good part of the collections of two other eighteenth-century theatrical bibliophiles: the bookseller Charles Chardin, who had been forced to sacrifice his collection in 1779, and Dominique Martin Méon, whose library had been sold in 1803. With the acquisition of Pont-de-Vesle's library, de Soleinne redoubled his efforts, replacing defective copies with better ones, filling in lacunae, attempting to collect all editions of a play rather than limiting himself to one. His ideal was to amass "*le répertoire universel du théâtre*," and he very nearly succeeded. De Soleinne originally intended to bequeath his library to the Comédie Française, but a scandal concerning the unauthorized sale of a number of items from that institution persuaded him to look elsewhere for a safer repository. In 1842, before new arrangements could be made, however, de Soleinne died. No buyer could be found who was willing to purchase all six thousand volumes, and the richest collection of dramatic works ever assembled was disposed of in smaller lots to the highest bidders. Auguste Rondel's understated description of the event as *"un malheur"* needs no translation (*La Bibliographie dramatique*, p. 12).

Although parts of the de Soleinne library found their way into the Bibliothèque Nationale (f.f. 9242–341), it no longer exists as a coherent collection. But its legacy lives on in the *Bibliothèque dramatique de M. de Soleinne*, a magnificent six-volume bibliography prepared by Paul Lacroix under the pseudonym "P. L. Jacob" and published 1843–1844. Brenner complained that it was badly printed and full of errors, omissions, and misprints, but Lancaster praised it as the most complete bibliography of plays in existence. Certainly it has not been replaced, and scholars continue to make extensive use of it. Marvin Carlson, for example, relies heavily on the de Soleinne *Bibliothèque* in his *Theatre of the French Revolution* (1966). (The anonymous *Essai d'une bibliographie générale du théâtre*, published in 1861, was intended to complement the de Soleinne *Bibliothèque* by providing a list of theatrical writings other than plays. See also Charles Brunet, *Table des pièces de théâtre décrites dans le catalogue de la bibliothèque de M. de Soleinne*.)

The chief rival of Pont-de-Vesle as a collector of playtexts in eighteenth-century France was Louis-César de la Baume Le Blanc, Duc de La Vallière (1708–1780), whose large library was catalogued in the *Bibliothèque du théâtre français depuis son origine* (1768). As the title suggests, La Vallière's library, like that of Pont-de-Vesle, was not limited to the eighteenth century, but contemporary pieces formed large parts of the collections of both men. Some second copies and inferior editions from La Vallière's library were sold in 1767, and other parts of the collection went on sale in 1773 and 1777. But the major part was acquired in 1784 by the Marquis de Paulmy d'Argenson, founder of the Bibliothèque de l'Arsenal (1754), where La Vallière's library now forms the basis of the theatre collection.

The dramatist Guilbert de Pixérécourt (1773–1844) was also a lover of books, and after his retirement to Nancy in 1835 he founded the Société des Bibliophiles Français. His library, which included a large amount of material from the time of the Revolution, was catalogued by Paul Lacroix and Charles Nodier, librarians at the Bibliothèque de l'Arsenal, in *Bibliothèque de M. Guilbert de Pixérécourt* (1838). The collection was used extensively by Henri Welschinger in his *Le Théâtre de la Révolution* (1880).

ARCHIVAL DOCUMENTS

We are here concerned with a multitude of official and semiofficial documents, mostly in manuscript, which are housed in the libraries, archives, and museums of France, but especially of Paris. (An invaluable guide to the main collections can be found in André Veinstein and Alfred S. Golding, eds., *Bibliothèques et musées des arts du spectacle dans le monde*.)

The Bibliothèque Nationale holds—along with a mass of printed material, including part of de Soleinne's library—a collection of manuscript plays associated with the Comédie Française, 1644–1786 (f.f. 9236–37), as well as a collection of plays from the period of the Revolution and Empire, 1789–1815 (f.f. 7005). Also included among its holdings are manuscript books by Henri Duval, le Chevalier de Mouhy, and François Parfaict (discussed later in this chapter). The Bibliothèque de l'Arsenal houses "Notices sur les oeuvres de théâtre" by the Marquis d'Argenson (3448–55) and a miscellaneous collection titled "Recueil d'anecdotes sur la Comédie Française, la Comédie Italienne et la Foire" (3534). A large collection of documents relating to the opera from 1669 is preserved in the Bibliothèque de l'Opéra. A rich basis was provided by the acquisition of a substantial portion of the collection of de Soleinne. This library is rich in theatricalia, including evidence concerning costume, decor, and the administration of the Opéra. (This material has been insufficiently examined and described. Spire Pitou, for example, in *The Paris Opera* (1983), makes use of "unpublished documents in the Opéra library," including evidently a manuscript logbook—the *Journal de l'Opéra*—but he does not describe the document or indicate its nature.) Most of the materials housed in the Bibliothèque de la Société des Auteurs et Compositeurs dramatiques relate to the period following the founding of the society in 1777. Included are journals and dramatic reviews; theatre annuals and almanacs; playtexts, often annotated by the authors; and programs and posters. But the greatest treasure is undoubtedly the remains of the account books of the original Bureau Dramatique, with marginal annotations and notes by Beaumarchais, Michel-Jean Sedaine, Favart, and other dramatists.

The two main Parisian repositories of theatrical material are, however, the Archives Nationales and the Archives de la Comédie Française. The archives du Minutier Central contains the records of the public notaries of Paris, a treasuretrove of information concerning the lives, fortunes, and business affairs of persons associated with the theatre. Veinstein and Golding summarize the contents and their uses:

Marriage contracts, wills, and *post mortem* estate inventories furnish information of a biographical nature about the actors and managers of the theatrical companies; the contracts of association of the performers, and those calling for the erection of a theatre or the installation of a performing hall within an existing building reveal details of the organization of the groups of players and the practice of their business. [*Bibliothèques et musées*, s.v. "Archives Nationales"]

Occasionally an "*inventaire après décès*" can provide more direct evidence concerning matters theatrical. For instance, that of Charlotte Sirop, first wife of the actor Henri-Louis Lekain, contains a list of Lekain's costumes in 1775. (This inventory is in the "Inventaire de la loge que ledit sieur Cain occupe à la Comédie François" in the Archives Nationales. See the article by Georges Naudet in *Revue d'Histoire du Théâtre*, 1950.) Of perhaps more direct relevance to the theatre are the Papiers de la Maison du Roi (Papers of the Royal Household) (serie O'), which record the regulations, ordinances, and decrees governing the various musical and theatrical institutions: the Royal Academy of Music or Opéra (O'613–29) and the Comédie Française, the Comédie Italienne, the Opéra-Comique (O'842–54). Also included are the records of the Premiers Gentilshommes de la Chambre, the officials charged with the supervision of the theatres. (An early but still useful survey of theatrical material in the Archives Nationales is provided by Henri de Curzon in *Bibliographe Moderne* I, 52–83.)

Thanks principally to the indefatigable researches of Emile Campardon, a great deal of this archival material relating to the theatres of Paris has been collected and published. Campardon (1837–1915) spent his entire professional life working in the Archives Nationales. (See his *Souvenirs d'un vieil archiviste*, 1906.) His expertise as an archivist was matched only by his love for the theatre, a circumstance for which several generations of scholars have cause to be grateful. His most important publications so far as the theatre of the eighteenth century is concerned are the following:

a. *Les Spectacles de la foire* (1877). This two-volume compilation of documents concerns the actors, managers, and theatres of the eighteenth-century fairs and boulevard.

b. *Les Comédiens du roi de la troupe française* (1879). The contents are arranged alphabetically by the names of the actors, but Campardon includes a chronological index to the documents, which date from 1613 to 1789. The documents include (i) *ordres de debut ou de reception* from the Premiers Gentilshommes de la Chambre; (ii) *brevets de pensions*, almost always accompanied by the baptismal records of the pensioners; (iii) *actes notaries* (e.g. marriage contracts, donations, etc.); (iv) *procès-verbaux judiciaires*. Campardon compared his documentary information with the accounts found in eighteenth-century journals and memoirs (those of Louis Petit de Bachaumont and Charles Collé, for example), and with early historical accounts by writers such as les frères Parfaict and Pierre David Lemazurier.

c. *Les Comédiens du roi de la troupe italienne* (1880). The contents are again arranged alphabetically by actors' names, and the work includes the same kind of information as the preceding work. But Campardon also includes in an appendix twenty-four documents concerning the troupe dating from 1684 to 1780: complaints to the police; proceedings of the Royal Academy of Music against the Comédie Italienne; lawsuits; the company's representations to the Premiers Gentilshommes de la Chambre. Of particular interest are the Acte de Société of 1719 (doc. 5), which established the Théâtre Italien, and the Royal Decrees of 1762 (doc. 13), which united the Comédie Italienne and the Opéra Comique, and of 1779 (doc. 23), which proclaimed a new constitution for the troupe.

d. *L'Académie royale de musique au XVIIIe siècle* (1884). These two volumes bring to a conclusion the results of nearly fifteen years of archival research. Some of the documents printed relate to the Academy as an institution, others to the private lives of the actors, singers, and musicians attached to it. Again, Campardon includes an interesting selection of *procès-verbaux judiciares*, where we find the complaints of seduced women and tricked husbands, the grievances of proprietors and porters. And again, Campardon consulted Claude Parfaict's *Dictionnaire des théâtres* (1756) and various contemporary periodicals in order to verify his documents.

Campardon's work is in the best tradition of nineteenth-century research, obsessed as it was with the collection and publication of data. His selection of documents for publication was based on diligent search, a sure knowledge of the archives, and above all a wide knowledge of the theatrical world of the seventeenth and eighteenth centuries.

The second principal repository is, of course, the Archives de la Comédie Française, which reflects the history and activities of that illustrious company over three centuries. Included are thousands of manuscript plays, stage directions, and administrative memoranda; the seventeenth-century account books of Lagrange La Thorillière, and Hubert (discussed in Ronald Vince, *Renaissance Theatre*, p. 151); minutes of the meetings of the company; letters, posters, programs, press clippings; and even twelve thousand models of scenery and costume. Much of this material, of course, dates from the nineteenth and twentieth centuries, but there is almost a complete run of *registres* from 1680, and the internal affairs of the company during the eighteenth century are well documented. (See Georges Monval, *Les Collections de la Comédie-Française, catalogue historique et raisonné*, [1897].) Once again scholarship has benefitted from the researches of a tireless archivist. Jules Bonnassies (1813–1880), an official in the Ministry of Public Instruction, was charged with regrouping and classifying the archives of the Comédie Française. He subsequently drew on this archival material in the preparation of his six books on the history of the Comédie Française. In the best known and most frequently cited of his works, *La Comédie-Française, histoire administrative* (1874), he analyzed the history of the company to 1757 in terms both of its relations with royal authority and its internal regulations. Of most importance for modern scholars is that Bonnassies printed the articles of regulation in their entirety. Indeed, his practice of citing and excerpting archival documents gives all his books their lasting value.

One final comment: French archives have not been immune to the ravages of modern warfare. During the siege of Paris in the Franco-Prussian War of 1870, fire destroyed a good many public documents. Studies published before that date sometimes include references to or even copies of manuscripts no longer in existence. Thus Victor Hallays-Dabot's *Histoire de la censure théâtrale en France* (1862), for example, includes numerous transcriptions of lost documents.

Theatrical Registers

Daily records of performances, receipts, and expenses are available to us for the Comédie Française and the Comédie Italienne for a good part of the eighteenth century. These *registres* are among the most precious and frequently consulted documents from the archives of the Paris acting companies. There are in addition large collections of *registres* in municipal and state archives outside France. Repositories in the Hague, in Amsterdam, and in other cities in Holland, for instance, provided much of the material for J. Fransen's *Les Comédiens français en Hollande* (1925). Belgian archives, especially the Archives Générales du

Royaume a Bruxelles, were exploited—not always accurately—by Frederic Jules Faber in the writing of his *Histoire du théâtre français en Belgique* (1878–1880) and by Henri Liebrecht in his *Histoire du théâtre français à Bruxelles* (1923). Both authors cite and quote archival documents liberally, although Liebrecht makes an effort to correct Faber's errors. From these records it is possible to learn the titles of plays performed, the dates of performance, the receipts, the number of spectators, the actors' and authors' shares of the receipts, the actors' parts, and the net profits. For some years there are monthly or annual summaries. On the basis of such information historians have been able to establish the repertory for each company, and to some extent to gauge the relative success of specific plays and playwrights.

In the Bibliothèque Municipale in Bordeaux, a document is preserved that, although perhaps not technically a *registre*, provides information of a similar kind. We find in it, after the day and date of performance, the titles of the plays played each evening, the announcement of *débuts*—of visits by famous actors— and at the end of each recorded season, a summary of the plays presented, as well as tables of the complement of the troupe. The "Manuscrit Lecouvreur" (ms. 1015) provides this information for each year from 1772 to 1794, with the exceptions of the seasons of 1776–1777 and 1782–1783. The document has been little used by historians. Henri Lagrave, who discussed it at a 1976 colloquium, noted only two previous references to it. (See his article in *La Vie théâtrale dans les provinces du midi*, ed. Yves Giraud, pp. 209–21.) Jean-Baptiste Gaussen-Couvreur, dit Lecouvreur, was an actor and, Lagrave suggests, a kind of La Grange of the Bordeaux troupe, the person responsible for keeping the company records. Programming methods, repertory, and the taste of the theatre public— all this can be derived from this invaluable document.

The *registres* of the Comédie Française are, of course, much better known. Preserved in the archives of that institution, they are complete for the years 1680–1793, except for the season 1739–1740. (A season normally ran from Easter to Easter.) The 169 *registres* between 1680 and 1774 provide daily accounts, as well as monthly or yearly reckonings. (They have been printed in part by Henry Carrington Lancaster in *The Comédie Française 1680–1701* and *The Comédie Française 1701–1774*.) Another twenty-eight, dating between 1761 and 1793, provide meticulous and detailed annual accounts, possibly all prepared by the same person. Those dating between 1769 and 1793 allow only a single page per month, where we are given daily details concerning the title of the play performed, the receipts, and the debuts of actors. Beginning with the 1757–1758 season, the custom began of having separate *registres* for receipts and expenses. As for the last *registre* for 1739–1740, our information concerning this season is derived indirectly from Charles de Fieux, Chevalier de Mouhy, who intimates in his *Tablettes dramatiques* (1752) that he had examined it, but who notes in the augmented version of his work, *Abrégé de l'histoire du Théâtre-Français* (1780–1783) that it had disappeared. A. Joannides in *La Comédie-Française de*

1680 à 1920 relied on Mouhy, and Lancaster on Joannides. And we rely on Lancaster. (Joannides, incidentally, reproduces facsimiles of *registres* for 1680, 1689, 1770, 1782, and 1784.)

The *registres* of the Comédie Italienne form part of the collection of the Bibliothèque de l'Opéra. (A microfilm copy is held in the Library of Congress.) The Théâtre Italien in 1793 became the Théâtre de l'Opéra-Comique National, and the *registres*, which were bound or rebound in the early nineteenth century, are stamped on the spines "Registres de l'Opéra-Comique" and are catalogued under that title. (The *registres* have been partially printed by Clarence D. Brenner in *The Théâtre Italien: Its Repertory, 1716–1793.*) The early records list in detail all daily expenses and receipts, but later accounts tend more and more to present expenses in a summary fashion, until 1772, after which time they are omitted entirely from the daily entries. The records were originally kept in Italian and were the responsibility of troupe members delegated the task for one- or two-month periods. As the years passed, French was used more frequently, often alternating with Italian as the responsibility passed from actor to actor. In 1741 Jean Baptiste Linguet became permanent treasurer of the company (a post he held until 1774), and thereafter the *registres* were written entirely in French. Most of the records—especially after Linguet—are fair copies of daily journal entries, and the process of transcribing the entries undoubtedly produced errors and omissions. Also, the practice of referring to plays by catchwords sometimes makes accurate identification difficult. (Brenner would not guarantee the accuracy of his identifications.) Missing *registres* are simply ignored, and those extant are numbered consecutively, beginning with number ten. (The first nine are discussed below.) The *registre* for the very first season is missing, but again we can learn something of its contents indirectly: It was evidently examined by Antoine d'Origny in the preparation of his *Annales du Théâtre Italien* (1788), where he reports receipts of 4,068 livres (I, 29).

As we have just noted, the *registres* do not begin until number ten, which deals with the 1717–1718 season. The first two numbered documents are identical in content, although written in different hands, and record the alterations in the Hôtel de Bourgogne undertaken with the arrival of the Italian troupe in 1716. The next two—similarly identical in content—contain a brief history of the Théâtre Italien in the seventeenth century. Numbers five and six list the debuts, receptions, and retirements of actors from December 1728 to September 1794, alphabetically by player. The next two contain copies of by-laws, official decrees, letters, and minutes dated between 1814 and 1823. The last, number nine, contains a miscellaneous collection of pamphlets, decrees, and regulations, mostly from the early years of the nineteenth century. (In *La Comédie Française*, Claude Alasseur notes [p. 201] the existence of an unedited manuscript *registre*, preserved in the library of the Société des Auteurs et Compositeurs, which contains annual receipts of the Comédie Italienne from 1740–1741 through 1757–1758 and daily receipts from the 1762–1763 season to the Revolution.)

WRITTEN EVIDENCE

The amount and variety of written evidence concerning the theatre reached unprecedented proportions in the eighteenth century. The theatre became the object of serious scholarship and the stuff of specialized history. Contemporary commentary on the theatre included critical observations on specific plays and performances, ongoing theoretical debates concerning the nature and function of dramatic performance, and formal treatises on the theatre and acting as arts. The numerous foreigners attracted to the French capital prompted the publication of tourist "guidebooks" which sought to instruct young strangers in the art of Parisian living and to warn them of potential hazards. Inevitably chapters were included on the theatres—valuable sources of information for the historian. Periodical literature increased in volume and, as the century wore on, tended to devote more and more space to theatrical affairs. Yearly theatrical almanacs from the second half of the century provide information concerning performance and the repertory of Parisian theatres. Finally, on a less formal level, we have myriads of published correspondence, memoirs, and journals written by persons whose connections with the theatre ranged from participant to observer to purveyer of gossip to indifferent chronicler. The discussion that follows provides an outline only of this material, and indicates some of the better-known and most frequently cited material.

History and Scholarship

Although Maupoint's *Bibliotèque [sic]* des théâtres appeared two years earlier, the first substantial work of theatrical scholarship in eighteenth-century France was Pierre François Godard de Beauchamps' *Recherches sur les théâtres de France* (1735). Maupoint's *Bibliothèque* is brief and anecdotal, arranged alphabetically by title, indicating the author and date of first performance for each play. In contrast, Beauchamps arranged his material chronologically, and although he makes no claim that the result is history—he preferred to think of the arrangement as a "useful order"—it is to Beauchamps that we owe the common notion of the chronology of the early French drama. The period before Jodelle is treated as a unit, followed by four "ages": Jodelle to Garnier, Garnier to Hardy, Hardy to Corneille, and Corneille to the "present" (i.e. 1735). Historians and bibliographers have continued to find Beauchamps arrangement useful, simply adding new "ages" as they were needed. It is the recognition implicit in these "ages" of dramatic change and development, a fundamentally historical perspective, that makes the order "useful." Beauchamps brought to his work as well both the historian's passion for precision and a healthy scepticism. He made a point of examining all the plays he discussed, noting the format, the edition, the place of publication, the name of the printer, and the date of the *privilège* or theatrical license. But this he considered only the beginning of his task. Distrustful of both authors and printers, he addressed himself to other questions as well: "The first, being to determine, if such a play had been performed, and in what theatre. The second, to discover assumed or disguised names. The third, to attribute anonymous plays to their true authors. . . . The fourth, being to establish fixed dates" (preface). Such work is fundamental to historical research.

Undoubtedly the most famous of early French theatre historians are the brothers Parfaict, François (1698–1753) and Claude (1701–1777), described by Emile Campardon as *"les pères de notre histoire dramatique"* (*L'Académie royale de musique*, I, vii). François' first published work, *Agendas historiques et chronologiques des théâtres de Paris* (1735–1737), contains a great deal of information, but it seems to have been hastily done and is badly organized. Another work, *Histoire de l'Académie royale de musique* remains in manuscript in the Bibliothèque Nationale (f.f. nouv. acq. 6532). Together, the brothers wrote an account of the evolution of the itinerant theatres of the fairs (*Mémoires . . . des spectacles de la foire*, 1743) and a history of the Théâtre Italien in France to 1697 (*Histoire de l'ancien Théâtre Italien*, 1753). Their most important contributions, however, are their *Histoire du Théâtre Français*, published in fifteen volumes between 1735 and 1749, and the *Dictionnaire des théâtres de Paris*, undertaken by Claude with the aid of Godin d'Abguerbe after the death of François and published in seven volumes in 1756. (The edition of 1767–1770 was reprinted by Slatkine in 1967.) *L'Histoire*—*"un ouvrage considerable"* (Auguste Rondel, *Les Bibliothèques dramatiques*, p. 6)—is arranged on a year-by-year basis by the titles of plays performed during the year, and provides some production details, rudimentary dramatic analysis, and extracts from the plays. Because the authors consulted the *registres* of the Comédie Française, the later volumes dealing with the eighteenth-century theatre are generally more reliable than the earlier ones. Unfortunately, although the brothers intended to bring their record up to 1752, volumes 14 and 15—covering the periods 1698–1708 and 1709–1721—were the last to appear. Nevertheless, the *Histoire* remains a mine of information. Besides titles, extracts, biographical sketches, critical commentary, and production notices, we find quotations from correspondence and from contemporary reviews in periodicals. Early in his career Claude Parfaict planned a vast dramatic dictionary, but the project never came to fruition. The *Dictionnaire* that appeared in 1756 presents information similar to that of the *Histoire*, but arranged alphabetically by play, playwright, and player rather than chronologically by year. Too, the *Dictionnaire* takes 1552 as its starting date, the year of Jodelle's *Cléopâtre captive*, and continues its account through to the date of its publication. Besides printing extracts from plays—entire scenes are included from non-published plays—and act-by-act sketches, there are, where possible, lists of actors and their roles, and lists of premiers and revivals. Taken together, the *Histoire* and the *Dictionnaire* provide essential data for the study of the Parisian stage during the first half of the eighteenth century.

A work of somewhat broader scope is Luigi Riccoboni's *Réflexions historiques et critiques sur les différents théâtres de l'Europe* (1738), translated into English as *An Historical and Critical Account of the Theatres in Europe* (1741). (The English version was reissued with some new preliminary matter in 1754 as *A General History of the Stage.*) Riccoboni (1675–1753) was the director of the Italian troupe invited back to France in 1716. An accomplished actor—best known as the interpreter of the mask Lelio—Riccoboni had in 1728 written an important book on the commedia dell'arte. With his *Réflexions historiques* he turned his attention to a comparison of the various national theatres and dramas of Europe. His perspective is unequivocally neoclassical, and he assumes the supremacy of the French theatre in this respect. While acknowledging the beauties of the English theatre, for instance, he can hardly dare hope that it will ever be able to regularize its beauty. "If some time or other the *English* Poets would submit themselves to the three Unities of the Theatre, and not expose Blood and Murder before the Eyes of the Audience, they would at least partake of that Glory which the other more perfect modern Theatres enjoy" (*A General History of the Stage*, pp. 180–81). Riccoboni is far more given to speculation than to the presentation of information, but he does offer interesting descriptions of several contemporary playhouses. (His discussions of the Venetian theatre and the Comédie-Française are printed by A. M. Nagler in *A Source Book in Theatrical History*, pp. 268–72, 285–88.)

Riccoboni is, nevertheless, something of an anomoly among eighteenth-century chroniclers of the stage. More typical are those works that carry on more or less in the tradition of Beauchamps and les frères Parfaict. The *Tablettes dramatiques* of Charles de Fieux, Chevalier de Mouhy, first published in 1752 and reprinted as *Abrégé de l'histoire du Théâtre-Français* in 1780–1783 provides sketchy information, often incomplete and faulty, on plays and performances, and provides alphabetical catalogues of authors and actors. (The same author's unpublished *Journal chronologique du Théâtre Français, 1749–1773* is housed in the Bibliothèque Nationale, f.f. 9229–35.) Antoine de Léris' *Dictionnaire portatif* (1754, 1763) attempts to cover the period 1400–1760 and provides alphabetical entries on plays, authors, musicians, and actors. Jacques Bernard Durey de Noinville's *Histoire du théâtre de l'Académie Royale de musique en France* (1753, 1757) is unreliable. Jean-Auguste Julien Desboulmiers, in *Histoire du théâtre de l'Opéra-Comique* (1769) and *Histoire anecdotique et raisonnée du Théâtre Italien* (1769) provide generally reliable information on the Italian players and repertory, as does Antoine d'Origny in *Annales du Théâtre Italien* (1788). Nicolas Toussant Des Essarts, the author of a large number of books on literature including a seven-volume literary history of France, *Les Siècles littéraires de la France* (1800–1803), is best known to theatre historians for *Les Trois Théâtres de Paris* (1777), a brief survey of the legal and regulatory history of the Comédie Française, the Comédie Italienne, and the Opéra, which also includes summaries and quotations from laws, decrees, statutes, regulations, and practices. Some documents are reproduced. A document of 9 June 1758, for example, refers to the establishment of *abonnements à vie* or life subscriptions to the theatre (p. 110). We must note too the work of the Abbé Joseph de la

Porte (1713–1779), whose *Anecdotes dramatiques* (with Jean Clement, 1775) and *Dictionnaire dramatique* (with S.R.N. Chamfort, 1776) are still cited by historians. Pierre David Lemazurier's *Galérie historique des acteurs du Théâtre Français* (1810) provides an alphabetical listing of actors with a biographical notice of each. And finally, Charles Guillaume Etienne and Alphonse Martainville give a full account of plays produced between 1789 and 1799 in *Histoire du théâtre français depuis le commencement de la Révolution jusqu'à la réunion générale* (1802). (Marvin Carlson makes a specific note of the usefulness of this work in *The Theatre of the French Revolution*.)

The overall usefulness of these dictionaries and handbooks can, of course, be called into question. A. M. Nagler notes that they "can hardly claim to have increased our knowledge of theatrical history" (*A Source Book in Theatrical History*, p. xx), while Henri Lagrave refers to them as "*un bonheur inegal*," a mixed blessing (*Le Théâtre et le public*, p. 13). Much of the information they provide—certainly the most "interesting" information—is anecdotal, much of it too good to be true, but if its factual basis can be confirmed from other sources there is no reason why use cannot be made of what Lagrave refers to as the "secondary information of an anecdote" (p. 13). There is, moreover, a level at which such material itself becomes the stuff of history, worthy of being recorded as part of the general theatrical milieu.

A special case is that of Thomas Simon Gueullette (1683–1766), amateur writer, author of "oriental" stories, editor of old books, sometime actor, and theatre addict, who occasionally found time to preside as a Paris magistrate. Gueullette claimed to have been a devotee of the Comédie Italienne from as early as 1694, and after the return of the Italians in 1716 he became a regular and assiduous playgoer and an intimate of many of the actors, including Riccoboni, Francesco Materassi, Jean Antoine Romagnesi, and especially Pierre François Biancolelli, the son of the great Harlequin Giuseppe Domenico Biancolelli. Following the death of Pierre François in 1734, Gueullette came into possession of a collection of scenes in the father's hand, which he proceeded to translate into French. (A copy of the translation is preserved in the Bibliothèque Nationale, ms. f.f. 9328.) Thus stimulated, he began at this time to collect materials for a history of the Théâtre Italien from 1577 to 1697. When in 1750 he started preparing this material for publication he decided to bring the account up to 1750 (eventually extended to 3 June 1762), and he added to his accounts of the players and their roles various engravings of performers and scenes as well as letters he had received from players. The project, however, was never completed, and in his will Gueullette left his manuscript in "*deux volumes de veau jaune*" to one M. Meunier. It was eventually acquired by M. de Soleinne and is now preserved in the Bibliothèque de l'Opéra. It was finally published in 1938 under the title, *Notes et souvenirs sur le Théâtre Italien au XVIIIe siècle*.

Gueullette's notes were evidently used extensively by the Parfaicts, especially in the preparation of their *Histoire de l'ancien Théâtre Italien* and in the Italian section of the *Dictionnaire des théâtres*. (Eugene Lintilhac, in *Histoire générale du théâtre en France*, actually credits Gueullette with the former work.) But little use was made of the manuscript before its publication. Less a history than a series of sketches, *Notes et souvenirs* is clearly a labor of love by a stage-struck amateur, but its sometimes naive judgments and comments provide a peculiarly intimate look at the actors, actresses, and performers of the Comédie Italienne.

An even more imposing work in eight manuscript volumes was at one time, in the nineteenth century, wrongly attributed to Gueullette. The *Notices sur les oeuvres de théâtre*, preserved in the Bibliothèque d'Arsenal (mss. 3448–55) has since been correctly assigned to René Louis de Voyer de Paulmy, Marquis d'Argenson. Henri Lagrave, who identified the author in 1963 and subsequently published a printed edition of the work, comments in *Le Théâtre et le public*: "This monument of living history, of amateur criticism, deserves to be in a class by itself, for its originality and for its wealth of interesting pieces of information, a great deal of which cannot be found elsewhere" (p. 13). The *Notices*, consisting of play titles and descriptions, analysis and criticism, and detailed extracts, are arranged alphabetically in volumes corresponding roughly to the types of theatre found in eighteenth-century Paris: 3448, Théâtre ancien; 3449–51, Théâtre français; 3452, Opéra; 3453, Opéra-comique; 3454, Théâtre italien; 3455, Parodies, théâtre anglais, théâtre danois. As Lagrave points out in the preface to his edition of the *Notices*, the work occupies an organizational niche between the alphabetical and the chronological, between a dictionary and a history. The result confers on the whole, he notes, "a certain harmony," and he suggests that the most appropriate label for the work is *répertoire historique* (p. 32). But beyond its organizational innovation, Argenson's work is valuable for its content. First, it is the only work undertaken in the century to provide a general view of all the various kinds of drama being performed, ancient and modern, French and foreign. Second, the point of view informing the author's criticism is that of a spectator in the theatre responding honestly to what he sees and hears. "The chief interest of the *Notices* is here," writes Lagrave, "in the spontaneous testimony, direct, sincere, of a representative of the public, that is to say, simply, of a man" (p. 51). We might add that Argenson represented the privileged segment of that public, but his attitude toward those in the *parterre* was tolerant and his observations on audience judgment and behavior clear-sighted. (Argenson's reputation, based mainly on his *Mémoires*, is somewhat at odds with the picture Lagrave derives from the *Notices*—see below.)

Another work, also in manuscript, should be noted. Henri Charles Duval (1770–1847), employed after 1797 in the Bureau des Arts and charged with the administration of theatres, prepared, probably after 1816, a fourteen-volume "Dictionnaire des ouvrages dramatiques depuis Jodelle jusqu'à nos jours" (Bibliothèque Nationale, ms. f.f. 15048–61; microfilm in Library of Congress). Duval examined the records of the police censor and was thus able to add considerably to our knowledge of the repertories of the fair theatres, particularly for the period 1770–1790.

One final contemporary work, on a specialized topic but central to the theatre, is Jean George Noverre's *Lettres sur la danse et sur les ballets* (1760). Noverre (1727–1810) was one of the great innovators in the dance, and his book was translated into English in 1783 and republished in 1803 in St. Petersburg. (A modern English translation, based on the 1803 edition, has been made by Cyril Beaumont.) He worked and taught in several countries: in Stuttgart (1760–1767); in London on several occasions (1755, 1780–1782, 1787); and in Paris, where he was appointed ballet master at the Opera in 1776. Considered the creator of the *"ballet d'action,"* Noverre decried what he found to be an overemphasis on technical virtuosity and stressed the importance of dramatically motivated dance. His *Lettres*, in the words of his translator, "considered as an exposition of the theories and laws governing ballet and dance representation, and as a contemporary history of dancing, have no equal in the whole of the literature devoted to that art" (Beaumont, p. xi). For the theatre historian, the value of the work is enhanced too by Noverre's evaluations of dancers during the first half of the eighteenth century, and by the valuable details he includes concerning production and costumes.

Critical Commentary

Theoretical and prescriptive commentary on drama and theatre in eighteenth-century France, while advocating and developing principles that led eventually to the overthrow of the neoclassical theories that had dominated the seventeenth century, continued the role of the older criticism in helping to determine dramaturgy and stage practice. Neoclassicism, it must be noted, died hard. François de Fenelon's *Lettre écrite a l'Académie Française* (1714), described by Marvin Carlson as "the first major poetics of the new century" (*Theories of the Theatre*, p. 142), is undeniably neoclassical in spirit. One hundred years later Jean François de La Harpe's *Le Lycée, ou Cours de littérature ancienne et moderne* (1818) surveyed literature from the Greeks through the eighteenth century from the perspective of a firm neoclassical taste. But the critical works appearing over the course of the century that were most influential in determining and that most accurately reflected actual practice were increasingly subversive of the neoclassical ideal. In the view of Eleanor Jourdain, whose *Dramatic Theory and Practice in France 1690–1808* (1921) remains a significant analysis of the period, the seeds of a changing aesthetic are to be found in the debate that began in the last years of the seventeenth century between ancients and moderns and that concluded with the triumph of the moderns. "The method of judgment," she notes, "tended to be less academic and to bring in the appeal to feeling, which, with a large public, prevails over reason. Thus the principles of judgment were recognized as themselves subject to change and development: and the direction of the change was in sympathy with the democratic movement of the eighteenth century" (p. 156).

As we noted earlier, the theatre became to some extent an instrument of social and political change, especially during the thirty years leading to the Revolution of 1789. As early as 1726 the Abbé Charles Irénée de Saint-Pierre, in an article first published in the periodical *Le Mercure*, and later reprinted in the author's *Oeuvres diverses* (1728–1730) proposed that a panel of knowledgable citizens be appointed to oversee and direct theatrical presentations in the interests of making society "every day milder, more peaceful and happier" (*Oeuvres diverses*, II, 192). In spite of the Abbé's undoubted good intentions—he was an outspoken critic of the absolutism of Louis XIV and of the tyranny of his ministers—nothing came of his project. And as future events would demonstrate, citizens can be quite as tyrannical as kings. The idea of controlling the drama for social and political reasons continued to inform writing about the theatre nevertheless; and however idealistic the expression (as in the writings of Sébastien Mercier for instance), there were always those who would improve society at the expense of freedom—that of the individual as well as that of the theatre. For Marie-Joseph Chenier, for example, the theatre was an important medium of instruction, the state's pulpit, and therefore must necessarily be controlled by the state (*La Liberté du théâtre en France*, 1789).

Tracing these ideas and evaluating their relationships to dramaturgy and theatrical organization can be difficult because dramatic criticism appeared in such diverse forms and places. In general, critical commentary during the early part of the century is found in prefaces to published plays, and to a lesser extent in periodicals. Later the prefaces were expanded to become pamphlets attached to plays, and later yet we find separate critical treatises. But pertinent material is also to be found in correspondence, in memoirs, and especially in Diderot's famous encyclopedia. There is as yet no systematic, complete survey, or even bibliography, of the dramatic criticism of eighteenth-century France. Pierre Peyronnet provides a partial list in *La Mise en scène* (pp. 163–64), and Jourdain (pp. 155–77) and Carlson (pp. 141–62) provide some discussion of the main documents. Otherwise it is in effect every scholar for herself/himself.

The case of Voltaire (1694–1778) illustrates some of the difficulties facing the historian. The great savant and littérateur dominated the cultural and intellectual life of eighteenth-century France as did no other. He was from an early date attracted to the theatre, and his passion for it continued throughout his long life. (His tragedy *Oedipe* was performed in 1718; his last play *Irène* in the year of his death.) Voltaire was a prolific writer, and he discussed drama and the theatre in his *Lettres philosophes* (1734), in his *Dictionnaire philosophique* (1764), in forty dedications and prefaces to his plays, and in hundreds of scattered references in his more than ten thousand letters. (See Voltaire's *Oeuvres complètes*, ed. Louis Moland, and his *Correspondence*, ed. T. Besterman.) An accurate analysis and estimate of Voltaire as a dramatic critic and polemicist necessitates an exhausting sifting of this mountain of material. Curiously, it appears that while the great man's reputation might prompt the effort, the results can be disappointing. Carlson points out that while Voltaire's general movement throughout the century was in the direction of the *comédie larmoyante* and the *drame bourgeois*, others preceded him, and he remained essentially a conservative theorist:

Taken as a whole, Voltaire's dramatic theory, despite his frequent claims of innovation, remains strongly conservative. A somewhat greater interest in visual spectacle (especially the exotic), though not to the extent of challenging unity of place; a somewhat greater freedom in expression, though not enough to erode traditional French poetic form; a somewhat greater freedom in subject matter, allowing figures from French history to join Greeks and Romans as possible subjects; and a new emphasis on the emotional, especially the sentimental—these essentially exhaust his innovations. [*Theories of the Theatre*, p. 147]

Just as it is unimaginable to conceive of the eighteenth-century French theatre without Voltaire, it is impossible to come to grips with it without taking into account Denis Diderot and his monumental *Encyclopédie*. Diderot (1713–1784) was a mediocre dramatist at best, but his interest in the theatre and its reform was a serious one, reflected even in his novel *Les bijoux indiscrets* (1748). His two plays, *Le fils naturel* (1757) and *Le père de famille* (1758) were each accompanied in publication by an essay explaining and justifying his new *drame bourgeois*. In the *Entretiens*, three discourses accompanying *Le fils naturel*, he expands on the English playwright George Lillo's defense of domestic tragedy in the Dedication to *The London Merchant* (1731), arguing for the truly tragic effect of "a realistic scene, true customs, discourse proportioned to the action, simple action, dangers before which it is impossible that you have not trembled for your parents, for your friends, for yourself" (Third *Entretien*). In his essay *Sur la poésie dramatique*, appended to *Le père de famille*, he continues to discuss the ways in which serious drama, or *drame* (*Le fils naturel*), and serious comedy (*Le père de famille*) help to fill the gap that he perceived between the established forms of tragedy and comedy. (Lillo's Dedication and an English translation of *Sur la poésie dramatique* are printed in *Dramatic Essays of the Neoclassical Age*, ed. Nenry Hitch Adams and Baxter Hathaway; Diderot's dramatic theory has been collected in *Diderot's Writings on the Theatre*, ed. F. C. Green.) Pierre Beaumarchais acknowledges Diderot's influence in his own defense of the *drame* in his *Essai sur le genre serieux*, prefaced to *Eugénie* (1767) (printed by Adams and Hathaway). Among the other writers on the theatre who took up Diderot's ideas was Pierre Jean Baptiste Nougaret (1742–1823), a man of prodigious memory and industry but little thought or critical principle, who in *De l'Art du théâtre en général* (1769) gave Diderot's theories a superficially naturalistic cast by stressing the surface appearance—notable of the lower classes of society— rather than the psychology of everyman that Diderot found in his middle-class protagonists.

The *Encyclopédie*, which appeared in seventeen volumes between 1751 and 1765, had in some respects an even more important role to play in the history of dramatic theory. Articles on drama and theatre were prepared by several different contributors, but the major articles were by Jean François Marmontel (1723–1799), mediocre dramatist, editor for two years of *Le Mercure de France* (1758–1760), and protégé of Voltaire, from whom he derived the liberal classicism that informs his articles in the *Encyclopédie*. (Marmontel later collected his contributions in *Eléments de littérature*, 1787.) Another article, innocently devoted not to the theatre but on "Geneva," by Diderot's co-editor d'Alembert, ironically helped to instigate a twenty-year debate on the morality of the stage and the necessity for reform or even censorship. D'Alembert had noted almost in passing that the city's suppression of the theatre in the interests of the morality of its young people was ill-advised. The comment called forth an almost immediate reply from Jean Jacques Rousseau (1712–1778)—who in his *Lettre à M. d'Alembert* (1758) drew on Plato and his own growing conviction of the corrupting influence of civilization—to defend his native city. The only theatre he approved of was that of celebratory open-air spectacle, a notion, Marvin Carlson suggests, that gave the leaders of the Revolution their idea of festival performance (*Theories of the Theatre*, p. 152). The ensuing debate—which found expression in pamphlets and multi-volume works alike and was carried on at various levels by writers as disparate as Beaumarchais, Nougaret, Rétif de la Bretonne, and Cailhava d'Estandoux—revolved around three questions: Is theatre necessary or desirable for the people? Who ought to judge plays? Can a professional actor be virtuous?

Such questions are unlikely to result in firm answers, but the debate provided occasion and context for serious proposals for theatrical reform, for even the defenders of the theatre were convinced that it should be changed to reflect more accurately the concerns of society and to provide social and political lessons. Among the most significant, and most frequently cited, of the reform theorists is Louis Sébastien Mercier (1740–1814), who developed his ideas in *Du Théâtre* (1773) and *De la Littérature* (1778). Mercier recognized the usefulness of the theatre as an instrument of moral teaching and agreed with Diderot and Beaumarchais that the representation of contemporary social conditions was essential to its function:

The stage is a picture; its aim is to make the picture useful, that is, to bring it to the threshold of the greatest number of people so that the image it presents will serve to bind men together by means of the all-conquering sentiments of pity and compassion . . . ; it is necessary that the moral purpose, without being either hidden or too open, should lay hold on the heart and establish itself there as ruler. [*Du Théâtre*, in *Dramatic Essays of the Neoclassic Age*, ed. Adams and Hathaway, p. 385]

He goes on: "I wish to see great masses, opposed tastes, mixed humors, and especially the consequences of contemporary manners. . . . What alone gives vitality to drama and weight to morality is the simultaneous and reciprocal action of all characters" (p. 393). Mercier found the theatrical traditions of French classicism detrimental to the theatre's mission as school to the masses. He saw in the privileged status of the Comédie Française another barrier to reform, attributing the actors' indolence and their unwillingness to produce new plays to a lack of competition. But such carping comments do not detract from Mercier's ideal vision of the stage and its role in furthering a national purpose and establishing and perpetuating a free society. His ideas are undoubtedly eccentric and utopian, but they are not contemptible. Carlson comments that he was ahead of his time and was pretty much ignored by his contemporaries, but that "he provided a crucial link between the patriotic manifestations that Rousseau considered perhaps the only form of spectacle suitable for his republic, and the pageants and dramas of the Revolution" (*Theories of the Theatre*, p. 159).

Much of what passed for theatrical theory and criticism in eighteenth-century France is barely worthy of the name. From a historical perspective it is important to note it as evidence of current and recurrent concerns about the nature and function of the theatre, but even the best of it contributes little of lasting significance to the history of ideas. On the other hand, the close association of criticism and playwriting, often undertaken by the same writer, makes a knowledge of at least the major documents essential for an understanding of the changes taking place in the theatre and in society at large.

Treatises on Acting

Extended discussions of the actor's craft are relatively rare before mid-century. Jean Léonor de Grimarest's *Traité du récitatif* (1707) is a general handbook on declamation and public speaking. Of more direct relevance to acting is Jean Dubos' *Réflexions critiques sur la poésie et sur la peinture* (1719). Dubos devotes several chapters to a discussion of declamation, movement, and gesture, arguing for an acting style based firmly on highly honed vocal skills and training in body movement, and for performance controlled by a kind of musical notation. The analogy of acting with painting and sculpture was widespread among eighteenth-century teachers and theorists. Not only did actors study the visual arts to learn appropriate postures and gestures, but painters and sculptors themselves used rules developed for actors in their representations of the human figure. The student of the history of acting must to some extent also be a student of the history of sculpture. Paintings and engravings of actors and stage scenes, on the other hand, must be used with caution, for the demands of pictorial art may necessitate changes in posture or gesture. On the positive side, it seems reasonable to speculate that iconographical analysis of such paintings in the light of information concerning actors available to us from other sources might help us to understand the relationship between the presentation of the human figure on stage and its representation in painting and sculpture.

As envisaged by Dubos, acting was an art to be tightly controlled by a conductor, the actor an instrument subordinated to the demands of the whole. Dene Barnett, in an important series of articles in *Theatre Research International*

(1977–1981), notes that eighteenth-century rules for actors, designed more or less to implement notions similar to those of Dubos, fall into three categories:

a. those concerned with the use of the arms, hands, face, head, and so on to represent or to externalize a particular passion;
b. those concerned with the use of the arms, hands, eyes, face, etc. to emphasize or to enforce important words or ideas during declamation; and
c. those designed to ensure grace and elegance of movement, and pictorial interest and beauty.

Although the rules for acting were codified in handbooks throughout Europe, and although they continued to be developed and taught well into the nineteenth century, by the middle of the eighteenth century their theoretical basis was already being undermined by the same forces that were causing changes in dramatic theory and practice.

The first indication that art and training might not be sufficient or even of first importance for good acting came from Luigi Riccoboni, the distinguished leader of the Comédie Italienne. In *Dell'arte rappresentativa* (1728) he argued for the necessity of study and training, but he also insisted that an actor must feel the emotion he is portraying. (See the translation and paraphrase in Toby Cole and Helen Krich Chinoy, eds., *Actors on Acting*, pp. 59–63.) By 1738 and the publication of *Réflexions historiques et critiques*, Riccoboni was even more convinced that acting without feeling was sterile, and he condemned the actors of the Comédie Française for their studied and artificial style. François Riccoboni (1707–1772) disagreed with his father and in *L'Art du théâtre* (1750) argued that in order for an actor to express himself effectively, he must be the master of the appropriate techniques. An actor who truly feels the passions he represents would not be able to act. (*L'Art du Théâtre* was translated into German in 1810 by Friedrich Ludwig Schröder for use as a training manual at the Hamburg theatre.)

But the disagreement between father and son was only a preliminary round. In 1749 Pierre Rémond de Sainte-Albine published *Le Comédien*, in which, among many other things, he generally supported the elder Riccoboni's position on the desirability of "natural" acting. The book was widely translated and was read in Germany, France, and the Netherlands. In England it served as the basis for John Hill's *The Actor* (discussed in chapter 1). Several years later Antonio Fabio Sticotti, an actor with the Théâtre Italien, translated Hill's book back into French as *Garrick ou les acteurs anglais* (1769), a truncated version that stresses Hill's discussion of the actor's natural attributes over those cultivated through training and study. Enter Denis Diderot. He first replied to Sticotti in *Observations sur Garrick ou les acteurs anglais* (reprinted in *Diderot's Writings on the Theatre*, ed. F.C. Green) but later elaborated his views in the single most famous treatise on acting of the eighteenth century: *Le Paradoxe sur le comédien*. (Although written about 1773, *Le Paradoxe* was not in fact published until 1830, forty-six years after its author's death.) In his earlier comments on acting, Diderot had actually been in agreement with Luigi Riccoboni, Sainte-Albine, and Sticotti, but *Le Paradoxe* was clearly written in sharp reaction to his earlier attitude. To move an audience, the actor must remain himself unmoved—thus the paradox of the title. "Were it otherwise," says Diderot, "the player's lot would be the most wretched on earth: but he is not the person he represents; he plays it, and plays it so well that you think he is the person; the deception is all on your side; he knows well enough that he is not the person" (*The Paradox of Acting*, tr. Walter Herries Pollock, pp. 19–20). The actor imitates an ideal type and thus creates an artistic reality quite distinct from himself. The actor's mimetic art is rooted in convention and acquired through training and discipline. In this, Diderot's ideas are remarkably close to some modern notions of stylization and defamiliarization.

The question remains, of course, as to the usefulness to the historian of Diderot's theoretical essay in estimating acting techniques and styles in eighteenth-century France. If we simply accept that *Le Paradoxe* presents its author's idea of what acting should be, not what it is or was, then as evidence for theatre history it belongs—if anywhere—to the nineteenth century, when it was published. But Diderot does illustrate his thesis with references to specific eighteenth-century players, and in at least two instances those players themselves would have recognized the accuracy of his analysis (without necessarily approving his conclusions). Diderot cited the actresses Mlle Clairon and Mlle Dumesnil as representatives of artful and emotional acting respectively, and in their *Mémoires* each of these renowned actresses writes of her acting in precisely the same terms as those used by Diderot. (Selections are printed in Cole and Chinoy, pp. 170–76.) Clairon: "How am I enabled to substitute the ideas, sentiments and feelings, which should distinguish those characters [Roxane, Amenaide, Viriate] in lieu of my own? It is by art alone that it can be done" (p. 172). Dumesnil: "To imbue oneself with great emotions, to feel them immediately and at will, to forget oneself in a twinkling of an eye in order to put oneself in the place of the character one wishes to represent—that is exclusively a gift of nature and beyond all the efforts of art" (p. 175). The language and the opposed assumptions of the dispute were certainly well established by the end of the eighteenth century and continued in pretty much the same vein through the nineteenth and even into the twentieth century. Lee Strasberg asserts in the Introduction to the Dramabook edition of *The Paradox* that Diderot's "demand for actor's discipline, for a technique of emotional experience" made him "one of the pioneers of the modern concept of the theatre" (p. xii). Denis Diderot and the Actors Studio?!

The discussions noted above are representative and are the most significant of French treatises on acting, but others might profitably be examined to provide a more detailed picture. Articles in the *Encyclopédie* by Diderot, Marmontel, Jean-Louis de Cahuzac, and others might be consulted, together with *Observations sur l'art du comédien* (1764, 1775) by Jean Nicolas Servandoni d'Hannetaire. Later discussions include Pierre Dorfeuille's *Les Elemens de l'art du comédien* (1799), Jean Marie Maudit La Rive's *Réflexions sur l'art théâtrale* (1801), and François Joseph Talma's "Réflexions sur l'art du comédien," prefaced to Lekain's *Mémoires* (1825). (Barnett lists and quotes most of the obviously pertinent material in his articles in *Theatre Research International*.) Other commentaries undoubtedly lie buried in less obvious places.

Periodicals and Almanacs

Periodical publications, many of them devoted to cultural and literary matters, first appeared in the seventeenth century. They carried announcements and commentary on theatrical performances and dramatic publications. But their number increased markedly in the eighteenth century, and as the years passed they allotted more and more space to theatrical affairs. Many of these publications were short-lived and sometimes went under several different names. Copies can be difficult to locate. (The Department des Arts du Spectacle of the Bibliothèque Nationale has a substantial collection, listing the titles of 650 periodicals published between 1713 and 1957. The most important are listed by Lagrave, *Le Théâtre et le public*, pp. 672–73, and Max Fuchs, *Lexique des troupes de comédiens ou XVIIIe siècle*, pp. xi-xii.) Early literary journals include *Le Journal Littéraire* (1713–1722, 1729–1736), *Le Journal des Savants* (1665–1792), and *Nouvelles Littéraire* (1715–1720). The playwright Pierre Marivaux edited three journals appearing intermittently between 1722 and 1734 (*Le Spectateur Français*, *L'Indigent Philosophe*, *Le Cabinet du Philosophe*). Of more importance are *La Gazette de France*, which appeared weekly from 1688, and *Corréspondence Litteraire* (edited by Friedrich Melchior, Baron Grimm, until 1773 and thereafter by J. H. Meister), which provides a reliable record of literary events between 1753 and 1826.

Perhaps the periodical most frequently cited by theatre historians is *Le Mercure de France*, founded on an irregular basis by Jean Donneau de Vise in 1672 as *Le Mercure Galant* and published monthly from 1678. It appeared under several different titles (*Le Nouveau Mercure Galant, Le Nouveau Mercure, Le Mercure*) before taking its best-known name in 1724. (For several years, beginning in 1758, it was edited by Jean Marmontel, dramatic critic, contributor to the *Encyclopédie*, and lover of Mlle Clairon.) Another important publication, devoted exclusively to the theatre, *Le Journal de Théâtres*, was known for part of its brief history (1776–1778) as *Le Nouveau Spectateur*. The editor, one M. Le Fuel de Mericourt, indicated that he would provide an examination of new plays by distinguished men of letters, and indeed the second issue (15 April 1776) included an article on the condition of French tragedy by Sébastien Mercier. Another equally short-lived journal devoted to the theatre was *Le Censeur Dramatique* (1797–1798), edited by Alexandre Grimod de la Reynière, a well-travelled, conservative gastronome who recalled with nostalgia the pre-revolutionary theatre of the elite.

There seems little doubt that the public was more and more interested in reading about the theatre, and it seems likely too that the interest was not confined to those who actually attended the theatre on a regular basis. The periodicals not only announced new plays and sometimes previewed or reviewed perfor- mances, but they also published *extraits*, which consisted of brief reviews, accompanied by long—sometimes very long—summaries of plays judged to be of particular interest. Lagrave notes that Pierre Mélèse recorded sixty-three such *compte-rendus* between 1659 and 1715, but that a similar count for the period 1715–1750 would run to many hundreds (*Le Théâtre et le public*, p. 13). By mid-century, whether or not members of the public attended plays, they were able to inform themselves about the latest productions.

About 1735 a special kind of periodical publication began to appear: the *calendrier dramatique*, or yearly almanac, which gave the complete repertory of all Paris theatres. These were compiled under various editors and under various names: *Agenda des théâtres*, *Tableau des théâtres*, *Almanach des spectacles*, *Année théâtrale*, *Annuaire dramatique*. These publications came and went, ov- erlapped, reappeared, but taken together they provide detailed records covering 180 years (1735–1914). (Auguste Rondel lists the major almanacs in *La Biblio- graphie dramatique*, pp. 6–7.) Among the better-known writers who produced these *calendriers dramatiques* is Pierre Nougaret, whose *Almanach forain* (1773– 1788) chronicled *"des principales villes de l'Europe"* as well as the theatres of the boulevards and the fairs. The longest running and most frequently cited, however, is Abbé La Porte's *Les Spectacles de Paris, ou Suite du calendrier historique et chronologique des théâtres* (1754–1778). *Les Spectacles* continued after La Porte's death in 1779 under different editorship; after 1800 its name was changed to the *Almanach des spectacles de Paris*.

Memoirs, Journals, and Correspondence

The memoirs and journals here discussed represent only a small proportion of such material produced, but they also represent the most frequently cited. Taken as a whole, they constitute primary evidence for the political, social, and cultural history of France, of which the theatre was a part. We saw earlier that historians have stressed the role of the theatre as a sociopolitical phenomenon. These memoirs, journals, and letters make such an interpretation possible. In- cluded are the writings of the court-centered nobility, the Parisian bourgeoisie, gossip-mongers and observers of contemporary city manners, playwrights and critics, actors and actresses.

The social and political life of France that found its centre in the courts of Louis XIV and Louis XV is recorded in several famous journals. The Marquis de Dangeau (1638–1720), an assiduous courtier, made a daily record of court activities between 1684 and 1714, including literary events insofar as they might interest the court. About 1730, his unpublished journal came into the hands of Louis de Rouvroy, Duc de Saint-Simon (1675–1755), who used it in the prep- aration of his own memoirs, which he had begun as early as 1694. The result is a voluminous record, written between 1740 and 1750, of the later years of Louis XIV. (A supplement that carried the record to the death of the aged Cardinal Fleury in 1743 is lost.) Saint-Simon may have been unhistorical in his animosities and biases and in his tendency at times to mix fact and gossip, but he had an eye for detail and a nose for intrigue, and the picture he paints of the court is vivid and probably unequalled among his contemporaries. He was especially good at descriptions of court ceremonials, a talent that makes his lack of interest in the arts in general or the theatre in particular a great pity. Saint-Simon's manuscript *Mémoires* was in turn used by Charles Pinot Duclos (1704–1772) in the preparation of his *Mémoires secrets sur les règnes de Louis XIV et de Louis XV* (1790).

The *Journal et mémoires* of René Louis de Voyer de Paulmy, Marquis d'Argenson (1694–1757), like those of Dangeau and Saint-Simon, was not published until after its author's death. Known at court as *"Argenson la bête,"* evidently to distinguish him from a more amiable brother, Argenson has a reputation among historians as a malcontent who saw everything in dark hues. His memoirs nevertheless are acknowledged as among the most important literary works of the eighteenth century. Although John Lough, in his primer on the economic and social history of France, *An Introduction to Eighteenth Century France*, notes the suspect nature of Argenson's account of affairs from 1735 to 1757 and cites the Duc de Luynes as "a more reliable if less interesting witness" (p. 32), it is significant that Lough quotes extensively from the unreliable Argenson and not at all from Luynes. Luynes (1695–1758), honest and commonsensical, also recounts the life of the court—particularly the details of manners, customs, and matters of etiquette—but sadly adds nothing directly to our knowledge of the theatre.

The later years of Louis XV and the reign of Louis XVI oddly lack any written observations comparable to those of Saint-Simon or Argenson. The closest approximation is probably the *Mémoires* of Jeanne-Louise Campan, first lady of the bedchamber to Marie-Antoinette.

These aristocratic *mémorialistes* had their counterparts among the bourgeoisie. The *Journal et mémoires* of Mathieu Marais (1664–1737) recounts news of the city, especially those items that were hostile to the court. Also included are anecdotes and comments on literary events of the day. The *Chronique de la Régence et du règne de Louis XV* by Edmund Barbier, better known as the *Journal de Barbier*, covers the years 1718–1762 almost in the manner of a newspaper addressing a readership. Barbier wrote of the life of Paris, the religious quarrels, the financial scandals, and the struggles of the magistrates against royal power. But as intriguing as it is concerning the legal profession, there is little in the *Journal* specifically concerning the arts.

The affairs and manners of the city itself, including its entertainments and arts, are far more interestingly chronicled in the *Mémoires secrets* of Louis Petit de Bachaumont (1610–1771), who for forty years between about 1730 and 1771 presided over the literary salon of Madame Doublet, a centre for the gathering and dissemination of news and gossip. Bachaumont was evidently in the habit of circulating bulletins to subscribers, but in 1762 he began the systematic synthesis of his material in the form of a chronicle. Six volumes were published in 1777, six years after his death, and the compilation was carried on by others to a total by 1789 of thirty-six volumes. Bachaumont was a gossip and a dilettante, and he and his successors exhibit little taste or critical ability beyond an urbane scepticism. The *Mémoires secrets* nevertheless contain a wide variety of materials useful to the historian: play summaries, reports on publications and performances, reviews, songs, sermons, and anecdotes—always anecdotes.

It seems hardly necessary to note that the voluminous writings of Voltaire, especially his letters and notebooks, are prime sources of information for the theatre historian. We can add the *Mémoires sur Voltaire et ses ouvrages* published by his two secretaries, Longchamp and Wagnière. But less luminous dramatists provide interesting and useful commentary as well. Charles Collé (1709–1783) offers lively portraits of many of his contemporaries—playwrights, actors, and actresses. (Nagler prints Collé's descriptions of Michel Baron and Mlle Lecouvreur in *A Source Book*, pp. 188–89.) Charles Simon Favart (1710–1792)—dramatist, director, and husband of the actress Marie-Justine Favart of the Théâtre Italien—in his *Mémoires et corréspondence littéraires, dramatiques et anecdotiques* contributes a large collection of letters to and from Marmontel, Mouhy, Voltaire, and especially his longtime friend Count Marcello Durazzo. The correspondence with Durazzo continued on a regular basis from 1759 to 1770 and provides valuable insights into the concerns of a working dramatist and man of the theatre. (Nagler prints extracts, pp. 304–5, 324.) The letters bespeak a warm and generous man. Garrick's comment in a letter to a mutual acquaintance that he loved Favart with all his heart but was embarrassed to write him in French (Favart, *Mémoires*, III, 9) seems to have been sincere. And finally, the world of letters and drama is the centre of Marmontel's *Mémoires*, undertaken near the end of his life and providing the great litterateur's considered estimates of his many distinguished contemporaries.

The famous *Mémoires* of Carlo Goldoni (1707–1793), who came to Paris in 1762 in order to revive the Comédie Italienne, are of far more significance for an understanding of the Italian theatre than for the French. Goldoni was 76 years old when he began writing them and he was 80 when they were published in 1787. He had little understanding of Paris or the French, his French was barely adequate, his memory failing, and he seemed determined to find fault with no one. The Italian years come off reasonably well, but as one of his biographers notes, "from the moment his narrative reaches his departure from Italy for Paris until the end of his narrative, Goldoni seems almost to have been intentionally inaccurate" (Joseph Kennard, *Goldoni and the Venice of His Time*, p. 202).

Like their counterparts in England, French actors and actresses were the subjects of innumerable anecdotes, epigrammes, and observations, many of them included in the memoirs and journals discussed above, and many in the pamphlets of the time. Surprisingly few of the famous performers, however, undertook to write their own memoirs. Among those who did were the great rivals, Mlle Clairon and Mlle Dumesnil. The actresses' differences of opinion concerning the art of acting were evidently of long standing. In Regnault-Warin's *Mémoires historiques et critiques sur F. J. Talma*, published in 1827, there is recorded a discussion that purportedly took place in 1787 among the actor Talma, his teacher Dugazon (Jean Gourgaud), the dramatist Marie-Joseph Chenier, and the two elderly actresses. (The discussion is printed in the English translation of Karl Mantzius, *A History of Theatrical Art*, V, 276–78.) Dumesnil argued for "natural" acting, Clairon for rules and conventions; Dumesnil argued for "reality," Clairon for "fiction." The same points of view are expressed at greater length in Clairon's *Mémoires*, first published in 1798, and those of Dumesnil, which appeared in 1800. Clairon's *Mémoires*, besides her reflections on acting, contain a modicum of information about her early life and career, but the title of Dumesnil's work, *Mémoires de Marie-Françoise Dumesnil, en réponse aux mémoires d'Hippolyte Clairon*, indicates her far more limited aims.

The memoirs of Henri Louis Lekain (1729–1798) are something of a disappointment. A very sketchy outline of the actor's life, notable only for a detailed description of Lekain's initial meeting with his mentor Voltaire, is padded with transcripts of letters, plot summaries and play descriptions, lists of names, petitions to the Premiers Gentilshommes de la Chambre du Roi, and other materials relating to Lekain's career. The information is interesting, but for the most part available elsewhere. Perhaps the most significant thing about Lekain's memoirs is that in the 1825 edition they are preceded by "Reflections on Lekain and on Theatrical Art," in which François Joseph Talma (1763–1826) pays tribute to the older actor and offers observations of his own on the actor's art. (Talma's piece is printed in *Papers on Acting*, ed. Brander Matthews.)

Even better known, especially among English speakers, are the *Mémoires* of Abraham Joseph Fleury (1750–1822), a mainstay of the Comédie Française from 1778 until 1818. First edited and published in 1836–1838 by J.B.P. Lafitte, the *Mémoires* were almost immediately translated into English as *The French Stage and the French People as Illustrated in the Memoirs of M. Fleury* (1841). Some scholars have expressed doubts as to the authenticity and reliability of the *Mémoires*. They were prepared some years after the actor's death and were reworked in the process by the editor Lafitte, who augmented them from other published memoirs and correspondence. But even if partly apocryphal, Fleury's *Mémoires* provide a lively picture of the late eighteenth-century theatre, and the information they provide can be used to verify if not to establish specific events or practices.

Miscellaneous

Travellers' diaries and journals are often useful sources of information. Two instances are of particular interest.

In May 1788 three actors from the Danish Royal Theatre undertook a trip to France and Germany in order "to see the most celebrated German theatres, but

above all the Parisian theatres'' and ''to deepen their knowledge and their com-
prehension of theatrical art.'' They were to observe theatrical equipment, scenic
arrangements, the repertory, and the acting, and to pay particular attention to
the roles they themselves played or might conceivably play. One of the three,
Joachim Daniel Preister, published an account of the five-month trip in 1789.
In it he referred to another journal kept by a second member of the trio, Michael
Rosing, but it was not until the beginning of World War II that this second
account was discovered and published by the Danish scholar Frederick Schyberg.
(Both accounts are, of course, in Danish. Fortunately, Solveig Schult Ulriksen
discusses the journals in some detail in French in the *Revue d'Histoire du Théâtre*,
1982.) Preister and Rosing are equally admiring of the management of the theatres
of Paris, but there seems to have been at least a partial division of labor, Rosing
concerning himself mainly with the regular theatre and Preister with the opera
and *opéra comique*. Rosing is an especially astute commentator on acting. Preister, who came from a family of painters and engravers and was possessed of a
remarkable visual memory, provides detailed information on decor and costumes.
Given that Preister's official account was destined for publication and the eyes
of his superiors, it is not surprising that the author sometimes pulls his punches,
in contrast to Rosing's unvarnished honesty. The fact that both were men of the
theatre and familiar with the French repertory makes their commentaries all the
more interesting and illuminating; although in the final analysis the real value
probably lies in what these accounts tell us about the emergent national theatres
of Scandinavia.

Of more immediate interest for the study of the French theatre is the account
of Dr. Charles Burney, who undertook a journey to France and Italy in 1770 in
preparation for his monumental *A General History of Music*. He published a
record of his travels as *The Present State of Music in France and Italy* (1771).
(This work, collated with the manuscript copy of Burney's original diary housed
in the Osborne Collection at Yale University, was edited by Percy Scholes and
was published in 1959 as *An Eighteenth-Century Musical Tour in France and
Italy*. See also *Music, Men and Manners in France and Italy 1770*, edited by
H. Edmund Poole, who provides a transcription of material from a second
manuscript in the British Library, add. ms. 35122.) Burney spent two weeks in
Paris and attended theatrical performances on four occasions: the Théâtre Italien
on June 13 and 23; the Opéra on June 15; and the Comédie Française on June
21. As we might expect, his chief interest was music, but he expressed considerable admiration for the comic actor Pierre Louis Dubus Preville of the Comédie
Française. Of the music at the theatres he comments: ''I perceived that the
overtures and act tunes of this theatre [Comédie Française], as of the *Théâtre
Italien*, were all either German or Italian; the French begin to be ashamed of
their own music every where but at the serious opera . . . '' (Scholes edition, p.
30). And he decided that in France good singing was never to be heard at the
theatres. In fact, Burney is unrelenting in his condemnation of French musical
performance, especially so after his return from Italy.

The accounts of foreign visitors can also throw light on theatrical practices that natives took for granted. A couple of English travellers, for instance, provide important evidence concerning the social composition of the audience of the *parterre*. Traditionally—and metaphorically—this French version of the English pit was associated with the less affluent classes. Marmontel in particular stresses the plebeian nature of the *parterre* audience. We nevertheless find Burney, writing to his daughter Fanny, reporting an entertaining visit to the Comédie Italienne during which he stood in the *parterre*. (See Fanny Burney, *The Early Diary*, I, xlvii.) And later Thomas Pennington, who travelled in France twenty years after Burney, records in his *Continental Excursions* (1809) the presence in the *parterre* of "well-dressed people" (I, 287). Social and economic status is not, of course, an absolute, and it is possible for Marmontel or Argenson to see plebeians where others might see merely more of the privileged classes. Lough points out that criticism of the "grands theatres," and especially of the Comédie Française, as being priced beyond their means was common in the latter part of the century. A manuscript "Mémoire sur les spectacles inferieurs" dated 1764 (Bibliothèque Nationale f.f. 9557) defends the boulevard theatres on precisely these grounds, that is, that they were the only form of entertainment poorer people could afford. (See Lough's discussion in *Paris Theatre Audiences*, pp. 209–10.) Coming to a meaningful conclusion on the basis of such evidence requires not only scholarly judgment but also an acute awareness of one's own perspective.

The historian who deals with questions concerning audiences and the theatre public must necessarily engage in a sophisticated form of historical sociology, constantly evaluating the evaluations of contemporary witnesses and commentators. The process is made more difficult in that the historian remains dependent for information on the almost accidental finding of relevant material in letters, pamphlets, petitions, memoirs, and even fiction. Lagrave cites *Jeanette seconde*, for example, a novel by Gaillard de la Bataille, as possibly the only source of a description of the *premières loges* of the opéra (*Le Théâtre et le public à Paris de 1715 à 1750*, pp. 243–44). Occasionally more obvious sources of sociological information can be consulted. Charles Pinot Duclos' *Mémoires pour servir à l'histoire des moeurs du XVIIIe siècle* (1751) provides interesting if guarded observations on the manners and customs of the time. But a far livelier and less inhibited picture is painted by Louis Sébastien Mercier in his *Tableau de Paris*, published in two volumes in 1781 but growing to twelve by 1788. (A selection has been translated by Wilfrid and Emilie Jackson, and an abridgment by Helen Simpson.) Mercier is the historian's reporter in the street, noting his impressions, recording his observations and his memories, and bringing to his portrayal of Parisian society a philosopher's intelligence and an experienced writer's flair for delineating manners and morals. The *Tableau* was described by Mercier's contemporary Jean François de La Harpe as "a mixture of absurdities, useful facts, extravagant paradox, pretentiousness, eloquence, and bad taste" (quoted in Jackson and Jackson translation, p. 4). Who could ask for anything more?

THEATRES AND THEATRE ARCHITECTURE

Parisian Theatres Before Mid-Century

Parisian theatres before mid-century were decidedly old-fashioned. The oldest was the Hôtel de Bourgogne, the principal home of the Comédie Italienne from 1716 to 1783, which had served dramatic art more or less continuously since 1548. The Palais-Royal, built in 1641, had undergone some renovations in 1670 and was to serve the Opéra until its destruction by fire in 1763. The newest theatre was that of the Comédie Française, erected in 1689 in the rue Neuve de Fossés, St.-Germain-des-Près, and used until 1770. The Salle des Machines, constructed in a wing of the Tuileries Palace by Gaspare Vigarini in 1660, was used only occasionally during the first half of the eighteenth century, although it was here that Jean Nicolas Servandoni designed some of his most elaborate spectacles in the early 1740s. In all of these structures, the right angle predominates. At a time when the U-shape of seventeenth-century theatres was being replaced with an oval or egg-shaped auditorium, the playhouses of Paris were reminiscent of the rectangular *jeux de paume* of an earlier age. Although the Palais-Royal and the Théâtre Français represented a kind of intermediate form, that of an elongated trapezium curved at one end, they remained essentially rectangular.

The theatres are discussed and described by various contemporary writers, but as Henri Lagrave ruefully notes, as loquacious as the writers are concerning the decorations of the auditoriums, they are oddly lacking in the kind of detail a theatre historian needs: the shape and dimensions of the stage and the *parterre*, the distribution of rooms, and the scenic arrangement (*Le Théâtre et le public*, p. 73). The main written and architectural evidence for these four theatres and for several court theatres is as follows.

Hôtel de Bourgogne

Although the oldest theatre in Paris, the Hôtel de Bourgogne is also the least well known. The principal evidence from the seventeenth century is a contract for renovations dated 17 April 1647, preserved in the Archives Nationales. (The document is printed by Wilma Deierkauf-Holsboer in *Le Théâtre de l'Hôtel de Bourgogne*, II, 183–86.) The earliest evidence from the eighteenth century is provided by two sketches of the theatre in James Thornhill's manuscript diary, acquired by the Victoria and Albert Museum in 1961. Thornhill visited the Hôtel de Bourgogne in March or April 1717, less than a year after the house had been refurbished for its new tenant, the Comédie Italienne. Thornhill was an experienced draughtsman and scene designer, and the drawings, however rough, are consequently of considerable value. (The sketches are reproduced and discussed by Graham Barlow in *Theatre Research International*, n.s., 1976.) A third sketch includes the cryptic notes, "The front cloth well painted wth gold[n] foliage," and "Flat scene of a pavil dropt down easy." "Whatever the technique or the function of the cloths," remarks Barlow, "clearly Thornhill was impressed by the expertise of their management" (p. 96). The interior of the theatre after the 1760 remodelling is represented in an engraving of a drawing by P. R. Wille, *fils* (reproduced by Barlow, pl. VI). But the only true architectural plan of the Hôtel de Bourgogne is that drawn by Gabriel Dumont for his *Parallèle de plans des plus belles salles de spectacles d'Italie et de France*. The plan, dated 1773, does not appear in all editions of Dumont's work, but it is included in the Composite Edition published by Benjamin Blom in 1968. The plan consists of one-half of the theatre only, but if the right edge-line is treated as the central axis, it is possible to reconstruct the complete ground plan. (See Lagrave, *Le Théâtre et le public*, fig. 14.) The players' complaint about 1781 that the theatre could accommodate only 1,528 spectators provides a final indication of its size. (See Brenner, *The Théâtre Italien*, p. 16.)

Palais-Royal

The earliest detailed description of the Palais-Royal is provided by Henri Sauval in his *Histoire et recherches des antiquités de . . . Paris* (II, 161). There is an anonymous plan for the theatre preserved in the Cabinet des Estampes of the Bibliothèque Nationale (Va 231e), and several paintings and engravings of the theatre's interior in the seventeenth century are available. (See Ronald Vince, *Renaissance Theatre*, pp. 170–71.) In the eighteenth century, only Jacques François Blondel among architects includes a plan and illustrations of the Palais-Royal (*L'Architecture française*, III). But these illustrations are limited to the ground-floor and first story, the scale is too small for the drawings to be of much help, and there is no accompanying written description. While Blondel is something of a disappointment, far more important evidence is provided by a collection of manuscript plans preserved in the Archives Nationales under the title, "Plans et coupes de l'ancienne salle de l'Opéra au Palais-Royal, brûlée le 6 avril 1763" (N III Seine 545/1–13). The thirteen plans are comprised of two series in two different hands of six and seven drawings respectively. The first series is not drawn to scale, but the second consists of carefully executed architectural drawings done to precise scale of plans for the *parterre*, the first, second, and third *loges*, and longitudinal and transverse sections. Lagrave, who reproduces six of the second series in *Le Théâtre et le public* (figs. 7–12), points out that these plans allow us to get an exact idea of the dimensions and the interior disposition of the theatre. The dimensions correspond fairly closely to those implicit in Dumont's *Parallèle de plans* as well.

Théâtre Français

The best-documented Parisian theatre of the eighteenth century is the *jeu de paume* renovated by the architect François d'Orbay in 1689 for the Comédie Française. The most complete written description is to be found in the third volume of Blondel's *Architecture français* (1752–1756), accompanied by plans, but the theatre is treated as well by André Roubo in *Traité de la construction des théâtres* (1777) and by les frères Parfaict in *Histoire du Théâtre Français*. (The latter work reproduces a manuscript description of a painting of the *"attributs du théâtre"* in the ceiling of the theatre—see Lagrave, p. 17n.) Once again, however, we find the most precious architectural evidence in theatrical archives. In the archives of the Comédie Française was discovered a carton labelled "Bâtiment de l'Ancienne Comédie" containing various memoranda, copies of notarized deeds, and most important of all, a complete set of plans by d'Orbay for the 1689 building. The existence of this treasure was theorized by Jules Bonnassies in *La Comédie-Française* (1874), and the prophecy was validated by its discovery by Nicole Bourdel and by its subsequent publication in the *Revue d'Histoire du Théâtre* in 1955. Included are an elevation of the façade, a cross section, and plans for the first and third *loges*.

Salle des Machines

This theatre in the Palais des Tuileries was the only French theatre in the early eighteenth century that was considered comparable to the great theatres of Italy, capable of inspiring astonishment and admiration. Useful descriptions are to be found in Sauval's *Antiquités de la ville de Paris* (II, 161–63) and in Germaine Brice's *Description de la ville de Paris*. Blondel's description in *Architecture française* (IV, 89–90), together with an elevation and a ground plan, provides a reasonably accurate estimate of the dimensions of the theatre, distribution and arrangement of seating, and decorations.

Court Theatres

Court theatres at Fontainbleau and Versailles during the early eighteenth century are also documented. The Marquis de Dangeau's *Journal* for 9 February 1718 mentions a performance of *Athalie* at the Louvre in April 1716, and a document in the Archives Nationales notes the construction of a temporary theatre in the Tuileries Palace in March of the same year. (See Alfred Marie's article, "Les Théâtres du château de Versailles" in *Revue d'Histoire du Théâtre*, 1951.) Other references are found in Beauchamps' *Recherches sur les théâtres de France* (1735) and *Le Mercure*. A small theatre at Versailles, constructed in the 1680s, continued to be used for court performances by the professional companies for much of the eighteenth century. The theatre is described by the Duc de Luynes in his *Mémoires* and by Blondel. The room was redecorated in 1724 and 1726, and the *loges* were enlarged in 1748. (P. Verlet refers to but does not reproduce two plans in the Archives Nationales in his discussion of these renovations in "L'Opéra de Versailles" in *Revue d'Histoire du Théâtre*, 1957.) Another small theatre at Fontainbleau is known from a plan dating from 1682, again preserved in the Archives Nationales. In 1725 this theatre was replaced with a true *"salle de spectacle,"* known to us through two sections in the Bibliothèque Nationale. (These 1725 plans, together with that of 1682, are reproduced by Marie in "La Salle de théâtre du château de Fontainbleau," *Revue d'Histoire du Théâtre*, 1951.) Three further plans in the Archives Nationales documenting renovations to the theatre in

1754 are to be found among the papers of the Royal Household (O' 1438). Bundled in the same carton was a document titled "State of boxes of the theatre at Fontainbleau relative to the alphabetical letters of the plans, following the arrangement ordered by H. M. in December 1754," with a note "approved this 20 December 1754." (For a detailed discussion of these plans and the court theatres in general see Lagrave, *Le Théâtre et le public*, pp. 129–70.)

The New Theatre Architecture

With the possible exceptions of the Salle des Machines and the theatre at Fontainbleau (especially after the modifications of 1754 made it a horseshoe-shaped ellipse), which were both specialized court theatres, Paris was contributing very little to the evolution of the comfortable, well-equipped public theatres that were becoming the norm throughout much of Europe. This was certainly the opinion of many Frenchmen, including Voltaire. Henri Lagrave draws attention to a pamphlet of 1749, *Des Embellissements de Paris* (Voltaire's *Oeuvres complètes*, XXIII), and to Voltaire's preface to *Sémiramis* (1748) titled *Dissertation sur la tragedie ancienne et moderne* (*Oeuvres complètes*, IV). Both pieces were prompted by the debacle of the performance of *Sémiramis*, during which Voltaire's spectacular scenic effects were rendered ludicrous by the presence on stage of a crowd of spectators. The incident determined Voltaire to rid the French theatre of this longstanding practice. "One of the greatest obstacles in our theatre," he fumed, "to all great or pathetic action, is the crowd of spectators mingled on the stage with the actors: this indecency was particularly apparent at the premiere of *Sémiramis*" (IV, 499). But in the *Dissertation* he goes beyond the immediate event to offer a more general discussion of theatre architecture. He begins by criticizing the Parisian theatres, their cramped facilities, and their lack of comfort, and he then proceeds to outline what was needed for the appropriate presentation of plays such as *Sémiramis*. The theatre needs to be very large. In order for the spectacular elements he envisaged to be accommodated and the action not reduced to a "long conversation," the stage must be large enough to represent part of a public edifice, "the peristyle of a palace, the entrance of a temple." The scene should be imposing in its majestic grandeur. As for the auditorium, all the spectators must be able to see equally well from all parts of the house. Whatever the effect of these demands on theatre architecture, by 1759 at any rate Voltaire saw the removal of spectators' benches from the stage of the Comédie Française. (See Lagrave, *Le Théâtre et le public*, pp. 112, 120–21.)

Voltaire's dissatisfaction with Paris theatres was widely shared. By 1760 an anonymous writer in *L'Année littéraire* could not conceal his exasperation. "But is it possible," he wrote, "that for a century we have not had the time to perceive that of all forms, the least advantageous for a theatre is that of a gallery or corridor a great deal longer than it is wide, where the best place for seeing is the worst for hearing and *vice versa*?" ("Réflexions sur les salles de spectacles," quoted by Lagrave, p. 123). By 1760, it is true, four new theatres had been constructed in France, but only one—Jean Monnet's Opéra-Comique de la Foire Saint Laurent (1752)—was in Paris. The remaining three—at Metz (1738) and Montpellier (1752), and the Théâtre de Lyon (built by Charles Soufflot 1754–56)—were among the earliest specifically designed, free-standing municipal playhouses that became sources of local civic pride throughout Europe. Alphonse Gosset was responsible for the Grand Théâtre de Rheims (1776); Claude-Nicolas Ledoux for the theatres of Besançon (1778) and Marseilles (1785); Victor Louis for the Grand Théâtre de Bordeaux (1780). In Paris M. de Moreau designed the new Opéra, Palais-Royal (1764); Charles Dewailly and Marie-Joseph Peyre the Théâtre de l'Odéon (1782); Jacques Molinos and Jacques Guillaume Legrand the Théâtre Faydeau (1788); and Victor Louis the Théâtre des Arts (1782), the Variétés Amusantes (later the Théâtre Français) (1787), and the Théâtre des Variétés (1790). At Versailles Jacques Ange Gabriel built a new Royal Opera in 1770. Moreover, during the Revolution there were twelve additional buildings built or renovated as theatres.

Even though some of these theatres continued into the twentieth century, renovation and restorations over the years have rendered them less useful for historical purposes than we might hope. Exceptions are Gabriel's Opéra Royal, which has been lovingly restored, and Louis' Grand Théâtre de Bordeaux. (See André Japy, *L'Opéra Royal de Versailles* and Margarete Baur-Heinhold, *The Baroque Theatre*, pls. 151–57.) Restoration necessarily involves historical reconstruction based on evidence other than the theatre being restored; otherwise restoration would not be necessary. Such evidence for French theatres built during the last half of the eighteenth century comes from two principal sources: national and municipal archives; and contemporary historical and theoretical works on theatre architecture, some of them written by the architects themselves.

Documents from the Royal Office of Construction in the Archives Nationales include reports on theatrical renovation and construction, particularly for those houses occupied by the Comédie Française, the Comédie Italienne, and the Opéra. Officially notarized minutes containing directives for the building of theatres are often accompanied by drawings. Gabriel's projected plans for the theatre at Versailles, preserved in the Archives Nationales (O' 1786–1787) are printed by Alfred Marie in "Les Théâtres du château de Versailles" in *Revue d'Histoire du Théâtre* III, 133–52) and by Pierre Verlet, "L'Opéra de Versailles" in the same journal for 1957. Verlet also provides an inventory of the Gabriel material in *Le Jardin des Arts* (1957). A large number of archival drawings and plans for Dewailly and Peyre's Odéon are reproduced by Monika Steinhauser and Daniel Rabreau in *Revue de l'Art* (1973). Similarly, municipal and departmental archives contain material relevant to provincial theatres. Those of Besançon and Doubs, for instance, contain the bulk of the projects, plans, memoirs, and accounts associated with the building of the Théâtre de Besançon in 1784. (See Hélène Leclerc's discussion and reproductions of drawings in "Au Théâtre de Besançon" in *Revue d'Histoire du Théâtre*, 1958.)

Two theatre architects—two of the most important—published descriptions and illustrations of their own work. Victor Louis, who designed four theatres including the Théâtre Français of 1787, produced his *pièce de resistance* with the Grand Théâtre de Bordeaux, a project that occupied him for seven years between 1773 and 1780. Not surprisingly, this large and luxuriously appointed house is richly documented with plans and with engravings of the interior. (See François Georges Pariset, ed., *Victor Louis 1731–1800: Dessins et gravures*.) And Louis himself contributed *Salle de spectacle de Bordeaux* (1782). (The most frequently printed plan of Louis' Théâtre Français, taken from Alexis Donnet's *Architectonographie des théâtres de Paris*, is not the original plan but rather the plan of the theatre as modified in 1799 by Jean Moreau to enlarge slightly the depth of the stage at the expense of the auditorium. See Georges Monval, *Les Collections de la Comédie-Française*, p. XIII, and Donald Mullin, *The Development of the Playhouse*, fig. 183.)

Claude-Nicolas Ledoux (1736–1806) designed theatres at Besançon and Marseilles and influenced Louis' design for the Théâtre Français, which resembles the house at Besançon more than it does that at Bordeaux. Shortly before his death, Ledoux published *L'Architecture sous le rapport de l'art, des moeurs et de la législation* (1804), which contains an exterior and a ground plan of the Théâtre de Besançon (reproduced by Leclerc in "Au Théâtre de Besançon" in *Revue d'Histoire du Théâtre*, 1958, pls. I, II).

Our principal sources of information, however, are the numerous historical and theoretical treatises on theatre architecture published in the latter half of the eighteenth century. These works provide most of the most frequently reproduced plans and elevations, and their commentaries provide much of the substance for modern interpretations of baroque and neoclassical theatre architecture. The most important are discussed here.

Jacques François Blondel (1705–1774)

A professor at the Académie Royale de l'Architecture, Blondel exerted considerable influence on the younger generation of theatre architects through his teaching and writing. In his *Cours d'architecture* (1771–1777) he taught that theatres should be independent structures, situated to facilitate a free flow of traffic and an ease of access. Sheltered terraces and colonnades would provide spectators with the opportunity to take some air between acts and to watch for carriages that would come for them after the performance. His notions concerning the shape of the auditorium suggest a solution to the concerns expressed by the author of "Réflexions sur les salles de spectacles." "In general," he wrote, "we think that the interior of the auditorium of these sorts of buildings ought to be circular or elliptical, in preference to the oblique form that has been given to them until now" (*Cours d'architecture*, II, 265). There were certainly precedents in Italy both for luxurious accommodation and for interiors based on the circle or the ellipse. But it seems equally certain that it was Blondel's teaching that helped to promulgate the ideas in France. Blondel's *Architecture française*

(1752–1756), a collection of engravings with commentary, includes a front elevation, plans, and sections of the Comédie Française, based on d'Orbay's plans (see above) but modified to reflect the state of the theatre in 1754. These engravings are the basis for those published in Diderot's *Encyclopédie*. (They are reproduced by Lagrave in *Le Théâtre et le public*, figs. 1–6.)

Charles Nicolas Cochin (1715–1790)

In his *Projet d'une salle de spectacle pour un théâtre de comédie* (1765), Cochin echoes once again the concerns expressed in the anonymous "Réflexions," pointing out that most theatres are too elongated, "so that the boxes at the end, which are the best for seeing the spectacle, and those for which the acting and décor are arranged, are too far away for anyone to be able to see and hear distinctly" (p. 4). His solution, however, was extreme. He proposed that an elliptically shaped auditorium face the stage the long way, with three proscenia arranged on the wide stage. (Cochin's plan and sections are reproduced in Mullin, *The Development of the Playhouse*, figs. 178–81.) Mullin notes that Cosimo Morelli based his design for the stage of the Teatro d'Imola on Cochin's plan (p. 106; figs. 137, 182) but that Morelli's experiment was not imitated elsewhere. In his *Parallèle de plans*, however, Gabriel Dumont includes a plan almost identical to Cochin's for a theatre constructed at the Court of Wurtemberg in Stuttgart after a design by Phillipe de la Guépierre. (This design bears no relation to that of the house built in Stuttgart by la Guépierre in 1759—see Mullin, fig. 141. Is this a case of mislabelling?)

Chevalier de Chaumont (fl. 1765–1775)

Chaumont cuts a relatively insignificant figure in this company. In his two volumes on the *Véritable construction d'un théâtre d'opéra* (1766, 1767), he notes the high current interest in theatrical construction and theories of theatre architecture, and he offers guidelines based on what he believes are Italian principles. He suggests that French stages need not be as large as those of Italy, which have to accommodate singers and dancers as well as actors. (Chaumont was savaged by Pierre Patte in his *Essai sur l'architecture théâtrale*—see below.)

Diderot's Encyclopédie

Thirty-one engravings illustrating theatre architecture and forty-nine engravings illustrating stage machinery were published in Volume X of the *Recueil de planches*, published in 1772. In addition, nine engravings of theatre architecture were published in a supplementary volume in 1777. (They are all collected in a convenient volume published in 1969 as *Theatre Architecture and Stage Machines*.) The following French theatres are represented: Lyon; Metz; Montpellier; Moreau's Opéra, Palais-Royal; the Salle des Machines; and d'Orbay's Théâtre Français. The engravings were evidently the work of Gabriel Dumont, who also contributed plans for a projected concert hall and a theatre to the 1772 volume, as well as the schematic plans contained in the 1777 supplement. The extremely valuable engravings of stage machinery, indoubtedly representing actual practice, were designed and explained by the architect M. Radel under the direction of M. Giraud, machinist at the Opéra.

Gabriel Pierre Martin Dumont (1720–after 1790)

Dumont worked for a considerable period of time in Italy, but returned to Paris in the 1760s as Professor of Architecture. Besides his work for the *Encyclopédie*, his main value for theatre historians lies in his *Parallèle de plans des plus belles salles de spectacles d'Italie et de France*, published in several editions between 1763 and 1774. (A composite edition was published in 1968.) The *Parallèle de plans* includes a good many plans and sections of Italian theatres—which Dumont clearly saw as superior to the theatres of France—and of other theatres throughout Europe. The French theatre is represented by the theatre at Lyon (9 plates); the Théâtre de Versailles; the Opéra-Comique de la Foire Saint Laurent; the Opéra, Palais-Royal; and the theatres at Montpellier, Nancy, and Metz. In addition, as we have already seen, Dumont includes plans of the Théâtre Français, based on Blondel, and a partial ground plan of the Hôtel de Bourgogne.

André Jacob Roubo (1739–1791)

Roubo, who describes himself as a master carpenter, published his *Traité de la construction* in 1777, a general historical and theoretical work usually dismissed as conservative and imitative. On the same grounds, it provides a compendium of received opinion useful to the historian. Roubo claims to consider the arts of the architect, the decorator, the machinist, and the carpenter in his discussion, and he bases his historical section on the work of, among others, Blondel, the Parfaict brothers, Beauchamps, Voltaire, Dumont, Cochin, Rousseau, and the *Encyclopédie*. He offers brief descriptions of Greek, Roman, and French theatres, drawing comparisons where appropriate, and he also describes the principal theatres of Italy, which he sees as providing models for all the modern theatres of Europe. He offers no description of the theatres of Germany, England, or Spain on the grounds that "they are of little consequence for the most part, and . . . their form differs little from those of Italy" (p. 36). Roubo's own project in fact offers little that is new.

Pierre Patte (1723–1814)

Patte is another of those knowledgeable teachers whose contributions are historical and theoretical rather than practical. Patte built little, but he wrote a good deal, including the final volume of Blondel's *Cours d'architecture* and his own *Essai sur l'architecture théâtrale* (1782). In his historical examination of theatres in the latter work—most of them Italian but including the Opéra and the Grand Théâtre de Bordeaux—the author reviews the various shapes that had been tried (circle, semi-circle, oval, bell, horseshoe, rectangle, and so on) and concludes that "the ellipse alone reunites all the advantages desired for a playhouse'' (p. 30). He also offers a summary review of his contemporaries who had written on theatre architecture. He objects to Cochin's projected plan, for example, on the grounds that the acoustical arrangement would result in the loss of the actor's voice, and the three scenes would lack continuity with the large auditorium and detract from the theatrical illusion (pp. 129–33). Patte's preference, based on the principles of geometry and the laws of physics, is justified by the superiority of *"la courbe elliptique"* for seeing and hearing. It is perhaps worth noting that Patte thought very little of English theatres, suggesting that they were so defective that they did not merit discussion (p. 118). George Saunders, in his *Treatise on Theatres* (1790), cites Patte's work, "which," he says, "pleased me much, as he was the first who attempted to lay down some principle on which to proceed. His theory, however, in my opinion is deficient, his examination of theatres is partial, and sometimes his comparisons are unfair" (p. ix). In his own examination of the principal theatres of Europe, Saunders expresses admiration for Louis' Grand Théâtre de Bordeaux, but comments on the Hôtel de Bourgogne that it is "universally condemned and is a disgrace to that polished nation" (p. 76). And Saunders opted for the circle over the ellipse.

Boullet (fl. ca.1760–1800)

Boullet (not to be confused with the architect Etienne Louis Boullée) is known only as the author of *Essai sur l'art de construire les théâtres, leurs machines et leurs mouvemens* (1801). He is described on the title-page as *"Machiniste du Théâtre des Arts"* and claims in his preface to have worked for forty years at the Grand Théâtre de Versailles and at the Opéra. This practical experience strongly informs his notions of appropriate theatre architecture. The great variety in the theatres built during the last twenty years of the eighteenth century, he argues, demonstrates the lack of a unifying theory. With the exception of the Odéon, built by Peyre and Dewailly in 1782, theatre architecture reflected the vain-glory and egotism of architects rather than providing appropriate facilities for those who mount performances. Boullet is, of course, thinking primarily of his own profession: "When theatres are constructed on faulty principles, they are handed over to the machinist who has never been consulted, and he is told: Do marvellous things. But by then the simplest things are very difficult to carry out" (p. 6). Boullet argues that the general dimensions of a theatre derive from the width of the proscenium, but then goes on to devote the bulk of his 108 pages to issues of space (corridors, passageways, foyers, storerooms), to the construction and storage of chariots, weights, scene frames and machines (especially the movement of stage machinery), and to questions of fire prevention and general security. (He recommends that a company of six armed guards maintain constant surveillance in the vicinity of the theatre.) Detailed drawings of the wooden framework and the machinery illustrate the text. All in all, this important source of information on the structural facilities of an eighteenth-century theatre has not received the attention it deserves. Happily, a recent translation by C. Thomas Ault augurs for a brighter future.

Lighting

A concern concomitant with the reform of theatre architecture in the second half of the eighteenth century was a new interest in theatre lighting, with its use as an element of stage décor and as an element essential for the comfort and convenience of the audience. The suggestions for changes and innovations indirectly indicate the fundamental nature of the lighting systems already in place, with their advantages and disadvantages. In the case of the Comédie Française we have as well an important document preserved in the Bibliothèque de la Comédie Française titled, "Dépense des Chandelles ord^{res} et des Lampions et Chandelles extraord^{res} à commencer aujourd'huy samedy 22e avril 1719." (Gösta M. Bergman offers a detailed analysis of this thirty-four page manuscript in *Lighting in the Theatre*, pp. 154–68.) But the published discussions that appeared after 1760 were based on aesthetic principles and were concerned with technical solutions to technical problems. Jean George Noverre in his *Letters on Dancing and Ballets* (1760) and Francesco Algarotti in his *Essay on the Opera* (French edition 1773) linked stage lighting with the art of painting. Cochin, Roubo, and Patte, in the works noted above, were all concerned with improving lighting systems for the auditorium and with lessening the dazzling effect of footlights. One of the most important lighting documents of the century is the text of a speech by Antoine Laurent Lavoisier to the Academy of Sciences in 1781. Lavoisier systematically addressed himself to the three areas of concern—the lighting of the auditorium, the lighting of the wing stage, and the lighting of the forestage. His technical solutions included the use of reverberators or reflecting lamps to intensify and diffuse light in the auditorium, the installation of screens to concentrate the light from footlights on the stage, and the introduction of "*réverbères paraboliques*" in the flies, whereby light could be directed to different parts of the stage. As Bergman points out, in Lavoisier's comments "we may discern a new feeling for the shades of the atmospheric play, a burgeoning romanticism of nature" (*Lighting in the Theatre*, p. 192). Nevertheless, the tension between the aesthetic and the social functions of the theatre remained unresolved as the eighteenth century ended. Boullet in 1801 noted that in Italy the auditorium was not illuminated during the performance. "In France," he writes, "and especially in Paris, there is on the contrary a desire for light. It can be pleasant to be seen as well as to see; but the stage action is thereby sacrificed" (*Essai sur l'art de construire les théâtres*, p. 94).

SCENE DESIGN

Scene designs are tricky things for the theatre historian to come to terms with. The bulk of them have survived in the form of engravings and prints, and they have long been prized and collected as works of art in their own right. Even in those instances where we possess sketches and drawings by the designers themselves, it is not always clear whether they were executed as directions for the scene painter or as models for the engraver. In order to evaluate what is clearly pictorial art in the theatrical context for which it was ostensibly created, it is necessary to determine the relationship between two-dimensional engravings or drawings and the three-dimensional stage setting the pictorial design purports to represent. It seems obvious from what we know of the mechanics of stage and scenic representation that many engravings function on a plane considerably removed from the possibilities of stage representation. ''The frozen, architectural music of baroque stage settings,'' comments Dunbar Ogden, ''often displays fantasies that their creators could not realize in genuine edifices. In the hundreds of sketches, fully executed drawings, and engravings of a theatrical nature . . . we witness the reach of their imaginations and the grandeur of their conceptions, given elegant expression through the skill of their draftsmanship'' (*The Italian Baroque Stage*, p. 1). Some of the ways by which these fantasies and conceptions were or might have been translated into stage practice are explained in the handbooks prepared by Italian practitioners such as Giulio Troili, Andrea Pozzo, Ferdinando Bibiena, and Baldassare Orsini (see Chapter 3), but for French practice it is advisable to compare these Italian works with the drawings of stage machinery in the *Encyclopédie*, with the comments of Boullet in his *Essai*, and with the work of Jean Nicolas Servandoni at the Palais-Royal and the Salle des Machines. Yet even then we are left with a generalized notion of stage design, for we are often at a loss to identify the particular work or performance for which the design was intended. Finally, although literally thousands of designs and prints relating to festivals, ballets, operas, and dramatic performances from the late seventeenth and the eighteenth centuries are preserved in the Bibliothèque Nationale, the Cabinet des Dessins of the Louvre, the Archives Nationales, the Bibliothèque de l'Opéra, and the National Museum in Stockholm, they are not easily studied as theatrical documents. We are for the most part dependent upon exhibition catalogues and specialized monographs for reproductions of a small proportion of these and other collections, and in most instances the basis for selection is not the usefulness of the designs to the theatre historian.

The best-known scene designers are those who were associated with the Opéra and the court, most of whom were designated ''Dessinateur de la Chambre et du Cabinet du Roi,'' the official responsible for royal *fêtes*, and *pompes funèbres*, as well as for scene design at the Palais-Royal. Among them were Jean I Berain (1637–1711), his son Jean II Berain (1678–1726), Jean Nicolas Servandoni (1695–1766), François Boucher (1703–1770), Charles Michel-Ange Challe (1718–1778), Pierre-Adrien Paris (fl. 1778–1800), and Louis René Boquet (1717–1814). (A fine selection of drawings and engravings by Berain père, Servandoni, Boucher, and Paris is provided by Nicole Decugis and Suzanne Reymond in *Le Décor de théâtre en France*, especially chapter IV, ''Les Spectacles de la Cour et l'Opéra.'')

Servandoni, who served his apprenticeship in Italy, is probably the most significant of the scene designers. He began designing for the Opéra in 1724, succeeding Jean II Berain as *premier peintre-décorateur* in 1728. Although he did not formally relinquish the post to Boucher until 1746, he had effectively ceased to design scenes for the Opéra by 1737. Between 1738 and 1742, and again between 1754 and 1758, he organized yearly spectacular shows at the Salle de Machines in the Tuileries Palace. Other "official" duties included court celebrations to mark royal occasions such as the birth of the Dauphin or the marriage of a princess. Servandoni and his work were known outside France, in Lisbon and Vienna, in London where he went in 1747 to work for Rich at Covent Garden, at Dresden where in 1754 August III of Saxony appointed him *premier peintre-décorateur*. Diderot referred to Servandoni as a great machinist, a great architect, a good painter, and a sublime designer. Unhappily, neither his talent nor his success was enough to ensure the survival of the bulk of his designs. Most of our information concerning his work at the Opéra is derived from detailed descriptions of twenty-one stage settings printed in the *Mercure* and from occasional discussions long after the fact. The ten *spectacles muets* mounted in the Salle des Machines are documented in the pamphlets that Servandoni himself published to commemorate the shows. In addition, Decugis and Reymond publish five maquettes from a private collection, which have been attributed to Servandoni or to one of his pupils and which they believe might have been intended as projects for the *spectacles muets* at the Tuileries Palace (pls. 43–47). But they also admit the possibility that the maquettes were done for a miniature theatre intended for the young Louis XV (p. 95). The literary journals add little to our knowledge here. Even the *Mercure*, which did not approve, says relatively little. Similarly the most famous of the royal celebrations—that of 1729 in recognition of the birth of the Dauphin, and that of 1739 in honor of the marriage of Louis XV's daughter Elisabeth—are known through official descriptions and *mémoires*, illustrated with a few engravings. (For a list of these and Servandoni's own descriptions, see Jeanne Bouché's article on Servandoni in the *Gazette des Beaux Arts*, 1910.) A very few of Servandoni's drawings are scattered throughout several collections both public and private, and in 1939 the French government acquired thirty colored sketches and models, purportedly the work of Servandoni. They are now preserved at the Château de Champs, Seine-et-mare. Finally, in the National Museum at Stockholm are three drawings of plans and elevations identified as the work of Servandoni. (They are reproduced by Per Bjurström in "Servandoni et la Salle des Machines" in *Revue d'Histoire du Théâtre*, 1959.) Bjurström believes that they are drawings for a *spectacle muet* at the Salle de Machines. "The plans," he writes, "give an idea of the way in which Servandoni performed his task from a purely technical point of view and, in much the same way, they are of great interest for an appreciation of his previous work" (pp. 222–23). Although not everyone agrees that these drawings relate to the Salle de Machines (see, for example, an article by Bert O. States in *Revue d'Histoire du Théâtre*, 1961), the evidence indicates nevertheless that Servandoni worked primarily as a theatrical as opposed to a pictorial artist. This may help to explain the paucity of surviving drawings and engravings.

PICTORIAL EVIDENCE

The theatrical enterprise in France, like that in England, gave rise either directly or indirectly to a large amount of artifactual material of widely ranging quality. The archives of the Comédie Française contain statues, busts, paintings, drawings, engravings, medals, and as Monval disarmingly notes in his catalogue, *"autre objets d'art ou de curiosité"* (p. 1, including the famous armchair from the production of Molière's *Malade imaginaire* of 17 February 1673). Convenient samplings of this material, together with some from other collections, especially that of the Bibliothèque de l'Arsenal, can be found in the fourth volume of Lucien Dubech's *Histoire générale illustrée du théâtre*, and in Volume IV of Heinz Kindermann's *Theatergeschichte Europas*.

Book Illustrations

It is sometimes held that engravings illustrating printed plays often depict scenes that the playwright did not write, that they represent an iconographic or a publishing tradition that may bear only an oblique relationship to the play or theatrical presentation. This clearly seems to have been the case with the engravings illustrating seventeenth-century editions of Corneille and Racine. At the same time, such illustrations ought not to be dismissed out of hand. Many of those from the eighteenth century, in particular, while of little artistic merit, seem to be modelled on stage scenes. Those illustrating the plays of Jean François Regnard, who wrote for the Comédie Française from 1694 to 1708, for example, suggest wings and perspective scenery, and depict actors in poses more characteristic of a dramatic scene than a pictorial composition (Dubech, IV, 15, 17, 21). On the other hand, some of the engravings accompanying Voltaire's plays, while ostensibly depicting specific actors in specific scenes, are more obviously composed pictures in their own right (Dubech, IV, 35, 39). Others (Dubech, IV, 113) are more artlessly theatrical. In some illustrations the costumes appear to conform to descriptions found elsewhere; in others they are clearly fanciful. In short, book illustrations provide a glimpse into stage presentation, but it is through a glass, darkly.

Theatre Interiors

The interiors of theatres, particularly toward the end of the century, are represented in several engravings. A performance of Voltaire's *Princesse de Navarre* in the theatre at Versailles on the occasion of the marriage of the Dauphin in 1745 is the subject of an engraving by Charles Nicolas Cochin reproduced by Dubech (IV, 37), who also includes an engraving depicting the "crowning" of the aged Voltaire in his box in the Salle des Machines after the sixth performance of his last play, *Irène*, shortly before the great man's death in 1778 (IV, 45). As we might expect, theatres designed by Victor Louis received considerable graphic attention. Dubech reproduces an interior and an exterior view of the Grand Théâtre de Bordeaux (IV, 9). But of more interest, and more often reproduced in general histories and handbooks, are two interior views of the theatre built by Louis in 1787 as the Variétés Amusantes, but known after 1799 as the Théâtre Français. The first presents a view of the auditorium from the scene back of the stage, on which three actresses are performing in an unknown play (Dubech, IV, 155). The second is even better known and depicts a scene from a spectacular production featuring a chase over a bridge (Dubech, IV, 156). Both engravings were done in 1790, before Moreau's renovations.

Perhaps the best-known engraving of a theatre interior, however, was executed in 1726 by François Joullain after a painting by Charles Coypel (Dubech, IV, 1; Molinari, *Theatre Through the Ages*, p. 195; Baur-Heinhold, *The Baroque Theatre*, p. 140). We are given a full frontal view of the stage before the curtain rises, with a partial view of occupied boxes on either side and spectators standing in the *parterre*. Prominent are two hanging candelabra, evidently lowered for trimming. The engraving is generally taken to represent the Comédie Française, although Dubech and Margarete Baur-Heinhold believe it to be the Palais-Royal. What has interested theatre historians most about the picture is the presence on the stage of spectators, some of whom are peeping from behind the curtain. (At least one scholar, however, identifies one of the figures behind the curtain as a "petit-maître." See Gösta M. Bergman, *Lighting in the Theatre*, p. 150.) Barbara Mittman has questioned the accuracy of the engraving on the ground that "there is no orchestra between the stage and the *parterre*, whereas all other evidence points to the existence of an orchestra pit at that juncture" (*Spectators on the Paris Stage*, pp. xvi–xvii). In defense of Coypel and Joullain it should be noted that a line of vertical bars just visible above the heads of the figures in the *parterre* suggests a demarcation between *parterre* and orchestra pit, and the perspective of the picture does not preclude a space between the bars and the stage. Nevertheless, the differences of opinion concerning the theatre depicted, the identity of at least one of the figures on the stage, and the absence or presence of an orchestra pit are indicative of the difficulties in arriving at an accurate reading of such evidence.

Theatrical Portraits and Scenes

Portraits of actors and paintings based on theatrical scenes can sometimes provide valuable information concerning gesture, costume, and stage deportment. Among the artists who contributed to the genre in eighteenth-century France were Claude Gillot (1673–1732), Antoine Watteau (1684–1721), Nicolas Lancret (1690–1743), Charles Antoine Coypel (1696–1751), Jean Louis de Faesch (or Fesch) (1697–1778), Charles Nicolas Cochin (1715–1790), and Gabriel Jacques de Saint-Aubin (1724–1780). Let us consider the examples of Watteau and Faesch.

Watteau, a native of Valenciennes, worked with Gillot for a time between

1702 and 1708. Gillot was especially interested in theatrical subjects, particularly the commedia dell'arte, and Watteau followed his lead. Many of Watteau's paintings, of course, are "theatrical" without being evidence for theatrical performance. "In their treatment of theatrical subjects," comments a recent art historian, "they tend to be loose in their ties to the details of the model seen on the stage . . . " (Donald Posner, *Antoine Watteau*, p. 54). A couple of early pictures are believed to record scenes from specific plays, however. *Arlequin Empereur dans la lune* (Posner, fig. 43) depicts a scene from an Italian comedy performed at the Foire Saint-Laurent in September 1707 and thus provides evidence of a continuing tradition of the commedia dell'arte even during the years of the Italian troupe's exile. *L'Ile de Cythère* (Posner, pl. 6) is usually related to *Les Trois cousines* by Florent Dancourt, but as Posner notes, "the representation lacks decisive specificity" (p. 54). In a couple of other instances it has proved impossible to identify the plays, but what is depicted are obviously dramatic scenes (Posner, figs. 45, 46, pl. 5). Otherwise, the inspiration and theme are theatrical, but the execution and composition are pictorial. This is true of the engraving depicting the departure of the Comédie Italienne from Paris in 1697 (Posner, fig. 42) and of two paintings of commedia dell'arte masks in forest settings (Posner, figs. 47, 49). Later paintings (Posner, pls. 7–9, 48) carry on this tradition of depicting commedia dell'arte actors "off-stage" in situations and poses intended to symbolize universal human actions and behavior. The atmosphere and the costumes of the theatre remain, but the content is no longer theatrical.

Five of Watteau's mature paintings, nevertheless, often find their way into books on theatre history:

a. *Harlequin, Pierrot and Scapin* (Posner, fig. 186). The five figures are shown in three-quarter, with the stage merely suggested by a curtain and a hint of scenery. The actors—not characters—are all gazing at the audience, as though taking a curtain call. (The painting is known only through prints and copies.)

b. *L'Amour au Théâtre Français* (Posner, fig. 190, pl. 54; Dubech, IV, 93). This painting is commonly taken as a depiction of an intermezzo from *Les Fêtes de l'Amour et de Bacchus* by Lully and Molière, revived in 1706 and again in 1716.

c. *L'Amour au Théâtre Italien* (Posner, fig. 191, pl. 55). Unlike the painting noted above, this companion piece is not modelled on a real performance or play. Instead, we are presented with an ideal group portrait of a theatrical company. The figure of Mezzetin has sometimes been identified as Luigi Riccoboni, but the likelihood seems remote. And in any event, we have no way of making a positive identification.

d. *Comédiens Italiens* (Posner, fig. 192; Brockett, 12.14). This famous painting is Watteau's most ambitious theatre-piece. Although it is known only through a copy, several preparatory drawings exist (Posner, figs. 194, 195). In one sense, the painting combines the curtain call of *Harlequin, Pierrot and Scapin* with the ideal portrait of *L'Amour au Théâtre Italien*. The entire company of actors is presenting itself to the audience at the end of a performance.

e. *Comédiens Français* (Posner, pl. 56; Brockett, 12.19; Dubech, IV, 159). This painting gives every indication of depicting a scene from a specific play, but the play has not been identified.

These late paintings are neither stupidly photographic nor imaginatively fanciful. They are idealized though accurate impressions of the profession of acting. They portray, in Posner's words, ''the stage and the cast, the costumes and the gestures . . . the individuals and the roles that characterize a theatre'' (p. 266). Properly read, they provide priceless insights into the world of the early eighteenth-century actor.

Jean Louis de Faesch presents quite a different case. As an artist Faesch is of little significance, rating no mention in standard histories of art. But as a painter and caricaturist of theatrical figures during the third quarter of the eighteenth century he garnered a modest contemporary reputation, and some of his watercolors regularly illustrate books on theatrical history, though sometimes unacknowledged. Faesch's subjects included English actors as well as French. He provided the drawings for the engravings in *Dramatic Characters, or Different Portraits of the English Stage*, published by Robert Sayer in 1770 and 1773. The same publisher issued a parallel collection of French actors in character after drawings by Faesch in 1772 (Dubech, IV, 32, 46, 55). But Faesch evidently executed his series of French actors in watercolors as well. (See Dubech, IV, 43, 81; Kindermann, *Theatergeschichte Europas*, IV, 366, 447; Molinari, *Theatre Through the Ages*, pp. 190, 193–95.) The actors portrayed are those active after mid-century: Brizard, Mme Favart, Mlle Dumesnil, Mlle Clairon, and above all Le Kain. Earlier performers had certainly been the subjects of paintings and especially engravings, and Faesch's favorites appear in other prints, but Faesch's portraits, particularly the watercolors, appear uncompromisingly theatrical in their bold and severe outlines, bordering on but still avoiding caricature. There is usually no background to detract from the figures of the performers. The gestures are exaggerated, flamboyant; the costumes carefully detailed. It is difficult not to see in these pictures the actors and actresses described by Diderot, Fleury, Clairon, Talma, and others.

Theatrical paintings and engravings exist, of course, in great numbers, and no respectable theatre collection is without hundreds or even thousands of them. Only a small fraction have been reproduced by theatre historians. Those with a claim to artistic merit, produced by artists of significance, are most likely to have been studied and analyzed by art historians and have thereby had a context provided for a ''reading'' by theatre historians. We are otherwise left to our own devices, and there are few rules to guide interpretation beyond the advice to treat each example on its own merit and the injunction to proceed with caution.

Costume

With a few exceptions, notably by Claude Gillot, most extant costume designs were prepared by the various ''Dessinateurs de la Chambre du Cabinet du Roi'' for productions at the Palais-Royal and the court theatres at Versailles and

Fontainbleau. Drawings and engravings by Jean Berain *fils*, Jean Baptiste Martin (1657–1735), François Boucher (1703–1770), Michel-Ange Slodtz (1705–1764), and Louis René Boquet (1717–1814) are to be found in the Bibliothèque de l'Opéra and scattered among other collections. (An important collection of material from the Opéra archives is to be found in Carlos Fischer, *Les Costumes de l'Opéra*, and a selection of drawings and engravings of costume is reproduced in Adolphe Jullien, *Histoire du costume du théâtre*.)

A good idea of the costumes worn at the Comédie Française and the Comédie Italienne can be derived from some of the theatrical paintings discussed above. Those of Faesch are particularly useful in this respect. Late in the century there also appeared a short-lived journal devoted to costume. *Costumes et Annales des Grands Théâtres de Paris* was published between 1786 and 1789, initially under the editorship of Michel René Hilliard d'Auberteuil but eventually under that of Jean Charles Levacher de Charnois, whose name is now inextricably linked to the periodical. Levacher de Charnois also published *Recherches sur les costumes et sur les théâtres de toutes les nations* (1790). Each number of *Costumes et Annales* included pictures of actors in character, followed by drawings of their costumes. Neither the journal nor the book is likely to be found in every undergraduate library, but Kindermann reproduces several of the engravings in *Theatergeschichte Europas* (IV, 383, 412, 414, 415, 435, 443, 460). Of particular interest is the print of Mlle Dumesnil as Jocaste in Voltaire's *Oedipe* (Kindermann, IV, 369), which bears a striking resemblance to Faesch's depictions of the actress; and also the famous picture of Mme Favart as Roxelane in her husband's play, *Les Trois Sultanes* (Kindermann, IV, pl. 36; Brockett, 12.26), which features the actress playing a harp and dressed in an "authentic" costume from Constantinople. With these illustrations, we may compare as well the written portraits and engraved illustrations in Antoine Vincent Arnault's *Souvenirs et regrets d'un vieil amateur dramatique* (1829), an odd collection of theatrical curiosities, but a book that occasionally casts an illuminating light on performers of the late eighteenth century.

REFERENCES

Adams, Nenry Hitch and Baxter Hathaway, eds. *Dramatic Essays of the Neoclassic Age*. New York, 1947.

Adhemar, Helene. *Watteau: Sa Vie—son oeuvre*. Paris, 1950.

Aghion, Max. *Le Théâtre à Paris au XVIIIe siècle*. Paris, n.d. [1926].

Alasseur, Claude. *La Comédie Française au 18e siècle, étude économique*. Préface J. Fourastié. Paris and the Hague, 1967.

Albert, Maurice. *Les Théâtres de la foire (1660–1789)*. New York, 1970. [1900]

———. *Les Théâtres des boulevards, 1789–1848*. Paris, 1902.

Algarotti, Count Francesco. *An Essay on the Opera Written in Italian*. London, 1767. [Italian ed. 1755, French ed. 1773]

Ancely, R., H. Tribout de Morembert, and R. Mesuret. "Pour un inventaire des affiches de théâtre." *Revue d'Histoire du Théâtre* V (1953), 183–88.

Argenson, Marquis de (René Louis de Voyer de Paulmy). *Journal et mémoires*. Ed.
    E.J.B. Rathery. 9 Vols. Paris, 1859–1867.
————. *Notices sur les oeuvres de théâtre*. Ed. Henri Lagrave. Studies in Voltaire and
    the Eighteenth Century. 2 Vols. Geneva, 1966.
Arnault, Antoine Vincent. *Souvenirs et regrets d'un vieil amateur dramatique; ou Lettres
    d'un oncle à son neveu sur l'ancien Théâtre Français*. Paris, 1861. [1829]
Bachaumont, Louis Petit de, et al. *Mémoires secrets pour servir à l'histoire de la re-
    publique des lettres en France de 1762 jusqu'à nos jours*. 36 Vols. London, 1777–
    1789.
Barbier, Edmond Jean François. *Chronique de la Régence et du règne de Louis XV (1718–
    1763)*. 8 Vols. Paris, 1857.
Barlow, Graham. "The Hôtel de Bourgogne According to Sir James Thornhill." *Theatre
    Research International* n.s. I (1976), 86–98.
Barnett, Dene. "The Performance Practice of Acting: The Eighteenth Century." *Theatre
    Research International* n.s. II, no. 3 (1977), 157–86; III, no. 1 (1977), 1–19; III,
    no. 2 (1978), 79–93; V, no. 1 (1980), 1–36; VI, no. 1 (1980–1981), 1–32.
Baur-Heinhold, Margarete. *The Baroque Theatre: A Cultural History of the 17th and
    18th Centuries*. New York and London, 1967.
Beauchamps, Pierre François Godard de. *Recherches sur les théâtres de France, depuis
    l'année 1161 jusqu'à present*. 3 Vols. Paris, 1735.
Beaumarchais, Pierre Augustin Caron de. *Théâtre complet*. Ed. R. d'Hermies. 1952.
Bergman, Gösta M. *Lighting in the Theatre*. Stockholm and Totowa, N.J., 1977.
Bernardin, Napoleon Maurice. *La Comédie Italienne en France et les théâtres de la foire
    et du boulevard (1570–1791)*. Geneva, 1969. [1902]
Bibliothèque du théâtre français depuis son origine. 3 Vols. Dresden, 1786. [La Vallière's
    Library]
Bjurström, Per. "Mises en scène de Sèmiramis de Voltaire en 1748 et 1759." *Revue
    d'Histoire du Théâtre* VIII (1956), 299–320.
————. "Servandoni, décorateur de théâtre." *Revue d'Histoire du Théâtre* VI (1954),
    150–59.
————. "Servandoni et la Salle des Machines." *Revue d'Histoire du Théâtre* XI (1959),
    222–25.
Blondel, Jacques François. *L'Architecture française*. 4 Vols. Paris, 1752–1756.
————. *Cours d'architecture*. 6 Vols. Paris, 1771–1777.
Boindin, Nicolas. *Lettres historiques sur tous les spectacles de Paris*. 5 Vols. Paris, 1719.
Boncompain, Jacques. *Auteurs et comédiens au XVIIIe siècle*. n.p., 1976.
Bonnassies, Jules. *Administration théâtrale: la censure dramatique*. Paris, 1873.
————. *Les Auteurs dramatiques et la Comédie-Française*. Paris, 1874.
————. *La Comédie-Française et les comédiens de province*. Paris, 1875.
————. *La Comédie-Française, histoire administrative, 1658–1757*. Paris, 1874.
————. *Comédie-Française, notice historique sur les anciens bâtiments*. Paris, 1868.
————. *Les Spectacles forains et la Comédie-Française*. Paris, 1875.
Borgerhoff, Elbert B. O. *The Evolution of Liberal Theory and Practice in the French
    Theatre 1680–1757*. Princeton and London, 1936.
Bouché, Jeanne. "Jean-Nicolas Servandoni." *Gazette des Beaux Arts* ser. IV, no. 4
    (1910), 121–46.
Boullet. *Essai sur l'art de construire les théâtres, leurs machines et leurs mouvemens*.
    Paris, 1801.

————. *Essay on the Art of Constructing Theatres, Their Machines and Their Operations*. Tr. C. Thomas Ault. In *Performing Arts Resources*, Vol. 11: *Scenes and Machines from the 18th Century: The Stagecraft of Jacopo Fabris and Cityoen Boullet*. Ed. Barbara Cohen-Stratyner. New York, 1986.

Bourdel, Nicole. "L'Etablissement et la construction de l'Hôtel des comédiens français rue des Fossés-Saint-Germain-des-Près (Ancienne Comédie) 1687–1690." *Revue d'Histoire du Théâtre* VII (1955), 145–72.

Brenner, Clarence D. *A Bibliographical List of Plays in the French Language, 1700–1789*. Berkeley, 1947.

————. *The Théâtre Italien: Its Repertory, 1716–1793. With a Historical Introduction*. Berkeley and Los Angeles, 1961.

Brereton, Geoffrey. *French Comic Drama from the Sixteenth to the Eighteenth Century*. London, 1977.

Brice, Germaine. *Description de la ville de Paris et de tout ce qu'elle contient de plus remarquable*. Ed. Pierre Codet. Paris and Geneva, 1971. [Reproduction of 9th edition of 1752]

Brockett, Oscar. *History of the Theatre*. 4th ed. Boston, 1982.

Brunet, Charles. *Table des pièces de théâtre décrites dans le catalogue de la bibliothèque de M. de Soleinne*. Paris, 1914.

Burney, Charles. *Dr. Burney's Musical Tours in Europe*, Vol. I: *An Eighteenth-Century Musical Tour in France and Italy*. Ed. Percy A. Scholes. London, 1959.

————. *Music, Men and Manners in France and Italy 1770*. Ed. H. Edmund Poole. London, 1969, 1974.

————. *The Present State of Music in France and Italy*. London, 1771; 2d ed. 1773.

Burney, Fanny. *The Early Diary, 1768–1778*. Ed. A. R. Ellis. 2 Vols. London, 1907.

Cailhava d'Estandoux, Jean François. *Causes de la décadence du théâtre et les moyens de le faire refleurir*. Paris, 1789.

————. *De l'Art de la comédie*. 4 Vols. Paris, 1772; 2 Vols. Paris, 1786.

Campan, Jeanne-Louise. *Mémoires sur la vie de Marie-Antoinette*. Ed. F. Barrière. Paris, 1876.

Campardon, Emile. *L'Académie royale de musique au XVIIIe siècle. Documents inédits découverts aux archives nationales*. 2 Vols. Paris, 1884.

————. *Les Comédiens du roi de la troupe française pendant les deux derniers siècles. Documents inédits recueillis aux archives nationales*. Paris, 1879.

————. *Les Comédiens du roi de la troupe italienne pendant les deux derniers siècles. Documents inédits recueillis aux archives nationales*. 2 Vols. Paris, 1880.

————. *Souvenirs d'un vieil archiviste*. Paris, 1906.

————. *Les Spectacles de la foire. Documents inédits recueillis aux archives nationales*. 2 Vols. Paris, 1877.

Carlson, Marvin. *The Theatre of the French Revolution*. Ithaca, N.Y., 1966.

————. *Theories of the Theatre: A Historical and Critical Survey, from the Greeks to the Present*. Ithaca, N.Y., and London, 1984.

Carmody, Francis J. *Le Répertoire de l'opéra-comique en vaudevilles de 1708 à 1764*. University of California Publications in Modern Philology, Vol. 16, no. 4. Berkeley and London, 1933.

Chamfort, Sebastien and Abbé Joseph de La Porte. *Dictionnaire d'anecdotes dramatiques*. 3 Vols. Paris, 1776.

Charpentier, Louis. *Causes de la décadence du goût sur le théâtre*. Amsterdam and Paris, 1768.

———. *Essais historiques sur les modes et sur les costumes en France*. Paris, 1776.

Chaumont, Chevalier de. *Véritable construction d'un théâtre d'opéra*. Paris, 1766. [Reprinted 1974]

———. *Véritable construction exterieure d'un théâtre d'opéra*. Paris, 1767. [Reprinted 1974]

Chenier, Marie-Joseph. *La Liberté du théâtre en France*. Paris, 1789.

Chevalley, Sylvie. "Le Costume de théâtre de 1685 à 1720 d'après le théâtre de Dancourt." *Revue d'Histoire du Théâtre* XVI (1964), 25–39.

Chevrier, François Antoine. *Observateur des spectacles sur le théâtre*. 3 Vols. Paris, 1755; new ed. 1762.

Clairon, Claire Josèphe Hippolye Leris. *Mémoires de Mlle Clairon*. New ed. Paris, 1822. [Reprinted 1968]

Cochin, Charles Nicolas. *Projet d'une salle de spectacle pour un théâtre de comédie*. London and Paris, 1765. [Reprinted 1974]

Cole, Toby and Helen Krich Chinoy, eds. *Actors on Acting: The Theories, Techniques, and Practices of the Great Actors of all Times as Told in Their Own Words*. Rev. ed. New York, 1970.

Collé, Charles. *Correspondence inédite de Collé*. Ed. Honore Bonhomme. Paris, 1864.

———. *Journal et mémoires*. Ed. Honore Bonhomme. 3 Vols. Paris, 1868.

Colson, Jean-Baptiste. *Manuel dramatique*. 3 Vols. Bordeaux, 1817.

———. *Répertoire du Théâtre-Français, ou details essentials sur 360 tragédies et comédies*. 3 Vols. Bordeaux, 1818.

Curzon, Henri de. "Etat sommaire des pièces et documents concernant le théâtre et la musique conservé aux archives nationales à Paris." *Bibliographe Moderne* I (1899), 52–83.

Dainville, François de. "Les Lieux d'affichage des comédiens à Paris en 1753." *Revue d'Histoire du Théâtre* III (1951), 248–60.

Danchin, Pierre. Review of Spire Pitou, *The Paris Opera* in *Theatre Survey* XXVI (1985), 90–93.

Dangeau, Marquis de (Philippe de Coucillon). *Journal*. Ed. E. Soulié and L. Dussieux. 19 Vols. Paris, 1854–1860.

Decugis, Nicole and Suzanne Reymond. *Le Décor de théâtre en France du moyen age à 1925*. Paris, 1953; London, 1954.

Deierkauf-Holsboer, S. Wilma. *Le Théâtre de l'Hôtel de Bourgogne*. 2 Vols. Paris, 1968–1970.

Desboulmiers, Jean-Auguste Julien, dit. *Histoire anecdotique et raisonnée du Théâtre Italien, depuis son rétablissement en France jusqu'à l'année 1769*. 7 Vols. Paris, 1769.

———. *Histoire du théâtre de l'Opéra-Comique*. 2 Vols. Paris, 1769.

Des Essarts, Nicolas Toussant. *La Comédie satirique au XVIIIe siècle. Histoire de la société française par l'allusion, la personalité et la satire au théâtre. Louis XV. Louis XVI. La Révolution*. Paris, 1885. [Reprinted 1970]

———. *Les Siècles littéraires de la France*. 7 Vols. Paris, 1800–1803.

———. *Les Trois Théâtres de Paris ou abrégé historique de l'établissement de la Comédie Françoise, de la Comédie Italienne et de l'Opéra*. Paris, 1777.

Desnoiresterres, Gustave. *La Comédie satirique au XVIIIe siècle*. Paris, 1885.

————. *Voltaire et la société française au XVIIIe siècle*. 8 Vols. Paris, 1867–1876.

Diderot, Denis. *Diderot et le théâtre*. Paris, 1984.

————. *Diderot's Writings on the Theatre*. Ed. F. C. Green. Cambridge, England, 1936.

————. *Encyclopédie ou Dictionnaire raisonné des sciences, des arts et des métiers*. 17 Vols. Paris, 1751–1765. *Plates*. 11 Vols. Paris, 1762–1772.

————. *Encyclopédie. Recueil de planches, sur les sciences, les arts liberaux, et les arts mechaniques, avec leur explication*. Vol. X. Paris, 1772. [Readex Compact Edition]

————. *Le Paradoxe sur le comédien*. Paris, 1830.

————. *The Paradox of Acting*. Tr. Walter Herries Pollock. New York, 1957.

Diderot, Denis and Jean le Rond d'Alembert. *Theatre Architecture and Stage Machines: Engravings from the "Encyclopedie, ou Dictionnaire raisonne des sciences, des arts, et des metiers."* New York and London, 1969.

Donnet, Alexis. *Architectonographie des théâtres de Paris ou parallel historique et critique de ces édifices*. Paris, 1821.

Dorfeuille, Pierre. *Les Elemens de l'art du comédien*. Paris, 1799.

Dubech, Lucien. *Histoire générale illustrée du théâtre*. 5 Vols. Paris, 1931–1934.

Dubos, Jean. *Réflexions critique sur la poésie et sur la peinture*. 2 Vols. Paris, 1719.

Duclos, Charles Pinot. *Mémoires pour servir à l'histoire des moeurs du XVIIIe siècle*. 2 Vols. Paris, 1751.

————. *Mémoires secrets sur les règnes de Louis XIV et de Louis XV*. Paris, 1790.

Dukore, Bernard F., ed. *Dramatic Theory and Criticism: Greeks to Grotowski*. New York, 1974.

Dumesnil, Marie Françoise. *Mémoires de Marie-Françoise Dumesnil, en réponse aux mémoires d'Hippolyte Clairon*. Paris, 1800.

Dumont, Gabriel Pierre Martin. *Parallèle de plans des plus belles salles de spectacles d'Italie et de France, avec des détails de machines theatrales*. New York, 1968. [ca. 1774]

Durey de Noinville, Jacques Bernard. *Histoire de théâtre de l'Académie Royale de musique en France depuis son etablissement jusqu'à présent*. Paris, 1753, 1757.

Essai d'une bibliographie générale du théâtre ou catalogue raisonné de la bibliothèque d'un amateur complétant le catalogue Soleinne. Paris, 1861. [Reprinted 1967]

Etienne, C. G., and A. Martainville. *Histoire du théâtre français depuis le commencement de la Révolution jusqu'à la réunion générale*. 4 Vols. Paris, 1802.

Faber, Frederic Jules. *Histoire du théâtre français en Belgique depuis son origine jusqu'à nos jours*. 5 Vols. Brussels, 1878–1880.

Favart, Charles Simon. *Mémoires et corréspondence littéraires, dramatiques et anecdotiques*. Ed. A.P.C. Favart. 3 Vols. Paris, 1808.

Fenelon, François de. *Lettre écrite a l'Académie Française*. In *Oeuvres*, Vol. I. Paris, 1822. [1714]

Fischer, Carlos. *Les Costumes de l'Opéra*. Paris, 1931.

Fleury, Abraham Joseph Bénard. *The French Stage and the French People as Illustrated in the Memoirs of M. Fleury*. Tr. Theodore Hook. 2 Vols. London, 1841.

————. *Mémoires de Fleury de la Comédie-Française, 1757 à 1820*. Ed. J.B.P. Lafitte. 6 Vols. Paris, 1836–1838.

Framery, Nicolas Étienne. *De l'Organisation des spectacles de Paris*. Paris, 1790.

Fransen, J. *Les Comédiens français en Hollande au XVIIe et au XVIIIe siècles*. Paris, 1925.

Fuchs, Max. *Lexique des troupes de comédiens au XVIIIe siècle*. Paris, 1944.

———. *La Vie théâtrale en province au XVIIIe siècle*. Paris, 1933. [Reprinted 1976]

Giraud, Yvres, ed. *La Vie théâtrale dans les provinces du midi*. Actes du 11e Colloque de Grasse, 1976. Tübingen and Paris, 1980.

Goldoni, Carlo. *Mémoires de Goldoni*. Preface Louis Jouvet. Intr. Marcel Lapierre. Paris, 1946.

———. *Mémoires pour servir à l'histoire de sa vie et a celle de son théâtre*. 3 Vols. Paris, 1787.

Grimarest, Jean Léonor de. *Traité du récitatif*. Paris, 1707.

Grimm, Baron von (Friedrich Melchior). *Corréspondence littéraire, philosophique et critique*. Ed. M. Tourneux. 16 Vols. Paris, 1677–1882.

Grimm, Johan Friedrich Karl. *Bemerkungen eines Reisenden durch Deutschland, Frankreich, England und Holland*. 3 Vols. Altenburg, 1775.

Grimod de la Reynière, A.B.L., ed. *Le Censeur dramatique, ou Journal des principaux théâtres de Paris et des départements*. 4 Vols. Paris, 1797–1798.

Gueullette, Thomas Simon. *Notes et souvenirs sur le Théâtre Italien au XVIIIe siècle*. Ed. J. E. Gueullette. Paris, 1938.

Gueullette, Thomas Simon, ed. *Théâtre des boulevards ou Recueil des parades*. 3 Vols. Paris, 1756.

Hallays-Dabot, Victor. *Histoire de la censure théâtrale en France*. Paris, 1862.

Hawkins, Frederick. *The French Stage in the Eighteenth Century*. 2 Vols. London, 1888. [Reprinted 1969]

Isherwood, Robert. "Entertainment in the Parisian Fairs in the Eighteenth Century." *Journal of Modern History* LIII (1981), 24–48.

Japy, André. *L'Opéra Royal de Versailles*. Versailles, 1958.

Jeudwine, Wynne. *Stage Designs*. London, 1968.

Joannides, A. *La Comédie-Française de 1680 à 1920*. Préface Jules Claretie. Paris, 1921. [First edition 1901]

Jourdain, Eleanor F. *Dramatic Theory and Practice in France 1690–1808*. New York, 1921. [Reprinted 1968]

Jullien, Adolphe. *La Comédie à la cour. Les Théâtres de société royale pendant le siècle dernier*. Paris, 1883.

———. *La Comédie de la cour de Louis XVI. Le Théâtre de la Reine à Trianon*. Paris, 1875.

———. *La Cour et l'opéra sous Louis XVI*. Paris, 1878.

———. *Histoire du costume au théâtre, depuis les origines du théâtre en France jusqu'à nos jours*. Paris, 1880.

———. *Histoire du théâtre de Madame de Pompadour dit Théâtre des petits cabinets* [Paris, 1874]; *Les Grands nuits de sceaux: Le Théâtre de la Duchesse du Maine d'après des documents inédits* [Paris, 1876]; *L'Opéra secret au XVIII siècle (1770–1790): Aventures et intrigues secrètes racontées d'après les papiers inédits conservés aux archives de l'état et de l'opéra* [Paris, 1880]. Geneva, 1978.

Kaufmann, Emil. *Architecture in the Age of Reason: Baroque and Post-Baroque in England, Italy, and France*. Cambridge, Mass., 1955.

Kennard, Joseph Spencer. *Goldoni and the Venice of His Time*. New York, 1920.

Kindermann, Heinz. *Theatergeschichte Europas*. Vol. IV: *Von der aufklarung zur romantik* (Part 1). Salzburg, 1961.

Lacroix, Paul [P. L. Jacob]. *Bibliothèque dramatique de M. de Soleinne*. 6 Vols. Paris, 1843–1844.

Lacroix, Paul, and Charles Nodier. *Bibliothèque de M. Guilbert de Pixérécourt avec des notes littéraires et bibliographiques*. Paris, 1838.

La Dixmerie, Nicolas Bricaire de. *Lettres sur l'état présent de nos spectacles*. Amsterdam and Paris, 1765.

Lagrave, Henri. "La Saison 1772–1773 au Théâtre de Bordeaux: études du répertoire." In *La Vie théâtrale dans les provinces du midi*. Actes du 11o Colloque de Grasse, 1976. Ed. Yves Giraud. Tübingen and Paris, 1980.

———. *Le Théâtre et le public à Paris de 1715 à 1750*. Paris, 1972.

La Harpe, Jean François de. *Correspondence littéraire*. 6 Vols. Paris, 1801–1807.

———. *Le Lycée, ou Cours de littérature ancienne et moderne*. 14 Vols. Paris, 1818.

Lancaster, Henry Carrington. *The Comédie Française 1680–1701: Plays, Actors, Spectators, Finances*. Baltimore, 1941.

———. *The Comédie Française 1701–1774: Plays, Actors, Spectators, Finances*. Transactions of the American Philosophical Society, n.s., Vol. 41, Part 4. Philadelphia, 1951.

———. *French Tragedy in the Reign of Louis XVI and the Early Years of the French Revolution, 1774–1792*. Baltimore, 1953.

———. *French Tragedy in the Time of Louis XV and Voltaire, 1715–1774*. Baltimore, 1950.

———. *Sunset: A History of Parisian Drama in the Last Years of Louis XV, 1701–1715*. Baltimore, 1945.

La Porte, Abbé Joseph de. *Almanach historique et chronologique de tous les spectacles*. Paris, 1752.

———. *Calendrier historique des théâtres de l'opéra et des comédies françoise et italiennes et des foires*. Paris, 1753.

———. *Les Spectacles de Paris, ou Suite du calendrier historique et chronologique des théâtres*. 27 Vols. Paris, 1754–1778.

La Porte, Abbé Joseph de, and Jean Marie Bernard Clement. *Anecdotes dramatiques*. 3 Vols. Paris, 1775.

La Porte, Abbé Joseph de, and S.R.N. Chamfort. *Dictionnaire dramatique, contenant l'histoire des théâtres*. 3 Vols. Paris, 1776.

La Rive, Jean Marie Maudit de. *Moyens de négénérer les théâtres, de leur rendre leur moralité et d'assurer l'etat de tous les comédiens, sans dépenses pour le gouvernement*. Paris, 1806.

———. *Réflexions sur l'art théâtrale*. Paris, an IX [1801].

La Vallière, Duc de. *Bibliothèque du théâtre françois depuis son origine*. 3 Vols. Dresden, 1768.

Lavoisier, Antoine Laurent. "Mémoire sur la manière d'eclairer les salles de spectacles." In *Oeuvres*, Vol. III. Paris, 1865.

Leclerc, Hélène. "Au Théâtre de Besançon (1775–1784)." *Revue d'Histoire du Théâtre* X (1958), 103–27.

———. "Les Bibiena: Une dynastie de scenographes baroques." *Revue d'Histoire du Théâtre* XXIII (1971), 7–39.

———. "Les Indes Galantes (1735–1952)." *Revue d'Histoire du Théâtre* V (1953), 259–85.

Le Couvreur, Adrienne. *Lettres de Adrienne Le Couvreur.* Ed. Georges Monval. Paris, 1892.

Ledoux, Claude-Nicolas. *L'Architecture sous le rapport de l'art, des moeurs et de la législation.* Paris, 1804.

Lekain, Henri Louis. *Mémoires de Lekain, précédé de réflexions sur cet acteur, et sur l'art théâtral, par M. Talma.* Paris, 1825.

Lemazurier, Pierre David. *Galérie historique des acteurs du Théâtre Français, depuis 1600 jusqu'à nos jours.* 2 Vols. Paris, 1810.

Léris, Antoine de. *Dictionnaire portatif, historique et littéraire des théâtres.* Paris, 1754; 2d ed. 1763.

Le Sage, Alain René, and d'Orneval. *Le Théâtre de la foire ou l'opéra comique.* 10 Vols. Paris, 1721–1737.

Levacher de Charnois, Jean Charles. *Costumes et Annales des Grands Théâtres de Paris.* 4 Vols. Paris, 1786–1789. [Periodical]

———. *Recherches sur les costumes et sur les théâtres de toutes les nations, tant anciennes que moderne.* 2 Vols. in 1. Paris, 1790; 2d ed. 1802.

Liebrecht, Henri. *Histoire du théâtre français à Bruxelles au XVIIe et au XVIIIe siècle.* Paris, 1923.

Lintilhac, Eugene. *Histoire générale du théâtre en France.* 5 Vols. Paris, 1904–1910.

Longchamp, S. G., and Wagnière. *Mémoires sur Voltaire et ses ouvrages, par L. et W., ses secretaires.* 2 Vols. Paris, 1826.

Lough, John. *An Introduction to Eighteenth Century France.* New York, 1960.

———. *Paris Theatre Audiences in the Seventeenth and Eighteenth Centuries.* London, 1957.

Louis, Louis Nicolas (Victor). *Salle de spectacle de Bordeaux.* Paris, 1782.

Luynes, Duc de (Charles Philippe d'Albert). *Mémoires sur la cour de Louis XV (1735–1758).* Ed. L. Dussieux and E. Soulié. 17 Vols. Paris, 1860–1865.

Mantzius, Karl. *A History of Theatrical Art.* Tr. Louise Cossel. 6 Vols. New York, 1936.

Marais, Mathieu. *Journal et mémories.* Ed. M.F.A. de Lescure. 4 Vols. Paris, 1863–1868.

Marie, Alfred. "La Salle de théâtre du château de Fontainbleau." *Revue d'Histoire du Théâtre* III (1951), 237–47.

———. "Les Théâtres du château de Versailles." *Revue d'Histoire du Théâtre* III (1951), 133–52.

Marmontel, Jean François. *Eléments de littérature.* In *Oeuvres complètes*, Vol. IV. Paris, 1819–1820. [1787]

———. *Mémoires d'un père.* In *Oeuvres complètes*, Vol. I. Paris, 1819–1820. [1787]

———. *Oeuvres complètes.* 7 Vols. Paris, 1819–1820. [1787]

Mastropasqua, Fernando. *Le feste della Rivoluzione Francese 1790–1794.* Milan, 1976.

Matthews, Brander, ed. *Papers on Acting.* Preface Henry W. Wells. New York, 1958.

Maupoint. *Bibliotèque [sic] des théâtres, contenant le catalogue alphabetique de pièces dramatiques, opéra, & opéra comique; & le tems de leurs réprésentations.* Paris, 1733.

Melcher, Edith. *Stage Realism in France Between Diderot and Antoine.* Bryn Mawr, Penn., 1928. [Reprinted 1976]

Mélèse, Pierre. *Le Théâtre et le public à Paris sous Louis XIV (1659–1713).* Paris, 1934.

Mercier, Louis Sébastien. *De la Littérature et des littératures.* Yverdon, 1778.

———. *Du Théâtre, ou Nouvel Essai sur l'art dramatique.* Amsterdam, 1773.

————. *The Picture of Paris Before and After the Revolution*. Tr. Wilfrid and Emilie Jackson. London, 1929.

————. *Tableau de Paris*. Nouvelle edition. 12 Vols. Amsterdam, 1782–1788. [Reprinted 1979]

————. *The Waiting City: Paris 1782–88*. Tr. Helen Simpson. London, 1933.

Mittman, Barbara. "Cinq documents partant sur l'enceinte de la balustrade de l'Ancienne Comédie." *Revue d'Histoire du Théâtre* XXXV (1983), 174–89.

————. *Spectators on the Paris Stage in the Seventeenth and Eighteenth Centuries*. Ann Arbor, Mich., 1984.

Molinari, Cesare. *Theatre Through the Ages*. Tr. Colin Hamer. London, 1975.

Monval, Georges. *Les Collections de la Comédie-Française, catalogue historique et raisonné*. Préface Jules Claretie. Paris, 1897.

Mouhy, Chevalier de (Charles de Fieux). *Abrégé de l'histoire du Théâtre-Français*. 4 Vols. Paris, 1780–1783.

————. *Tablettes dramatiques, contenant l'abrégé de l'histoire du Théâtre-Français, l'établissement des théâtres à Paris, un dictionnaire des pièces et l'abrégé de l'histoire des auteurs et des acteurs*. Paris, 1752.

Mullin, Donald C. *The Development of the Playhouse: a Survey of Theatre Architecture from the Renaissance to the Present*. Berkeley and Los Angeles, 1970.

Nagler, A. M., ed. *A Source Book in Theatrical History*. New York, 1959.

Naudet, Georges. "Les Costumes de Le Kain en 1775." *Revue d'Histoire du Théâtre* II (1950), 463–67.

Niklaus, Robert. *A Literary History of France: The Eighteenth Century 1715–1789*. Gen. Ed., P. E. Charvet. London and New York, 1970.

Nougaret, Pierre Jean Baptiste. *De l'Art du théâtre en général*. 2 Vols. Paris, 1769.

————. *Les Spectacles de foires et des boulevards de Paris [Almanach forain]*. 8 Vols. Paris, 1773–1788.

Nouveau recueil choisi et mêlé des meilleures pièces du théâtre françois et italien. 8 Vols. The Hague and Utrecht, 1733–1743.

Noverre, Jean George. *Letters on Dancing and Ballets*. Tr. Cyril W. Beaumont. London, 1930. [1760]

————. *Lettres sur la danse et sur les ballets*. Paris, 1760.

Oenslager, Donald. *Stage Design: Four Centuries of Scenic Invention*. New York, 1975.

Ogden, Dunbar. *The Italian Baroque Stage: Documents by Giulio Troili, Andrea Pozzo, Ferdinando Galli-Bibiena, Baldassare Orsini*. Berkeley, 1978.

Origny, Abraham Jean Baptiste Antoine d'. *Annales du Théâtre Italien, depuis son origine jusqu'à ce jour*. 3 Vols. Paris, 1788.

Parfaict, Claude, and Godin d'Abguerbe. *Dictionnaire des théâtres de Paris*. 7 Vols. Paris, 1756. [Edition of 1767–1770 reprinted 1967]

Parfaict, François. *Agendas historiques et chronologiques des théâtres de Paris*. 3 Vols. Paris, 1876. [1735–1737]

Parfaict, Francois and Claude. *Histoire de l'ancien Théâtre Italien depuis son origine en France, jusqu'à sa suppression en l'année 1697*. Paris, 1753.

————. *Histoire du Théâtre Français depuis son origine jusqu'à present*. 15 Vols. Paris, 1735–1749. [Reprinted 1967]

————. *Mémoires pour servir à l'histoire des spectacles de la foire par un acteur forain*. 2 Vols. Paris, 1743.

Pariset, François Georges, ed. *Victor Louis 1731–1800: Dessins et gravures*. Bordeaux, 1980.

Patte, Pierre. *Essai sur l'architecture théâtrale*. Paris, 1782. [Reprinted 1974]

Pennington, Thomas. *Continental Excursions: or Tours into France, Switzerland and Germany in 1782, 1787, and 1789*. 2 Vols. London, 1809.

Petitot, C. B., ed. *Répertoire du Théâtre Français*. 23 Vols. Paris, 1803–1804. 50 Vols. 1813; 25 Vols. 1817; *Supplément* 8 Vols. 1819–1820.

Peyronnet, Pierre. *La Mise en scène au XVIIIe siècle*. Paris, 1974.

Pitou, Spire. *The Paris Opera: An Encyclopedia of Operas, Ballets, Composers, and Performers. Genesis and Glory, 1671–1715*. Westport, Conn., 1983.

———. *The Paris Opera: An Encyclopedia of Operas, Ballets, Composers, and Performers: Rococo and Romantic, 1715–1815*. Westport, Conn., 1985.

Posner, Donald. *Antoine Watteau*. Ithaca, N.Y., 1984.

Pougin, Arthur. *Un Directeur d'opéra au dix-huitième siècle*. Paris, 1914.

———. *L'Opéra-Comique pendant la Révolution, de 1788 à 1801*. Paris, 1891.

Pozzo, Andrea. *Rules and Examples of Perspective*. Tr. John James. London, 1707.

Rétif de la Bretonne, Nicolas Edme. *La Mimographe*. Présentation de Martine de Rougemont. Paris and Geneva, 1980.

———. *La Mimographe, ou Idées d'une honnête femme pour la réformation du théâtre national*. Amsterdam, 1770.

Riccoboni, François. *L'Art du théâtre*. Paris, 1750.

Riccoboni, Luigi. *De la réformation du théâtre*. Paris, 1747.

———. *Dell'arte rappresentativa*. London, 1728.

———. *A General History of the Stage*. 2nd ed. London, 1754. [Reprinted 1978]

———. *An Historical and Critical Account of the Theatres in Europe*. London, 1741.

———. *Réflexions historiques et critiques sur les différents théâtres de l'Europe*. Paris, 1738.

Riccoboni, Luigi, ed. *Le Nouveau Théâtre Italien ou Recueil général de toutes les pièces représentées par les comédiens de S.A.R. Mgr. le duc d'Orléans*. 10 Vols. Paris, 1751. [Earlier editions 1716, 1718, 1725, 1729, and 1733]

Rondel, Auguste. *La Bibliographie dramatique et les collections de théâtres en France*. Firenze, 1914.

———. *Les Bibliothèques dramatiques et les collections de théâtre*. Lille, 1913.

Root-Bernstein, Michèle. *Boulevard Theater and Revolution in Eighteenth-Century Paris*. Ann Arbor, Mich., 1984.

Roubo, André Jacob. *Traité de la construction des théâtres et des machines théâtrales*. Paris, 1777.

Rousseau, Jean Jacques. *Lettre à M. D'Alembert sur son article Genève*. Ed. Michel Launay. Paris, 1967. [1758]

———. *Politics and the Arts: Letter to M. d'Alembert on the Theatre*. Tr. Allan Bloom. Ithaca, N.Y., 1968.

Sainte-Albine, Pierre Rémond de. *Le Comédien*. Paris, 1749.

Saint-Pierre, Abbé Charles Irénée de. "Projet pour rendre les spectacles plus utile a l'état." In *Oeuvres diverses*, Vol. II. Paris, 1728–1730.

Saint-Simon, Duc de (Louis de Rouvroy). *Mémoires*. Ed. A. de Boislisle. 43 Vols. Paris, 1879–1930.

———. *The Memoirs of the Duke of Saint-Simon on the Reign of Louis XIV and the Regency*. Tr. Bayle St. John. 2 Vols. New edition. New York, 1936.

Saunders, George. *A Treatise on Theatres*. London, 1790. [Reprinted 1968]
Sauval, Henri. *Histoire et recherches des antiquités de la ville de Paris*. 3 Vols. Paris, 1724.
Scholz, János, ed. *Baroque and Romantic Stage Design*. Intr. A. Hyatt Mayor. New York, 1949. [Reprinted 1962]
Servandoni, Jean Nicolas, dit Hannetaire. *Observations sur l'art du comédien, et sur d'autres objets concernant le théâtre en général*. Paris, 1764, 1775.
States, Bert O. "Servandoni et la Salle des Machines." *Revue d'Histoire du Théâtre* XIII (1961), 42–44.
Steinhauser, Monika, and Daniel Rabreau. "Le Théâtre de l'Odéon de Charles de Wailly et Marie-Joseph Peyre, 1767–1782." *Revue de l'Art* XIX (1973), 9–49.
Sticotti, Antonio Fabio. *Garrick ou les acteurs anglais*. Paris, 1769.
Théâtre françois, ou Recueil des meilleures pièces de théâtre. 12 Vols. Paris, 1737.
Ulriksen, Solveig Schult. "Le Théâtre parisien en 1788, vu par trois acteurs danois." *Revue d'Histoire du Théâtre* XXXIV (1982), 169–85.
Veinstein, André, and Alfred S. Golding, eds. *Bibliothèques et musées des arts du spectacle dans le monde./Performing Arts Libraries and Museums of the World*. 3d ed. Paris, 1984.
Verlet, Pierre. "Gabriel et la construction de l'Opéra de Versailles." *Le Jardin des Arts* XXXIII (1957), 555–61.
———. "L'Opéra de Versailles." *Revue d'Histoire du Théâtre* IX (1957), 133–54.
Vince, Ronald W. *Renaissance Theatre: A Historiographical Handbook*. Westport, Conn., and London, 1984.
Voltaire [François Marie Arouet]. *Oeuvres complètes*. Ed. Louis Moland. 52 Vols. Paris, 1877–1885.
———. *Voltaire's Correspondence*. Ed. T. Besterman. 107 Vols. Geneva, 1953–1965. 2d ed. 135 Vols. Geneva, 1968–1977.
———. *Voltaire's Notebooks*. Ed. T. Besterman. 2 Vols. Geneva, 1952.
Welschinger, Henri. *Le Théâtre de la Révolution 1789–1799, avec documents inédits*. Paris, 1880. [Reprinted 1968]

THE THEATRE OF EIGHTEENTH-CENTURY ITALY

INTRODUCTION

Theatre historians have seldom been able to find a satisfactory unifying theme in the history of the Italian stage in the eighteenth century and have usually turned instead to the elucidation of a particular aspect of the Italian theatrical world: scene and stage design, the opera, Carlo Goldoni's "reform" of the commedia dell'arte, or the beginnings of a national drama in the work of Scipione Maffei, Vittorio Alfieri, Goldoni, and Carlo Gozzi. The difficulties of providing a single comprehensive picture are compounded by the political and cultural diversity among a people characterized by local loyalties and dominated by Hapsburg emperors. Only republican Venice could make any claim to being a cultural and theatrical capital comparable to Paris or London. But whatever the focus, the tendency is to center discussion on particular figures: the Bibiena family, for instance, for scene design; Metastasio for opera; Goldoni and Gozzi for comedy; Maffei and Alfieri for tragedy.

Thus Jean C. L. Simonde de Sismondi, in his *Historical View of the Literature of the South of Europe* first published in 1846, praises Metastasio as "the most pleasing, and the least difficult of the Italian poets" (I, 506); refers to Goldoni as the reformer "whose genius was capable of making a stronger impression [than lesser writers] on the minds of his countrymen" (I, 516); and writes of Alfieri that his creation of "a new Italian drama . . . is a phenomenon which strikes us with astonishment" (I, 569). (Nearly a century later, Joseph Kennard organized *The Italian Theatre* [1932] around the same dramatists, adding only Carlo Gozzi to the list.) However, when Simonde de Sismondi goes on, in the same breath, to describe Alfieri both as sharing characteristics with the great French tragic writers and as being "wholly Italian in his genius" (I, 570), he introduces two issues central to the historiography of the Italian theatre. The first concerns the interpretation of the theatre in terms of the national genius of the Italian people; the second deals with the nature and value of the influence of the neoclassical drama of France on the theatrical expression of that genius. What composes the genius of Italy? And what sort of theatre most accurately exemplifies it? How crucial to the development of Italian drama was the French influence, and was it beneficial or harmful?

The questions are in fact inextricably linked, although few historians have been able to juxtapose French influence and Italian genius with the bland indifference illustrated by Simonde de Sismondi. Nor have they been able to identify so unequivocally the "true" national theatre of Italy. The English writer Violet Paget, who wrote under the name Vernon Lee, tried later in the nineteenth century to provide a key to the understanding of eighteenth-century Italian theatre by identifying music as the central theatrical art. *Studies of the Eighteenth Century in Italy* (1880, 1887) is not an easy book to evaluate. The writing is often precious, the arguments sometimes confused and inconsistent, but the observations are occasionally very penetrating and for English readers, at least, shed much-needed light on "this obscure period." "Italy in the last century," wrote the author, "got her drama and her comedy neither from Paris nor from London, but from her own intellectual soil, where they had been germinating for centuries," and produced "a drama as national as the English drama of the days of Shakespeare and the Spanish drama of the days of Lope de Vega" (pp. 3–4). The drama to which Vernon Lee refers is, of course, the opera, which she interprets as the natural product of native spontaneity:

The opera, as elaborated by Apostolo Zeno and perfected by Metastasio, is not a classical production like the French and Italian tragedy . . . : it is . . . a romantic product, born unnoticed by the learned and suffered to grow up unmolested by them, and only given an outer semblance of classic correctness when already fully and individually developed. [p. 165]

The other natural form, the commedia dell'arte, had by the eighteenth century begun to lose its power:

The life of the style was fast ebbing; no new types appeared; the old became stereotyped; the jokes and gestures and acrobatic feats became traditional; the Comedy of Masks began to be considered as legitimately enthroned as perpetual sovereign of the Italian comic stage; its days of battle and adventure were over. [p. 244]

Still, there was enough life left in the old form to provide the basis for the development of Goldoni's comic genius, which remained spontaneous and true to its origins until the playwright was goaded into suppressing all improvisation and rejecting the masks, "into appealing to French models with which his own style had nothing in common" (p. 269). For Vernon Lee, "the great Venetian comic writer" died with Goldoni's abandonment of his native land in 1760 and his transformation into the Italian Molière. In the final analysis, opera was the "national and spontaneous" drama of Italy. Save for the young Goldoni all else was academic, artificial, "pseudo-classic and eclectic" (p. 4), in the neoclassical mold of "the too eloquent Racine or the overwitty Molière" (p. 40).

Twentieth-century historians have explored similar issues but with a lesser tendency to French-bashing and in terms less emotion-laden. In *The Italian Stage from Goldoni to D'Annunzio* (1981), for instance, Marvin Carlson explains the famous quarrels between Goldoni and Pietro Chiari and later between Goldoni and Gozzi during the 1750s as part of a general struggle during the eighteenth century between those who cherished the native theatrical traditions exemplified in the commedia dell'arte (the conservatives) and those who looked to French precepts and models in their efforts to revitalize the Italian theatre (the liberals). According to this interpretation, which enjoys a general currency, the emergence near the end of the century of Alfieri as the great Italian tragedian is traceable to the efforts of earlier writers, such as Pier Jacopo Martelli and especially Scipione Maffei, to impose a neoclassical structure on tragedy. Opera was rescued from garish spectacle by the liberals' insistence on a literate and informing text, the result of which were Metastasio's librettos. Goldoni's reforms place him in the liberal camp, while Gozzi—whose plays did not, in the view of Simonde de Sismondi, "represent the national spirit of the Italian people" (I, 539) and whom Vernon Lee describes as "whimsical, sentimental, metaphysical" (p. 275)—becomes the conservative champion of traditional Italian theatre. Which is the "national and spontaneous" theatre here, and which the "pseudo-classic and eclectic"?

The surface similarity between modern and nineteenth-century concerns, however, should not blind us to important differences. Vernon Lee's work is the product of a nineteenth-century aestheticism, a movement that was itself the product of post-romantic assumptions concerning spontaneity and that was contemptuous of what it viewed as the artificiality of neoclassicism. Carlson, on the other hand, bases his analysis on what eighteenth-century Italians themselves thought, and finds in their numerous writings the stuff of their theatrical history and the evidence for its interpretation. He thus includes in his examination of the period, besides playtexts, various pamphlets and pastiches, memoirs and letters, travellers' accounts and commentaries, journals and the proceedings of sundry societies and academies that sprang up at intervals during the century. In the process, he has occasion to refer to theatres, acting companies, and audiences—subjects pretty much ignored by nineteenth-century scholarship.

Still, the overall thrust of Carlson's study follows earlier lines of exposition in its emphasis on Gozzi, Alfieri, and especially Goldoni as the founders of a truly Italian repertory. (Carlson is interested primarily in the spoken drama as opposed to the opera.) Giuseppe Guerzoni, for instance, in *Il teatro italiano nel secolo XVIII* (1876) concentrates almost exclusively on in-depth discussions of the works of Metastasio, Goldoni, and Alfieri, differing from Carlson and other modern historians only in what strikes us as a disproportionate emphasis on the tragedian. (Fully one-half of the book's 670 pages are devoted to Alfieri.) A similar emphasis on playwrights and plays is evident in Ernesto Masi's *Studi sulla storia del teatro italiano nel secolo XVIII* (1891) and in the more specialized study by A. Galletti, *Le teorie drammatiche e la tragedia in Italia nel secolo XVIII* (1901). In fact, so far as the regular drama is concerned, there has been little of historiographical interest added in the twentieth century. A recent collection of papers originally presented at Fontainbleau in 1982 explores the relationship of the Italian theatre during the seventeenth and eighteenth centuries to that of the rest of Europe as part of what we might call the new internationalism. (See Christian Bec and Irene Mamczarz, eds., *Le Théâtre italien et l'Europe*.) But otherwise, scholars have turned instead to the study of theatre architecture and scenography.

The discussion that follows sketches and evaluates the principal evidence for the study of Italy's contributions to world theatre in the four areas by which she is best known: Venetian comedy, the opera, theatre architecture, and scene design.

WRITTEN EVIDENCE

Tragedy and Neoclassic Theory

During the last decade of the seventeenth century, a group of like-minded reformers in Rome founded the Arcadian Academy, ostensibly devoted to *semplicitá* ("simplicity"), but in practical terms determined to "purify" the opera and reinstitute tragedy in the light of neoclassical precept and French example. One of the founders of the Arcadian Academy, Giovanni Maria Crescimbeni (1663–1728), in 1700 wrote *La Bellezza della volgar poesie,* in which he castigated the irregularities and extravagances of seventeenth-century opera for the breakdown of the classical genres of tragedy and comedy. Another founder, Gianvencenzo Gravina (1664–1718)—perhaps best known as the discover and patron of Pietro Trapassi, whom he renamed Metastasio—in his *Della tragedia* (1712) called for a return to the neo-Aristotelian unities. Scipio Maffei (1675–1765), the author of the successful tragedy *Merope* (1713), and Apostolo Zeno (1669–1750), who established the conventions of the *opera seria,* collaborated in the founding of the *Giornale dei Letterati d'Italia* (1710), a journal similarly dedicated to neoclassical principles. Metastasio too at the end of his life felt compelled to write a commentary on Aristotle (1782), and even Alfieri commented on dramatic theory and especially on tragedy in his autobiography (1804) and in his miscellaneous writings. From a strictly theoretical standpoint, none of these treatises or commentaries is of great importance, and they are unlikely to be conveniently anthologized or even discussed in standard histories of criticism, but the historian who neglects such work risks misinterpreting the genesis and thrust of theatrical reform in eighteenth-century Italy.

Comic Controversy

For most students of the theatre, eighteenth-century Italian comedy means Goldoni and his theatrical wars with Chiari and Gozzi. Thus the plays, librettos, letters, pamphlets, and prologues from the turbulent 1750s have been searched out and analyzed and the story told many times over. (Goldoni House in Venice holds twenty thousand works pertaining to Goldoni; the theatre museum at La Scala holds many of his letters.) The quarrel was truly literary and theatrical. In 1749 Chiari parodied Goldoni's *La vedova scaltra* (*The Cunning Widow*) with *La scuola delle vedove* (*The School for Widows*). Goldoni immediately replied in a pamphlet. He describes in his memoirs how he shut himself up in his room and wrote until he felt himself avenged. Three thousand copies of his *Apologetical Prologue to 'The Cunning Widow'* were subsequently distributed, with the result that Chiari's piece was suppressed and the government instituted theatrical licensing. Still in a pique, Goldoni promised to write sixteen new plays for the 1751 season. The first of them was *Il teatro comico*, performed in 1751 at the Teatro San Angelo. The setting is the rehearsal of another play, and the dramatist used the opportunity to present his ideas about comic drama. (He intended, he reports in his *Mémoires*, to place it at the head of a new edition of his plays, in itself an indication of the close connection in Goldoni's mind between the play as performed and the play as printed—an important consideration for the theatre historian.) Later, in a mock almanac, *La Tartana degli influssi* (1757), Gozzi attacked both Chiari and Goldoni as charlatans, interested in controversy merely for financial gain. Goldoni replied in a poem. And so the quarrel continued, in "a snowstorm of pamphlets, epistles, poems and plays spreading across literary Europe so that in Paris Voltaire came to Goldoni's defense and in London Guiseppe Baretti . . . championed Gozzi" (Carlson, *The Italian Stage*, p. 12). Nevertheless, the principal sources of information concerning the Goldoni-Gozzi controversy are the memoirs that each of the antagonists produced near the end of his life. Indeed, even without the contemporary documentation noted above, it is possible to reconstruct the substance of the quarrel, and the personal and ideological bases for it, from these two autobiographical works.

The Memoirs of Goldoni and Gozzi

Goldoni wrote his *Mémoires*—in French—at Versailles between 1783 and 1787, thirty years after the eventful decade of the 1750s. He discusses his life and career in three stages: the early years to 1747; the years in Venice, 1747–1762; and the years in France, 1762–1787. Later research has shown the *Mémoires* to be contradictory and occasionally inaccurate so far as precise detail is concerned, but possibly a greater disappointment evolves from the author's reluctance or inability to deal with anything but surface events, and even on this level to shy away from controversy. Rather than naming names and recounting quarrels, Goldoni delights in his successes in Venice and then passes quietly into France. The events are alluded to, but seldom do we get a sense of the intensity of the theatrical world. We do get a sense of a busy playwright and of a thriving commercial theatre, but the author is vague and inoffensive where we might have expected—and preferred—precision and passion.

In retrospect, at least Goldoni had some notion of his own role in the development of the Italian theatre. Noting his return to Venice in 1747 to write for the Medebac company, he comments: "I had there lain [*sic*] the foundation of an Italian theatre, and it was there I intended to labour in the construction of that new edifice" (Black translation, p. 234). He also realized that his most significant contribution to Italian comedy was the suppression of the masks. He acknowledged their antiquity, and that of the *commedia improvviso*, indeed he claimed to possess a fifteenth-century manuscript containing 120 *scenari* calling for the traditional masks (a manuscript about which we know nothing). But things had changed: "The mask must always be very prejudicial to the action of the performer. . . . He can never convey by the countenance, which is the interpreter of the heart, the different passions with which he is inwardly agitated. . . . The actor must, in our days, possess a soul; and the soul under a mask is like a fire under ashes" (p. 300). Besides his successes, his unnamed enemies, and his reform of comedy, Goldoni turns often to the printing of his plays—a concern that both editors and historians must take into account when trying to determine the acted version of a play. For instance, having encountered difficulties with his one-time theatrical manager Girolamo Medebac and his publisher Bettinelli—"I had . . . to contend against the director, who contested the right of property of my pieces, and against the bookseller, who was empowered to publish them" (pp. 281–82)—Goldoni published his own edition and, to foil Medebac and Bettinelli, announced several corrections and alterations that *their* versions would not have. Which version approximates the acted text?

In his *Memorie inutile* (1797–1798), Goldoni's rival Carlo Gozzi exhibits none of the former's bland reticence, and while undoubtedly intending the work as a literary monument to himself, offers a close and detailed description of his long association with the acting troupe of Antonio Sacchi, an association that spanned forty years. And it is this narrative, rather than Gozzi's reflections on Chiari and Goldoni, that makes his work particularly valuable for students of the eighteenth-century theatre. Nevertheless, the comments on his rivals are sharp enough, and are the most easily remembered. He describes the Chiari-Goldoni quarrel as a "whirlwind of comedies, tragi-comedies, and tragedies, composts of imperfections . . . a diarrhea of dramatic works, romances, critical epistles, poems, cantatas, and apologies" (*Useless Memoirs*, ed. Philip Horne, p. 169). Of Chiari he wrote: "In him I found a brain inflamed, disordered, bold to rashness, and pedantic. . . . I found him one of the most turgid, most inflated, nay, the most turgid, the most inflated, of this century" (p. 71). Goldoni comes off little better. He had, writes Gozzi, "an abundance of comic motives, truth, and naturalness":

Yet I detected a poverty and meanness of intrigue; nature copied from the fact, not imitated; virtues and vices ill-adjusted, vice too frequently triumphant; plebeian phrases of low double meaning . . . ; surcharged characters; scraps and tags of erudition, stolen Heaven knows where, and clumsily brought in to impose upon the crowd of ignoramuses. Finally, as a writer of Italian . . . he seemed to me not unworthy to be placed among the dullest, basest, and least correct authors who have used our idiom. [1890 ed., pp. 169–70]

(We might remember Goldoni's comment in his *Mémoires*: "I was perpetually reproached with the original sin of Venetianism," p. 312.)

It is comments of this sort, together with Gozzi's admittedly less-than-attractive relationships with women, that have given the *Memorie inutile* a bad name. But Gozzi has other strikes against him as well. Historically, he is a figure of reaction, opposed to the reforms that historians later approved of. His autobiography was apparently undertaken as a defense against the attacks of Antonio Gatarol, an exiled Venetian diplomat, and is consequently viewed as self-serving and unreliable. His English translator, John Addington Symonds, made no attempt to conceal his contempt for the man and his work. These are the unscholarly prejudices that must be overcome if Gozzi's *Memorie inutile* is to receive just treatment as a document of theatre history.

Contemporary History and Commentary

We are here concerned with a miscellany of writings by theatre professionals, casual observers, theorists, historians, *literati*, and foreign visitors. As varied in tone and treatment as such sources are, they have served, together with the memoirs of Goldoni and Gozzi, as the focal points for reconstructions of eighteenth-century Italian theatrical life. A constant motif is the need for theatrical reform—reform of opera, reform of tragedy, reform of comedy.

Benedetto Marcello's *Il teatro alla moda* (1720), for instance, is a small gem of a book, by an author who was a musician and composer as well as a Venetian judge. It offers a tongue-in-cheek, mildly satirical picture of the musical theatre of the time, ridiculing the pretentions of the *virtuosi*, the poets, the composers, and above all the singers, whose tyrannies cow both the composer (who tailors the aria to the singer) and the director (whose lack of control matters little given that he is both deaf and dumb). (An English translation of *Il teatro alla moda* appears in *Musical Quarterly*, 1948–1949.) The unhappy relationship among poet, composer, and performers was a constant theme among those who would reform the opera. It is also a prime concern of Francesco Algarotti, in *Saggio sopra l'opere in musica* (1755; English tr. 1767), a book that became the reformer's bible and anticipated Gluck's famous preface to *Alceste* (1769), in which the subjugation of music to poetry formed the basis of a new operatic aesthetic.

So far as the commedia dell'arte and the regular theatre were concerned, the parameters of subsequent discussion were set out by Luigi Riccoboni in his *Histoire du théâtre italien* (1730–1731), in which the author advocates the "re-

gularizing'' of the traditional improvised comedy by providing the actors with
written texts:

During the entire sixteenth century, until the beginning of the seventeenth we see two
different theatres: the one taken up by the professional players, who played *impromptu*
with Arlequino and the other masked actors: and the other taken up by the academicians,
who acted regular written dramas, which sometimes passed to the theatre of the professional actors. At the beginning of the seventeenth century the decadence of *belles lettres*
in Italy brought about the decline of good [i.e. regular] theatre, and the professional
players, who had never abandoned their improvisation and their masked actors, surren-
dered themselves to the corruption, in separating tragedy and regular comedy from their
theatre. Towards the end of the seventeenth century and the beginning of the eighteenth
an attempt was made to rehabilitate the Italian theatre, by restoring tragedy and regular
comedy; but it soon relapsed and perhaps the deplorable state it is in today is to be
expected. [I, 89–90]

This analysis would not be out of place in a modern textbook. It certainly provides
a suitable and oft-painted backdrop to the achievements of Goldoni and Alfieri.
    A work that appeared at the same time as Riccoboni's history initiates a long
series of accounts by visitors from England and France, accounts which provide
a running commentary on the Italian theatre through much of the century. (In
fairness, we should note that Joseph Addison had published his *Remarks on
Several Parts of Italy* in 1705; but however much he later commented on Italian
opera in the *Spectator*, in this early travel book he tells us only that he attended
his eighth opera in Florence and that modern Italian actors sometimes wore
masks that covered the entire head.) Edward Wright's *Some Observations Made
in Travelling through France, Italy, etc.* was published in 1730 and includes
descriptions of Italian comedy, Venetian masking, the *ridotto* or life in the foyer,
and carnival entertainments. As for the opera, Wright was favorably impressed
with the stage machinery he saw in Venice, but less favorably impressed with
the behavior of members of the audience, whom he describes as noisy and
inattentive, given to playing cards and spitting. Nor did he think much of the
regular drama: "Their Tragedy borders upon the Bombast; and the Comedy is
much upon the same Speed in the Theatre as it is on the Mountebanks Stage"
(p. 85). Similar observations on the opera are made by the French writer Charles
de Brosses, whose *Lettres écrites* record his travels through Italy in 1739 and
1740. (Most of the letters were in fact composed fifteen or twenty years after
the fact—a discovery not made until 1922—and they were not published in an
authorized edition until 1836. This does not necessarily invalidate them as evidence, but it is something that the researcher must take into account.)
    The opinions of Samuel Sharp, who visited Italy in 1765–1766, echo the
comments of Riccoboni and Wright. "The present state of the stage here," he
writes, "is what it always must have been in its infancy, before it became
polished, and whilst the audience were a rude and illiberal people ... (*Letters
from Italy*, p. 94). He thought little of the comedies he witnessed—"generally

dull, where they are not farcical'' (p. 279)—and although he praised the acting
of the tragedians as "more sweet and pathetick" than the French, given the low
state of Italian culture, he saw little hope for Italian tragedy itself (pp. 245–46).
Sharp was also a keen observer and recorder of theatrical practices and effects.
He marvelled at and estimates the size of the King's theatre in Naples, but notes
that it is much more pleasing to the eye than the sound of the singers' voices
was to the ear. He makes the usual complaint about the inattentiveness of the
audience. At a burletta opera house—"hardly better than a cellar"—he records
an audience consisting mainly of "men in dirty caps and waistcoats," who were
also given to spitting (p. 93). Sharp found the stage dances "tedious," "vulgar,"
and "buffoonish"; he considered the scenes, costumes, and actors to be generally
indifferent. But his eye was keen. He noted that only the stage was lighted at
the opera house in Naples, "which renders the spectacles frightfully dark and
melancholy" (p. 88). He writes of the salaries of singers and the role of the
impressario. And he records that the dancers wore black drawers. (He is not
sure why.)

Understandably, Sharp's criticisms aroused the ire of London's Italian-in-
Residence, Giuseppe Baretti, who replied in *An Account of the Manners and
Customs of Italy* (1768). Baretti is best known for his condemnation of Goldoni
and his exaltation of Gozzi, whose genius he describes as "the most wonderful
. . . next Shakespeare, that ever any age or country produced" (I, 191). But his
attack on Sharp is also, in a grotesque way, an attack on the concerns of twentieth-
century theatre historians. Castigating the Englishman for failing to discuss "our
[Italian] theatrical abilities, as poets," he sneers at the "miserable trifles" that
concern Sharp: "the extent of our stages; the width of the boxes; their price and
disposition; the gaudiness of the scenery; its illumination, or no-illumination;
the salary of the singers; the length of the dances; the inattention of the audience"
(I, 147). "What do we care," thunders Baretti, "whether industry or mere
accident threw these particulars in his way?" (I, 151). The modern scholar might
well ask the same question with respect to Baretti, and point out that Sharp tells
us far more about the theatre than does Baretti. If we consider these books as
documents apart from the theatrical history we wish to understand, this evaluation
is undoubtedly true. But if we consider them as *part* of that history, they have
in fact equal claim on our attention.

Other writers wrote of their travels in Italy during the same decade, including
Tobias Smollet (1766) and Laurence Sterne (1768). L'Abbé Jérôme Richard's
six-volume *Description historique et critique de l'Italie* (1769) is regularly mined
by theatre historians for information concerning the theatre. And all of these
works, together with those by Addison, Wright, Baretti, Sharp, Brosses (in
manuscript), and others were used by Joseph Jérôme Lalande in the preparation
of his eight-volume *Voyage d'un François en Italie* (1769), a fact that, taken
into account with Brosses' prolonged preparation of his *Lettres écrites*, indicates
that travel literature in the eighteenth century as a genre was likely written as
much with an eye to convention as from direct observation. Lalande is, never-

theless, a much more amiable and tolerant observer than Sharp (whose *Letters*, he writes, are "filled equally by precise information and bad humour" [I, xxi]). He praises the performances in Naples of operas, especially those based on the librettos of Zeno and Metastasio, noting that the many musical settings composed for the small number of librettos is due to the large number of fine composers and the paucity of fine poets (VI, 351–52). He notes that tragedy has not emerged in Italy, and he reports that the renown of the Venetian theatre is due less to its playhouses than to its excellent music and to the talent of its comic actors (VIII, 204). While few of Lalande's observations concerning the theatre are profound, he dutifully notes visits to theatres in Milan, Parma, Bologna, Florence, Rome, Naples, Turin, and Venice, and he usually offers at least a brief comment on the size, shape, and general structure of the playhouses. He asserts, for example, that only Soufflot's theatre at Lyon is comparable to the theatre at Turin, built in 1740, and he cites Cochin in support of his valuation; he describes the Teatro d'Argentina in Rome as shaped like a "truncated egg, square at one end, and round at the other," but also as one of the most beautiful theatres in Italy (V, 180). In fact, his only real complaint, of this theatre as of most of the Italian houses, is that the decorations are poor and there is little in the way of stage machinery. (But compare the remarks by Wright in 1730.)

Dr. Charles Burney's *The Present State of Music in France and Italy* (1771) records the great musicologist's observations during his tour of the previous year. (The work has been edited by Percy Scholes as *An Eighteenth-Century Musical Tour in France and Italy*.) Burney echoes Wright, Brosses, and Sharp on the noisy behavior of Italian audiences, noting that the boxes and rooms are furnished with fireplaces and pharo tables: "Indeed, music at the theatres, and at other public places in Italy seems but an excuse for people to assemble together, their attention being chiefly placed on play and conversation, even during the performance of a serious opera" (p. 257). The author's comments on music are, of course, important, but for the theatre historian there is the added value of his cool and dispassionate descriptions and evaluations of the several playhouses he visited at Turin, Brescia, Padua, Florence, and Naples. Of the San Carlo theatre in Naples, for instance, he notes the immense size of the stage, the oval or egg-shaped auditorium, the size and apportionment of the boxes, balconies, and pit; he dubs the theatre "a noble and elegant structure," superior in its scenes and decoration to the "great French opera at Paris" (pp. 271, 277). Burney also describes a commedia dell'arte performance in the ancient Roman amphitheatre at Verona:

The stage was erected in the middle of the arena; there were only two boxes, one on each side of the stage: the area before the stage made a kind of pit, where the better sort of company sat on chairs. The next best places were on the steps, about twelve deep, railed off from the rest of the steps, which may be regarded as the upper gallery; but all this in the open air, and seats the naked marble. [p. 94]

We have here a nice imposition on an ancient structure of an eighteenth-century conceptual frame of reference. The variety of theatrical performance in Italy is attested as well by Hester Lynch Piozzi's report in 1789 of a performance that she witnessed in Naples of *Il trionfo di Policinello*, "a pageant of prodigious size, set on four broad wheels like our waggons, but larger" (*Observations and Reflections Made in the Course of a Journey Through France, Italy, and Germany*, p. 365).

Finally, we must take note of an ambitious early attempt at writing a complete history of the theatre. Pietro Napoli Signorelli began his *Storia critica dei teatri* as early as 1776; a six-volume edition was published 1787–1790 and a ten-volume edition in 1813. The wonder is not that the work is uneven and flawed—it is—but that it is so wide-ranging in its treatment of the theatre and, perhaps of most importance, that it is in fact the first "history" of western theatre as an autonomous institution. The theatre—or better, dramatic literature—Signorelli believed, expresses the full maturity of a society, but was generated by theatre itself and in turn generated theatre. In his first two volumes (of the six-volume edition) Signorelli speculates on the origins of dramatic poetry and tries to establish what various theatres have in common. He continues in the third volume with a discussion of Oriental, pre-Columbian American, Greek, and Latin theatres. Then, in the last three volumes, Signorelli deals with the drama of modern Europe from the fourteenth through the eighteenth centuries. (Eighteenth-century Italian drama is discussed in the final volume.) In the eighteenth century only Riccoboni and the Englishman Charles Dibdin approach Signorelli's breadth of treatment, and neither approximates his historiographical innovations.

DRAMATIC TEXTS: SCENARIOS, LIBRETTOS, MUSICAL SCORES

To speak of a dramatic text from eighteenth-century Italy is in fact to speak of a chimera, particularly if as theatre historians we are referring to the written dialogue and stage directions that form either the script for or the record of a performance. The performance traditions of the opera and the commedia dell'arte militated against the preservation of a constant text and encouraged instead constant improvisation and change. And neither copyright law nor publishing conventions were precise enough or universal enough for us to hazard more than tentative generalizations concerning the texts that we habitually consult. The situation is less painful, however, once we look to the performance tradition itself as the object of our investigations, and once we cease to regard commedia dell'arte scenarios, opera librettos, or even Goldoni's published plays as literature.

Commedia dell'arte

In spite of the early efforts of Luigi Riccoboni to adapt improvisation to literary drama and the later attempts at reform of the Italian comedy by Goldoni, the traditional commedia dell'arte persisted through the eighteenth century. Each troupe inherited from its predecessors a supply of scenarios, or plot outlines with brief directions for properties, characters, entrances, and so on, and then altered them, or added new ones, to suit changing needs and circumstances. Occasionally, performances were based on conventional dramatic texts, and sometimes there was a kind of mixed form, in which written passages were stitched together with scenes of pure improvisation. (Evaristo Gherardi's *Le Théâtre italien*, published in 1694, is a collection of this sort.) More than one thousand *scenari* are extant, preserved in several manuscript collections and in a printed edition of 1611. (The collections are discussed in detail by Kathleen Lea in *Italian Popular Comedy*.) Some of these scenarios can be associated with specific companies, but it seems likely that such skeleton outlines could be and were traded, pirated, adapted, and recreated over the years for specific uses. Each performance was in effect unique. Nevertheless, the way they were used in practice clearly did not change over the years. In 1728, writing of Flaminio Scala's 1611 collection, *Il teatro delle favole rappresentative*, Riccoboni notes: "They are not so concise as those we use and hang upon the wall of the theatre behind the scenes; neither are they so prolix that the actor can obtain the least suggestion of dialogue from them. They explain only what the scene is about, what the actor is to do, and no more" (*Histoire du théâtre italien*, quoted by Pierre Louis Duchartre, *The Italian Comedy*, p. 51). The persistence of this practice into the second half of the eighteenth century is attested by Carlo Gozzi at the end of the century:

The subject which serves as guide for these excellent players is written entirely on a small slip of paper and posted under a little light for the greater convenience of the troupe. It is astonishing to think that, with such a trifling aid as this, ten or twelve actors are able to keep the public in a gale of laughter for three hours or more and bring to a satisfactory close the argument which has been set for them. [Quoted by Duchartre, p. 51]

A modern scholar obviously needs more than "such trifling" aid to reconstruct a performance.

Goldoni's Comedies

We can derive some notion of the nature and value of more traditional dramatic texts from Goldoni's *Mémoires*. We have seen that the playwright was concerned about the printing of his plays and paid close attention to their publication and distribution. We learn as well that the law in Italy and in particular in Venice may not have been as clear as it ought to have been on copyright and performance rights. For example, when the theatre manager Medebac claimed the rights to Goldoni's plays and arranged for their publication on his own behalf, there was little that the dramatist could do save to arrange the publication of his own edition outside Venice. The fact that he incorporated changes in this edition to differentiate it from Medebac's is also of significance. From incidents such as this we can surmize several things: first, that piracy in publishing in some form was not only possible in Italy but also probable; second, that a playwright like Goldoni, looking for profits from publication as well as performance, probably prepared his texts especially for printing; and third, that whatever served as copy text (e.g. Medebac's playhouse text or Goldoni's revised text), the versions of Goldoni's plays printed during his lifetime reflect playhouse practice as the playwright knew it, however much specific details might have been altered by the author or might fail to reflect the improvised changes that actors trained in impromptu performance undoubtedly rang on the text in a given production.

Opera Librettos

Patrick J. Smith in *The Tenth Muse* estimates the number of extant librettos from seventeenth- and eighteenth-century Italy at over twenty thousand. They are to be found in collections of varying size in libraries throughout Italy, France, and Great Britain, but the two largest and most important collections are the Rolandi Collection, housed in the Giorgio Cini Foundation Institute in Venice, and the Schatz Collection in the Library of Congress. Ulderico Rolandi, the Italian physician responsible for the collection bearing his name, also wrote one of the few studies of the opera libretto to appear before Smith's landmark volume of 1970. *Il libretto per musica attraverso i tempi* (1951) deals in some detail with specific characteristics of the librettos in the collection: changes in appearance and format, variants, parodies, the effects of censorship, and so on. While the collection has been superbly catalogued, the catalogue has not yet been published. The collection in the Library of Congress, assembled in the nineteenth century by the German Albert Schatz, was acquired early in the present century on behalf of the library by Oskar T. Sonneck, who in 1914 published his *Catalogue of the Librettos Written Before 1800* (reprinted by Burt Franklin, 1967). This triply-referenced—by title, librettist, composer—and annotated work remains, according to Smith, "the single most valuable work on the libretto" (p. 412). The Schatz collection differs from that of Rolandi principally in its inclusion of more German librettos and Italian works in German.

Actually, in spite of their seemingly great number, it is a wonder that opera librettos have survived at all. They were printed and distributed or sold as throwaways, intended for the immediate use of audiences rather than for the benefit of posterity. As Smith puts the case:

Not only have most copies, therefore, disappeared, but those which have survived are in far less than perfect condition, and the effects of time upon the inferior paper used in their production has led to further deterioration. Finally, libraries have all too often allowed such examples as they have to molder unattended because other facets of their collections demand prior attention and expenditure of funds. [pp. 411–12]

He goes on to point out that as a consequence the collections tend not to be consulted, and historians and critics turn instead to the texts printed in the vocal or orchestral scores, texts which may in fact differ markedly from the original librettos. Smith dismisses these texts on the ground that they were beyond the control of the librettist, but for a theatre historian the issue is not so clear.

Individual librettos were often set to music by several composers, and during performances changes were introduced to accommodate virtuosi singers. Metastasio's twenty-seven librettos, for instance, were set to music more than one thousand times during the eighteenth century, some of them by as many as twenty different composers, and a single composer might well set the same libretto two or three times. Moreover, each libretto was subjected to further changes each time it was performed, as recitatives and arias, ensembles and choruses were added or deleted at the whim of director or performer. The continual alteration of the libretto under these circumstances resulted not only in a "staggering" number of variant readings for any given libretto (the adjective is Smith's), but also ultimately in the creation of a kind of opera known as *pasticcio*:

an opera which had migrated from city to city, undergoing patching and alteration at every stage, until it might one day arrive at London (its usual final home) with a libretto in which Metastasio shared honors with "Zeno, Goldoni, Stampiglia, Rossi, and other librettists," while "Gluck, Ciampi, Galuppi, Cocchi, Jommelli, Latilla, Handel and several more might be pasted together" in the same musical score. [Donald Jay Grout, *A Short History of Opera*, p. 190]

Given these conditions, the libretto printed with the music—where it is available—might very well be a more accurate indication of what was actually performed than a text supervised by the librettist. It is true that in the eighteenth century there was a reading public for opera librettos. But here as always there is a distinction to be made between a reading text and a performance text. Establishing or discovering an "authoritative" or "true" text is less important to a theatre historian than determining as closely as possible the variant performed at a particular time and place. Moreover, as the century wore on and words and music moved closer to a state of equilibrium, there was a greater likelihood of a particular musical setting's being identified with a given libretto. Patrick Smith notes, for example, that Goldoni's *La Buona Figliola* was best known in the musical version by Niccolo Piccinni (*The Tenth Muse*, p. 110).

Music

Opera music itself is even more difficult to track down and identify than are the librettos. Grout's lament of twenty years ago is still true: "Almost none of the music was printed; hundreds of manuscripts have been lost, and hundreds of others exist only in rare copies; only an infinitesimal fraction of it is accessible in modern editions'' (*A Short History of Opera*, p. 185). And he might have added that much of what we do have consists solely of arias. The Estense Library in Moden, for example, has 425 volumes in manuscript and another 165 printed volumes of arias, as opposed to 278 manuscript volumes and 95 printed volumes of *melodrammas*. (See Veinstein and Golding, *Bibliothèques et musées des art*, s.v. "Italy.") Since for the *opera seria* of the first half of the century the aria was the dramatic centre-piece, this is perhaps not so serious a limitation as it might otherwise be, but as recitative and ensemble came into greater prominence, the inadequacy of the aria as a basis from which to reconstruct a performance becomes clearer.

The principal composers of opera music during the century were Niccolò Porpora (1686–1766), Leonardo Leo (1694–1744), Johann Adolph Hasse (1699–1783), Niccolò Piccinni (1728–1800), Giuseppe Sart (1729–1802), Antonio Sacchini (1730–1786), Antonio Salieri (1750–1825), and Alessandro Scarlatti (1660–1725). (For a list of some modern editions see Grout, *A Short History*, pp. 769–86.)

THEATRES AND STAGE DESIGN

Our information concerning the more than forty important playhouses built or in use in Italy during the eighteenth century is derived from several sources: the accounts of travellers and visitors (see above); occasional paintings and engravings; a handful of surviving theatres; contemporary works on theatre architecture and stage design. The remarks of foreign visitors to Italian theatres, while anecdotal, subjective, and sometimes prejudiced, are usually based upon observations made during a performance, and thus leave impressions of a playhouse in use. Such impressions can contribute to an understanding of theatre dynamics in a way that architectural drawings and even engravings can seldom do. In any event, the number of published engravings and paintings of Italian theatres is not large. An engraving of 1780 of the Teatro d'Imola is printed by Dunbar Ogden in *The Italian Baroque Stage* (p. 75); another of the Teatro San Benedetto in Venice, dating from 1782, is in Baur-Heinhold's *The Baroque Theatre* (pl. 110); and a painting by P. D. Olivero, dating from about 1740, of the Teatro Regio in Turin, is reproduced by Allardyce Nicoll in *The Garrick Stage* (no. 24). Clearly a great deal more can be learned by examining extant theatres dating from the eighteenth century. Although they have all been renovated since their initial construction, the basic structure remains intact for the most part, and skilled investigators are sometimes able, by a kind of architectural archaeology, to determine many of the original details. Baur-Heinhold includes photographs of four extant theatres in *The Baroque Theatre*:

a. Teatro Grande, Padua (1748–1751): designed by Antonio Cugini and remodelled in the nineteenth and again in the twentieth century (pl. 114).

b. Palace Theatre at Caserta (1752): designed by Luigi Vanvitelli for Charles VII of

Naples (pl. 108). (In addition, the Metropolitan Museum possesses drawings of a plan and three sections of the theatre, evidently prepared by an unknown French artist about 1775. Donald Oenslager reproduces one of the sections in *Stage Design*, fig. 61.)

c. Teatro Communale, Bologna (1756–1763): designed by Antonio Bibiena (pls. 117–21).

d. Teatro La Fenice, Venice (1790–1792): designed by Giovanni Antonio Selva; renovated by Tommaso and Giovanni Battista Meduna (pls. 111–13).

To these we should add the famous Teatro alla Scala, built in Milan in 1778 by Giuseppe Piermarini, extensively remodelled in 1837, modernized in 1920, and reconstructed after severe bomb damage during World War II. (See Luigi Lorenzo Secchi, *Il teatro alla Scala, 1778–1978*; Gianni Mezzanotte, *L'architettura della Scala nell'età neoclassica.*)

The Bibiena family—especially Ferdinando, Antonio, Francesco, and Giuseppe—were responsible for the design of many theatres and theatre interiors in Italy, Germany, and Austria. Their contributions, surveyed by A. Hyatt Mayor in *The Bibiena Family*, consist principally of the following:

a. Court Opera House in Vienna (Mayor, pls. 14, 18): designed and built by Francesco in 1704; destroyed in 1747. (Sketches and engravings are reproduced in Baur-Heinhold, *The Baroque Theatre*, pls. 162, 164.)

b. Opera House in Nancy: built between 1707 and 1709 by Antonio and burnt sometime before 1745. (A drawing of the proscenium is held in the Louvre.)

c. Teatro Filarmonico: built in 1720; burnt in 1749; rebuilt to the same plan 1760; interior altered 1874. (See Baur-Heinhold, *The Baroque Theatre*, pls. 115, 116; Mullin, *The Development of the Playhouse*, fig. 76.) Mayor reproduces part of a large engraving by Giuseppe Zucchi showing various sections of the theatre (p. 19). Martin Hammitzsch records in *Das Moderne Theaterbau* (1907) that he saw three elevations of the theatre in the Filarmonico archives in 1901, which may have been Francesco's original drawings, but the only drawings now known to exist are copies made by Giuseppe Charmont (1699–1768), preserved in Cooper Union (Mayor, pls. 20–21). (Corrado Ricci published a photograph of the renovated playhouse in *La scenografia italiana*, pl. 44.)

d. Teatro Aliberti: the work of Francesco, built in 1720. It is discussed by Francesco Milizia in his *Architteti* (translated in 1826 as *Lives of the Celebrated Architects*) and by J. J. Lalande in *Voyage d'un François en Italie* (II, 182).

e. Teatro del Castello, Mantua: designed and built by Ferdinando between 1732 and 1735, this theatre was also a victim of fire in 1781. Ferdinando's plan is reproduced by Hammitzsch (fig. 70) and Mullin (fig. 77).

f. Bayreuth Opera: the only theatre for which a Bibiena was at least partially responsible, to survive to the present. Bayreuth was actually designed by Joseph St. Pierre, with the interior decorated by Giuseppe Bibiena in 1748. (See Mayor, pls. 22–25; Hammitzsch, fig. 107; Baur-Heinhold, pls. 163, 165–75, colorplate XV.)

g. Dresden Opera House: Giuseppe also created plans for a new opera house in Dresden

(Hammitzsch, figs. 113–16), but the house was never built. Instead, in 1750, he redecorated the old house, which unhappily burnt in 1849.

h. Teatro della Pergola: again, an instance of redecoration, this time by Antonio, of a theatre originally erected in 1657 and altered since Antonio's renovations of the 1750s. Lalande offers a description (II, 358).

i. Teatro Communale, Bologna: begun by Antonio Bibiena in 1756 and opened in 1763; the facade was never finished, and the interior was redone in 1866. L. Capponi's *Pianta e spaccato del Nuova Teatro di Bologna* (1771) includes five large engravings of the theatre, together with its facade as frontispiece.

j. Teatro Rossini, Lugo: built 1758–1761 by Antonio Bibiena and F. Petrocchi.

k. Teatro de'Quattro Cavalieri in Pavia: again, a published work, *I desegni del Nuovo Teatro de Quattro Cavalieri* (1773), provides an engraved frontispiece and three copperplate engravings.

It must be noted, however, that very often the Bibienas allowed visual aesthetic considerations to take precedence over acoustics. Although the Teatro Filarmonico was admired for its acoustics, it remains an anomaly. Donald Mullin points out that it was more usual for the Bibienas to design "theatres of glittering grandeur without reference to acoustical studies" (*The Development of the Playhouse*, p. 89). Yet even their baroque grandeur was ultimately held against the Bibiena theatres, and most of them were demolished, or remodelled in accordance with neoclassical taste. As early as 1766 Lalande in his *Voyage* complained that the forty-five-year-old Teatro Aliberti was ugly, because "it swarmed with excrescences" (quoted by Mayor, p. 18).

The Bibienas not only designed playhouses, but also wrote about theatre design. Ferdinando published *L'architettura civile* in 1711, a book that went through several editions and is frequently cited by theatre historians still; his undated *Varie opere di prospettiva* appeared between 1703 and 1708. Francesco wrote but never published *L'architettura maestra dell'arti che la compangono*. And Giuseppe contributed *Architetture e prospettive* (1740–1744; translated by A. Hyatt Mayor, 1964). (Ferdinando's *L'architettura civile* is discussed below.)

As in France, historical and theoretical works dating from the late eighteenth and early nineteenth centuries add immeasurably to our understanding of theatre architecture. Gabriel Dumont in his *Parallèle de plans* publishes plans of the Teatro Reale in Naples (1750), the Teatro Ducale in Parma (remodelled 1760), the Teatro Ducale in Milan (destroyed 1776), and the Teatro di Tor di Nona (1771) and the Teatro Aliberti in Rome. He devotes considerable attention to two theatres in particular—the Teatro d'Argentina, erected in Rome in 1732, and the Teatro Torino, built in 1740. Besides ground plans and cross sections for these theatres, he provides as well cross sections with details of the framework for the machinery, and details of the construction. George Saunders in *A Treatise on Theatres* similarly publishes plans of the Teatro d'Argentina, the Teatro Torino, and the theatre at Milan, but he adds the Teatro San Carlo at Naples (1737), the Teatro Communale at Bologna (1756), and the Teatro San Benedetto in Venice. He also includes plans for Cosimo Morelli's theatre at Imola (pl. 7, fig. 3), inspired, as we have seen, by Cochin's 1765 project, and built in 1779.

Italians too contributed to the theoretical discussion. Conte Vincenzo Arnaldi in his *Idea di un teatro* (1762) argued for a semi-circular auditorium and against the *parterre* and the *loges*. The architect Francesco Milizia (1725–1798), in an oddly negative and moralistic work, *Trattato completo, formale e materiale del teatro* (1771), vigorously attacked both the architectural form of contemporary theatres and the immorality of the theatrical institution itself. Giulio Ferrario (1767–1847) in 1830 published *Storia e descrizione de'principali teatri antichi e moderni*, an elaboration and commentary on Pierre Patte's *Essai sur l'architecture théâtrale* (1782), a work that of course also included a good deal of Italian material. Ferrario includes observations on "the famous architect and scene painter Paolo Landriani" (1757–1839), who between 1815 and 1824 published his *Osservazione sui di fetti prodotti nei teatri*, in which, from the vantage of a working scene designer, he offers an intelligent critique of stage design and of the relationship between the stage and the auditorium. Other works from the late eighteenth century that can be consulted are Vincenzo Lamberti's *Le regolata construzione de teatri* (1787) and Francesco Riccati's *Della costruzione de'teatri secondo il costume d'Italie* (1790).

Stage design and the mechanics of scenic practice in fact—the concerns of those who must translate two-dimensional designs into three-dimensional stage sets—were the subjects of several treatises by Italians during the eighteenth century, but these works were in turn the inheritors of a seventeenth-century tradition, represented in the writings of Leone de'Sommi, Nicolà Sabbattini, Joseph Fürttenbach, and Fabrizio Carini Motta. (See Ronald Vince, *Renaissance Theatre*, pp. 13–15.) The basics of single-perspective rectangular scene design are set out by Giulio Troili (1613–1685) in his *Paradossi per pratticare la prospettiva* (1672), a practical handbook that served as a starting point for later theorists and practitioners. Andrea Pozzo's *Prospettiva de'pittori e architetti* (1693–1700) is particularly valuable as a source of information concerning the way that the stage picture was actually apportioned among the several wings. As Dunbar Ogden points out in *The Italian Baroque Stage* (where pertinent selections from Troili and Pozzo are printed in English translation): "He [Pozzo] is the first to present exact procedures according to the laws of perspective for the transfer of scene designs onto wing surfaces, and he gives more precise rules for the employment of oblique wings than did his predecessor Troili" (p. 15). The practicality of Troili and Pozzo takes second place to aesthetic considerations in *L'architettura civile* by Ferdinando Bibiena, published in 1711. Bibiena's main contribution to stage design was the *scena veduta per angolo*, the system whereby scenes are viewed from a forty-five-degree angle, using two or more perspective vanishing points, thereby effectively separating the stage space from that of the auditorium. What Bibiena neglects to do is precisely what Pozzo was at pains to do—explain exactly how the scene was to correspond to the various wings. In a later work, *Direzione della prospettiva teoria* (1732), Ferdinando does describe a sketch-to-set process that Ogden (p. 47) identifies as a prophecy of a future emphasis in scene design on performance environment rather than on pictorial illusion.

A particularly important source of information concerning the Italian system of stagecraft and stage design in use during the first half of the eighteenth-century—and perhaps even earlier—is *Instruction in der Teatralischen Architectur und Mechanique* by Jacopo Fabris (1689–1761), an Italian-trained designer who spent most of his working life outside Italy. In 1746 he was appointed to the court of Frederick V of Denmark; the manuscript of his five-volume *Geometrisch-Perspectivisch Architectischen Lectionem* (1760) is to be found in the Royal Library at Copenhagen. The *Instruction* is volume four. (The treatise was published in German by Torbin Krogh in 1930; an English translation by C. Thomas Ault was published in 1986.) Fabris differs from Troili, Pozzo, and especially Ferdinando Bibiena in that he lacks their inventiveness; as a consequence, he describes practices that were undoubtedly commonly in use in theatres throughout Italy, Germany, and France.

If the usefulness of the *Instruction* comes from Fabris's technical competence and unimaginative practicality, the value of Baldassare Orsini's writings on scene design can be attributed to the author's scholarly credentials and a well-thought-out theoretical perspective. Orsini (1732–1810), Director of the Academy of Design at Perugia, was the author of guidebooks to Perugia and Ascoli, several studies of Etruscan monuments, and a biography of the late fifteenth-century painter Pietro Perugino; the translator of Vitruvius; and the editor of the architectural works of Leon Baptista Alberti, Vincenzo Scamozzi, and Leonardo da Vinci. In 1801, he published a Vitruvian dictionary. So far as scene design is concerned, Orsini includes a chapter on the subject in *Della geometria e prospettiva pratica* (1771–1773), but provides his most extensive treatment in *Le scene del nuovo Teatro del Verzaro* (1785), which he wrote as a consequence of his experience designing the stage and scenery for the new theatre in 1781. *Le scene* is significant on two counts. First, Orsini describes and illustrates thirteen different stock scenes and includes information on the ways that the scenes were apportioned among the wings and backscenes. (The scenes he included—royal chamber, salon, gallery, royal hall, palace, temple, street, courtyard, dungeon, villa, piazza, harbor, woods—might be compared to the lists in the Covent Garden inventory of 1744 and the 1758 pamphlet, *The Case of the Stage in Ireland*—See chapter 1.) Second, he provides detailed descriptions of the process of scene painting, including information on colors, pigments, light and shadow, and the use of chiaroscuro. Such technical detail is rare. But, like Fabris, Orsini does not record major innovations. He gives us what had become standard theatrical practice in the last quarter of the eighteenth century. Dunbar Ogden, whose exerpts from *Le scene* and commentary provide the best introduction to the Italian designer in English, points out that his work "provides us with a summary of and a conclusion to developments that had taken place since the time of Aleotti and that had been recorded by perspectivists before him"

(*The Italian Baroque Stage*, p. 72). "With Orsini, he concludes, "we are come to the end of an era that had reached its heights in the work of Pozzo and the Bibienas" (p. 4).

SCENE DESIGN

Italian scene designers dominated European scene design for two centuries, and common sense dictates that the subject should occupy a central place in the discipline of theatre history. The truth seems to be, however, that the centre will not hold. The study of scene design threatens always to move to the periphery of the historian's concern, or even to detach itself completely and either move into a closer proximity to the history of art or remain an independent study, hovering precariously between theatre and art. The reasons are not difficult to discern. Evidence for the ephemeral scenes that graced stages for particular productions consists of hundreds of sketches, drawings, and engravings whose relationship to actual stage sets and to specific productions is at best problematic. Further, most scene designers were pictorial artists first and stage artists second; they obviously sought a more permanent medium for the preservation of their art than the wings and backscenes that, by Orsini's reckoning, could be counted on to last no longer than ten years. Most designs as we have them—as we noted earlier—reflect their creators' fantasies as much as or more than their stage realization. Divorced then from the theatres and machinery by which they were realized, and from the performances and theatrical works for which they were intended, scene designs have found their final artistic context in picture books and exhibitions. The imaginative retreat from artistic rendering to stage set, with little chance of certitude, is a process that few historians have been willing, or able, to undertake.

But if specific designs seldom illuminate specific performances, the designs taken *en masse* can be analyzed to allow generalizations concerning the recurrent stage pictures of the eighteenth century. The list of stock scenes provided by Orsini, for instance, indicates the predominance of architectural settings used, and the extant designs of Pozzo, Filippo Juvara, Pietro Gaspari, and the Galliari, Quaglio, and Bibiena families bear out the impression. Morever, the practical handbooks of Troili, Pozzo, Ferdinando Bibiena, and Orsini discussed above describe the making of architectural stage settings. In a sense, scene designers had found a way to indulge their architectural fantasies unimpeded by the practical restraints of building in real stone and marble.

Specialized studies devoted to Italian scenography are plentiful, as the references appended to this chapter attest, but the following volumes provide excellent introductions to the designs: János Scholz, *Theatrical Designs from the Baroque through Neo-Classicism* (1940); the same author's *Baroque and Romantic Stage Design* (1949); Donald Oenslager, *Stage Design* (1975). There are, of course, collections of drawings and engravings of scene designs in libraries and museums on both sides of the Atlantic, but private collectors from an early date have been attracted to such material. The bulk of the designs published by Scholz, for example, came originally from two collections: that of Michael Mayr (1796–1870), stage designer to the Princes Eszterhazy in Eisenstadt, Austria, a collection which illustrates the German tradition of Italianate scene design from the Bibienas to the mid-nineteenth century; and that of Giovanni Piancastelli (1844–1926), a large collection assembled during the latter half of the eighteenth century. Large parts of both collections eventually found their way to the United States and into several collections. Historians might on occasion lament the difficulty of locating specific designs, but it is often thanks to private collectors and their willingness to invest time and money in the acquisition of drawings and engravings that they can be located at all.

Some Major Scene Designers

The following scene designers are representative, and they were important during the eighteenth century, but of course their work represents only a fraction of that available in libraries and archives. (The most convenient source of information concerning designs and their locations is the *Enciclopedia dello spettacolo*, published in nine volumes and a *Supplement*, between 1954 and 1966.)

Filippo Juvara (1676–1736)

Juvara's most important work was done for the theatre that he constructed in the Palazzo Cancellaria in Rome at the request of Cardinal Pietro Ottoboni. One hundred and twenty-six of his *Pensieri di scene apparecchie* are contained in a single volume now in the Victoria and Albert Museum. (See Mercedes Viale Ferrero, *Filippo Juvara*.)

Vincenzo Re (d. 1762)

Re designed scenes for hundreds of productions at the Teatro San Carlo in Naples over a twenty-five-year period. His designs also appear in *Narrazione delle solenni reale feste*, a festival book of 1748.

Paolo Landriani (1757–1839)

Perhaps most famous for his *Osservazione* (discussed above), Landriani has also left us a sketchbook containing 211 stage designs prepared for La Scala over a period of twenty-five years between 1792 and 1817.

Bibiena Family

Easily the best known of Italian scene designers, the various members of the Bibiena family—notably Ferdinando (1657–1743), Francesco (1659–1739), Giuseppe (1696–1757), Antonio (1700–1774), and Carlo (1728–1787)—created a constant and recognizable style that found expression in hundreds of scene designs throughout Italy and northern Europe from the 1680s to the 1780s. Only a handful of their finished drawings survive (most of them reproduced by A.

Hyatt Mayor in *The Bibiena Family*), but the Bibienas' work survives in hundreds of etchings and engravings. There are in addition several sketchbooks preserved in libraries and museums in Europe and America: the Austrian National Library in Vienna; the Accademia di San Luca in Rome; the Theatre Museum of Munich; and Harvard University Library.

Quaglio Family

After the Bibienas the most prolific and influential of the great families of Italian scene designers, the Quaglios worked mainly in northern Italy, southern Germany, and Austria through seven generations, from the middle of the seventeenth century to the middle of the twentieth. In all, fifteen members of the family had careers as scene designers. Most of their work is preserved in the Theatre Museum of Munich.

Galliari Family

The last notable family of Italian scene designers, the Galliaris, like the Bibienas, worked in close collaboration with one another, and it is therefore rarely possible to differentiate the work of the various family members. The best known are Bernardino (1707–1794), Fabrizio (1709–1790), Giovanni Antonio (1714–1783), and Gaspare (1761–1823). Bernardino designed for the Teatro Regio Ducale in Milan; Fabrizio and Giovanni Antonio for the Teatro Regio and the Teatro Carignaro in Turin; Gaspare at La Scala. Donald Oenslager notes that in one respect the Galliari designs are unique: their sketches are often enclosed within lines indicating a proscenium drapery, reflecting the fact that they worked "almost exclusively behind the theatre's proscenium arch" (*Stage Design*, p. 96). (See Mercedes Viale Ferrero, *La scenografia del '700 e i Fratelli Galliari*.)

Giovanni Battista Piranesi

Piranesi has always presented a problem for the theatre historian. His work is clearly theatrical in style, even in inspiration, but he had a limited association with actual theatre production, and relatively few of his designs were intended for the stage. As a consequence, because they *appear* to be stage designs, his engravings are sometimes reproduced as such with no hint of their true provenance; on the other hand, there is an even better chance that they will be ignored, on the grounds that they were in fact not intended specifically for the theatre. The most useful view lies somewhere in between. Piranesi's style owes a good deal to the theatrical designs of Juvara and the Bibiena family, but his own work—especially *Carceri d'invenzione* (ca. 1745; reworked 1761), fantastic imaginary prisons—had an even greater effect on subsequent scene design. Joseph Roach, in an article in *Theatre Survey* (1978), argues persuasively that Piranesi's talent for transforming "commonplace experience into spectral nightmare" (p. 102) had an immediate effect on scene design throughout Europe, and he traces the influence of *Carceri* on the 1760 revival of Rameau's *Dardanus* at the Opera, on Vincenzo Mazzi's *Cappricci di scene teatrali* (1776), on the work of Charles Michel-Ange Challe in the 1770s, on Francesco Chiaruttini's 1786 design for a prison scene (reproduced in Oenslager, fig. 96), and on De Loutherbourg's maquette of a prison, as well as on many scene designers of the early nineteenth century. "Piranesi," writes Roach, "by creating an atmospheric version of Baroque scenography that appealed directly to Romantic taste, bridged the gulf between the quaint conventions of seventeenth-century operatic design and the theory of the modern stage" (p. 115). Piranesi's etchings of Roman ruins in his *Vedute* similarly influenced scene design in the late eighteenth and early nineteenth centuries. (See A. Hyatt Mayor, *Giovanni Battista Piranesi.*)

REFERENCES

Addison, Joseph. *Remarks on Several Parts of Italy, &c. in the Years 1701, 1702, 1703*. In *The Works of the Right Honourable Joseph Addison*, Vol. I. Ed. Henry G. Bohn. London, 1856. [1705]

Alfieri, Vittorio. *Lettere edite e inedite*. Turin, 1890.

————. *Memoirs*. 1810 Trans. Rev. E. R. Vincent. London, 1961.

Algarotti, Count Francesco. *An Essay on the Opera Written in Italian*. London, 1767. [Italian ed. 1755]

————. *Saggio sopra l'opere in musica*. Leghorn, Italy, 1755.

Arnaldi, Conte Vincenzo. *Idea di un teatro*. Vicenza, 1762.

Baretti, Giuseppe Marc'Antonio. *An Account of the Manners and Customs of Italy*. 2 Vols. London, 1768.

Baur-Heinhold, Margarete. *The Baroque Theatre: A Cultural History of the 17th and 18th Centuries*. New York and London, 1967.

Bec, Christian and Irene Mamczarz, eds. *Le Théâtre italien et l'Europe*. Paris, 1983.

Bibiena, Ferdinando Galli. *L'architettura civile*. Ed. Diane M. Kelder. New York, 1971. [1711]

————. *Direzione della prospettiva teoria*. 1732.

————. *Varie opere di prospettiva*. Bologna, n.d. [1703–1708]

Bibiena, Giuseppe Galli. *Architectural and Perspective Designs*. Ed. A. Hyatt Mayor. New York, 1964. [1740–1744]

Brosses, Charles de. *Lettres écrites d'Italie à quelques amis en 1739 et 1740*. Paris, 1836.

————. *Lettres historiques et critiques sur l'Italie*. 3 Vols. Paris, 1799.

————. *Lettres historiques et critiques sur l'Italie*. Ed. Yvonne Bezard. 2 Vols. Paris, 1931.

Burney, Charles. *Dr. Burney's Musical Tours in Europe*, Vol. I: *An Eighteenth-Century Musical Tour in France and Italy*. Ed. Percy A. Scholes. London, 1959.

————. *Memoirs of the Life and Writings of the Abate Metastasio*. 3 Vols. London, 1796. [Reprinted 1971]

————. *Music, Men and Manners in France and Italy 1770*. Ed. H. Edmund Poole. London, 1969, 1974.

————. *The Present State of Music in France and Italy*. London, 1771; 2d ed. 1773.

Capponi, L. *Pianta e spaccato del Nuovo Teatro di Bologna*. Bologna, 1771.

Carlson, Marvin. *The Italian Stage from Goldoni to D'Annunzio*. Jefferson, N.C., 1981.

Crescimbeni, Giovanni Maria. *La Bellezza della volgar poesie*. Rome, 1700.

Duchartre, Pierre Louis. *The Italian Comedy*. Tr. Randolph T. Weaver. New York, 1966.
[1929]

Dumont, Gabriel Pierre Martin. *Parallèle de plans des plus belles salles de spectacles d'Italie et de France, avec des details de machines théâtrales*. New York, 1968.
[ca. 1774]

Enciclopedia dello spettacolo. Founded Silvio D'Amico. 9 Vols. Rome, 1954–1962. *Supplement 1955–1965*. Rome, 1966.

Fabris, Jacopo. *Instruction in Theatre Architecture and Mechanics*. Tr. C. Thomas Ault. In *Performing Arts Resources*, Vol. 11: *Scenes and Machines from the 18th Century*. Ed. Barbara Cohen-Stratyner. New York, 1986.

————. *Jacopo Fabris Instruction in der Teatralischen Architectur und Mechanique, Udgivet og Forsynet med Inledning af Torben Krogh*. Copenhagen, 1930.

Ferrario, Giulio. *Storia e descrizione de'principali teatri antichi e moderni*. Milan, 1830.

Ferrero, Mercedes Viale. *Filippo Juvara*. New York, 1970.

————. *La scenografia del '700 e i Frattelli Galliari*. Turin, 1963.

————. *La scenografia della Scala in eta neoclassica*. Milan, 1983.

Galletti, A. *Le teorie drammatiche e la tragedia in Italia nel secolo XVIII*. Cremona, 1901.

Giorgi, Felice. *Descrizione istoria del Teatro di Tor di Nona*. Rome, 1795.

Goldoni, Carlo. *Mémoires de Goldoni*. Preface Louis Jouvet. Intr. Marcel Lapierre. Paris, 1946.

————. *Memoirs of Carlo Goldoni*. Tr. John Black. New York, 1926. [1787]

————. *Opere complete di Carlo Goldoni*. Ed. G. Ortolani, E. Maddalena, and C. Musatti. 40 Vols. Venice, 1907–1960.

Gozzi, Carlo. *The Memoirs of Count Carlo Gozzi*. Tr. John Addington Symonds. 2 Vols. London, 1890.

————. *Useless Memoirs of Carlo Gozzi*. Tr. John Addington Symonds. Ed. Philip Horne. Intr. Harold Acton. London, 1962.

Gravina, Gianvencenzo. *Della tragedia*. Naples, 1715.

Grosley, Pierre John. *New Observations on Italy and Its Inhabitants*. 2 Vols. London, 1769.

Grout, Donald Jay. *A Short History of Opera*. 2d ed. New York, 1965.

Guerzoni, Giuseppe. *Il teatro italiano nel secolo XVIII*. Milan, 1876.

Hammitszch, Martin. *Das Moderne Theaterbau*. Berlin, 1907.

I designi del Nuovo Teatro de Quattro Cavalieri eretto in Pavia. Pavia, 1773.

Kelder, Diane. *Drawings by the Bibiena Family*. Philadelphia, 1968.

Kennard, Joseph Spencer. *Goldoni and the Venice of His Time*. New York, 1920.

————. *The Italian Theatre*. 2 Vols. New York, 1932.

Kerman, Joseph. *Opera as Drama*. New York, 1956.

Lalande, Joseph Jérôme. *Voyage d'un François en Italie fait dans les années 1765 & 1766*. 8 Vols. Paris, 1769.

Lamberti, Vincenzo. *Le regolata construzione de teatri*. Naples, 1787.

Landriani, Paolo. *Osservazione sui di fetti prodotti nei teatri*. 4 pts. Milan, 1815–1824.

Lea, Kathleen. *Italian Popular Comedy: A Study in the Commedia Dell'Arte, 1560–1620, with Special Reference to the English Stage*. 2 Vols. New York, 1962. [1934]

Leclerc, Hélène. *Les Origines italiennes de l'architecture théâtrale moderne*. Paris, 1946.

Lee, Vernon [Violet Paget]. *Studies of the Eighteenth Century in Italy*. London, 1880; new ed. 1887. [Reprinted 1978]

Maffei, Scipio and Apostolo Zeno. *Giornale dei Letterati d'Italia*. Verona, 1710.

Mamczarz, Irene. *Les Intermèdes comiques italiens au XVIIIe siècle en France et en Italie*. Paris, 1972.

Mancini, Franco. *Scenografia italiana*. Milan, 1966.

————. *Scenografia napoletana dell'eta barocca*. Naples, n.d. [1964].

Marani, E. *Il teatro di Antonio Bibiena in Mantova e il polazzo accademico*. Mantua, 1979.

Marcello, Benedetto. *Il teatro alla moda*. Ed. Andrea d'Angeli. Milan, 1956. [1720]

————. *Il teatro alla moda*. Tr. Reinhard G. Pauly. *Musical Quarterly* XXXIV (1948), 371–403; XXXV (1949), 85–105.

Mariani, Valerio. *Storia della scenografia italiana*. Florence, 1930.

Marotti, Ferruccio. *Lo spazio scenico. Teorie e tecniche scenografiche in Italia dall'eta Barocca al settecento*. Rome, 1974.

Masi, Ernesto. *Studi sulla storia del teatro italiano nel secolo XVIII*. Florence, 1891.

Mayor, A. Hyatt. *The Bibiena Family*. New York, 1945.

————. *Giovanni Battista Piranesi*. New York, 1952.

————. *Tempi e aspetti della scenografia*. Turin, 1954.

Mezzanotte, Gianni. *L'architettura della Scala nell'età neoclassica*. Milan, 1982.

Milizia, Francesco. *Lives of the Celebrated Architects, Ancient and Modern, With Observations on Their Work and on the Principles of the Art*. Tr. Edward Cresy. 2 Vols. London, 1826.

————. *Trattato completo, formale et materiale del teatro*. Rome, 1771.

Monteverdi, Mario. *La Scala: Four Hundred Years of Stage Design*. Milan, 1971.

Mullin, Donald C. *The Development of the Playhouse*. Berkeley and Los Angeles, 1970.

Nicoll, Allardyce. *The Garrick Stage, Theatres and Audiences in the Eighteenth Century*. Ed. Sybil Rosenfeld. Manchester, 1980.

Oenslager, Donald. *Stage Design: Four Centuries of Scenic Invention*. New York, 1975.

Ogden, Dunbar. *The Italian Baroque Stage: Documents by Giulio Troili, Andrea Pozzo, Ferdinando Galli-Bibiena, Baldassare Orsini*. Berkeley, 1978.

Orsini, Baldassare. *Della geometria e prospettiva pratica*. 3 Vols. Rome, 1771–1773.

————. *Dizionario universale d'architteturo vitruviano*. 2 Vols. Perugia, 1801.

————. *Le scene del nuovo Teatro del Verzaro*. Perugia, 1785.

Patte, Pierre. *Essai sur l'architecture théâtrale*. Paris, 1782. [Reprinted 1974]

Pauly, Reinhard G. "Benedetto Marcello's Satire on Early 18th-Century Opera." *Musical Quarterly* XXXIV (1948), 222–33.

Piozzi, Hester. *Observations and Reflections Made in the Course of a Journey Through France, Italy, and Germany*. Dublin, 1789.

Piranesi, Giovanni Battista. *The Prisons by Giovanni Battista Piranesi*. Ed. Philip Hofer. New York, 1973.

Pozzo, Andrea. *Rules and Examples of Perspective*. Tr. John James. London, 1707.

Rabany, Charles. *Carlo Goldoni: Le Théâtre et la vie en Italie au XVIIIe siècle*. Paris, 1896.

Rasi, Luigi. *I comici italiani, biografia, bibliografia, iconografia*. 2 Vols. in 3. Florence, 1897, 1905.

Riccati, Francesco. *Della costruzione de' teatri secondo il costume d'Italie vale a dire divisi in piccole logge*. Bassano, 1790.

Ricci, Corrado. *La scenografia italiana*. Milan, 1930.

Riccoboni, Luigi. *Histoire du théâtre italien*. 2 Vols. Paris, 1730–1731.

Richard, L'Abbé Jérôme. *Description historique et critique de l'Italie*. 6 Vols. Paris, 1769.

Roach, Joseph R., Jr. "From Baroque to Romantic: Piranesi's Contribution to Stage Design." *Theatre Survey* XIX (1978), 91–118.

Rolandi, Ulderico. *Il libretto per musica attraverso i tempi*. Rome, 1951.

Saunders, George. *A Treatise on Theatres*. London, 1790. [Reprinted 1968]

Schnapper, Antoine, ed. *La scenografia barocca*. Bologna, 1982.

Scholz, János, ed. *Baroque and Romantic Stage Design*. Intr. A. Hyatt Mayor. New York, 1949. [Reprinted 1962]

———. *Theatrical Designs from the Baroque through Neo-Classicism*. Intr. George Freedley. 3 Vols. New York, 1940.

Secchi, Luigi Lorenzo. *Il teatro alla Scala, 1778–1978*. Milan, 1978.

Sharp, Samuel. *Letters from Italy, Describing the Customs and Manners of that Country in the Years 1765 and 1766*. London, 1766.

Signorelli, Pietro Napoli. *Storia critica dei teatri antichi e moderni*. 6 Vols. Naples, 1787–1790. 10 Vols. Naples, 1813.

Simonde de Sismondi, Jean Charles Leonard. *Historical View of the Literature of the South of Europe*. Tr. Thomas Roscoe. 4th ed. 2 Vols. London, 1895. [1846]

Smith, Patrick J. *The Tenth Muse: A Historical Study of the Opera Libretto*. New York, 1970.

Smollet, Tobias. *Travels through France and Italy*. London, 1766.

Sonneck, Oskar T. *Catalogue of the Librettos Written Before 1800 in the Schatz Collection of the Library of Congress*. Washington, 1914. [Reprinted 1967]

Soubies, Albert. *Le Théâtre italien au temps de Napoléon et de la Restauration*. Paris, 1910.

Sterne, Laurence. *A Sentimental Journey through France and Italy*. London, 1768.

Strunk, Oliver, ed. *Source Readings in Music History*. New York, 1950.

Tafuri, Manfredo and Luigi Squarzina. *Teatri e scenografie*. Milan, 1976.

Veinstein, André and Alfred S. Golding, eds. *Bibliothèques et musées des arts du spectacle dans le monde./Performing Arts Libraries and Museums of the World*. 3d ed. Paris, 1984.

Villeneuve, Josse de. *Lettre sur le mechanisme de l'opéra italien*. Paris and Florence, 1756.

Vince, Ronald W. *Renaissance Theatre: A Historiographical Handbook*. Westport, Conn., 1984.

Wright, Edward. *Some Observations Made in Travelling through France, Italy, etc. in the Years 1720, 1721 and 1722*. 2 Vols. in 1. London, 1730.

THE INTERNATIONALIZATION OF EIGHTEENTH-CENTURY THEATRE: A MISCELLANY

The history of the theatre in England, France, and Italy during the eighteenth century is largely the history of professional theatres; the theatres of all three countries could build on traditions dating from the early seventeenth century and even earlier. London and Paris were theatrical centres that both attracted and nourished theatrical artists, and they have similarly served to focus the attention of theatre historians. Italy, as we have seen, was in a somewhat different position in that it lacked a cultural and geographical focus for its professional theatre. Partly as a consequence, Italian professionalism was subject to a kind of centrifugal action which sent Italian actors, singers, and scene designers to the farthest reaches of the European continent. Such "internationalizing" of the theatre was not, however, exclusively an Italian phenomenon, nor was it a one-way process. International travel was not limited to paripatetic Italian scene designers. English actors performed in Germany in the seventeenth century, and their influence was still being felt in the eighteenth. French actors performed in Germany, Russia, and Scandinavia; German actors in Russia, Poland, and Hungary; Italian actors and singers in England, Germany, Russia, France, and Spain. Repertories were increasingly international, and new dramatic forms resulted from complex interactions among the theories and practices of various national theatres and theatrical traditions.

French neoclassicism, which dominated Europe for nearly two centuries, also served to focus debate in those parts of Europe struggling to establish independent theatres. Much of the history of the theatre in Northern and Eastern Europe can be seen in terms of a struggle for national independence, a struggle that was fundamentally cultural and even political. It is possible to trace throughout the eighteenth century a slowly growing opposition to what had become a Franco-Italian hegemony in the theatre, perpetuated by the presence—in most of the

European courts—of French and Italian acting troupes and designers who set
the standards of style and repertory, often to the detriment of any indigenous or
"national" drama. It is essential to understand this if we are to understand
theatrical developments throughout Europe. (The theatre of Spain in the eighteenth century presents a special case.)

It is, of course, almost a truism that political, geographical, and economic
conditions affect cultural and artistic development. Writing of the German theatre
in 1700, Walter H. Bruford, for instance, observes: "In a country without
political, social, religious or cultural unity . . . , it could not be expected that the
arts should display a unified style, least of all an art so inescapably social as
that of the theatre. There was as yet no accepted type of German drama, as there
was a French tragedy and comedy, still less was there an accepted tradition in
the production and acting of plays" (*Theatre Drama and Audience in Goethe's
Germany*, p. 1). Such circumstances—which were prevalent in much of Eastern
Europe as well as in the German-speaking territories—not only have been subjected to historical analysis but also have in turn prompted among some European
scholars the development of a theatre historiography self-consciously nationalistic
and closely allied with social and political history. Edith Császár Mályusz, who
is concerned with the development of national theatres in Austria, Czechoslovakia, and Hungary, states the position very clearly:

I do not consider the history of theater to be the history of drama or the history of theatrical
productions, and even less the success stories, or only the schematic linking together of
the biographies of actors; but primarily a certain directional manifestation in the development of society. Because the theatre develops from society as its foundation, or, if
one wishes, we might say a superstructure, it develops and grows according to the
economic situation and psychological reactions of the society. The actors themselves step
forth from the society, and the theater reacts upon them episodically, not immediately
heating them up to the heights of political agitation. [*The Theater and National Awakening*,
p. 3]

To the extent that the emergence of national theatres and dramas in the countries
of Northern and Eastern Europe at or near the end of the eighteenth century
represents in general a triumph over the internationalizing tendencies of neoclassical taste and principles, the subject lies outside the range of our present
concerns. But to the extent that it affected and was affected by the Pan-European
nature of dramatic theory, scene design, repertory, and performance style, the
nationalistic theatrical movements must be taken into account.

The purpose of this chapter is to provide a brief sketch of the central topics
of concern to the theatre historian in Spain, Germany, and Russia during the
period and to outline, again in brief, the elements that reflect the internationalization of theatre architecture and stage design.

SPAIN

To a certain degree, Spain stands apart from the generalizations that apply with more or less validity to the countries of Northern and Eastern Europe. Unlike them, Spain at the beginning of the eighteenth century could look back on over a century of a mature theatrical tradition. The Golden Age still cast its glow (or pall) over theatrical expectation. Contemporary commentators saw a similarity between the theatres of Spain and England, and contrasted them both with that of France. Neoclassical theorists like Thomas Rymer, John Dennis, and Charles Gildon disapproved equally of the irregularity of Elizabethan plays and the Spanish *comedia*. In 1743 James Ralph noted the similarity of the two dramas, not only in their disregard of the rules but also in the manner of the typical defense of their irregularity, "which is excused by some of the best *Spanish* Writers, in the same Manner that we excuse *Shakespear*, that is to say, by alledging [*sic*] that ordinary Writers, are bound by Rules, but that great Wits are above them" (*Case of our Present Theatrical Disputes*; quoted by John Loftis in *The Spanish Plays of Neoclassical England*, p. 19). In a famous letter to the French Academy in 1776, Voltaire not only noted the resemblance between English and Spanish plays but attributed the crude irregularity of the seventeenth-century theatre (outside France of course) to the infection of Spain. Lope de Vega, his contemporaries and predecessors, Voltaire wrote, "made of the Spanish stage a monster that pleased the rabble. This monster was paraded in the theatres of Milan and Naples. It was impossible that this contagion would not infect England; it corrupted the genius of all those who worked for the theatre long before Shakespeare" (*Oeuvres complètes* XXX, 364). Although Voltaire undoubtedly misjudged the influence of the Spanish drama, his exceptionally strong aversion to the *comedia* of the Golden Age was shared by most neoclassicists in the eighteenth century, including those in Spain. What distinguished Spanish theatre history from that of Germany and Russia, therefore, is that Spanish nationalists, rather than looking forward to a new theatre that would embody and express their sense of nationhood, were driven to cling to the theatre of the past in opposition to an imposed neoclassicism.

There appears to be agreement among modern scholars that in spite of the efforts of neoclassical theorists, there was little change in dramatic form or repertory until after mid-century. What sometimes does appear to be at issue is the relative worth of the older *comedia* and its eighteenth-century imitations, and the newer products of neoclassical principles and practices. Eighteenth-century Spanish theatre is explained either as a slowly developing but necessary neoclassical reaction to the bad taste and extravagance of the *comedia*, or as a period in which theatrical freedom and native traditions were sacrificed to the rules of a foreign doctrine and the plays of the great Spanish dramatists were slowly replaced by pale imitations of French masterpieces. Early, principally Spanish, scholarship reflects the latter view. More recent studies are generally concerned with the introduction and acceptance of neoclassicism in Spain and consciously or unconsciously adopt the neoclassical viewpoint. But in fact, such value judgments are irrelevant where they are not actually misleading. At the very least they tend to oversimplify both the historical and the historiographical processes. If the history of the theatre teaches us anything, it teaches that the success or quality of drama does not depend directly on the presence or absence of specific dramatic conventions or theories of production. Certainly references to the "rigidity" of neoclassical doctrine, or to the "extravagance" of the *comedia*, have limited explanatory power.

The Spanish scholars most intimately associated with the nationalist position are Marcelino Menéndez y Pelayo and Emilio Cotarelo y Mori. The former author's monumental *Historia de las ideas estéticas en España*, which appeared during the 1880s, remains a touchstone of Spanish nationalistic taste. Menéndez y Pelayo searched out passages in the works of eighteenth-century Spanish writers that express admiration for the drama of the Golden Age, finding even in its harshest critics an acknowledgement of the worth and power of the *comedia*, and tracing through the century the signs of a continuing tradition that would once again burst forth in the romanticism of the nineteenth century. For Menéndez y Pelayo neoclassicism was foreign to the Spanish national character and could not forever suppress the national spirit. He interpreted Feijóo as a precursor of romanticism, cited passages in Luzán favorable to the *comedia*, and attributed the characteristic tone of Moratín's comedies at the end of the century to Terence rather than to the French Diderot.

Cotarelo y Mori in a series of books published at the turn of the present century consistently minimized the effect of the neoclassical movement in Spain and insisted on the continued success of Golden Age dramas on the stage. But perhaps of more significance, he brought the detailed knowledge and methodology of the theatrical researcher to bear on the issue. He examined the production records of Madrid's two theatres for a forty-year period ending about 1780 and reported the results in *Iriarte y su época* (1897). One-half of the offerings were by Calderón, another one-quarter by other Golden Age dramatists, and a large percentage of the remainder were *saintes*, *zarzuelas*, and heroic comedies by Ramón de la Cruz, the most popular dramatist of the century and one given to continuing native forms. "The Spanish people," concludes Cotarelo y Mori, "continued to be faithful to their great poets, and, if not in real life, at least on the stage, they wanted to see that national romanticism which reminded them of their days of glory" (p. 333; translated and quoted by John Cook, *Neo-Classic Drama in Spain*, p. 249).

Interpretations of eighteenth-century Spanish theatre more sympathetic to the neoclassical reforms have generally found more favor among non-Spanish scholars. (An exception is Graf von Schack, who in his *Geschicte der Dramatischen Litteratur und Kunst in Spanien* [1845–46] expressed little sympathy with French theory and practice, but nevertheless provides a less heated survey of theatrical conditions than Cotarelo y Mori was later to do.) Modern reactions to the native Spanish tradition actually began with R. E. Pellissier's *The Neo-Classic Move-*

ment in Spain during the XVIIIth Century (1918), a relatively neutral treatment of a historical phenomenon. But the arguments were advanced more vigorously twenty years later by Paul Merimée, whose critical stance in *L'Influence française en Espagne au dix-huitième siècle* (1936) clearly reflected his nationality. (He complains, for instance, of Schack's anti-French bias: "The author does not lose any opportunity to abuse the French theatre and French authors; at times his partiality is such that it detracts oddly from his authority in matters of substance" [p. 77n.].) Merimée is of course concerned with more than simply the theatre, but he does not exclude that institution from the process of assimilation of French culture by the Spanish, which he sees completed by 1765. His attitude toward the theatre and the ultimate failure of French neoclassicism to reform it, is made clear in his near lament on Leandro Fernandez de Moratín, "whose work, impregnated with French influences, if it had been more abundant, would have been able to give to the struggles of the two dramatic schools a conclusion acceptable to both of a bourgeosie comedy of Spanish manners" (p. 6). (Compare Menéndez y Pelayo on Moratín, above.) Merimée admits the existence of innumerable attacks on neoclassicism, but finds them generally motivated more by a hatred of French literature than by an aversion to the rules. This general line of thought reached its zenith (or nadir) in an article by Charles Blaise Qualia that appeared in the *Publications of the Modern Language Association* in 1939:

To introduce classicism into the theatre, it was necessary to teach a fixed set of rules that required intellectual ability to appreciate and understand. The *vulgo* that ruled the taste of the Spanish stage did not possess this ability. Hence, neither the actors . . . nor the audiences could tolerate a type of drama that required technical learning to be understood, and the movement to introduce neo-classical drama into Spain resolved itself into a struggle between Gallophile intellectuals on the one hand and the *vulgo* and the actors on the other. [*PMLA* LIV, 184]

Spanish nationalist historians were thus placed in the camp of the stupid and the ignorant. The picture is rendered little better by the current commonplace, represented in nonspecialist introductions to the subject, that the eighteenth-century Spanish stage produced only degenerate imitations of Lope de Vega and Calderón de la Barca and that eighteenth-century Spanish theatre audiences were merely parochial and conservative. (See, for example, R. Merritt Cox, *Eighteenth-Century Spanish Literature*, p. 80.)

Fortunately, the most substantial work—in English at least—on the theatre of eighteenth-century Spain for the most part substitutes detailed analysis and scholarly detachment for easy generalization and polemic. In *Neo-Classic Drama in Spain* (1959), John A. Cook takes issue with Menéndez y Pelayo and especially with Cotarelo y Mori regarding both the value and the effect of the neoclassical movement, arguing that the nationalists' bias prevented them from correctly interpreting evidence and blinded them to the positive features of neoclassicism. "The author of this study feels," he writes, "that neoclassicism represented a natural and inevitable reaction against the affected style, bad taste, and irregularity into which Golden Age drama had degenerated'' (p. vii). Specifically, he challenges the Spanish scholars' reading of the tone of some of the works they discuss, and in the case of Cotarelo y Mori, the use of statistical evidence. He points out, for example, that one of Luzán's responses to criticism of his *Poética* is characterized by Menéndez y Pelayo as "discourteous," but that Pellissier found in it "perfect affability" (p. 67). While estimates of tone are to a certain extent subjective and depend upon an ability based on a close familiarity with both text and milieu, Cook is quite right to point out this area of disagreement, for such estimates affect the evaluation of evidence. He also questions Cotarelo y Mori's conclusion that plays of the Golden Age continued as the greater part of the theatres' repertories throughout the century. The Spanish scholar had based his contention on the number of older plays produced and the percentage of the total repertory they represented. Cook argues that such figures are not relevant, that "in evaluating the popularity of plays the number of performances of a given play and the amount of money it produced are much more important . . . " (p. 249). And he consequently argues that translations, recasts, and other plays in the neoclassical mode consistently outdrew the *comedia* at the box-office during the last two decades of the eighteenth century. "The Golden Age comedies," he concludes, "had not been driven from the stage by neoclassic propaganda; they were dying a slow death because they no longer reflected Spanish customs, and therefore had lost their appeal to the public" (p. 231).

Principal Contemporary Documents of the Controversy

The evidence for the foregoing interpretations of Spanish theatre history consists mainly of treatises, prefaces, and periodical articles which appeared on a fairly regular basis over a period of over seventy-five years, culminating in the attempt at the end of the eighteenth century to impose neoclassical standards through government control of the theatres. (See Cotarelo y Mori, *Biblioteca de las controversias sobre la licitud del teatro en España*.)

It is generally agreed that a critical influence on Spanish intellectual history was provided by the Benedictine monk, Benito Jerónimo Feijóo (1676–1764), whose interests lay principally in theology, philosophy, and science. Feijóo's attempt to strike a balance between native culture and imported intellectual traditions has made him a saint in both camps. Menéndez y Pelayo and Cotarelo y Mori see him as a precursor of romanticism; Cook views him as the principal source for whatever success neoclassicism came to enjoy in Spain. The unwary student of the theatre who turns with anticipation to Feijóo's *Teatro crítico universal*, published in eight volumes between 1726 and 1739, however, is certain to be disappointed. The work is not concerned with the theatre—there is no evidence to indicate that its author had an interest in it—but with a critical examination of ideas. Feijóo certainly argued in favor of science and rational thought, and he fought hard against ignorance and superstition, but he makes only one reference to the theatre: he discusses very briefly, and with satisfaction, the influence of Spanish comedy on the French theatre, citing as his authority the French critic Charles de Saint-Evrémond.

A far more direct and significant influence on neoclassical thought in Spain was Ignacio de Luzán's *Poética* (1737). Drawing largely on Aristotle and French and Italian critics, Luzán provided the basis for nearly all subsequent renderings of the neoclassical rules by Spanish writers. Luzán bases his discussion of the drama on the ubiquitous neoclassical principle of verisimilitude, and he derives the unities of time, place, and action logically from that principle, in much the same fashion as Castelvetro had done more than a century and a half earlier. Italianate scene changing, he charges, is merely an extravagant device for avoiding the discipline of the unities. Nevertheless, his own solution falls far short of the common French practice of limiting the setting to a single place. Instead, he suggests dividing the stage horizontally into the requisite number of settings, a notion reminiscent of the medieval *décor simultané* and of Mahelot's designs at the Hôtel de Bourgogne during the early years of the seventeenth century. Luzán indicates as well the possibility of vertical or perpendicular divisions, an idea that was to surface a few years later in the Parfaicts' description of medieval staging in their *Histoire du théâtre français*. But such fancies ran counter to Luzán's determined neoclassicism. Upon his return from a visit to France, he published *Memorias literarias de París* (1751), in which he roundly castigated French scenic practice for allowing changes in perspective: "The stable and fixed scene is more appropriate, more verisimilar and more in keeping with the unity of place interpreted in its strictest sense. . . . It is true that the fixed scene requires that the poet exert greater effort to conciliate the verisimilitude of the plot with the stability of place, but that is as it should be" (*Memorias literarias*, p. 116; translated and quoted by Cook, pp. 70–71). There is evidence too that Luzán's exposure in Paris to the *comédie larmoyante* changed his attitude toward the rigid separation of genres, but Menéndez y Pelayo's contention that the experience softened the critic's attitude toward the *comedia* is rightly challenged by Cook (pp. 73–76), who points out that tearful comedy was not the same as Spanish tragicomedy and that both Luzán and French critics like Diderot could and did defend it in neoclassical terms. If, as Cook notes, Luzán's *Poética* became the manifesto of the neoclassical movement in Spain, we should perhaps be grateful that Spanish staging practice was little affected by his theories of staging, in either their fanciful or severe modes.

The year following the publication of Luzán's *Poética*, there appeared in Paris a volume titled *Extraits de plusieurs pièces du théâtre espagnol avec des réflexions, et la traduction des endroits les plus remarquables*. The author, Du Perron de Castera, evidently intended his work as a source of material for the French theatre. Unfortunately, he combined an infuriating (to Spanish nationalists at least) condescension towards the Spanish drama with three specific charges: (i) that the Spanish *comedia* disregarded the unities; (ii) that the inclusion of so much material in a single play made the drama monstrous; and (iii) that the

Spanish had never produced proper tragedies. The effect of this little volume on Spanish criticism was not merely to pique Spanish sensibilities but to set the debate in neoclassical terms. In answering these criticisms, Spanish critics fell into the trap of attempting a neoclassical defense of dramatic forms that had in fact evolved outside the rules. Both sides assumed the validity of neoclassical principles, and the way was prepared for the eventual recasting of Golden Age drama in neoclassical form. The most important replies to Du Perron came from Blas Antonio Nasarre and Agustín Montiano y Luyando.

Nasarre, the royal librarian, in the preface to his *Comedias y entremeses de Miguel de Cervantes Saavedra* (1749), tried to make of Cervantes an exponent and practitioner of neoclassical principles and ventured to claim that Spain had comedies that "are in no way inferior to those of the famous Molière; to those of his imitator Wycherley, who is the English Molière, nor to those of Maffei and Riccoboni in Italy" (p. 38; translated and quoted by Cook, p. 93). But this defense of Spanish drama not surprisingly turned into a virulent condemnation of that drama—mainly by Lope de Vega and Calderón—which seemed indefensible in neoclassical terms. Montiano in his *Discurso sobre las tragedias españoles* (1750) tried to defend Spanish tragedy in the way that Nasarre had defended comedy, arguing that the genre had a long and honorable history in Spain. But, like Nasarre, in the final analysis he cannot refrain from damning the *comedia*. In a second *Discurso*, published a couple of years later, Montiano expands his discussion—and his usefulness to theatre historians—by making specific recommendations concerning theatrical programming and by including a consideration of acting and stage apparatus. Of particular interest are his comments on Madrid's theatres, both of which had recently been remodelled:

Our theatres have the material proportions which any play may require, because within an oval form or shape, with reasonably good architecture, there is a vestry, or scene of fair dimensions, which leaves free an adequate forum when such is necessary; a good-sized proscenium or *tablado*; a space for the wings or lateral machinery; a place above and below for the *appearances*; and in short, all the conveniences needed by the actors and the audience. . . . [*Discurso II*, p. 31; translated and quoted by Cook, pp. 128–29]

Montiano's comments, together with those of Leandro Moratín (see below), provide important information concerning the redesigned Teatro de la Cruz (1743) and Teatro del Principe (1745).

So far as formal treatises are concerned, the neoclassicists generally had their own way. Luis Velázquez continued the attack on Lope de Vega and Calderón in his *Orígenes de la poesía castellana* (1754), and in 1762 and 1763 the dramatist Nicolas Fernández de Moratín published three vitriolic attacks on the Spanish theatre and fellow playwright Ramón de la Cruz, who at the time virtually controlled the theatres of Madrid and who the neoclassicists believed, probably wrongly, was responsible for keeping their plays off the stage. Moratín's *Desengaños al teatro español (Censure of the Spanish Theatre)* established its author, in the words of Cotarelo y Mori, as "the most furious of all those who at that time swore by the authority of Boileau" (quoted by Cook, p. 217). The idea that the *comedia* should be suppressed and neoclassical drama officially supported by government action, first broached by Luzán, began to be picked up by other writers. Even Ramón de la Cruz echoed the sentiment in the preface to one of his operas (1757). Another notion, also first suggested by Luzán, was to recast Golden Age plays according to the rules. Thus Tomás Sebastián y Latre in *Ensayo sobre el teatro español* (1772) encouraged playwrights to rework the old *comedias*. Not until 1800, however, did a recast meet with public approval. The persistence on the stage of the *comedia* in the face of neoclassical opposition is attested by the demand of Mariano Luis Urquijo—who was later responsible for the *mesa censoria* of 1799—that it was time that the *comedia* be abandoned. The time was 1791.

The apologists for the *comedia* were for the most part less organized and less articulate than their opponents, and the actors and audiences spoke with performances and applause, not in literary documents. In 1764 there appeared an anonymous work, *La nación española defendida de los insultos del Pensador y sus secuaces (The Spanish Nation Defended)*, with a foreword by Mariano Nipho, to whom the work is sometimes attributed. The author—whoever he was—presents himself as a Spaniard who long has lived abroad and who has come to a recognition of the superiority of the Spanish drama, and he proceeds to demonstrate that superiority by a judicious selection of extracts from French critics. In fact, according to Cook, "the principal value of *The Spanish Nation Defended* lies, not in its defence of Golden Age comedy, but in the fact that it served to acquaint the reading public with the changes that had taken place in dramatic criticism in France" (p. 205). Another defense of the Spanish theatre, *La escena Hespañola defendida en el prólogo del teatro Hespañol* (1786), by García de la Huerta, is simply a diatribe against French dramatists and anyone who sees anything but good in the Spanish theatre.

Periodicals

The controversy was also carried on in several periodicals throughout the century, most of them of short duration and difficult to locate. Consequently the present discussion depends upon the analyses in Cook, *Neo-Classic Drama in Spain*, and Qualia, "The Campaign to Substitute French Neo-Classical Tragedy for the Comedia, 1737–1800," *PMLA* (1939). Although theoretical controversy was an important ingredient in their composition, the periodicals could also include reviews of plays and productions and commentary on actors and theatres. None of them present a complete picture of theatrical activity in Madrid, even for the few years of their publication, but they are valuable in establishing the repertory and the relative success of plays performed in Madrid theatres, especially in the last part of the century. (See Ada M. Coe, *Catálogo bibliográfico y crítico de las comedias anunciadas en los periódicos de Madrid desde 1661 hasta 1819.*)

Luzán's *Poética* had no sooner appeared than the first substantial Spanish periodical devoted to the criticism of literature from a neoclassical perspective appeared. *El Diario de los literatos* (1737–1742) modelled itself on contemporary French journals and announced its intention to steer a moderate course in its reviews of books, but its fundamental position was made clear very early on when it printed a lengthy review of and commentary on Luzán's *Poética*. Although the journal actually printed reviews of only two *comedias*—by Juan Ruiz de Alarcón and Tomás de Añorbe y Corregel—the practice of reviewing plays and performances in the light of the neoclassical rules was continued in Juan Mercadal's *El duende especulativo sobre la vida civil*, which appeared weekly for seventeen numbers in 1761. A more significant publication, *El Pensador* (1762–1767) was similarly the work of a single editor, the French–educated José Clavijo y Fajardo, who modelled his essays on Joseph Addison's *Spectator* papers. Once again, Luzán is cited as an authority in a campaign against the *comedia* and in favor of neoclassical standards of dramaturgy and taste. And again there is call for government intervention. Underlying the criticism are two concerns that remained constant among the reformers: the insistence on the moral function of the theatre, and the desire to bring Spain into the circle of civilized nations whose prime representative was France. *El Pensador* stimulated some nationalist replies. Besides that contained in *La nación española defendida* (see above), another defense was launched by Juan Christóbal Romea y Tapia in a short-lived periodical, *El Escritor sin título*. It is worth noting that Romea y Tapia's defense is limited to the dramatic texts of the *comedia* and does not extend to its performance. In this respect his only recommendation was to raise the price of admission and convert the theatre into an aristocratic institution, thereby, one assumes, endowing it with morality and taste. Several years later *El Censor* (1781–1786), a periodical published in the form of discourses, restated the charges of naivete, barbarousness, and immorality against the *comedia*.

With Mariano Nipho's *El Diario extranjero* (1763), we leave generalized theory and return to specific theatrical reviews. John Cook argues that this journal is "the first Spanish periodical to attempt a regular criticism of plays performed on the Spanish stage" (*Neo-Classic Drama in Spain*, p. 181). Nipho went beyond the modest beginnings in *El Diario de los literatos* and *El duende especulativo* by devoting considerable space to the specifically theatrical conventions of performances. He commented frequently on the quality of the acting and on the lives and training of actors, advocating government control of the theatres and adequate salaries for the actors. Still, the periodicals that had thus far appeared were limited in point of view, in breadth of interest, and in duration of publication, and could not really be compared with those of France. It was not until 1784 that a journal appeared to match the early *Diario de los literatos* in tone and dignity and to equal the French journals in longevity and sophistication.

The *Memorial literario* (1784–1808) announced its policy in its first number:

"In these articles we propose to give the argument or constitution of the comedies that are being performed on the stage and to collect the opinions of men of good judgment with reference to their good qualities or their defects" (translated and quoted by Cook, p. 314). It need hardly be said that the men of good judgment invariably had neoclassical tastes, or that the bible for critical principles was Luzán's *Poética*. The periodical was nevertheless moderate in the opinions and evaluations it printed, even as it pressed for immediate reform of the theatre to counter the bad taste of the audiences and the laziness of the actors. The only other periodical comparable to the *Memorial literario* in quality and longevity was the *Diario de Madrid* (1788–1818), which opened with a series of articles by the neoclassical playwright Candido María Trigueros and in 1789 promised a series of one hundred articles covering the rules for comedy, tragedy, and opera. Although the journal published articles opposed to as well as in favor of neoclassicism, the editorial thrust of the journal was never in doubt, and Luzán remained a major influence. (Cook relies on the *Diario de Madrid* as a check on the lists of performances provided by Cotarelo y Mori.)

Two shorter-lived periodicals that appeared briefly near century's end complete our present survey. *El Correo de Madrid* (1786–1790) and *La Espigadera*, both firmly neoclassical and reformist, were particularly critical of the acting and staging conditions at the theatres. The first article to appear in *La Espigadera* was devoted to a denunciation of Spanish performances, which the anonymous author considered coarse, indecent, and disordered. The stage sets were absurd, the stage directions confused, the acting ridiculous: "Theatrical performances . . . in Madrid have reached such an extreme of irregularity and ridiculousness that if the culture of a capital were to be judged by that of its theatre . . . ours could not fail to pass for the most uncultured and uncivilized in Europe" (translated and quoted by Cook, p. 325). And the prime cause of this theatrical chaos was the "enthusiasm and fury" of the *comedia*. Little had changed since Luzán.

Government Action and the Reform Plan of 1799

Calls for some sort of official action in the reform of the theatre, first suggested by Luzán, were a constant theme in the neoclassical program throughout the century. La Academia del Buen Gusto, established in 1749, seems to have been a combination of *salon* and academy, and like its predecessors in France and Italy was devoted to providing a dictionary and a grammar for the native language and a poetics for the native literature. The minutes of the Academia, which included Luzán, Nasarre, and Velázquez among its members, are preserved in manuscript in the Biblioteca Nacional. The imperviousness of the theatre to reform, however, clearly called for more official measures. In the Conde de Aranda, prime minister under Carlos III (r. 1759–1788), the reformers found a sympathetic ally with the power to act.

As early as 1763 Mariano Nipho had been asked to draw up a plan for theatrical reform (discussed briefly by Cook, p. 207), in which the author concentrated on the improvement of acting and theatrical management, but the plan was never implemented. In 1767 Aranda asked Bernardo de Iriarte to select from the old *comedia* those plays that adhered to neoclassical rules most closely to form a basic repertory. Iriarte's manuscript report (Biblioteca Nacional, ms. 9327) lists seventy-three *comedias* that could be recast in the neoclassical form with a minimum of revision, including twenty-one by Calderón, but only three by Lope de Vega and none by Tirso de Molina. (The manuscript is cited and discussed by Cotarelo y Mori in *Iriarte y su época*, p. 421, and by Cook in *Neo-Classic Drama in Spain*, pp. 226–27.) Aranda also established theatres at the royal residences (*Sitios Reales*) at Aranjuez, San Lorenzo, and La Granja, with Clavijo y Fajardo as general director. (The royal theatres were closed in 1777.) In Madrid the Frenchman Luis de Azema y Reynauld was appointed director of theatres. The *Instrucción para el Director de los Teatros de Madrid, Dr. Luis Reynaud*, dated April 1771 (preserved in the Archivo Municipal, Madrid), includes regulations concerning rehearsals, casting, and actor discipline.

In 1790, Gaspar de Jovellanos published his *Memoria para el arreglo de la policía de los espectáculos y diversiones públicas*, a report commissioned by the Academy of History at the request of the Supreme Council of Castile as a prelude to reform. Jovanellos roundly condemned the *comedia* on moral grounds and recommended dramatic contests as the means by which the old drama might be replaced by regular neoclassical drama. He also commented extensively on the reform of the physical theatre and on the acting profession. In 1791, Mariano Luis Urguijo published a preface to his translation of Voltaire's *La Mort de César*, in which he advocated the establishment of an official body

to examine for itself all the old and modern dramas; to order corrected those that are susceptible of emendation; to prohibit the performance of those that are bad; and, by bestowing laurels, prizes, and honors upon good poets who distinguish themselves, to encourage the youth of the nation to study such an important science. [translated and quoted by Cook, p. 371]

Finally, Leandro de Moratín in 1792 wrote two letters to the king criticizing the conditions of the Madrid theatres and recommending himself for the position of director of theatres. The magistrate of Madrid's reply suggested that Moratín's concerns were exaggerated but that two censors, one clerical and one lay, had been appointed. (The letters are printed in Antonio Canovas del Castillo, *Arte y letras*, pp. 282–98.) Further administrative details were worked out over the next several years, including the formation of a Board of Control consisting of a director, a censor, and teachers of declamation and music, and the plan whereby Madrid's theatres were to be nationalized in March 1800 was approved by royal order on 29 November 1799. The plays approved for performance were published in 1800 as *Teatro nuevo español*. The theatres were returned to the city on 24 January 1802. The neoclassical movement had failed. (For details see the article by C. E. Kany in *Revista de la Biblioteca, Archivo y Museo* VI [1929].)

*   *   *

The attempts of the neoclassicists to reform the Spanish theatre, so well documented throughout the century and still debated among modern scholars, tend to overshadow other concerns and other sorts of evidence. Early historians were themselves neoclassical in orientation. The Italian Pietro Napoli Signorelli, whose *Storia critica dei teatri* (1787–1790) we have already noted, lived in Spain for some time and during the 1770s and 1780s was a member of a celebrated *tertulia* or literary club, which included the playwrights Nicolás de Moratín and Tomás de Iriarte. The *Storia critica* in fact was written at the suggestion of the *tertulia*, to formalize the group's ideas concerning the reform and renewal of the theatre. (Leandro de Moratín discusses the *tertulia* in his *Vida de Don Nicolás Fernández de Moratín*.) The younger Moratín himself wrote a historical work, *Orígenes del teatro español*, first published posthumously in his *Obras* (1830–1831). This work, together with an essay on the history of the Spanish theatre in the eighteenth century with several appended catalogues of plays, is highly regarded by nationalist and neoclassicist alike. Casiano Pellicer's *Tratado histórico* (1804) is similarly neoclassically oriented, but based as it is on original archival research, continues to be cited as a valuable work of scholarship. Both Signorelli and Moratín had the advantage—and disadvantage—of recording history that they had witnessed and to a certain extent had helped to shape; Pellicer had access to some documents that are no longer extant. Less privileged historians must rely on less direct sources of information, especially archival documents and playtexts.

Fortunately, Spanish archives and libraries have long been repositories for theatrical material, and theatre historians since Pellicer have consulted and sometimes printed documents from the Archivo de la Diputación, the Archivo Historico de Protocolos, the Archivo del Palacio Nacional, and especially the Biblioteca Municipal and the Biblioteca Nacional—all in Madrid. The many publications of Emilio Cotarelo y Mori are particularly valuable for their discussion and publication of archival documents. The fact that the theatres were under municipal control has ensured the preservation in the municipal archives of a good deal of information concerning the management and upkeep of the *corrales*. (Oddly we have very little information concerning the theatres in the *Sitios Reales*.) And the neoclassical campaign to involve the national government in the reform of the theatre has resulted in various reports and documents concerning the theatre being preserved in the Biblioteca Nacional and the Biblioteca Municipal. Finally, that most pervasive effect of government involvement, censorship, has meant that hundreds of manuscript plays with the censor's *imprimatur* are to be found in both the national and the municipal libraries. (See, for example, A. Paz y Melia, *Catalogo de las piezas de teatro que se conservan en el departamento de manuscritos de la Biblioteca Nacional*.)

The theatre historian, therefore, faces the task of comparing these manuscript copies with the published versions of the plays (if they exist) in the light of the practices of the acting troupes and the various reviews and descriptions of plays and performances in order to come to some conclusion as to the version that was actually performed. We would like to think that the approved manuscript version represents what was performed, but there is evidence to suggest that the actors may have learned their parts before the script was submitted to the censor, who is unlikely to have attended a performance in any event.

The study of these manuscript texts can sometimes yield interesting results indeed. Heinrich Richard Falk, for instance, notes the repeated references in the plays of the second half of the century to actors and theatrical events, and he notes the tendency in many of the *sainetes* (short farces) of Ramón de la Cruz for the performers to play the parts of actors or even themselves in theatrical situations. Such plays are obviously important sources of information concerning theatrical practices, personnel, and audiences. But the manuscript texts of Cruz's plays—most of them housed in the Biblioteca Municipal—are even more revealing. Cruz evidently had specific actors and actresses in mind when he wrote the plays, for he almost invariably provides the names of specific actors instead of the names of characters in speech headings and stage directions. These manuscripts, notes Falk, "constitute an invaluable source of information on Spanish actors during the last half of the eighteenth century. The careers of most performers on the Madrid stages can be established with virtual certainty solely from the evidence of these manuscripts" (in *Educational Theatre Journal* XXVIII, 302n.).

For the most part, however, the theatre of eighteenth-century Spain has not attracted much attention among English-speaking theatre historians, nor is it given much space in general histories and textbooks. John Cook's *Neo-Classic Drama in Spain* (1959) and I. L. McClelland's *Spanish Drama of Pathos: 1750–1808* (1970) remain the only substantial works in English. Pity.

GERMANY

It might well be argued that neoclassicism fared worse in Germany than in Spain, not, it is true, because it encountered an entrenched native tradition, but because it was only one of several elements that contributed to the development of the German theatre. At the beginning of the eighteenth century, what we might very loosely refer to as the German theatre was as confused and diverse as the more than three hundred duchies and territories that were ostensibly "German." John Prudhoe sums up the situation:

One by one foreign traditions had been haphazardly adopted. To that of the English Comedians were added those of the *comedia* and the theatre of machines. In the seventeenth century Dutch touring companies brought the neo-classicism of [Joost van den] Vondel together with elaborate mimed interludes in lavish costume. French and Spanish plays were also imported, though, of course, heavily adapted. The total result was an unedifying, inartistic confusion. [*The Theatre of Goethe and Schiller*, p. 14]

Few commentators would quarrel with Prudhoe's last sentence. The history of the German theatre is most commonly interpreted as the successive efforts of theatre managers, dramatists, and critics to bring an edifying, artistic order out of the confusion. It is worth noting that although early attempts at reforming the German theatre were initiated and led by those who advocated a neoclassicism on the French model, efforts soon passed into the hands of actor-managers who were as concerned with the viability and respectability of the acting profession as they were with repertory. A new phase was introduced with the establishment, during the final thirty years of the century, of so-called national theatres. Finally, the "classicism" developed by Goethe and Schiller at Weimar at the end of the century, however it is interpreted or explained, has little in common, either in dramaturgy or in acting style, with the neoclassical rules as advocated early in the century by Gottsched. The discussion that follows notes only those documents that are indispensable for the study of the German theatre in the eighteenth century.

Gottsched and the Neubers

Johann Christoph Gottsched (1700–1766), Professor of Poetry at Leipzig University, early in his career established himself as a leader in eighteenth-century rationalism and as an unswerving proponent of neoclassicism. While still in his twenties, he edited two influential journals, *Die vernünftigen Tadlerinnen* (1725–1726) and *Der Biedermann* (1727–1729). The most complete—and best-known—statement of his principles is to be found in his *Versuch einer kritischen Dichtkunst* (1730; printed in *Schriften zur Literatur*, 1972). The work reveals a staunch admirer of a French criticism that was even in 1730 decidedly old-fashioned. The most frequently cited authorities are Dacier, Corneille, d'Aubignac, and Voltaire, and Gottsched's insistence on the moral function of drama and on the prime necessity of verisimilitude is expressed in a most simple-minded and pedantic form. In what has become the most famous passage in the work, we find the heart of Gottsched's poetic:

First of all, select an instructive moral lesson which will form a basis for the entire plot in accordance with the goals which you wish to achieve. Next, lay out the general circumstances of an action which very clearly illustrates the chosen instruction. . . . Next, you must determine what effect you wish to achieve in this creation. . . . Everything will influence the names given to the characters who will appear in it. . . . If you want to make a comedy . . . the characters must be citizens, for heroes and princes belong in a tragedy. [pp. 97–98; translated and quoted by Marvin Carlson, *Theories of the Theatre*, p. 165]

The arguments for the unities are, of course, based on the necessity of verisimilitude and are reminiscent of Jean Chapelain's report on behalf of the French Academy on Corneille's *Le Cid* almost a century before. In fact, not since Castelvetro had the unities been advocated and defended so rigidly and on such a narrowly naturalistic basis. (The most extensive discussion of Gottsched's theories in English is by Betsy Aikin-Sneath in *Comedy in Germany in the first Half of the Eighteenth Century*, pp. 7–29.)

Professorial theories nevertheless are seldom heeded in the immediate hurley-burley of the practical work-a-day world, and we might expect Gottsched's ideas to remain in the arena of debate. But this was no ordinary professor. He was determined to bring enlightenment to his countrymen and in a very practical way. In 1727 he succeeded in establishing an association with an acting troupe newly formed by Caroline and Johann Neuber. Together Gottsched and the Neubers set out to reform the German theatre. The relationship is best understood through a study of sixteen letters written by the Neubers to Gottsched. (The letters are printed in F. J. von Reden-Esbeck's *Caroline Neuber und ihre Zeitgenossen*, which also includes a dozen of the Neubers' programs.) A main concern of Gottsched and the Neubers was to establish a body of drama to replace the crude improvised comedies of the German professional troupes. In the preface to Gottsched's play *Cato* (1732), there is a reference to eight plays in the company's repertory, most of them translations from the French. Over the next ten years about twenty more were added. A contemporary periodical records the repertory in 1741, and we find that three-quarters of the plays still are translations of French dramas, mostly by Corneille, Racine, Voltaire, Molière, Regnard, Marivaux, and Destouches. (See Reden-Esbeck, p. 259; Walter H. Bruford, *Theatre Drama and Audience in Goethe's Germany*, pp. 61–64.) The process of "regularizing" the repertory was formalized in the publication, between 1740 and 1745, of *Die deutsche Schaubühne nach den Regeln und Exempeln der Alten*, six volumes of plays either translated from or modelled on French drama, under the supervision of Gottsched. This and subsequent collections published throughout the century provide valuable records of what acting troupes actually performed.

Actors and Managers

Johann Friedrich Schönemann (1704–1782), one-time actor in the Neubers' company and after the breakup of that troupe leader of his own, like Gottsched also published the principal plays of his repertory. The seven volumes of *Schönemannsche Schaubühne*, published between 1748 and 1755, contain a preponderance of French plays in German translation, although the proportion of comedy and *comédie larmoyante* shows an increase over that of Gottsched's collection. Of equal significance are the prefaces to these volumes, in which Schönemann discusses the difficulties besetting an actor-manager. He complains of the ignorance of the low-brows, the snobbery of the Francophiles, and the stifling moral concerns of the clergy. He points bitterly to the pedantry he found in the universities and to the boorishness of their students, who blow tobacco smoke onto the stage. And he criticizes the extravagance, ingratitude, conceit, and lifestyle of actors. (Some things never change.)

The great actor Konrad Ekhof (1720–1778), like the Neubers, was concerned to raise the professional status of the actor in Germany. He acted with Schönemann's company for seventeen years, constantly honing his craft and deepening his understanding of the actor's art. In 1753 he founded a short-lived Acting Academy in Schwerin. Although the institution was not a success, the minutes of its meetings and Ekhof's *Grammatik der Schauspielkunst*, or plan for training actors, are preserved in the Hofbibliothek in Gotha and represent important evidence for the state of the acting profession before Ekhof's time and the ways in which it was changing. (Ekhof's writings are difficult to locate. Reden-Esbeck quotes from his work in *Caroline Neuber* and Heinz Kindermann discusses the *Grammatik* in *Theatergeschichte Europas* IV, 514–15.)

During the last three years of his life, Ekhof was in charge of play production at the Gotha court theatre. The administrative director was the court librarian, Heinrich August Ottakar Reichard (sometimes confused with the musician Johann Friedrich Reichard), who also edited two important publications during the last quarter of the century: *Theaterjournal für Deutschland* (1777–1784) and *Theaterkalender* (1775–1800). These periodicals record in some detail the establishment and repertories of the growing number of so-called national theatres, from the fourteen noted in the first number of *Theaterkalender* to the more than thirty recorded in the 1790s.

A few actors wrote autobiographies. Johann Christian Brandes' *Meine Lebensgeschichte* (1800), described by Bruford as "the most informative theatrical autobiography of the century" (*Theatre Drama and Audience in Goethe's Germany*, p. 184), provides the theatre historian with a good picture of the organization and activities of a German theatre company during the latter part of the century. August Wilhelm Iffland (1759–1814), actor and director of the National Theatre at Mannheim in 1785–1792 and later of that in Berlin, also describes his theatrical career in *Über meine theatralische Laufbahn*, written during the final years of his life. Finally we turn to Friedrich Ludwig Schröder (1744–1816), the actor who introduced Shakespeare to Germany and one of the most distinguished theatrical figures of the century. Schröder's biography was written by his friend Friedrich Ludwig Wilhelm Meyer (1819).

Contemporary Theatre History

Several works written late in the century provide at least partial histories of the German theatre. Christian Heinrich Schmidt's *Chronologie des deutschen Theaters* was published in 1775, and J. F. Schütze's *Hamburgische Theatergeschichte* in 1794. But the first, best-known, and most important is Johann Friedrich Löwen's *Geschichte des deutschen Theaters* (1766). Löwen (1729–1771), Johann Schönemann's son-in-law and described by W. H. Bruford in *Theatre Drama and Audience* as "an extremely conceited man, with a bee in his bonnet and a passion for intrigue" (p. 103), was instrumental in the founding of the Hamburg National Theatre in 1767. His *Geschichte*, together with a preliminary notice concerning the coming theatre and an *Address* to the theatre's staff on the occasion of his taking over the directorship, presents his analysis of the current state of the German theatre and outlines his plans for its future. (All three documents are printed in the edition of the *Geschichte* prepared by H. Stumke in 1903.) The historical part of Löwen's work, prepared in collaboration with Ekhof, concentrates on the careers of the Neubers and their successors Schönemann, Heinrich Koch, and Konrad Ackerman. The analysis of the defects of the German theatre stresses the cupidity of managers, the uncouthness of actors, the indifference of the princes and the large towns, the opposition of the clergy, and the lack of a German repertory. (Some things never change.) Löwen's solution included proposals to set up a permanent, nonprofit theatre with a salaried director, to establish a training school for actors, to provide decent salaries and pensions for actors, and to encourage native dramatists by offering prizes. Löwen was not the first to point out either the problems or the possible solutions, but he made his points at the right time, and the national theatres that emerged over the following thirty years were modelled more or less on the plan he outlined in his *Geschichte des deutschen Theaters*.

Lessing

The man engaged as resident advisor and dramaturg at the Hamburg National Theatre was Gotthold Ephraim Lessing (1729–1781), a dramatist and critic who had been engaged in theatrical and dramatic issues for almost twenty years before taking up his position at Hamburg in 1767. As editor of several theatrical periodicals between 1750 and 1761, Lessing had offered theatrical news of Paris and Berlin, but is probably best known for his rejection in an article in *Literaturbriefe* (1759–1761) of Gottsched's neoclassicism, and his advocacy of English rather than French dramatic models. The range of his theatrical interests as well as their general direction is illustrated too in the translation that engaged him during this period: François Riccoboni's *L'Art du théâtre*, John Dryden's *Essay of Dramatic Poesy*, Pierre Sainte-Albine's *Le Comédien*, Luigi Riccoboni's *Histoire du théâtre italien*. His translations of Diderot's *Entretiens* and *De la Poésie dramatique* indicate his awareness of the reaction even in France against the old-fashioned neoclassicism championed by Gottsched.

By far the most significant document to come from Lessing's pen, however, was the *Hamburgische Dramaturgie*, a journal in which the author not only chronicles the short history of the Hamburg National Theatre, but also sums up the best eighteenth-century thought on the theatre. Historians of the theatre and of dramatic theory have been equally impressed. Thus W. H. Bruford in *Theatre Drama and Audience* notes that the *Hamburg Dramaturgy* "shows us a leading German theatre in action at a critical period, informs us about its repertoire, and how it was received both by the public and by the ablest critic of the day, and it gives us vivid impressions of the acting" (p. 136). And Marvin Carlson in *Theories of the Theatre* comments: "In addition to reviewing individual productions, these essays ranged widely over questions of dramatic theory and technique; they provided, in their totality, the critical foundation for the establishment of a modern German theatre'' (p. 168). The general thrust of the work is to demonstrate the inferiority of French neoclassicism by comparing it unfavorably with English and Greek drama, and by appealing directly to Aristotle's *Poetics* as a counter to the neoclassical rules:

No nation [writes Lessing in his final essay] has more misapprehended the rules of ancient drama than the French. They have adopted as the essential some incidental remarks made by Aristotle about the most fitting external division of drama, and have so enfeebled the essentials by all manner of limitations and interpretations, that nothing else could necessarily arise therefrom but works that remained far below the highest effect on which the philosopher had reckoned in his rules. [tr. Helen Zimmern, in Bernard F. Dukore, *Dramatic Theory and Criticism*, p. 436]

Diderot, it is true, continues to be cited with approval; French plays are prominent in the Hamburg repertory; and Shakespeare is nowhere to be seen. But the groundwork had clearly been laid for Schröder's introduction of the bard as well as for the uniquely German classicism of Goethe and Schiller.

Goethe

Johann Wolfgang von Goethe (1749–1832), Germany's greatest man of letters, was involved with the theatre as playwright, critic, theorist, and manager for forty years, and his writings touching on dramatic art both comment on the history of the German theatre and are themselves the stuff of that history. A historian who would come to grips not only with the facts of German theatrical history from 1775 to 1815 but also with its motivating spirit could do no better than to become steeped in Goethe's works—in his dramas, his fiction and his autobiography as well as in those writings and observations concerned directly with theatrical management and production. The material of the early *Wilhelm Meisters theatralische Sendung*, written about 1777 but not published, was later incorporated into the semiautobiographical *Wilhelm Meisters Lehrjahre* (1795), which relates in its first six books the experiences of a stage-struck young man on tour with a theatrical company. While Goethe goes far beyond the conventional limitations of the picaresque novel, in these early episodes *Wilhelm Meister* is clearly in the tradition of Augustín de Rojas' *El viaje entretenido* (1603) and Paul Scarron's *Le Roman comique* (1651, 1657). Goethe's autobiography, *Dichtung und Wahrheit* (translated by John Oxenford), published at intervals between 1811 and 1831, breaks off in 1775, but includes a brief discussion of the state of the German stage and Schröder's Shakespeare adaptations in Book XIII. Between 1823, when Goethe was seventy-four, and 1832, the year of his death, he engaged in a series of conversations with a young man named Johann Peter Eckermann (1792–1854), who subsequently published transcriptions of the conversations in 1838. (The standard English translation is by John Oxenford.) The conversation on 22 March 1825, following the fire that had the previous night destroyed the Weimar theatre, is especially significant for the light it sheds on the theatre and its management when Goethe had first been appointed director in the early 1790s. Again on 14 April of the same year Goethe explained to Eckermann his method for selecting actors. Other comments are scattered throughout the *Conversations*. Finally, we have Goethe's famous *Regeln für Schauspieler* (*Rules for Acting*), which Eckermann edited from notes made in 1803 by two actors, Pris Alexander Wolff and Karl Gruner, and published in 1824. The *Rules* were intended to eliminate regional dialects; to instruct actors in proper enunciation; to provide principles for recitation and declamation, movement, and blocking; to outline procedures for rehearsals; and to offer advice to actors on proper social behaviour. (A complete translation of the *Rules for Acting* is provided by Marvin Carlson in an appendix to *Goethe and the Weimar Theatre*, itself the best introduction in English to Goethe's career as a theatre manager and director.)

RUSSIA AND EASTERN EUROPE

The historiography of the theatre of Eastern Europe is to a disconcertingly large extent a closed book to most English-speaking students of the theatre. And the main reason, of course, is that most of us are not familiar with the languages of Eastern Europe. English and French are the generally accepted languages of international theatre history; German retains some claim in American graduate schools as the language of scholarship; Spanish and Italian are widely taught. But rare indeed is the young theatre historian who deliberately sets out to add to these languages Polish or Russian or Serbo-Croatian or Hungarian. The field has been left to native speakers and to a handful of specialists who may or may not report their findings in English or French. Denied access to on-going scholarly discourse and to original source materials, therefore, theatre historians concerned with the overall dimension of European theatre history must perforce gain their knowledge at an unprofessional remove. The pertinent chapters in Heinz Kindermann's *Theatergeschichte Europas* that are devoted to the Slavic and Hungarian theatres are valuable introductions, but the nature of Kindermann's work precludes extensive references to primary materials, and the works cited in the notes and bibliographies are almost exclusively secondary sources. The difficulties of coming to terms with primary materials is only partially mitigated by the penetration into Slavic and Hungarian-speaking territories of French, Italian, and German theatre, with some attendant documentation in those languages.

Russia almost automatically turned to foreigners and foreign models to develop a secular theatre. Johann Gottfried Gregory, a priest from the German quarter of Moscow, was recruited in 1672 to produce court plays, but the experiment came to an end with Gregory's death in 1675. (Boris V. Varneke in his *History of the Russian Theatre* points out that the prototypes of Gregory's dramas are to be found in the anthology *Englische Comedien und Tragedien*, published in 1620.) In 1701 under Peter the Great, Johann Kunst and his German troupe were brought from Danzig, but by 1707 their theatre too had disbanded. The court theatre revived under the Empress Anna in 1730, and the succession of foreign acting companies at the Russian court between that date and 1758 is indicative of the general line of development that the Russian theatre was to take. The first to arrive were Italian *commedia dell'arte* companies, followed in 1740 by a German company under Caroline Neuber, which introduced neoclassical acting and repertory. Neuber's troupe was in turn replaced in 1743 by a French company with a French repertory. The "official" inauguration of Russian neoclassical drama came in 1747 with the publication of *Khorev*, a tragedy by Alexei Petrovich Sumarokov (1718–1777), a playwright hailed by German and French neoclassicists alike as the Racine of Russia. *Khorev* was performed in 1749 by the students of the Cadet Academy, but seven years later the first Russian professional acting company came into being under Sumarokov and Fyodor Volkov, a talented actor from Yaroslavl who had been invited to train at the Cadet Academy. Although the repertory was as varied as a strict censorship would allow, the main influences continued to be contemporary French and German plays. (The Legislative Act of 30 August 1756, which established the company, is printed in full in Boris V. Varneke, *History of the Russian Theatre*, pp. 71–72.) Russian theatre was not immune to the changes affecting theatre and drama in France and Germany, but neoclassicism continued as the dominant mode well into the nineteenth century. Simon Karlinsky argues that the neoclassical drama that began with *Khorev* reached its "natural termination" in Alexander Griboedov's *Gore ot uma* (1824), variously translated as *The Misfortune of Being Clever* or *The Trouble With Reason* (*Russian Drama from its Beginnings to the Age of Pushkin*, p. 61). Any doubts concerning the demise of neoclassicism were put to rest by the publication six years later of Pushkin's *Boris Godunov*.

Much of the evidence for this history consists of official and semiofficial reports, letters, records, decrees, and petitions. (Many are cited and quite a few are quoted by Boris Varneke, although the author is not always scrupulous in noting the source or location of a given document.) A series of petitions between 1749 and 1767, for example, asking for permission to stage plays in various leased premises and for police protection against riots during the performances, indicates the persistence of theatrical enterprises independent of the court (Varneke, pp. 59–60). We can add to such material newspaper notices and theatrical posters, but relatively few eyewitness accounts of productions or theatrical memoirs—so important to the study of the English and French stages—are available much before the end of the century. Varneke prints a passage by the actor Yakov Yemelyanovich Shusherin (1753–1813) on rehearsals (p. 90), and quotes contemporary descriptions of the actors Peter Plavilshchikov (1760–1812) and Anton Mikhailovich Krutitsky (1751–1803) (pp. 94–95), but he adds little else that would bring us the nitty-gritty of performance. The dearth of material from the provinces is even more acute. Varneke is thrown back on the theatre historian's oldest and weakest crutch: "We have to be satisfied with incomplete and fragmentary information, and console ourselves with the supposition that the nature of theatrical development in all cities was essentially the same, while differing in details" (p. 96).

During the early years of the nineteenth century, a trio of theatre enthusiasts sought to preserve something of the Russian theatrical world of the late eighteenth century, and the results of their efforts provide important information for theatre historians. Stepan Zhikharev (b. 1788), as a seventeen year old with a prodigious memory, began in 1805 a series of interviews with various theatrical celebrities of the day, and for almost two years kept a diary of his conversations and of his theatregoing. Among those who talked to him were the actors Ivan Dmitrevsky (1733–1821) and Peter Plavilshchikov, the playwright and director Alexander Shakhovsky (1777–1846), and in Karlinsky's words, "an elderly prompter who remembered much theatrical lore of the end of the eighteenth century" (*Russian Drama*, p. 184). (The diary was first published in the 1850s but has been more recently edited by B. M. Èikhenbaum. Unhappily, there is no English translation.) Sergei Aksakov (b. 1791) similarly cultivated the acquaintance of playwrights and actors, but waited until much later to write his memoirs concerning the Russian theatre between 1807 and 1826. (They are published in his *Sobranie sochinenii*, 1952–1956.) Finally, Pimen Arapov (1796–1861), a theatre administrator and publisher, compiled a posthumously published *Letopis' russkogo teatra* (*Chronicle of the Russian Theatre*), covering the period 1673–1825. (Varneke reports that the old actor Dmitrevsky had earlier submitted a history of the Russian theatre to the Russian Academy but that it was subsequently destroyed by fire.)

Simon Karlinsky notes in his introduction to *Russian Drama* that at one time he contemplated translating Sergei Danilov's *Ocherki po istorii russkogo dramaticheskogo teatra* (*Essays in the History of Russian Dramatic Theatre*). The reasons he gives for not doing so and for proceeding instead with his own project are perfectly legitimate, but the pity is that Danilov's work remains unavailable to those who do not read Russian. Published in 1948, *Ocherki* is in fact a true history of the theatre, concerned with performance arrangements and theatrical conditions in a way that Karlinsky is not. And in spite of the conventional Soviet jargon and jingoism—added, in Karlinsky's words, "to protect the author and the book from extermination"—the study represents an even-handed treatment of its subject. Karlinsky is equally admiring of Vsevolod Vsevolodsky-Gerngross's *Istoriia russkogo teatra* (1929), which, although thoroughly Marxist in approach, is written with real scholarly integrity. But he offers a warning concerning much of Russian scholarship in cultural and theatrical history since 1930:

For half a century now, distortion of cultural history has been practiced in the Soviet Union on a scale that is unimaginable to anyone who has not had a chance to compare pre- and post-revolutionary sources. Few people in the West have had that chance. This lack of comparison leads to uncritical acceptance by Western commentators, at times rather knowledgeable ones, of events unknown to history and manufactured in recent decades by career-minded Soviet scholars. [*Russian Drama*, p. xvi]

All the more reason to regret the unavailability in English of the work of Vsevolodsky-Gerngross and Danilov.

The studies that are available in Western languages are not numerous. Boris Vasilevich Varneke's *History of the Russian Theatre*, first published in 1908, is available in a translation of the third edition of 1939. Varneke remains useful for the amount of original source material he cites and quotes. Although he might be a trifle old-fashioned in his emphasis on the development of realism, "which constitutes the fundamental and the most productive tendency of our entire art" (p. x), any distortion of history that we might sense is the result of his thesis, not of deliberate falsification of evidence. Indeed his conclusion to the section on the eighteenth century, which celebrates the growth of the theatre from aristocratic entertainment to the mirror of the people's joys and sorrows, bears little relation to the documented survey that precedes it. The only English-language survey to rival that of Varneke, Marc Slonim's *Russian Theater from the Empire to the Soviets* (1961), is a popular account, devoid of scholarly notes and references and occasionally given to error. Karlinsky notes, for instance, that Slonim repeats the story, first recorded by Jacob von Stahlin in the eighteenth century but disproved in the nineteenth century, that Czar Alexei's daughter Sophia involved herself in the court theatre in the 1670s (*Russian Drama*, p. 51n.). Moreover, the entire history of the Russian theatre to the end of the eighteenth century is covered in fewer than twenty-five pages. Karlinsky himself, although more concerned with dramatic literature than theatrical history, presents a valuable survey of eighteenth-century Russian drama. The standard history of the Russian theatre in a Western language, however, remains Ettore Lo Gatto's detailed and well-illustrated *Storia del teatro Russo* (1952; 2d ed. 1963).

Elsewhere in Eastern Europe the German theatre was more influential than the French. Reichard's *Theaterkalendar* notes the presence of German companies in Prague, Bratislava, Riga, Warsaw, Pomerania, and Hungary. These German "national" theatres evidently offered more attractive models for central European nationalists than did the French. "For the young Central European national theatres," writes Edith Mályusz, "only English drama and the professional German theatres, which served as the intermediary, could be useful as an example. . . . The German theatre did not become popular in Bohemia and Hungary because it enjoyed the favor of the government. . . . It obtained its leading role because it was filled with action, was modern and was easy to understand" (*The Theatre and National Awakening*, p. 8). This explanation undoubtedly has some truth in it, but it is just as clearly incomplete. The process of internationalization and its effect on or acceptance by various linguistic and cultural groups throughout Europe is a complex story that has yet to be told.

In Hungary György Bessenyei (1747–1811), who was familiar with French neoclassical tragedy in Vienna, is credited with launching Hungarian dramatic literature with his *Agis Tragédiája* (pub. 1772), but the first public dramatic performance in the Hungarian language had to wait until 1791, when Hungary's first professional theatre company under László Kelemen began its short-lived career (1791–1796). Kelemen's experiment was an important forerunner of the Hungarian National Theatre that finally opened in 1837. And it also inspired the work of Hungary's first theatre historian. János Endrődy's *A magyar játékszín* (*The Hungarian Theatre*) was published in three volumes (1792–1793). The work is particularly valuable for the light it sheds on Kelemen and the vicissitudes of the Hungarian theatre in Pest in the 1790s. Other important documents relating to the company include the following:

a. a "Request for Assistance" addressed to the county authorities of Pest, perhaps in Kelemen's own hand, preserved in the Pest County Archives (reproduced in József Bayer, *A nemzeti játékszín története* [*The History of the National Theatre*], I, 146ff.);

b. a Memorandum on the Hungarian theatre prepared in 1792 by the German Julius Karl Horst, concerned mainly with the problems of management (Bayer, I, 74);

c. a petition recording Kelemen's expulsion from the company in 1795;

d. an inventory of the Kelemen troupe dating from the autumn of 1792;

e. theatrical regulations and financial accounts in the Pest County Archives; and

f. Kelemen's diary (edited in 1960 by Géza Staud).

Edith Mályusz was able, partially on the basis of this information, to reconstruct the performance of András Dugonics' *Mária Bátori*, the text of which survives in three manuscript copybooks as well as in the first edition of 1795 (*The Theater and National Awakening*, pp. 137–42). (For those who read Hungarian, the following volumes also contain important documentary materials: Béla Váli, *A magyar színészet története* [1887]; József Bayer, *A magyar dráma története* [1897]; Tibor Kardos and Tekla Dömötör, *Régi magyar drámai emlékek* [1966].)

THEATRE ARCHITECTURE AND SCENE DESIGN

In the areas of theatre architecture and scene design, as we have seen, Italian artists and technicians held sway. Nevertheless, during the eighteenth century the processs of internationalization resulted in work that was international in spirit and style, the product of designers who adapted, borrowed, or were influenced by one another's work. Andrea Pozzo's influential *Prospettiva de' pittori e architetti*, for example, was truly a Pan-European phenomenon. Originally published in both Italian and Latin, it subsequently appeared in a French translation in 1700, in a Latin-German edition in 1706, in an English translation in 1707, and in a French-Flemish edition in 1709. In 1737 a Chinese translation was presented to the Academy of St. Petersburg by Portuguese Jesuits. We have seen too the interrelationships among architectural theorists and historians, who freely commented on one another's work and tended to treat theatre architecture in an international context, contrasting and comparing theatrical design throughout Europe. The hundreds of extant scene designs, many of them associated with the court theatres established throughout the continent, also offer substantial evidence of an international style. This style was not, of course, static throughout the entire period. Scholars have had little difficulty tracing the development of a Baroque style in architecture and scene design through the seventeenth and early eighteenth centuries, culminating in the work of the Bibienas, and in tracing a reaction to this style, led by the Italian-trained but French-born Jean Nicolas Servandoni. Servandoni's work in Paris during the 1750s and the slowly waning influence of the Bibiena family (whose last member, Carlo, died in 1787) were the preludes to a neoclassical style evident in the work both of architects—such as Robert Adam, Claude Nicolas Ledoux, and Victor Louis—and of scene designers—such as the Quaglio family and Paolo Landriani. (The term *neoclassical* is here used as it is in art history. As a literary or theatrical term it refers to a movement that antedates Servandoni by a century.)

There is little point in attempting to trace the surviving evidence for all the theatres known to have been built in Europe during the eighteenth century, even if it were possible to do so. (Donald Mullin in *The Development of the Playhouse* provides a selective survey of some of the most architecturally significant houses, and Margarete Baur-Heinhold in *The Baroque Theater* includes a wide variety of photographs and engravings of theatres and stages of the period.) The most important evidence, of course, consists of those houses that have survived in one form or another to the present day, but even in these instances, we have no readily available information on the number or their condition. We have already noted some of the theatres that are extant in France and Italy. The following examples are from Germany and Eastern Europe:

a. Theatre at Ludwigsburg (Germany). Built by Donato Giuseppe Frisoni (1683–1735) in 1730 and painted by Giuseppe Baroffio, the house was completely renovated in 1810 by Friedrich Nicolaus Thouret (1767–1845). Its baroque interior was gutted and the auditorium was rebuilt in a lyre shape with neoclassical decoration. (See Baur-Heinhold, pls. 188–90.)

b. Schlostheater Schönbrunn (Vienna). This private theatre was built in 1766 by Nicolas Pocazzi for Maria Theresa. In 1926 the original proscenium arch was moved back to allow the addition of more seats, and a metal safety curtain was installed. The house was restored following damage during World War II. (See Baur-Heinhold, pls. 124–28.)

c. Altes Residenztheater (Munich). Designed by Lorenzo Quaglio and built by François de Cuvilliés 1750–1753, the Residenztheater is described by Mullin as "a court playhouse of limited size but spectacular appointment" (p. 60). The theatre was destroyed during World War II, but plans and photographs of the original structure allowed its reconstruction—using salvaged remains of the original—on a different site. (See Baur-Heinhold, pls. 177–85, colorplate XVI; Mullin, figs. 89–91.)

d. Česky Krumlov (Czechoslovakia). An ornate court theatre constructed in the Schwar-

zenberg Palace in 1766, the house remains virtually intact. Of particular importance
are the surviving scenic wings and their undercarriage. (See Baur-Heinhold, pls. 73,
75, 131, 132.)

e. Nostitz Theatre (Prague). Similarly extant but completely remodelled is a theatre built
in 1783 by Count Nostitz, now known as the Tyl Theatre. Baur-Heinhold publishes
a watercolor of the theatre from about 1830 (pl. 133). The house opened with a
production of Lessing's *Emilia Galotti*, but is probably best known as the locale of
Mozart's premières.

Even these very few examples serve to illustrate the international nature of
eighteenth-century theatre architecture and the difficulties of preserving architecture in any form given the human predilection for destruction.

Drottningholm and Gripsholm

Easily the best known of the extant eighteenth-century theatres are two Swedish
court theatres, at the royal residences at Drottningholm and Gripsholm. The
pictorial and graphic evidence for both theatres is printed and discussed in detail
by Agne Beijer in *Court Theatres of Drottningholm and Gripsholm* (1933; rpt.
1972).

At Drottningholm, a small baroque theatre erected in 1754 or 1755 was destroyed by fire in 1762. A plan and elevation of this theatre by George Greg-
genhoffer in the Nordic Museum in Stockholm (Beijer, pl. 2) is dated 1754, but
another plan at the Royal Board of Works (pl. 3:D), differing in some important
respects, is dated 1755. Several plans for remodelling the older house are preserved in the Nordic Museum (pl. 3:A,B,C), but the remodelling was evidently
never carried out. The man responsible for these plans, Charles Frederick Adelcrantz, was the architect commissioned to design the new playhouse, which
opened in 1766. (Some of his unused designs, held in the Royal Palace Archives,
Stockholm, are reproduced by Beijer as well [pl. 4:A,B,C].)

The plans for the new playhouse consist of the following:

a. three facade designs in the Royal Palace Archives (pl. 5:A,B,C);

b. two stage plans in the Nordic Museum (pl. 6:A,B);

c. two ground plans, one in the Nordic Museum (pl. 6:C) and one in the Uppsala
University Library (pl. 7);

d. a longitudinal section, corresponding to the ground plans, in the Uppsala University
Library (pl. 8);

e. a cross section of the auditorium contemporaneous with the façade designs, in the
Royal Palace Archives (pl. 9).

There are minor discrepancies among these drawings and between the drawings
and the theatre as it now exists, but the relationship of the plans to the structure
of 1766 is clear.

Under King Gustav III (r. 1771–1792), however, certain renovations were undertaken in the Drottningholm theatre. The king was himself a poet and playwright and sought to bring Sweden into the European mainstream. And this meant emulating the French theatre. French actors had in fact performed regularly in Stockholm since 1699, and the theatre at Drottningholm was built with the French players in mind. After Gustav came to the throne in 1771 the French troupe alternated between its *jeu de paume* in the capital and the court theatres at Drottningholm and Ulriksdal (also designed by Adelcrantz but no longer extant). But Gustav went further. A new company of French actors under J. M. Boutet de Monvel was imported in 1781. The Swedish Academy was founded in imitation of its French counterpart in 1786. Gustav's great ambition was to create a national theatre based on the French model, but his efforts appear not to have had the desired effect, at least so far as the drama itself was concerned. The vast majority of plays performed between 1772 and 1796 were translations or "localized" adaptations of foreign plays, principally French. (See Marie-Christine Skuncke, *Sweden and European Drama 1772–1796*.)

Of most significance for the theatre at Drottningholm, however, was the appointment in 1784 of the French scene designer Louis Jean Desprez (1743–1804) as official set designer at the royal theatres, a position he held until his death. The renovations actually carried out at Drottningholm in 1791 under Desprez' supervision were relatively minor in nature, consisting principally of a "*Sallon pour les festins et les ballets*" and a new reception room. (The plans are reproduced in Beijer, pls. 10, 11, 12.) Again, it appears that the completed changes were less ornate than those originally projected, but the relationship between the plans and the present structure is clear.

The theatre in the castle at Gripsholm was the work of the architect Eric Palmstedt, who enlarged and refurbished a smaller, earlier house in order to accommodate Bautet de Monvel's company. Several drawings that Palmstedt made in 1781 have been preserved in double-scale copies made in 1802 and authenticated by the then-President of the Swedish Academy of Liberal Arts. They include the following:

a. a survey drawing of the older theatre (Beijer, pl. 13:A);

b. a plan for the new theatre [an original drawing, minus the auditorium, is held at Gripsholm Castle] (pl. 13:B);

c. a longitudinal section of the auditorium (pl. 14);

d. a drawing of the stage opening as conceived by Palmstedt (pl. 15:A);

e. two drawings of the auditorium in 1781, the second of which incorporates its appearance after the changes of 1786 (pl. 15:B,C).

The 1786 changes are detailed in two sets of Palmstedt's original drawings now in the Uppsala University Library: a longitudinal section, cross section, and plan (pl. 16); and details of the auditorium (pl. 17).

Neither the Drottningholm theatre nor the Gripsholm theatre was long in use. Monvel's French troupe departed after Gustav's death in 1792, and by 1800 Drottningholm had fallen into complete disuse. Gripsholm's active life was even shorter. There is a record of its being used only once after the renovations of 1786, in the autumn of 1800. Ironically, the theatres' utter neglect has made them, quite literally, museums, of inestimable value to theatre historians. When they were rediscovered in 1921, intact, unrenovated, unmolested for 120 years, they gave historians a direct insight into an eighteenth-century playhouse. (Agne Beijer, for many years Director of the Drottningholm Theatre Museum, confessed that few moments in his life had been so full of emotion as were those during the spring of 1921 when the stages at Drottningholm and Gripsholm were first revealed to modern eyes. See his article in *Revue d'Histoire du Théâtre*, 1956.) Both theatres have been measured and surveyed afresh, and new plans and sections drawn. (These are reproduced in Beijer, *Court Theatres*, pls. 18–34, 35–41.) In addition, a careful photographic record has been made of the exteriors and interiors. (These too are published in *Court Theatres*, pls. I–XV.)

It is difficult to overestimate the importance and value of the thirty or so stage settings preserved at Drottningholm. Scene designs are in most cases available to us only through two-dimensional drawings, prints, and engravings, which must be imaginatively interpreted in terms of three-dimensional stage sets. We are aided somewhat in the process by the information concerning the transfer of designs to wings in Andrea Pozzo's *Prospettiva de' pittori e architetti* and Baldassare Orsini's *Le scene del nuovo Teatro del Verzaro*, but the task depends upon an often uncertain relationship between drawing or engraving and realized stage set, and the results are equally uncertain. At Drottningholm, however, the stage scenes are preserved on wings that actually formed the picture on the stage. In several instances we have as well the original sketch on which the painted scene was based and can therefore compare conception with execution. In his 1956 article on Drottningholm and Gripsholm in the *Revue d'Histoire du Théâtre*, Beijer draws attention to three maquettes by Desprez, one of which, discovered at Gripsholm, is for the first act of J. H. Kellgren's *Queen Christina of Sweden*. The same design is preserved not only in a stage setting at Drottningholm, but also in two sketches by the artist. The importance of the comparison thus made possible, Beijer suggests, is that it allows us to estimate the reliability of the many theatrical maquettes that have come down to us. (The maquette is pictured in Beijer's article, fig. 39; the stage setting is reproduced in *Court Theatres*, pl. XXXVIII.)

Ultimately, the value of the Drottningholm theatre goes beyond the simple presence of stage and machinery, designs and stage sets. As a working theatre from the past, it offers a rare opportunity for experiment, especially in the realm of lighting and stage setting. Agne Beijer is typically eloquent:

If we seek to determine the most valuable contribution of Drottningholm and Gripsholm to the history of the theatre, it is perhaps necessary to consider before all else the opportunity that they offer to our imagination to recreate the thousands of designs and engravings of scenes that the centuries have left us. They reveal to us the secret of the magic the spectators experienced, generation after generation, as we restore to them their third dimension and again bathe them in the delicate light of the candles—as we are able to invoke the fourth dimension of the theatrical vision of the seventeenth and eighteenth centuries. [*Revue d'Histoire du Théâtre*, VIII, 227]

The Schouwburg of Amsterdam

Amsterdam's Schouwburg has never featured prominently in studies of theatre design or as a centre of important dramatic activity; nevertheless, in its own way this theatre—or rather the three structures that have gone by that name—is as valuable to the theatre historian as the court theatre at Drottningholm. Amsterdam in general and the Schouwburg in particular reflected the cultural influences successively of Italy, England, France, and Germany without themselves ever assuming a cultural or theatrical leadership. The Schouwburg, writes a recent commentator, "was normative rather than egregious in its performance method, a style-follower rather than a fashion guide. . . . Thus, over the course of time the Schouwburg became a repository of a conventional stage practice which it had imported and assimilated into its own theatrical tradition" (Alfred Siemon Golding, *Classicistic Acting*, p. x). It is as custodian of customary theatrical practice that the Schouwburg is most valued by historians.

The first Schouwburg, designed by Jacob van Campen and built by Nicholaes van Campen in 1638, is known to us principally through two etchings of the stage and auditorium by Jacob Lescaille after drawings executed shortly following the theatre's erection by Salomon Savry, and through a ground plan drawn and etched in 1658 by W. van de Laegh. (All three etchings are preserved in the Archief Bibliotheek, Amsterdam, and are reproduced in Mullin, *The Development of the Playhouse*, figs. 33–35, and in Bamber Gascoigne, *World Theatre*, pp. 186–87.) In addition, we have a contemporary oil painting by H. J. van Baden of the interior from the viewpoint of a box on the left side of the house, and an engraving of the exterior. The former is in the Amsterdam Theatre Museum (Golding, *Classicistic Acting*, p. 183 n.3), the latter in the Archief Bibliotheek (Mullin, fig. 32). The theatre's records and accounts are also extant. (See J. A. Worp, *Geschiedenis van het Amsterdamschen Schouwburg*, pp. 87–88.) The designer, Jacob van Campen (1595–1657), an admirer of the work of Andrea Palladio and Vincenzo Scamozzi, had studied in Italy, and the design of the Schouwburg reflects a compromise between the older *rederijker* stage and the modified classical Vitruvian architecture of the Teatro Olimpico. But the stage depicted in Savry's etching is also strongly reminiscent of the stage at the Hôtel de Bourgogne as pictured in Mahelot's stage settings. (See the edition of the *Mémoire de Mahelot* by H. C. Lancaster.)

Campen's theatre was torn down and rebuilt in 1664. This second Schouwburg was extensively illustrated and described before its destruction by fire in 1772.

The auditorium is illustrated in engravings reproduced in Mullin (figs. 167, 169), the stage in engravings printed in Mullin (fig. 170) and in Brockett's *History of the Theatre* (fig. 13.24). Several contemporary descriptions of the house are cited and quoted in Worp's *Geschiedenis van het Amsterdamschen Schouwburg*. We have as well an often reproduced ground plan (Mullin, fig. 168; Kindermann, V, 446), which indicates a combination of oblique and parallel wings similar to plans for the Teatro di Tor di Nona in Rome being built at about the same time (Gascoigne, *World Theatre*, p. 311). Golding points out (pp. 188–89 n.16), however, that the plan was originally published in the *Atlas van de Stad Amsterdam*, a collection of contemporary views of Amsterdam in 1774, and goes on to argue that the plan reflects extensive alterations made between 1765 and 1769. We thus have an explanation for the contradictions sometimes noted between the plan and written descriptions of the theatre. (These same alterations are undoubtedly responsible for the variations in the portrayals of the theatre's interior—compare Mullin's fig. 167 with his fig. 169.) The gradual movement away from emblematic stage representation and toward neoclassical verisimilitude is reflected in the second Schouwburg in the arrangement of wings in strict perspective. "Instead of a relatively shallow acting area and a more or less permanent architectural facade to thrust into prominence symbolic elements in the speech, action and scene picture, the stage was reconstructed to furnish a more natural scenic illusion" (Golding, p. 44). By 1765 the standard stage settings at the Schouwburg included four different court scenes, an Italian street, a town, an ordinary neighborhood, a chapel or dungeon, a hell scene, and a sea scene (Golding, p. 191 n.27).

The third Schouwburg was constructed in 1774 on the Leidseplein, designed by the Amsterdam city architect Jacob Eduard deWitte and decorated by Pieter Barbiers the Elder and Jurriaen Andriessen. Again, prints and etchings are among our primary sources of information. (Several are reproduced in Ben Albach, *Helden Draken en Comedianten*, opp. pp. 64, 81, 96.) The engraving most likely to be encountered, however, differs from the majority in depicting a fourth balcony (Mullin, fig. 171; Kindermann, V, 450). Kindermann does little to clarify the situation by labelling the building "*der 'alten' Schouwburg*," thereby identifying it as the 1664 structure. There is little doubt, however, that the architectural details correspond with those otherwise known of the third Schouwburg or that the dress of the spectators dates from a period shortly after the turn of the nineteenth century. Mullin's estimate of 1805 is probably not far off. Golding conjectures (pp. 191–92 n.30) that the fourth balcony may have been added during the renovations of 1801. Two series of etchings in the Amsterdam Theatre Museum record the stage settings devised to replace those lost in the 1772 fire. Included are street scenes, a church, a chapel, middle-class and peasant dwellings, a palace, a dungeon, a garden, and a tent. We can compare this list with that noted above and with the Covent Garden inventory of 1744 and with Baldassare Orsini's list in *Le scene del nuovo Teatro del Verzaro*. Later and more romantic settings were provided by François Joseph Pfeiffer, who was commissioned in 1797 to create additional scenery. Some of his designs have survived among the maquettes constructed for a contemporary model of the Schouwburg. This model, with its many sets of scenery and working details, has been described by Richard Southern as "one of the most valuable and informative of theatre relics" (*Changeable Scenery*, p. 226).

CONCLUSION

The various and complex processes contributing to the internationalization of the theatre in eighteenth-century Europe have yet to be identified, mapped, or analyzed: the process by which common performance practices and acting styles were disseminated by precept and example over much of Europe; the process by which repertories were formed through translation, adaptation, and imitation, and changed under the pressures of local circumstances and nationalism in the countries of Eastern and Northern Europe; the process by which common principles and practices of theatre architecture and stage design spread throughout Europe; and the process by which styles of scenic design developed and were transmuted; the process by which neoclassical theory and practice interacted with, modified, and were modified by both older and newer theoretical principles in areas of vastly differing theatrical traditions. Some of this work has, of course, been done with respect to various national theatres, but the Pan-European picture has yet to be filled in. Historians of the future may very well find themselves interpreting a given theatrical event not only as an event in time but also as an event in space; that is, in terms of a historical sequence intersecting with a geocultural dimension, each event illuminating and being illuminated by parallel and contemporaneous events as well as by past and future events. Such a model might also stimulate the internationalization of theatre historiography. Only convention decrees that specialization must be determined on the basis of language or political boundaries.

REFERENCES

Aikin-Sneath, Betsy. *Comedy in Germany in the First Half of the Eighteenth Century.* Oxford, 1936.
Aksakov, Sergei. *Sobranie sochinenii.* 4 Vols. Moscow, 1952–1956.
Albach, Ben. *Helden Draken en Comedianten. Het Nederlandse Toneelleven voor, in en na de Franse Tijd.* Amsterdam, 1956.
Andioc, René. *Sur la querelle du theatre au temps de Leandro Fernández de Moratín.* Bordeaux, 1970.
Arapov, Pimen Nikolaevich. *Letopis' russkogo teatra.* St. Petersburg, 1861.
Baur-Heinhold, Margarete. *The Baroque Theatre: A Cultural History of the 17th and 18th Centuries.* New York and London, 1967.
Bayer, József. *A magyar dráma története.* 2 Vols. Budapest, 1897.
———. *A nemzeti játékszín története.* 2 Vols. Budapest, 1887.

Beijer, Agne. *Court Theatres of Drottningholm and Gripsholm*. Tr. G. L. Frolich. New York, 1972. [1933]

———. "Les Théâtres de Drottningholm et de Gripsholm." *Revue d'Histoire du Théâtre* VIII (1956), 215–27.

Brandes, Johann Christian. *Meine Lebensgeschichte*. Ed. W. Francke. Munich, Germany, 1923. [1800]

Brockett, Oscar. *History of the Theatre*. 4th ed. Boston, 1982.

Bruford, Walter H. *Germany in the Eighteenth Century: The Social Background of the Literary Revival*. Cambridge, England, 1935.

———. *Theatre Drama and Audience in Goethe's Germany*. London, 1950.

Burney, Charles. *Dr. Burney's Musical Tours in Europe*, Vol. II: *An Eighteenth-Century Musical Tour in Central Europe and the Netherlands*. Ed. Percy A. Scholes. London, 1959.

Cánovas del Castillo, Antonio. *Arte y letras*. Madrid, 1887.

Carlson, Marvin. *Goethe and the Weimar Theatre*. Ithaca, N.Y., and London, 1978.

———. *Theories of the Theatre: A Historical and Critical Survey, from the Greeks to the Present*. Ithaca, N.Y., and London, 1884.

Coe, Ada M. *Catálogo bibliográfico y crítico de las comedias anunciadas en los periódicos de Madrid desde 1661 hasta 1819*. Baltimore, 1933.

Cohn, Albert. *Shakespeare in Germany in the Sixteenth and Seventeenth Centuries: An Account of English Actors in Germany and the Netherlands and of the Plays Performed by Them During the Same Period*. New York, 1971. [1865]

Cook, John A. *Neo-Classic Drama in Spain: Theory and Practice*. Dallas, 1959.

Cotarelo y Mori, Emilio. *Biblioteca de las controversias sobre la licitud del teatro en España*. Madrid, 1904.

———. *Don Ramón de la Cruz y sus obras*. Madrid, 1899.

———. *Iriarte y su época*. Madrid, 1897.

———. *Isidoro Máiquez y el teatro de su tiempo*. Madrid, 1902.

———. *María del Rosario Fernández (La Tirana)*. Madrid, 1897.

Cox, R. Merritt. *Eighteenth-Century Spanish Literature*. Boston, 1979.

Danilov, Sergei. *Ocherki po istorii russkogo dramaticheskogo teatra*. Moscow, 1948.

De la Huerte, García. *La escena Hespañola defendida en el prólogo del teatro Hespañol*. Madrid, 1786.

Dukore, Bernard F., ed. *Dramatic Theory and Criticism: Greeks to Grotowski*. New York, 1974.

Du Perron de Castera. *Extraits de plusieurs pièces du théâtre espanol avec des réflexions, et la traduction des endroits les plus remarqables*. Paris, 1738.

Endródy, János. *A magyar játék színnek történetei kezdetétöl fogva az utóbbi kormány ozásig [A magyar játékszín]*. 3 Vols. Pest, 1792–1793.

Englische Comedien und Tragedien. Wolgast (?), Germany, 1620; 2d ed. 1624.

Falk, Heinrich Richard. "Actors, Audiences, and Theatrical *Sainetes*: A Formula for Success on the Eighteenth-Century Spanish Stage." *Educational Theatre Journal* XXVIII (1976), 299–311.

Feijóo, Benito Jerónimo. *Cartas eruditas*. Ed. Agustín Millares Carlo. Clásicos Castellanos, 85. Madrid, 1958.

———. *Teatro crítico*. Ed. Agustín Millares Carlo. 3 Vols. Clásicos Castellanos, 48, 53, 67. Madrid, 1953–1958.

Gascoigne, Bamber. *World Theatre*. Boston, 1968.

Glendinning, Nigel. *A Literary History of Spain: The Eighteenth Century*. Gen. ed. R. O. Jones. London and New York, 1972.

Goethe, Johann Wolfgang von. *The Autobiography of Goethe, Together With His Annals*. Tr. John Oxenford and Charles Nesbit. New ed. London, 1881–1882.

———. *Conversations and Encounters*. Ed. and tr. David Luke and Robert Pick. Chicago, 1966.

———. *Conversations of Goethe with Eckermann and Soret*. Tr. John Oxenford. 2 Vols. London, 1850.

———. *Goethes Werke*. 143 Vols. Weimar, 1887–1920.

———. *Travels in Italy*. Tr. C. Nesbit. London, 1883.

———. *Wilhelm Meister's Years of Apprenticeship/Wilhelm Meisters Lehrjahre*. Tr. H. M. Waidson, 3 Vols. London, 1977–1979.

Golding, Alfred Siemon. *Classicistic Acting: Two Centuries of a Performance Tradition at the Amsterdam Schouwburg, to Which is Appended an Annotated Translation of the "Lessons on the Principles of Gesticulation and Mimic Expression" of Johannes Jelgerhuis, Rz*. Lanham, N.Y., and London, 1984.

Gottsched, Johann Christoph. *Die deutsche Schaubühne nach den Regeln und Exempeln der Alten*. 6 Vols. Leipzig, 1740–1745; 2d ed. 1746–1750.

———. *Gesammelte Schriften von Johann Christoph Gottsched*. Ed. Eugen Reichel. 6 Vols. Berlin, n.d. [1902–1912]

———. *Schriften zur Literatur*. Stuttgart, 1972.

Gregor, Joseph. *Geschichte des Österreichischen Theaters. Von seinen Ursprungen bis zum Enmde der ersten Republick*. Vienna, 1948.

———. *The Russian Theatre*. London, 1930.

Heitner, Robert P. *German Tragedy in the Age of Enlightenment: A Study in the Development of Original Tragedies, 1724–1768*. Berkeley and Los Angeles, 1963.

Hillestrom, Gustaf. *Drottningholmsteatern förr och nu/The Drottningholm Theatre—Past and Present*. Photographs Lennart af Petersens. Stockholm, 1956.

Iffland, August Wilhelm. *Über meine theatralische Laufbahn*. Ed. H. Holstein. Heilbronn, 1886.

Jovellanos, Gaspar Melchior de. *Memoria para el arreglo de la policía de los espectáculos y diversiones públicas*. In Jovellanos, *Prosa Escogida*, ed. Felix Herrero y Salgado. Madrid, 1976.

———. *Obras completas*. 2 Vols. Biblioteca de Autores Españoles, 46, 50. Madrid, 1963, 1952.

Kany, C. E. "Plan de reforma de los teatros de Madrid." *Revista de la Biblioteca, Archivo y Museo*, VI, no. 23 (1929), 245–84.

Kardos, Tibor and Tekla Dömötör. *Régi magyar drámai emlékek*. 2 Vols. Budapest, 1966.

Karlinsky, Simon. *Russian Drama from its Beginnings to the Age of Pushkin*. Berkeley, 1985.

Kindermann, Heinz. *Theatergeschichte Europas*. 10 Vols. Salzburg, 1957–1974.

Kürschner, Joseph. *Conrad Ekhofs Leben und Wirken*. Vienna, 1872.

Lancaster, Henry Carrington, ed. *Le Mémoire de Mahelot, Laurent et d'autres decorateurs de l'Hôtel de Bourgogne et de la Comédie Française au XVIIe siècle*. Paris, 1920.

Lessing, Gotthold Ephraim. *Gesammelte Werke*. 10 Vols. Berlin, 1968.

———. *Hamburgische Dramaturgie*, in *Gesammelte Werke*, vol. VI. Berlin, 1968.

Limon, Jerzy. *Gentlemen of a Company: English Players in Europe 1590–1660*. Cambridge, England, 1986.

Loftis, John. *The Spanish Plays of Neoclassical England*. New Haven and London, 1973.

Lo Gatto, Ettore. *Storia del Teatro Russo*. 2d ed. 2 Vols. Florence, 1963.

Löwen, Johann Friedrich. *Geschichte des deutschen Theaters*. Ed. H. Stumke. Berlin, 1903. [1766]

Luzán, Ignacio de. *Memorias literarias de París, actual estado y methodo de sus estudios*. Madrid, 1751.

———. *Poética*. Ed. J. Cano. Toronto, 1928. [1737]

McCabe, William H. *An Introduction to the Jesuit Theater*. St. Louis, 1983.

McClelland, I. L. *The Origins of the Romantic Movement in Spain*. Liverpool, 1937.

———. *Spanish Drama of Pathos: 1750–1808*. 2 Vols. Toronto, 1970.

Mályusz, Edith Császár. *The Theater and National Awakening*. Tr. Thomas Szendrey. Atlanta, 1980.

Marker, Frederick J. and Lise-Lone Marker. *The Scandinavian Theatre: A Short History*. Oxford, 1976.

Menéndez y Pelayo, Marcelino. *Estudios y discursos de crítica histórica y literaria*. 7 Vols. Edición nacional de las obras completas, 6–12. Santander, 1944–1949.

———. *Historia de las ideas estéticas en España*. 5 Vols. Edición nacional de las obras completas, 1–5. Santander, 1944–1949.

Merimée, Paul. *L'Influence française en Espagne au dix-huitième siècle*. Paris, n.d. [1936]

Meyer, Friedrich Ludwig Wilhelm. *Friedrich Ludwig Schröder*. 2 Vols. Hamburg, 1819. [Reprinted 1923]

Moratín, Leandro Fernández de. *Obras*. 4 Vols. in 6. Madrid, 1830–1831.

———. *Vida de Don Nicolas Fernández de Moratín* in *Obras*, New Ed. Biblioteca de Autores Españoles, 2. Madrid, 1944.

Moratín, Nicolas Fernández de. *Desengaños al teatro español*. Madrid (?), 1762–1763.

Mullin, Donald C. *The Development of the Playhouse: a Survey of Theatre Architecture from the Renaissance to the Present*. Berkeley and Los Angeles, 1970.

La nación española defendida de los insultos del Pensador y sus secuaces. Madrid, 1764.

Pascal, R. *Shakespeare in Germany, 1740–1815*. Cambridge, England, 1937.

Paz y Melia, Antonio. *Catalogo de las piezas de teatro que se conservan en el departamento de manuscritos de la Biblioteca Nacional*. 2 Vols. Madrid, 1934–1935.

Pellicer, Casiano. *Tratado histórico sobre el origen y progresos de la comedia y del histrionismo en España*. 2 Vols. Madrid, 1804.

Pellissier, R. E. *The Neo-Classic Movement in Spain during the XVIIIth Century*. Stanford, 1918.

Prudhoe, John. *The Theatre of Goethe and Schiller*. Oxford, 1973.

Qualia, Charles Blaise. "The Campaign to Substitute French Neo-Classical Tragedy for the Comedia, 1737–1800." *Publications of the Modern Language Association* LIV (1939), 184–211.

Reden-Esbeck, F. J. von. *Caroline Neuber und ihre Zeitgenossen*. Leipzig, 1881.

Reichard, August Ottakar, ed. *Theaterjournal für Deutschland*. Gotha, 1777–1784.

———. *Theaterkalendar*. Gotha, 1775–1800.

Robertson, J. G. *Lessing's Dramatic Theory, Being an Introduction to and Commentary on his Hamburgische Dramaturgie*. Cambridge, England, 1939.

Schack, Graf von. *Geschichte der Dramatischen Litteratur und Kunst in Spanien*. 3 Vols. Berlin, 1845–1846.

Schmidt, Christian Heinrich. *Chronologie des deutschen Theaters*. Ed. P. Legband. Berlin, 1902. [1775]

Schönemann, Johann Friedrich. *Schönemannsche Schaubühne*. 7 Vols. Leipzig, 1748–1755.

Schröder, Freidrich Ludwig. *Beitrag zur deutschen Schaubühne*. 3 Vols. Berlin, 1786–1790.

Schütze, J. F. *Hamburgische Teatergeschichte*. Hamburg, Germany, 1794.

Sebastián y Latre, Tomás. *Ensayo sobre el teatro español*. Zaragoza, 1772.

Signorelli, Pietro Napoli. *Storia critica dei teatri, antiche e moderne*. 6 Vols. Naples, 1787–1790.

Skuncke, Marie-Christine. *Sweden and European Drama 1772–1796: A Study of Translations and Adaptations*. Stockholm, 1981.

Slonim, Marc. *Russian Theater from the Empire to the Soviets*. Cleveland, 1961.

Southern, Richard. *Changeable Scenery: Its Origin and Development in the British Theatre*. London, 1952.

Straumanis, Alfreds, ed. *Baltic Drama. A Handbook and Bibliography*. Prospect Heights, Ill., 1981.

Teatro nuevo español. Madrid, 1800–1801.

Tezla, Albert. *An Introductory Bibliography to the Study of Hungarian Literature*. Cambridge, Mass., 1964.

Thomas, R. Hinton. *The Classical Ideal in German Literature 1755–1805*. Cambridge, England, 1939.

Ulriksen, Solveig Schult. "Le Théâtre parisien en 1788, vu par trois acteurs danois." *Revue d'Histoire du Théâtre* XXXIV (1982), 169–85.

Urguijo, Mariano. *La Muerte del César*. Madrid, 1791.

Váli, Béla. *A magyar színészet története*. Budapest, 1887.

Varneke, Boris Vasilevich. *History of the Russian Theatre: Seventeenth through Nineteenth Century*. Tr. Boris Brasol. Rev. and ed. Belle Martin. New York, 1951.

Velázquez, Luis. *Orígenes de la poesía castellana*. Madrid, 1754.

Voltaire [François Marie Arouet]. *Oeuvres complètes*. Ed. Louis Moland. 52 Vols. Paris, 1877–1885.

Vsevolodsky-Gerngross, Vsevolod. *Istoriia russkogo teatra*. 2 Vols. Moscow, 1929.

Weiner, Jack. *Mantillas in Muscovy: The Spanish Golden age Theatre in Tsarist Russia 1672–1917*. Lawrence, Kansas, 1970.

Williams, Simon. *German Actors of the Eighteenth and Nineteenth Centuries: Idealism, Romanticism, and Realism*. Westport, Conn., and London, 1985.

Worp, J. A. *Geschiedenis van het Amsterdamschen Schouwburg 1496–1772, uitgegeven met aanvulling tot 1872 door Dr. J. F. M. Sterck*. Amsterdam, 1920.

———. *Geschiendenis van het Drama en van her Toonel in Nederland*. 2 Vols. Groningen, 1908.

Zhikharev, Stepan P. *Zapiski sovremennika*. Ed. B. M. Èikhenbaum. Moscow, 1955.

INDEX

About the Author

RONALD W. VINCE is Professor of English and a Member of the Instruction Committee on Dramatic Arts at McMaster University in Hamilton, Ontario. He is the author of *Ancient and Medieval Theatre* and *Renaissance Theatre* (both Greenwood Press, 1984).